Beyond 1

BEYOND
1492

*Encounters in Colonial
North America*

JAMES AXTELL

New York   Oxford
OXFORD UNIVERSITY PRESS
1992

Oxford University Press

Oxford   New York   Toronto
Delhi   Bombay   Calcutta   Madras   Karachi
Kuala Lumpur   Singapore   Hong Kong   Tokyo
Nairobi   Dar es Salaam   Cape Town
Melbourne   Auckland

and associated companies in
Berlin   Ibadan

Copyright © 1992 by James Axtell

Published by Oxford University Press, Inc.,
198 Madison Avenue, New York, New York 10016-4314

Oxford is a registered trademark of Oxford University Press

Library of Congress Cataloging-in Publication Data
Axtell, James.
Beyond 1492 :
encounters in colonial North America /
James Axtell.
p.   cm., Includes bibliographical references and index
ISBN 0–19–506838–6
ISBN 0–19–508033–5 (pbk.)
1. North America—History—Colonial period, ca. 1500–1775.
2. Indians of North America—History—Colonial period, ca. 1500–1775.
3. Columbus, Christopher—Influence.
4. America—Discovery and exploration—Spanish.
I. Title., 970.02—dc20   91–45411

6 8 9 7 5
Printed in the United States of America
on acid-free paper

For Susan
*Amie de la douceur perpetuelle
et l'éclat infini*

Preface

After 1492 the world became a very different place. Western Europe's "discovery" of and imperial thrust into the equally old world of the Americas set in rapid motion the final stages of the human and biological exposure of the earth's constituent parts to each other and the tying of those parts together with nautical lines.

Before Columbus, various ancient worlds—Africa, Asia, Europe, and the Americas—lay largely isolated from each other, shrouded in tantalizing mystery or blissful ignorance. Asians knew parts of Africa and even Europe (and the Chinese at least had the technology and knowledge to exploit both), but chose largely to stay home. North Africans certainly knew Europe and had colonized the Iberian peninsula for nearly eight centuries. But Western Europeans, driven by economic forces, social restlessness, and an evangelical religion, did the most to systematically intrude themselves and their ways of life into the known, inhabited parts of the world. Save for a few readers of ancient Norse sagas, no one knew of the Americas, and the Americans knew nothing of the rest of the world.

In 1492 Cristoforo Colombo, a Genoese sailor in the

employ of the Spanish crown, launched himself into the
midst of this long-ongoing process but had the skill and
fortune to "discover" for Europe the richly populated
newness of the American continent (though he may never
have fully realized the novelty of what he found). He did
not give birth to Western imperialism, colonialism, ethnocentrism, or racism, as some of his past and especially
current detractors have charged; he found them already in
place and was too much a man of his times to transcend
their limitations. But by yoking the Americas and the rest of
the known world in common fate, he did help to accelerate
the global irruption of social and cultural conflict, war, and
human suffering.

On the other hand (the scholar's justly favorite phrase),
the global encounters that Columbus initiated or inspired
(or merely preceded) were not uniformly deleterious either
to the earth's biota or to its human population. Like the vast
majority of historical events, each encounter was a mixed
bag of losses and gains, even for the African and American
natives who collectively lost the most. For the contest was
never conducted along strictly racial, ethnic, or national
lines: the outnumbered invaders knew the principle of
"divide and conquer," and the invaded, who practiced the
same thing in their own conflicts, could seldom resist the
West's blandishments or break their own habits long
enough to coordinate and solidify their resistance. Some
Africans and Indians gained at the expense of their brethren; others profited from the introduction of European
technology or the explanatory power of a universal religion.

The quincentenary of Columbus's epochal voyage is a
perfect time for the citizens of the "global village" he helped
create to reassess the initiation, conduct, and long- and
short-term results of those encounters. We need to learn to

live together on an increasingly shrinking planet. One way is to avoid the mistakes of the past; another is to draw more positive lessons from past encounters which were not so lopsided that each side could not reap some advantages. It might be satisfying to drag Columbus and other European colonists before our moral bar and to condemn them for not living up to our more enlightened standards (whoever "we" are and however those standards are defined). But it is more important—because more humanizing—for us to *understand* the actors of the past in their full complexity and humanity, just as we would like to be appraised by future historians. Straw men and cardboard women are unworthy subjects and incapable of teaching us anything of value.

This book is an attempt to understand the nature and moral consequences of some of the encounters, many of them tragic, between Europeans, Africans, and Indians primarily in North America in the three hundred years after 1492. It is a collection of essays on a common theme, all but one of which began as lectures, as I explain in the headnotes to each chapter. Like my previous book of essays, *After Columbus*, this book was unplanned.* It simply took on a life of its own as I was drawn (quite willingly) into the Quincentenary vortex of commemoration and cerebration.

When I sent the manuscript of *After Columbus* to press in 1987, I fully intended it to be my only contribution to the Columbian moment. But I did not foresee—historians tend to look in the rear-view mirror—the growing demand for speakers who were prepared by teaching and publication to discuss the grand theme of this century's centenary, the Columbian "Encounter." Since most of my life's work has been devoted to the ethnohistory of Indian-European contact in colonial North America, since I teach both "The

After Columbus: Essays in the Ethnohistory of Colonial North America (New York: Oxford University Press, 1988).

Age of Exploration" and "The Invasion of North America,"
and since I was a founding member and later chairman of
the American Historical Association's Columbus Quincentenary Committee, I was a likely candidate, particularly
because it was known that I could and liked to talk to
audiences of non-specialists. Most requests I was happy to
accept, even if it meant a certain loss of freedom for four
years and the postponement—yet again—of the completion of the second volume of my Oxford trilogy, *American
Encounter: The Confluence of Cultures in Colonial North
America.**

By training and perhaps instinct, ethnohistorians try to
view intercultural encounters from both (or all) sides of the
frontier: they are intellectually bifocal. And they use evidence generated by one culture to understand the other(s)
as well. In fact, it could be said that their major subject of
study is "otherness," the often ineluctable differences perceived in one group by another. Obviously, in ethnohistory
perspective—vantage point—is everything. The following
essays were written from four different perspectives. A few
try to view the "invasion" of North America through Indian
eyes, or at least over Indian shoulders: the lack of direct
evidence and the complexity of cross-cultural translation
make these attempts both risky and difficult. Other essays
interpret the "colonization" of the "New World" from a
contemporary European perspective, a task no less fraught
with challenges. At least three essays attempt to examine
American encounters through a bifocal lens. And another
trio of chapters focuses more on the present and how we are
succeeding or failing in our attempts to understand the
Columbian Encounter.   ₒ

---

*The trilogy is entitled "The Cultural Origins of North America," and its first
volume, *The Invasion Within: The Contest of Cultures in Colonial North America*, was
published by Oxford in 1985.

Together, I hope these essays give the reader an ample taste of the richness of research, insights, and perspectives that awaits the student of post-Columbian America. If they fail to convey the pleasure and excitement I have had in writing and delivering them, I have "botched it big time," as my students and sons might say.

Williamsburg   J.A.
October 1991

Acknowledgments

Ever since I discovered the "community of scholars" as an undergraduate at Yale, I have been a firm believer in that international, mutual-aid society of lifelong learners. Without the example, stimulation, constructive criticism, tolerance, and generosity of their colleagues, most scholars would cease to function, and all but the most reclusive would take much less pleasure from their work (which, in their company, becomes well-disguised but veritable play).

The community of scholars is responsible for this book. They invited me to speak its chapters, economically and emotionally supported its research and writing, applauded, criticized, and supplemented its oral and written results, and inspired its publication. So, with sincere thanks, I return it to them. But I also offer it to the larger community of readers often described as "general" but whom I prefer to regard as "ideal." I share Margaret Atwood's image of the ideal reader: someone "intelligent, capable of feeling, possessed of a moral sense, a lover of language, and very demanding."* If I could meet the high (often overlapping)

*Margaret Atwood, *Second Words: Selected Critical Prose* (Boston, 1984), 346.

standards of both communities at the same time, I would rest content—at least until the next book had to be written.

None of the essays in this book would have been written or improved without the impetus and vital audiences provided by several universities, colleges, and historical organizations who invited me to lecture on post-Columbian themes. I am grateful to the following institutions and people for putting bees in my bonnet and for unfailing courtesy, gracious hospitality, and frank exchange when I arrived to let them out:

—The New Jersey Historical Commission and its Associate Director, Richard Waldron
—Loyola University of Chicago, History chairman Joseph Gagliano, and Dean of Humanities Thomas Ranck
—Northwestern University and Timothy Breen, lecture impresario and *bon penseur et vivant*
—The membership of the American Society for Ethnohistory which elected me their president for 1988–89
—Mary Washington College and Professors John Pearce and Carter Hudgins (former graduate student and ace troweler)
—Oberlin College and the Mead-Swing Lectureship Committee chaired by Gary Kornblith
—Kutztown University, Christine Styrna (former graduate student and fierce volleyballer), and John Updike-lookalike Gordon Goldberg, chairman of History
—University of Tulsa, Barnard Professor of Western History and boon companion James Ronda, and History chairman Lawrence Cress
—Arizona State University and History chairman Robert Trennert
—University of Minnesota, Stuart Schwartz and Lucy Simler of the Center for Early Modern History, Jean O'Brien and Carla and William Phillips of the History Department

—University of Florida, Michael Gannon of the Institute for Early Contact Period Studies, History chairman Kermit Hall, and Kathleen Deagan and Jerald Milanich of the Florida State Museum
—The Maine Humanities Council and its director Dorothy Schwartz
—The American Historical Association's Columbus Quincentenary Committee, former chairwoman Helen Nader, and Carla Rahn Phillips and David Weber, co-editors extraordinaire
—University of Wisconsin System, Loretta Webster and Ronald Satz
—Vanderbilt University, the Robert Penn Warren Humanities Center, and Vivien Fryd of the Art Department
—Carleton College and History chairman Kirk Jeffrey
—Carleton University (Ottawa), Kerry Abel, Dean Maggie Lodge, History chairman Franz Szabo, and John Taylor and the Ottawa Historical Association
—Marquette University and John Krugler, brainy moviegoer and fellow lover of outdoor history
—State University of New York at Albany, Fundacion Xavier de Salas, and Jorge Klor de Alva (now at Princeton) and Gary Gossen of the Institute of Mesoamerican Studies
—Washington and Lee University, History chairman Robert McAhren, and the Society of Cincinnati.

I am also beholden to the maecenasian staffs and treasuries of the National Endowment for the Humanities and the American Council of Learned Societies, which allowed me to devote two semesters to the research which undergirds many of these essays.

I am even more grateful to my own university, William and Mary: first, for a semester research leave and two summer research grants; second, for the leadership of Dean (now Provost) Melvyn Schiavelli and History chairman John Selby, who generously upholstered a chair in which I could work; third, for the efficient service of Carol Linton and the Interlibrary Loan office of Swem Library; fourth, for the keen editorial eye of Michael McGiffert and the staff of the *William and Mary Quarterly;* and finally, for the Institute of Early American History and Culture which has allowed me to loft several trial balloons in their midst.

The scholarly community of Williamsburg is not only my intellectual home but a model of what it can be at its best. In my happy experience, the local congregation of early Americanists who ply their callings at Colonial Williams-burg, the Institute, the Jamestown-Yorktown Foundation, and the College gives added resonance to "Colonial Capi-tal."

Penultimately, I would like to thank two mentors who never taught me in the classroom but have been teaching me almost since I first stepped into my own. William Eccles and David Quinn, emeritus professors of history at the universities of Toronto and Liverpool, have served me constantly for nearly twenty years as exemplars of scholarly energy, excellence, and integrity. But I am even more thankful for their steadfast friendship, generosity, and still-frank criticism. They did not teach me to paddle my own scholarly canoe—just keep it upright and headed in the right direction.

But we all know that there are some things more impor-tant than scholarship and the writing of books. Whenever I need reminding, my two grown sons, Jeremy and Nathan-iel, seem to arrive, ready with wicked wit to prick my "scholarly" pretensions. They are aided and abetted on a daily basis by our silly-sly golden retriever ("The Rain Dog") who thinks that scholars are made only for long walks and tugs-of-war. And while the mother of the ménage has learned over thirty years to honor, even nourish, my scholarly idiosyncrasies, she has enough leprechaun beneath her benign freckles to frequently join the rest of the family in keeping me honest. For her tender ministrations, sage counsel, and abiding friendship, I count myself graced.

Contents

1. History as Imagination   3

Views from the Shore

2. Imagining the Other: First Encounters in North America   25
3. The Exploration of Norumbega: Native Perspectives   75
4. Native Reactions to the Invasion of America   97

Encounters Light and Dark

5. The First Consumer Revolution   125
6. Agents of Change: Jesuits in the Post-Columbian World   152
7. Humor in Ethnohistory   171

1492 and Beyond

8. Europeans, Indians, and the Age of Discovery in American History Textbooks   197
9. The Columbian Mosaic in Colonial America   217
10. Moral Reflections on the Columbian Legacy   241
11. Beyond 1992   267

Notes   317
Index   365

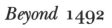

Beyond 1492

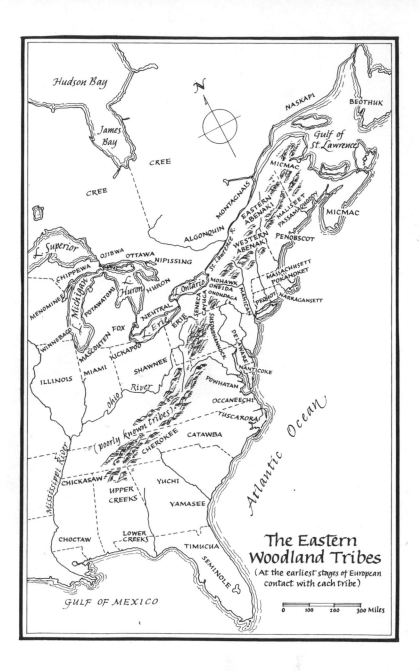

The Eastern Woodland Tribes

(At the earliest stages of European contact with each tribe)

CHAPTER ONE

History as Imagination

EXCEPT IN THE PRIVACY OF THEIR OWN CLASSROOMS, HIS-
torians seldom have an opportunity to declaim upon their disci-
plinary practices and credos. If they write history as well as teach
it, they spend the vast majority of their time and effort on the
past, not their own present. This is as it should be. But disciplines
are protean, living things which constantly change, and their
practitioners should from time to time take stock of how and why
they do what they do. One way is to follow the philosophical and
methodological debates that pepper their professional journals
and conferences. Another is to put pen (or word processor) to
paper to summarize their own beliefs and practices.

On an icy evening in January 1987, after twenty years of historical practice, I was given the pleasant opportunity to talk
about how and why I spent my waking hours as an historian. The
previous spring three other William and Mary professors and I
had been given endowed chairs, and the university, in a fit of
ritual exuberance, asked us to deliver inaugural lectures. Despite
the inclement weather, a kind and curious audience of townspeople and collegians filled a large lecture hall to hear the new
William R. Kenan, Jr., Professor of Humanities sing for his sup-
per. With the exception of the first three paragraphs, which were
rewritten for publication in *The Historian* in August 1987, the
following medley was presented to that audience.

3

Because of the oral and ceremonial nature of the occasion, I felt—for the first time in my professional life—that footnotes were not required. On this one occasion, as Samuel Eliot Morison said on another, my audience could "take a certain amount of erudition for granted."* *The Historian* did not require them either. But for this volume I feel that some readers might be curious to know where I borrowed some of the more authoritative expressions of my own convictions. I have therefore sought—sometimes in vain—to reconstruct my sources, long after the fact. In two instances, the reader will have to complete the reconstitution of my intellectual history from his or her own imagination.

M OST HISTORIANS ARE PROFESSIONAL SCHIZOPHRENics. Now that the nineteenth-century chimera of historical "science" has dissipated, their self-identities and allegiances are torn between the humanities and the social sciences. The symptoms of their dilemma are everywhere.

On the one hand, most historians turn to the National Endowment for the Humanities rather than the Social Science Research Council for funding. They regard their writing as a species of literature, and recognize their assumptions about humankind, time, and the cosmos as philosophical. And the major statements on the humanities in the past thirty years have spoken of history's centrality to the humane enterprise. Howard Mumford Jones's *One Great Society: Humane Learning in the United States,* the 1959 report of a thirteen-man Commission on the Humanities convened by the American Council of Learned Societies, regarded history as the "essence" of the humanities because they "depend for their very existence upon perspective in time.[1] Two decades later, the Rocke-

---

*Samuel Eliot Morison, *The Oxford History of the American People* (New York, 1965), vii.

feller Foundation commissioned thirty-two distinguished men and women to conduct a study subsequently entitled *The Humanities in American Life.* They, too, concluded that "while the medium in the humanities is language, the turn of mind is toward history."[2]

At the same time, in most colleges and universities, history is listed with the social sciences for the purpose of satisfying distributional or "liberal arts" requirements. And many historians are happy with that placement because the dominant mode or fashion in history is social history, which relies heavily on the techniques, methodologies, and jargon of the social sciences.

Another obstacle to thinking of history as one of the humanities is the widespread lay opinion that history is a dull, lifeless pile of cold, objective facts about the past, without social significance or human interest. Such a bad press is partly the fault of historians, for their huge audience, throughout its schooling, has been subjected to an unrelenting dose of objective-sounding, fact-ridden textbooks, and bombarded with so-called "objective" tests on an assortment of scarcely related names, dates, and events.

If they manage to survive that obstacle course with any interest in history intact, their search for good books of history will be frustrated by the current book market. The number of true histories that make their way to the revolving-door shelves of the be-malled chain stores can be counted on one hand. And in most used book stores and on the long tables of college alumnae book sales, without question the dullest, least attractive section is marked "History," not because good histories don't exist even in used form, but because the shop owners and alumnae sorters still regard history as those ponderous, dull-brown or faded-blue textbooks of yesteryear, double-columned, pocked with puerile subtitles, and studded with grainy black-and-white pictures of dyspeptic diplomats, stolid soldiers, and purse-lipped presidents. "Factual" books go under History; anything lively or interesting about the past goes under Biography, Ethnic Studies, Literature, Religion, Anthropology, or Travel. Even the History Book Club gravitates toward biographies, geographies, and military campaigns, as if its readers couldn't cope with—or wouldn't buy—riskier interpretations of larger and messier subjects.

Against such odds, can anyone argue persuasively that history in essence is one of the humanities, one of those artful disciplines that explore, explain, and celebrate human beings in their full collective and individual humanity? I would like to make that argument by suggesting that a major component of the historian's equipment, indeed his most important tool, is his imagination, not unlike the poet's or the novelist's.

I realize that some cultural heavyweights would find such a notion strange if not downright ludicrous. Through the mouth of a young divinity student from Salamanca, Cervantes argued that "it is one thing to write like a poet, and another thing to write like an historian. The poet can tell or sing of things, not as they were but as they ought to have been, whereas the historian must describe them, not as they ought to have been but as they were, without exaggerating or suppressing the truth in any particular."[3] Dr. Johnson simply snorted that "in historical composition all the greatest powers of the human mind are quiescent. . . . Imagination is not required in any high degree."[4] And from the "scientific" seminars of the nineteenth-century German universities came the Rankean battlecry: Write history *"wie es eigentlich gewesen*—as it had really been,"* as if total immersion in the archives would skim off any dangerously inventive cells from the historian's brain.

I prefer the notion of history dropped as an aside by George Steiner and supported by a host of practicing historians, past and present. In a review of a book by a French medievalist, Steiner characterized history as "exact imagining," and I know of no better encapsulation.[5]

In order to carry the battle into the enemy camp, we need our own supply of pithy quotations from eminent sources. Leading the charge to disarm the followers of Leopold von Ranke is a good nineteenth-century Prussian, Johann Gustav Droysen, who told his readers that "History is the only science enjoying the ambiguous fortune of being required to be at the same time an art."[6] Garrett Mattingly, the artful stylist of *The Armada* and far from a quixotic romantic, turned it around when he said "History is the most difficult of the belles lettres, for it must be true."[7] And to parry Dr. Johnson we have the unassailably English academic, G. M. Trevelyan, who was convinced that "the appeal of history to us all is in the last analysis poetic. But the poetry of history does not consist of imagination roaming at large," he cautioned, "but of imagination pursuing the fact and fastening upon it."[8]

Most people will have no trouble accepting that historians pursue facts—the "exact" half of Steiner's "exact imagining." That's always the first phase (and, unfortunately, often the last) of what we are taught in academic history courses, certainly as freshmen and as first-year graduate students. Perhaps without ever saluting the tattered flag of positivism, we learn that history is a kind of science, or at least a rigorous methodology, for the collection and verification of facts about the past and their logical and chronological relations. We learn to pray at the altar of Research, as John Livingston Lowes catechized, with "rigorous exactness in both the employment and the presentation of one's facts; scrupulous verification of every statement resting on authority; wise caution in drawing inferences; [and constant] vigilance which overlooks no evidence."[9] We learn to arrange events in strict temporal order so as to be able to distinguish causes from effects. We learn that total accuracy is a duty, not an option, particularly when putting words in dead men's mouths. We learn to rely on primary sources from participants and eyewit-nesses, but also to distrust those with crossed eyes, forked tongues, and interests to serve. We learn to circumnavigate a subject from all sides and angles, seeking closure and comprehensiveness of vision. And while we're at it, we look for contrary evidence, in hopes of finding the gaps in our armor before a deadly reviewer does.

After shamelessly ransacking virtually the whole university for methodologies and angles of vision, we collect our precious nuggets, those hard-core facts from the past. Contrary to popular opinion, they're not all as desiccated as royal genealogies, Civil War battles, or the provisions of the Hawley-Smoot tariff. Perfectly respectable historians have been known to scrounge for "facts" such as lost land-scapes in Tahiti, the color of a dead queen's underwear, the death rate of cats in a French working-class parish, the changing price of peasants' bread, gun barrel and pipe stem bores, the salt content of roily river water and the shell content of native pottery, the forgotten meaning of familiar words, and that most elusive of all quests, the mo-tivations behind human behavior, normal and abnormal, individual and collective. These are all "facts," but their mere mention suggests that the search for them is far from simple or dull.

While the historian does rummage around the past for his facts, he is not an indiscriminate pack rat. Some facts are worth more than others, some may be worth nothing. The reason is simple: history—what historians write—is not a three-dimensional reproduction of all that transpired in the lives of all people from the beginning of human time; that's the past. "History is not the past," Henry Glassie reminds us, "but a map of the past drawn from a particular point of view to be useful to the modern traveler."[10] In their collection and use of facts, historians are very selective, not only by choice but also of necessity. For the remains of the past are fragmentary, flawed, fugitive, and fragile.

Our best evidence about human history, people's words, have almost wholly vanished into thin air because they were spoken and not written down. The fortuitous fragment that did reach paper has suffered from the cruel and largely random action of vermin, dampness, heat, wars, fires, floods, rebuilding, stupidity, venality, absentmindedness, acid paper, taste, and fashion. The record that survives is often seriously flawed and one-sided. Institutions, the literate, and the upper classes leave the heaviest documentary tracks. And most written documents were produced by myopic, careless, self-interested, or insensitive observers or by indifferent factota in great impersonal bureaucracies. Nor are the records of the past equally accessible. One-of-a-kind books, manuscripts, and paintings are buried in exclusive libraries and private collections; governments, heirs, and principals restrict access and use; fads and fashions of scholarship consign whole genres of documents to limbo until the winds change. And if the ravages of the past were not enough, the record is continually being lost: archaeological and historical sites are bulldozed for condominiums and parking lots; frescoes are flooded, paintings slashed or stolen; documents are burned or shredded; languages die out with native speakers; stone monuments disintegrate from auto emissions and acid rain.

For most historians, the major problem is not research into the past, which despite its myriad enemies always seems to yield an excess of usable facts, but writing about it. "Research is endlessly seductive," as Barbara Tuchman knew, "but writing is hard work."[11] The reason writing is so hard is that it calls upon the historian's imagination at literally every stage.

After our research has been completed and our note-cards piled high, the mute data must be summoned to life through active acts of imagination. The first task in writing history is to *reanimate* the known facts, which come lifeless from the page. We must *revivify, resurrect,* and *re-create* the past for ourselves, in our mind's eye, before we can ever hope to transmit that vision to others. We must take the raw materials of our searches, as Paul Horgan has said, "through the crucible fires of our own achieved awareness."[12] Like poets and novelists, we must seize the opportunity and take the courageous step—to imagine what we know. For "without that intuition which we call 'historical insight,' but which is really a specially controlled exercise of the creative imagination," Garrett Mattingly noted, "most of the past can never be said to exist as history but only as the unorganized material from which history can be evoked."[13]

Lest this be thought a peculiarly romantic or modern notion, listen to the Reverend Ezra Stiles, Puritan president of Yale in the eighteenth century and a man deeply versed in history. "Fidelity in narrating *Facts* is a great and principal thing," he said,

> but then only is this species of writing perfect, when besides a well digested series of authenticated Transactions and Events, the motives and *Springs of Action* are fairly laid open and arise into view with all their Effects about them, when characters are made to live again, and past scenes are endowed with a kind of perpetual Resurrection in History.[14]

The main reason we must constantly seek to resurrect and reanimate the past is that, as the novelist L. P. Hartley noticed, "the past is a foreign country; they do things differently there."[15] While people in the past bore familiar human shapes and responded to essentially the same human needs we do, their minds and sensibilities were very different from ours. We simply cannot assume that "human nature" is unchanging and universal, except in the most uninteresting and uninformative generic sense, because cultures and what used to be called *Zeitgeists*— "spirits of the times"—mold and fashion the relatively plastic givens of human psychology and even biology into different species. Without a strenuous act of imagination, how could a modern historian, who has never known hunger for more than a few hours or been wracked by paralyzing fear of the plague or the devils of absolute, pitch-black night, possibly understand the intellectual and emotional climate of a sixteenth-century peasant or a seventeenth-century Huron? How else could a white female historian from one of the Seven Sister colleges come to grips with the alien lives of male slaves in the eighteenth century, or a black historian, born and raised in a northern city, get inside the heads and hearts of white slave owners in the Antebellum South?

It is ironic that while our knowledge of the present is but a partial and imperfect guide to the past, it's the only guide we have. But deep research and the liberal exercise of intuition and empathy can help reduce its limitations. After immersing ourselves in the recorded thoughts, feelings, and actions of the past, we must try to identify with its actors, to rethink their thoughts, re-experience their emotions, relive their deeds. In her imaginative biography of the emperor Hadrian, Marguerite Yourcenar urged us "through hundreds of note cards [to] pursue each incident to the very moment that it occurred. . . . Strive to read a text of the Second Century," she said, "with the eyes, soul, and feelings of the Second Century; let it steep in that mother solution which the facts of its own time provide; set aside, if possible, all beliefs and sentiments which have accumulated in successive strata between those persons and us."[16]

The only way we can achieve that re-creation is to draw on what Jack Hexter calls "the second record." Entirely personal and individual, the second record is

> everything [the historian] can bring to bear on the record of the past in order to elicit . . . the best account he can render of what he believes actually happened in the past. Potentially, therefore, it embraces his skills, the range of his knowledge, the set of his mind, the substance, quality, and character of his experience—his total consciousness.[17]

Paul Horgan said much the same: "The historian's sense of actuality is achieved by a feeling for humanity which has been finely honed from the very beginning of his studies, indeed of his independent life as a sentient human being. . . ."[18]

It is no coincidence that the historian's penetration of the foreignness of the past bears an uncanny resemblance to the anthropologist's imaginative entry into other cultures and to the novelist's forging of historically plausible though ultimately imaginary worlds and populations. All must find, fashion, and re-create alien presences in their imaginations before attempting to share them with their readers.

Frequently the records of the past, while abundant in general, are thin in specifics that the historian would like to know in order to tell a reasonably full and accurate story. He is thus forced to fill those lacunae with educated, or, as I would prefer, *imaginative,* guesses by extending the well known to the unknown. Controlled imagination is the only resource which permits us to read a person's character from a portrait or a diary, to reconstruct a dwelling from a buried foundation or a probate inventory, to piece together a battle, riot, or lover's quarrel from one-sided evi-

dence, or to repopulate a town from birth, death, and marriage registers. Once the historian acquires through his
research what John Updike calls the "fundamental fea-
sibilities" of a specific place-in-time, he can, like the novelist, "imagine freely there" to close the gaps in his understanding, which of course is larger and more valuable than
mere knowledge.[19]

The third role that imagination plays is in helping the
historian conjure the choices and alternatives that historical actors faced before they chose specific paths of action.
One of the hardest things for historians to remember is
that events now long in the past were once in the future.
Although history is lived forwards, facing down the stream
of time into uncertainty, it is understood and written only
in retrospect. We know the end before we consider the
beginning, and we can never wholly recapture what it was
like to know only the beginning. But there are two reasons
why it is important to "restore to the past its lost uncertain-
ties," in Hugh Trevor-Roper's words, to "reopen the doors
which the *fait accompli* has closed."[20]

First, historians no less than other humanists must constantly demonstrate that free will is not a mere philosophical axiom but a fact of life. While it is true that people are
bound by the constraints of heredity, society, and culture,
their choices are almost never limited to one course of
action. Only the blessed curse of hindsight prompts us, in
moments of intellectual weakness or indolence, to speak of
historical "inevitability" and other forms of determinism.
As Alexander Solzhenitsyn, who surely knows, admon-
ishes, "We must not hide behind fate's petticoats; the most
important decisions in our lives, when all is said, we make
for ourselves."[21]

And second, if written history is to capture the raw and
complex reality of the past, it must communicate what
William Bouwsma calls "the sense of contingency and,

therefore, suspense—the sense that the drama might have turned out otherwise—that belongs to all human temporal experience."[22] With imagination applied to deep knowledge, we can establish the real choices that people had in the past, rather than anachronistic, moralistic, or wishful ones. To expect a seventeenth-century Jesuit, for example, to treat his Indian neophytes as a modern social worker, trial lawyer, Peace Corpsman, or anthropologist might is to suffer from congestive failure of the imagination. His culture and even his order allowed him to play several roles, but these weren't among them.

Thus far we have spoken of imagination's role in ferreting and fleshing out particular historical details. But it has an even more vital part to play in discerning the larger patterns, structures, and meanings behind particular events and facts which contemporaries were not able to see. Here hindsight is indispensable for pulling into a single field of vision the beginning and the dénouement of the historical plot. But it is largely the synoptic imagination which completes the plot, which sees relations where the eye sees only facts, which sees the lines of form that strike through seeming chaos, which sees underlying unity in apparently diverse phenomena. Imagination has three major functions: (1) to originate, (2) to re-create, and, equally important, (3) to relate diverse elements of life to each other. Without imagination, historians would never see the woods for the trees—or the trees for the leaves; their meticulous minds would remain mired in the minutiae of their natty note cards.

Bernard Bailyn spoke recently of the historian's grasp of the whole, and pointed to Charles McLean Andrews, Ronald Syme, Perry Miller, and Lewis Namier as exemplars. The distinguishing mark of their work, Bailyn argued, was their "capacity to conceive of a hitherto glimpsed world, or of a world only vaguely and imperfectly seen before . . . a vision of a total world." From "occasional glimpses of reality" in the past record, "they had sensed, had pictured, and had conceived whole, the entire world that lay below."[23]

Perhaps the most famous synoptic vision in American history (analogous to Gibbon's among the "bare ruin'd choirs" of the Roman Empire) is Perry Miller's insight among a load of fuel drums in the African Congo. There, in 1926, while unloading a shipment of American case oil, Miller was suddenly caught by a vision of "the uniqueness of the American experience" and the pressing need to expound to the twentieth-century reader "the innermost propulsion of the United States." He knew he needed "a coherence with which [he] could coherently begin" and he quickly found it in the intellectual history of the Puritan migration from Europe to what he would mistakenly call "the vacant wilderness of America." His two-volume portrait of *The New England Mind,* incredibly rich in nuance and detail, is a splendid realization of that "sudden epiphany" on the banks of the Congo.[24]

With his understanding of the past largely achieved, the historian begins to plan his writing. Again, imagination is indispensable. But even before sketching an outline and certainly well before inserting the first sheet of intimidatingly blank paper into the typewriter, he should fix in mind the specific audience he plans to address. This takes another act of imagination because, as Father Ong has observed, "The Writer's Audience Is Always a Fiction." [25] Not to know for whom you are writing is to invite literary disaster, or at least an unfortunate mélange of missed signals and mixed messages.

In 1951 Louis Wright, in one of his charming newsletters from the Folger Library, complained that "too much scholarly publication gives the appearance of having been written for no discernible audience."[26] Things are no better now and much of the blame belongs to the doctoral dissertation, which gets young historians into the bad habit of writing either for a disembodied, pedantic muse or for a handful of academic specialists. It is better for all students of the humanities to write for an "ideal reader," someone (in Margaret Atwood's description) "intelligent, capable of feeling, possessed of a moral sense, a lover of language, and very demanding"—qualities which will constantly draw their like from the author.[27]

Since history at its best is shared discovery, the historian's final and most important task is to *translate* his vision, his "achieved awareness" and understanding, of the past for the modern reader. This is far from easy, for two reasons. First, the historian's goal must be to tell his story in such a way that the reader will actually *experience* the past rather than simply hear about it. And second, the historian must find a way to translate the foreign idiom of the past into that of his own time, without breaking faith with the past.

Returning from the "foreign country" of the past, the historian confronts an artistic problem similar to that of the anthropologist returning from field work in a foreign culture. Like the denizens of the past, the anthropologist's natives have their own ways of doing things, relating to each other, and making sense of the universe. They view the world through unique lenses and classify its movements and parts according to their own consistent schemes. The input of their minds and the output of their tongues are keyed to a complex code of meaning, which can be deciphered only after long study and with great sensitivity. If the participant-observer, the scholar, manages to break the code, to understand finally what makes the natives tick, he must then translate his understanding into the modern idiom of his own culture, which operates according to a very different code. In other words, the historian must respect the contextual integrity of the past while transmuting it through his art. Such a delicate agenda, of course, depends heavily on the writer's imagination.

At every stage the literary genesis of a book of history is a work of imagination. What matters most in history, Lewis Namier reminded us, is "the great outline and the significant detail; what must be avoided is [a] deadly morass of irrelevant narrative" in between.[28] As for any art, the solution of form for a work of history is the most important of the many aesthetic acts that must be performed. For the past has no shape; as John Updike recognized, "billions of consciousnesses silt history full, and every one of them the center of the universe."[29] Only literature has shape, and historical writing that is not literature is quickly consigned to deserved oblivion.

In earlier centuries, the best histories were written and read as literature. Gibbon, Prescott, Parkman, and Bancroft were best-selling authors among educated classes much smaller than ours. But since the professionalization of scholarship at the turn of the century, most historians have dropped their literary mantles fleeing in terror from that academic hobgoblin, "popular history." The public hunger for history has thus been fed largely by non-academic historians and historical novelists who write to be read, not by history professors whose increasingly specialized monographs reach tens of readers. The old sour-grape response of the academics simply will not wash: many of the so-called "popularizers" *do* do their homework, usually in the primary sources and in the professors' own monographs. But they reshape the facts they find into intelligible and eminently readable stories. They know what the poet-librarian Philip Larkin knew, that "readability to a large extent is credibility."[30]

Clearly, academic historians could improve their art by

paying closer attention to the work of their imaginative brethren, the novelists. Two of my favorite historians of an earlier generation—Paul Horgan and Bernard DeVoto— were also novelists who struggled daily with the quest for form. Both recognized the need for artistic form in history.

Horgan, whose two-volume biography of the Rio Grande River through three cultures and four centuries posed enormous problems of design and focus, believed that the most essential elements in the historian's make-up are "his imagination, his grasp of the whole, and his projection of form." For "design itself," he knew, "becomes a [crucial] reference—to information, to a point of view, to a flow of proper proportion between the parts, and to a just placing of emphasis."[31]

DeVoto once complained to a correspondent who had admired his *Across the Wide Missouri* that "very few historians of our time, practically no academic historians, realize that history is not only knowledge, not only knowledge and wisdom even, but is also art. I do," he asserted. "My books employ the methods and techniques of literature and especially they have structure as literature. They have form. What's more to the point . . . that form is used to reveal meaning. The meaning is the end in view."[32]

The structure of a book usually takes shape piece by piece, while the research is proceeding, but, since the imagination doesn't keep regular hours, it can change even after the writing has been launched. Witness Harold Nicolson, British diplomat and historian. In his diary for September 14, 1949 he wrote: "I work the whole time on Chapter VI and finish with the death of King Edward VII just before dinner. But in my bath I decided that I must make two chapters of it. This is depressing, but right. One simply must be firm with oneself about getting the architecture of books right."[33]

Somewhere along the way in our historical educations,

usually too late to prevent a good deal of mental mischief, we learn that history is not only a collection of hard facts but a congeries of soft interpretations. For many students this revelation can be disturbing because it seems to threaten the cool objectivity and calm authority of their textbooks. But for neophyte historians it gives the subject a new lease on life and introduces them to the humane and imaginative possibilities of the discipline. Where memorization of facts was the dominant mode of learning before, analysis of literary strategies must dominate after the discovery of interpretation.

All histories are interpretive unless they are dull and shapeless. If they have a point, they have a plot, a storyline that connects the value-free facts of the past into an intelligible pattern of meaning. Since most historical sequences or collections of facts about past events can be "emplotted" in a number of different ways so as to provide different interpretations, the historian makes an *aesthetic* choice based on the perceived fit between the facts as he knows them and a number of pre-coded plots. These plots boil down to the four archetypal forms of narrative fiction, dissected by Northrop Frye in *The Anatomy of Criticism*—romance, tragedy, comedy and satire. They are "extended metaphors" for reality, "verbal fictions" which constitute what Hayden White calls "the deep structure of the historical imagination."[34] They are vital to the historical enterprise because they serve as *explanations* of the past; in DeVoto's words, "the meaning is the end in view."[35] Only the historian's imagination can prefigure that goal and thereby provide histories with coherent form from beginning to end.

The plots of my own histories of Indian-white relations tend toward gentle satire, of which irony is the major expression, though some subplots and story events are played as comedy or tragedy. They are structured that way

because the larger story cast in the ironic mode gains whatever effects it has by frustrating normal expectations about
the kinds of effects created by the smaller stories cast in the
comic or tragic mode. As I have studied the record of the
past, I have become convinced that the visions of the world
represented by romance, comedy, and tragedy are ultimately inadequate to express the hopes, possibilities, and
truths of human existence. Something like genial skepticism is called for, rather than airy optimism or cynicism. I
know of no better way to regard the spectacle of Europeans dashing to America to "reduce the savages to civility"
by cutting the Indians' hair and making them wear pants,
only to find hundreds of those civilizing intruders being
converted with deceptive ease to the Americans' allegedly
"savage" way of life.[36]

A boundless resource, the imagination spares no detail
while working away at the grand design. With the anticipated end in view, the historian will have ready criteria for
selecting facts that will contribute to and not detract from
it. As he attempts to translate each fact, each thought, into
his own idiom, he is unconsciously creating his own inimi-
table style. There has been a lot of twaddle written about
style. Style is not, as most undergraduates believe, rhetori-
cal frosting on angel food facts; it is inseparable from content. I like Alfred North Whitehead's definition: "Style,"
he said, "is an aesthetic sense, based on admiration for the
direct attainment of a foreseen end, simply and without
waste."[37] The greatest possible merit of style," Hawthorne
knew, "is to make the words absolutely disappear into the
thought."[38] As the bridge to substance, style is the art of
the historian's science. Style pervades a historian's whole
work, from the choice and definition of subject through
the research to the final literary expression. But as Carl
Becker cautioned, "good style in writing is like happiness

in living—something that comes to you, if it comes at all, only if you are preoccupied with something else; if you deliberately go after it you will probably not get it."[39]

What the historian should be preoccupied with are the qualities of good historical writing: accuracy, clarity, conciseness, disinterestedness, and vigor. Perhaps above all, vigor. Jack Hexter is right to charge that "dull history is bad history to the extent to which it is dull."[40] Like his ideal reader, the historian should be a great lover of words. "A perfect writer," said Walt Whitman, "would make words sing, dance, kiss, do the male and female act, bear children, weep, bleed, rage, stab, steal, fire cannon, steer ships, sack cities, charge with cavalry or infantry, or do anything that man or woman or the natural powers can do."[41] He should even be as persnickety about punctuation as Oscar Wilde, who claimed that he had spent Saturday taking a comma out of something he had written and Sunday putting it in again.

When all the elements of style have received the necessary attention, the well-written history, like all good literature, should be a book that can be satisfactorily read aloud. If it cannot, it should be passed once more through the writer's imagination.

Of course, historians have no monopoly on scholarly imagination. But they have no *less* need of imagination than do other students of the humanities—or, it should be added, of the social or the physical sciences. For as Whitehead recognized, the proper function of a university in all its parts is the "imaginative acquisition of knowledge." "The whole point of a university, on its educational side," he said, "is to bring the young under the intellectual influence of a band of imaginative scholars." The scholar's deadliest enemies are pedantry and inert ideas, which are "merely received into the mind without being utilized, or tested, or thrown into fresh combinations."[42] As history has sometimes shown, the best way to combat these foes is to illuminate our teaching and our scholarship not only with the facts but with what Emily Dickinson called the "phosphorescence" of learning.[43]

Views from the Shore

CHAPTER TWO

Imagining the Other: First Encounters in North America

THE FOLLOWING ESSAY HAS HAD A LONG EVOLUTION. IT sprang from a twelve-page invitation from a Spanish foundation to contribute a paper on North America to a tripartite conference called "In Word and Deed: Interethnic Encounters and Cultural Developments in the New World." I was recruited for a session intriguingly entitled *"Asombro y duda ante los otros"* (Amazement and doubt in the presence of the other). Furthermore, two parts of the conference were to be held in Trujillo, Spain, and a princely sounding honorarium of *pesetas* was held out as an additional carrot. So I signed on with unseemly haste, even after learning that the site of the initial conference of which I was to be a part was Albany, New York, more than familiar to me from fifteen years of attending the annual meetings of the Conference on Iroquois Research.

At the bilingual conference in October 1988, I gave a brief version of my paper per instructions, but later submitted an expanded version for publication in the conference proceedings. Replete with annoying anthropological-style "footnotes," again per instructions, it eventually appeared in *Interethnic Images: Discourse and Practice in the New World,* edited by Gary H. Gossen and J. Jorge Klor de Alva.*

*Albany and Austin: Institute of Mesoamerican Studies and the University of Texas Press, 1992.

25

In 1990 I inherited the chairmanship of the American Historical Association's Columbus Quincentenary Committee, on which
I had served since its founding in 1985. With it I fell heir to much
delayed plans for a four-pamphlet series, "Essays on the Columbian Encounter," designed to acquaint history teachers and students with the major issues, best bibliography, and salient information, old and new, on the American aftermath of 1492. In
order to launch the series without further delay, the committee
chose a much extended and revised version of my Albany essay
as the first title. After running the editorial gauntlet of Carla
Rahn Phillips and David Weber, the series co-editors, it was published by the AHA in the winter of 1991. I trust that it will
interest readers well beyond the historical guild.

W HEN CHRISTOPHER COLUMBUS, "ADMIRAL OF THE
Ocean Sea," stumbled across the Taíno people of Guanahaní island on October 12, 1492, he unwittingly launched
the most massive encounter of foreign peoples in human
history. Five centuries later we are taking stock of that
momentous meeting of the so-called "Old World" with the
"New," of Europe (and quickly Africa and Asia) with the
Americas.

Since the late 1960s and early '70s, when the unpopular
war in Southeast Asia, the civil rights movement, and
American Indian protests shook our consciousness and re-
focused our imaginations, our interpretations of those
early American encounters have become increasingly bifocal and sensitive to native perspectives. We have come to
see with virtually new eyes that the Indians discovered Columbus and his world as surely and as importantly as he
did them and theirs. With good reason, the theme of the
Columbian quincentenary is the *mutuality* of discovery and

acculturation during five hundred years of ongoing "encounter."

The theme of the quadricentenary in 1892 was far different. In Spain and the United States particularly, the dominant cause of celebration (not mere commemoration or reflection) was the *progress* of Western technology, Christian religion, and democratic institutions over the Western Hemisphere, particularly among the "benighted" and "primitive" peoples Columbus "discovered" (as if they were lost). The heroic historical stature of the great discoverer himself was symbolized in countless marble statues; the human subjects of his discovery and exploitation were remembered only in sanitized museum cases highlighting their exotic aboriginality or in live demonstrations of their newfound civility, literacy, and industry. Unacknowledged were the cataclysmic ravages of disease, warfare, injustice, and dispossession that were the major (but not only) legacy of that encounter. No accounting was made of the frightful human toll of history, the incalculable costs of "progress," "civilization," and "empire."

Textbook Firsts

Before the reorientation of the '60s and '70s, North Americans knew something of the outlines of the debit side of the encounter (with the exception of disease) from their textbooks. But they tended to assume, with the textbook authors, that any warfare or bloodshed was the result of "savages" hopelessly resisting the inexorable incursion of "civilized" explorers and colonists bent on delivering them from native despotism, false religion, and cultural backwardness. In their collective mind's eye, a vision that many of us still share, they saw countless depictions of in-

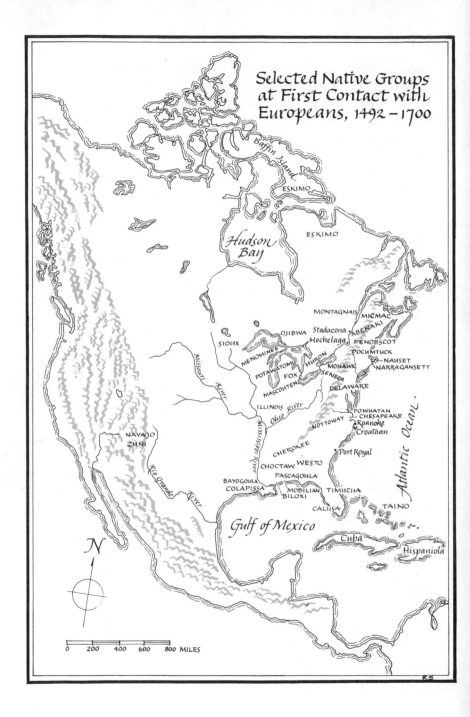

Selected Native Groups
at First Contact with
Europeans, 1492–1700

Baffin Island

ESKIMO

ESKIMO

Hudson
Bay

MONTAGNAIS   MICMAC

OJIBWA   Stadacona   ABENAKI
SIOUX   Hochelaga   PENOBSCOT
MENOMINEE   POCUMTUCK
POTAWATOMI   HURON   MOHAWK   NAUSET
FOX   SENECA   NARRAGANSETT
MASCOUTEN   DELAWARE
ILLINOIS   Ohio River
POWHATAN
NOTTOWAY   CHESAPEAKE
Roanoke
CHEROKEE   Croatoan
CHOCTAW   WESTO   Port Royal
BAYOGOULA   PASCAGOULA
COLAPISSA   MOBILIAN   TIMUCHA
BILOXI
CALUSA   TAINO

Missouri River

Rio Grande

River

Gulf of Mexico   Cuba
Hispaniola

Atlantic Ocean

N

0   200   400   600   800 MILES

trepid Europeans wading ashore in a hail of flint-tipped arrows and throat-catching war whoops. They remembered all too vividly how the Roanoke colonists were lost to history after numerous attacks by chief Wingina's naked minions in 1585–87, how the Chesapeakes of Cape Henry crept up "like Beares, with their Bowes in their mouthes" to assault the first wave of Virginia settlers in 1607, and how Nauset warriors pelted arrows at the poor Pilgrims who initially landed on Cape Cod in 1620 before finding shelter and religious toleration at Plymouth.[1]

But what the Pilgrims called "The First Encounter" was not, except for them. Fresh from European ports, the Pilgrims could not know that the natives who received them so ungraciously were not acting out of some atavistic racial hatred or primitive xenophobia but from a well-founded sense of revenge for injuries inflicted by earlier European visitors. By 1607 or 1620, when most textbooks before the '70s began the American story, many of the native peoples of the Atlantic seaboard had experienced fifty or a hundred years of contact with European ships, men, and erstwhile colonies. Predictably, many of those contacts ended in suspicion, fear, and conflict.

If we hope to plumb the long-term significance of the cultural encounters set in motion by the Columbian advent in 1492, we must do two things. First, we must search carefully for the very earliest Indian-European encounters, before either party had been forced into pugnacity or unbending distrust by conflict with the other. This will entail a certain amount of chronological backpeddling into the sixteenth century, but because of the uneven character of American exploration, even in the East, it is possible to find such innocent moments well into the seventeenth and even eighteenth centuries. And second, if we hope to recapture the palpable reality of those earliest encounters, we must, like the actors themselves, try to look squarely into the

"others'" faces and to hear, not just listen to, the halting
dialogues—or sad monologues—they carried on. Since
"the imaginations which people have of one another are
the solid facts of society," we must try to imagine the imaginations that Europeans and Indians had of each other.[2]

This will be no easy task because the great majority of
documents we have been left were written by the European
invaders of the Americas and not by the Indians. Thus we
have plenty of European depictions of the alien faces and
conduct they saw and the strange words they heard, but we
have too few Indian visions of the European intruders.
The temptation is to use what is easily available, but, in this
case particularly, we should firmly resist it. For it would
hoodwink us to the fact that *all* peoples are ethnocentric,
that cultural judgments are always relative, and that every
"other" we objectify is at the same time a first-person
subject, an "I." When reading early contact accounts, we
should keep in mind Michel de Montaigne's sly observation that "Each man calls barbarism whatever is not his own
practice. . . . Barbarians are no more marvelous to us
than we are to them, nor for better cause." In America as in
ancient Greece, language often constituted the first sign of
difference. As the apostle Paul warned the Corinthians: "If
I know not the meaning of the voice, I shall be unto him
that speaketh a barbarian, and he that speaketh shall be a
barbarian unto me."[3]

Imagining the "Other"

Before the "barbarians" of Europe and America actually
met, they each had some notion of what the "other" would
probably be like. Thanks to their own recent experience of
peoples and places and to the rediscovered libraries of the
ancient world, Europeans had a rich "cabinet of curi-

osities," accumulated over many centuries on three continents, from which to draw. From Marco Polo's thirteenth-century travels in particular, they continued to learn of immense empires and fabulous riches in the Far East. To resourceful fleets of Portuguese seamen, Africa gradually revealed its cultural secrets. Christian crusaders heading for the Holy City and pilgrims of every stripe left their footprints all around the sun-drenched rim of the Mediterranean. Hot on the heels of all these adventurers were eager avatars of trade, fanning out from the commercial capitals of Europe in search of useful knowledge as well as luxury goods and mineral wealth.

Beneath this growing knowledge of cultures and geographies lay a bedrock of ancient precedent—the Old and New Testaments and the classical heritage of Greece and Rome recently regained by the scholars of the Renaissance—and an even denser stratum of medieval legend. While the second-century Egyptian astronomer Claudius Ptolemy gave sixteenth-century Europeans a workable heaven by which to navigate and the fifth-century B.C. traveler-historian Herodotus a way to write the history of "others," credulous tale-tellers of the Middle Ages topped their imaginations with a bestiary of human monsters, monstrosities, and wild hairy men.

Accordingly, peoples of black, brown, yellow, and white skin, religions as diverse as Buddhism, pantheism, and atheism, and a spectrum of polities from divine monarchy to natural anarchy could be found in the collective wisdom of Europe. But also present, for learned and credulous alike, were strange people who ate human flesh, peered at the world from one large eye in the middle of their chests, and barked rather than spoke from canine snouts. To Europeans, "others" might appear in an infinite variety of shapes, hues, and habits, but they were always and distinctly unlike Europeans and, for the most part, therefore

Medieval travel books prominently featured archtypal human monstrosities, who presumably lived in exotic, unexplored countries.
Among the oddities in Gregor Reisch's menagerie were a sciapode
("who is shading himself under his only foot"), a cyclops, a little
dicephalus (two-headed person), an acephalus (with his face in his
chest), and a cynocephalus (dog-headed). From Reisch, *Margarita Philo-
sophica* (Basel, 1517).

regarded as inferior. Before and after 1492, the occidental
wall between "them" and "us" was high, and only a few
thinkers like Montaigne in the sixteenth century were
available to give fellow Europeans a leg up.[4]

The relatively isolated natives of the Americas, by contrast, were prepared by experience to see in "others"
largely faithful reflections of themselves or of the anthro-
pomorphic deities who populated their pantheons. While
Europeans found "others" to be different and usually inferior, the "others" the Indians knew tended to be similar or

superior. This is not to say that Indian cultures were bless-edly lacking in ethnocentrism: they were as hide-bound as the next group. But their human experience was limited solely to other Indian peoples, so their ethnographic cate-gories appear to have been relatively few, perhaps some variation on three.

The Indians' first category consisted of their own imme-diate social group, whether band, tribe, chiefdom, or con-federacy. As if to celebrate their ethnocentrism, the names many, perhaps most, groups (Iroquois, Navajo, Penobscot) gave themselves meant "the original people" or "the true men," in other words, the only folks who mattered. Their enemies and neighbors, on the other hand, were called names (Eskimo, Sioux, Nottoway) that meant "raw meat-eaters," "bark-eaters," or "rattlesnakes." In cultural retro-spect, most of these perceived differences were minor or nonexistent and were simply inflated or invented by poli-tics and inherited hatreds. Beneath the reciprocal epithets were brown-skinned Americans whose lives were strikingly similar, all things considered.

Even the third category of "others"—the spiritual beings with whom the Indian people closely shared the world—did not vary greatly from group to group. While these "supernatural" (a distinction they did not make) persons could easily change appearance and voice, particularly when encountered in dreams or induced trances, the In-dians of North America shared a belief that all living things possessed "souls" or "spirits" capable of unrestricted move-ment in time and space and of harming or helping other "persons." Because the magnitude of their power was largely unknown and because they might appear in a strange guise, each "person" had to be treated with respect and circumspection, often in formal ceremonies of sup-plication and thanksgiving. Thus, when Europeans first appeared at the edge of the water, woods, plains, or desert, the Indians were prepared to treat with extraordinary "persons" whose physical manifestations might be very different from, but certainly not inferior to, their own.[5]

Native Prophecies and Memories

Even before the first white men materialized, they may have impressed themselves upon the Indian imagination. Shamans who were thought capable of seeing into the future and other prescient people may have prophesied the coming of the Europeans. I say "may have" because these prophecies were recorded only after contact with the literate newcomers. In 1540 Francisco Vázquez de Coronado was glad to hear from Zuni elders in the desert Southwest that "it was foretold them more than fifty years ago that a people such as we are would come, and from the direction we have come, and that the whole country would be conquered." It is not unlikely that the natives' memories were jogged by the 1,700 men in the Spanish entrada, including 250 heavily armed horse-soldiers. A year later, under similar conditions, six leaders from an Indian town near the Mississippi visited Hernando de Soto's camp, saying "they were come to see what people [the Spanish] were and that they had learned from their ancestors that a white race would inevitably subdue them."[6]

A *wiochist* or shaman had a similar message for the Powhatans as they confronted English bellicosity in early Virginia after 1607: he predicted that "bearded men should come & take away their Country & that there should none of the original Indians be left, within . . . an hundred & fifty" years. Another shaman was somewhat more ambiguous when he informed the "emperor" Powhatan that "from the *Chesapeack* Bay a Nation should arise, which should dissolve and give end to his Empier." While the apparently feckless Jamestown colonists looked on, Powhatan exterminated the whole tribe of *"Chessiopeians"* to hedge his bets.[7]

Confronting a different English challenge, natives in New England were given a prophecy appropriate to their circumstances. During the lethal plague that preceded the arrival of the Plymouth pilgrims in 1620, a Nauset man on Cape Cod dreamed of the advent of "a great many men" dressed in what proved to be English-style clothes. One of them, dressed all in black, stood on an eminence with a book in his hand and told the assembled Indians that "God was *moosquantum* or angry with them, and that he would kill them for their sinnes. . . ."[8]

More prevalent than prophesies were oral traditions regarding the Europeans' arrival, a few collected shortly after contact, most of them several centuries later. When the natives recalled their first encounters with European "others," it was novel "persons" like their own deities whom they remembered. In 1633 a young Montagnais on the north shore of the St. Lawrence related the story his grandmother had told him of the Indians' astonishment at seeing a French ship for the first time. Like many natives before and after, they thought it was a "moving Island." Having seen the men aboard, however, the Montagnais women began to prepare wigwams for them, "as is their custom when new guests arrive," and four canoes bade the strangers welcome. The French gave them a barrel of ship's biscuits and probably offered them some wine. But the natives were appalled that these people "drank blood and ate wood" and promptly threw the tasteless biscuits into the river. Obviously more impressed by French technology than cuisine, the Montagnais henceforth called the French *ouemichtigouchiou,* "men in a wooden canoe or boat."[9]

The Micmacs were equally unimpressed by French fare,

as they recalled in the nineteenth century. When the first Frenchmen arrived in the Gaspé, presumably in the early sixteenth century, the Micmacs "mistook the bread which was given them for a piece of birch tinder." When wine was proffered, perhaps a nice Bordeaux red, the natives became convinced that the strangers were "cruel and inhuman, since in their amusements . . . they drank blood without repugnance. . . . Therefore they remained some time not only without tasting it, but even without wishing to become in any manner intimate, or to hold intercourse, with a nation which they believed to be accustomed to blood and carnage."[10]

   Further west, perhaps around Lake Superior, an Ojibwa prophet dreamed that

> men of strange appearance have come across the great water. They have landed on our island [North America]. Their skins are white like snow, and on their faces long hair grows. These people have come across the great water in wonderfully large canoes which have great white wings like those of a giant bird. The men have long and sharp knives, and they have long black tubes which they point at birds and animals. The tubes make a smoke that rises into the air just like the smoke from our pipes. From them come fire and such terrific noise that I was frightened, even in my dream.

At once a flotilla of trusted men was sent through the Great Lakes and down the St. Lawrence to investigate. On the lower river they found a clearing in which all the trees had been cut down, which led them to conjecture that "giant beavers with huge, sharp teeth had done the cutting." The prophet disagreed, reminding them of the long knives in his dream. Knowing that their stone-headed axes could not cut such large trees so smoothly, they were "filled with awe, and with terror also." Still more puzzling were "long, rolled-up shavings" of wood and scraps of "bright-coloured cloth," which they stuck in their hair and wound around their heads. Farther down the river they finally came upon the white-faced bearded strangers with their astonishing long knives, thunder tubes, and giant winged canoes, just as the prophet had foretold.

Having satisfied their curiosity and fulfilled the prophet's dream, the Indians returned home with their trophies: each villager was given a small piece of cloth as a memento. To impress their neighbors, the Ojibwas followed an old custom. Just as they tied the scalps of their enemies on long poles, "now they fastened the splinters of wood and strips of calico to poles and sent them with special messengers" from one tribe to another. Thus were these strange articles passed from hand to hand around the whole lake, giving the natives of the interior their first knowledge of the white men from Europe.[11]

White Deities

The Indians regarded the Europeans' ability to fashion incredible objects and make them work less as mechanical aptitude than as spiritual power. When the Delawares, who once lived along the New Jersey-New York coast, met their first Dutch ship in the early seventeenth century, they concluded that it was a "remarkably large house in which the Mannitto (the Great or Supreme Being) himself was present." Thinking he was coming to pay them a visit, they prepared meat for a sacrifice, put all their religious effigies in order, and staged a grand dance to please or appease him. Meanwhile, the tribal conjurers tried to fathom his purpose in coming because their people were all "distracted between hope and fear." While preparations went forward, runners brought the welcome news that the visitors were humans like themselves, only strangely colored and oddly dressed. But when the Dutchmen made their appearance, graced the assembly with a round of liquor, and distributed iron and cloth gifts, the natives were confirmed in their original belief that every white man was an "inferior Mannitto attendant upon the Supreme Deity"— the ship's captain—who "shone superior" in his red velvet suit glittering with gold lace.[12]

The earliest European objects of native awe corroborated native testimony about their godlike reception. The gentle inhabitants of the West Indies, Columbus assured his sovereign sponsors, were "very firmly convinced that I, with these ships and men, came from the heavens, and in this belief they everywhere received me after they had mastered their fear." Even the Taínos he kidnapped as guides and interpreters and took to Spain to support his discoveries were "still of the opinion that I come from Heaven, for all the intercourse which they have had with me. They were the first to announce this wherever I went . . . 'Come! Come! See the men from Heaven!'"[13]

Four survivors of the ill-fated Florida expedition of Pánfilo de Narváez (1528) also traded on their reputation for divinity as they walked from eastern Texas to Mexico. After some success in curing Indians with Christian prayers, elementary surgery, and the power of positive thinking, Alvar Nuñez Cabeza de Vaca and his three cohorts were regarded wherever they went as "children of the sun." The crowds of native acolytes who accompanied them swore at each new village that the Spaniards "had power to heal the sick and to destroy," just like their own shamans. In order to preserve their tremendous influence over the natives, the Spanish "gods" cultivated an inscrutable public silence, letting their black servant, Estevánico, make their mundane arrangements. The strange caravan of white and black beings, apparently endowed with extraordinary spiritual power and attended by an adoring cast of hundreds, sometimes thousands, gave them "control throughout the country in all that the inhabitants had power, or deemed of any value, or cherished."[14]

Having read the accounts of his Spanish predecessors before launching his own gold-seeking entrada into the Southeast in 1539, Hernando de Soto burnished his divine attributes to a high lustre. Whenever he came to a new province and needed bearers, food, and guides, he announced through his interpreter that "he was a son of the sun and came from where it dwelt," that he and his men were immortal, and that the natives could hide nothing because the face that appeared in the mirror he held before them "told him whatever they were planning and thinking about." Only when Soto visibly weakened and took to his bed did a chief near the Mississippi call his bluff, "saying that with respect to what he said about being the son of the sun, let him dry up the great river and he would believe him." Nor, when Soto died three days later, did the natives swallow the Spanish story that he was not dead but had only "gone to the sky as he had often done before."[15]

In the seventeenth century, Indians who first encountered French and English explorers also regarded them as deities from a familiar cosmos. When the English at Roanoke failed to sicken during Indian epidemics and seemed to show no sexual interest in native women—and had no women of their own—several of the local Indians "could not tel whether to thinke [them] gods or men." Believing in general that "all the gods are of humane shape," others thought the English immortal because they "were not borne of women." Likewise, when French traders and missionaries canoed into the upper Great Lakes in the 1660s, the Indians "often took them for spirits and gods." Having heard that the French were "a different species from other men," the Potawatomis near Green Bay were astonished to see in Nicolas Perrot, a French emissary, that the strangers possessed human form and "regarded it as a present that the sky and the spirits had made them in permitting one of the celestial beings to enter their land." Forty years later, wrote a missionary in 1700, the French in Louisiana had some difficulty in disabusing the Bayogoulas of the notion that "we are spirits descended from heaven, and that the fire of our cannon is the same sort as celestial fire."[16]

Welcoming the Strangers

The welcome and treatment the natives lavished on them convinced the Europeans even further that they were regarded as the bearers of divine tidings or at least of special human talents that were nonexistent or in very short supply in native society. It is difficult to tell from credulous European sources when the natives first realized that the intruders in their midst were not gods from another realm but were humans nonetheless possessed of extraordinary "spirits" or "souls," on a par with their own shamans and witches who practiced the black and white arts. In large part, the Europeans were treated as any native dignitaries would have been, but some aspects of their reception were clearly intended to honor celestial rather than earthly visitors.

Europeans first realized that Indians had placed them in a category by themselves when they caused a sensation by walking into native villages. When Columbus sent two of his men to explore a large island town, the inhabitants "touched them and kissed their hands and feet, marveling and . . . attempting to see if they were, like themselves, of flesh and bone." After a five-day stay, the men returned to the ship but had some difficulty persuading five hundred natives not to accompany them in hopes of seeing them "return to the heavens." The southwestern Indians who wanted to touch Cabeza de Vaca's band of wandering medicine men "pressed us so closely," he half-boasted, "that they lacked little of killing us; and without letting us put our feet to the ground, carried us to their dwellings. We were so crowded upon by numbers, that we [escaped] into the houses they had made for us."[17]

The natives of the Great Lakes and upper Mississippi also "devoured [the first Europeans] with their eyes." In the 1660s the Green Bay Potawatomis did not "dare look [Nicolas Perrot] in his face; and the women and children watched him from a distance." About the same time, Father Claude Allouez felt slightly more discommoded by the villagers at Chequamegon on Lake Superior. "We were so frequently visited by these people," he recalled, "most of whom had never seen any Europeans, that we were overwhelmed" and religious instruction went slowly. He was happier with the visits of the teachable children, who came to him "in troops to satisfy their curiosity by looking at a stranger." Eight years later, Father Jacques Marquette was likewise showered with attention by the Illinois not far from the Mississippi. "All these people, who had never seen any Frenchmen among them," he wrote, "could not cease looking at us. They lay on the grass along the road; they preceded us, and then retraced their steps to come and see us again. All this was done noiselessly, and with marks of great respect for us." When the Frenchmen were walked through the three-hundred-house village after a feast, "an orator continually harangued to oblige all the people to come to see us without annoying us."[18]

Even relative latecomers among the English sometimes had to endure the astonished stares of native hosts. In 1674 three Englishmen in two different parts of the Southeast met Indians who had apparently not laid eyes on their like. At the Westo village on the Savannah River, the chief's house could not hold the crowd that wanted to admire

Henry Woodward, a surgeon and early planter of South
Carolina. The smaller fry solved the problem by climbing
up on the roof and peeling it back to get a clear view.
Meanwhile, beyond the Great Smoky Mountains, a town of
western Cherokees welcomed two servants of a Virginia
gentleman-trader "even to addoration in their cerrimonies
of courtesies." The visitors' equally unusual packhorse was
tethered to a stake in the middle of town and given a royal
diet of corn, fish, and bear oil. Similarly, the white guests
were invited to squat on a specially built scaffold so that the
natives "might stand and gaze at them and not offend
them by theire throng." None of these celebrated Europeans ever talked about his embarrassment or self-
consciousness under such exposure, but we can well imagine that even the most self-possessed and arrogant men
must occasionally have developed a healthy blush.[19]

An even surer sign that the first Europeans were exalted
in Indian eyes was the official welcome they received.
Those who arrived by water were first guided to the best
anchorages and landings. If smaller boats then could not
reach dry land, the natives often plowed into the surf or
stream to carry the sailors piggyback. On Hispaniola in
1492, villagers "insisted on carrying [Columbus and his
men] on their backs . . . through some rivers and muddy
places." French officers in sixteenth-century Florida traveled to an important chief's village perched on the shoulders, not merely the backs, of several Indians who sought
to keep them out of the marshy mire surrounding it. In
1535, en route to Hochelaga on the upper St. Lawrence,
wiry Jacques Cartier had been lifted from his longboat by a
husky Indian and carried to shore in the man's arms "as
easily as if he had been a six-year-old child." Having been
carted around in a red blanket on other occasions, Nicolas
Perrot and a French companion drew the line at being

Indian hospitality to the first Europeans is depicted in this 1556 engraving of Jacques Cartier's approach to the St. Lawrence Iroquois village of Hochelaga (present-day Montreal). Two Indians carry the French piggyback while other natives welcome Cartier and his men at one of the (fancifully drawn) palisade gates. Engraver Giacomo Gastaldi worked from Cartier's written description rather than personal observation, but he captured the spirit of native kindness to strangers. From Giovanni Battista Ramusio, *Terzo volume della navigationi et viaggi* (Venice, 1556).

piggybacked. They politely told their Mascouten hosts that "as they could shape . . . iron, they had strength to walk." Few other Europeans let pride get in the way of a free ride.[20]

If getting there was half the fun, the arrival must have been somewhat discomfiting to those who had no idea what to expect. As soon as the newcomers were deposited in the village square or the chief's house, a startling round of touching and rubbing began, the import of which was not immediately clear. On their eight-year trek through the Southwest after 1528, Cabeza de Vaca and his comrades received at least two different greetings. One village, after quelling their fear of the strangers, "reached their hands to our faces and bodies, and passed them in like manner over their own." Another group somewhat farther west greeted the Spaniards "with such yells as were terrific, striking the palms of their hands violently against their thighs," a response that would have scared the wits out of Europeans less accustomed to native ways.[21]

Fortunately for most landed immigrants, the former gentle greeting was much more typical in eastern America. On the Gaspé Peninsula, both the Micmacs and the visiting Stadaconans who met Cartier "rubbed his arms and his breast with their hands" in welcome. Fifty years later, in 1584, Arthur Barlowe was greeted at Roanoke by Granganimeo, the local chief's brother, who struck his head and chest and then Barlowe's "to shewe [they] were all one." Several hundred miles away, on the icy coasts of Baffin Island, Eskimo traders were initiating relations with John Davis and his crew by pointing to the sun, striking their chests "so hard that [the sailors] might heare the blow," and crying *"Iliaoute"* in a loud voice. When Davis stuck out his hand to greet one of them English-style, the man kissed it instead.[22]

The customary greeting in South Carolina, as the English noted in the late 1660s, was the "stroaking of our shoulders with their palmes and sucking in theire breath the whilst." In Louisiana the French experienced a variation on the same theme. At their first camp near Biloxi in 1699, Pierre LeMoyne d'Iberville and his officers had their faces rubbed with white clay before being saluted in friendly fashion, which was, he wrote, to "pass their hands over their faces and breasts, and then pass their hands over yours, after which they raise them toward the sky, rubbing them together again and embracing again." Antoine de Sauvole, the fort commander, obviously found one party of Pascagoulas almost too much for his Gallic sensibilities.

"I have never seen natives [*sauvages*] less inhibited," he confided to his journal. "They have embraced us, something that I have never seen the others do." The most sensual treatment, however, was reserved for Europeans who had hiked into Indian country: their hosts massaged their feet, legs, joints, and even eyelids with soothing bear oil.[23]

But the cosseting had only begun. The visitors were next seated on fresh skins or reed mats, "harangued" (as they put it) with unintelligible speeches, entertained with dancing, singing, and games, and feasted to surfeit on such delicacies as *sagamité* (corn meal mush seasoned with fat) and roasted dog. An Illinois master of ceremonies, recalled Father Marquette, "filled a spoon with sagamité three or four times, and put it to my mouth as if I was a little child." After removing the bones from the second—fish—course and blowing on some pieces to cool them, the genial host put them in the Frenchmen's mouths "as one would give food to a bird." They passed on the dog course, as "gods" had some leave to do, but happily chewed the fat buffalo morsels again placed in their mouths. Most European guests, however, were allowed to feed themselves and so could take more time to appreciate native foods, upon which most of them would be dependent far longer than they could imagine.[24]

Becoming Americanized

Next came the serious business of assimilating the strangers into native society, of making the "others" even more like themselves, and securing peace until the newcomers displayed behavior that was less than "divine" or even, in native terms, "human." Throughout much of east-

Marche du
Calumet de Paia

ern America in the seventeenth and eighteenth centuries, the major vehicle of peaceful alliance was the calumet, a four-foot-long wood and stone pipe richly decorated with paint and a fan of long feathers. (After his Canadian experience, Iberville brought his own to Louisiana, an iron one "made in the shape of a ship with the white flag adorned with fleur-de-lis and ornamented with glass beads.") The Europeans soon learned that possession of a calumet was a passport through even hostile Indian country, and that sharing its consecrated smoke was the major ticket to diplomatic success. To refuse a calumet ceremony—which in the lower Mississippi Valley invariably lasted three days— was to declare war upon, or at least to risk affronting, the offering party. In 1701 Iberville took such a risk in passing a village of Mobilians because he did not have three days to spare. But he managed to unfurrow their brows by distributing several presents and taking a chief with him to receive the hospitality of Fort Biloxi.[25]

As early as the sixteenth century, smoke played another key role in welcoming the godlike Europeans. In native America, tobacco was sacred, and on its smoke prayers were lifted to heaven. The best way to honor any great-spirited being, therefore, was to offer it tobacco or smoke. When Father Allouez advised a Fox man to have his dangerously ill parents bled, the man poured powdered tobacco all over the priest's gown and said, "Thou art a spirit; come now, restore these sick people to health; I offer thee this tobacco in sacrifice." A dusty gown was small enough price to pay for such status, but other Frenchmen paid more dearly. In another part of the Great Lakes, Nicolas

(*Left*) French visitors await a line of Natchez dignitaries during a three-day calumet ceremony in early Louisiana. From Antoine Simon Le Page du Pratz (who lived among the Natchez from 1720 to 1728), *Histoire de la Louisiane*, 3 vols. (Paris, 1758).

Perrot had smoke blown directly into his face "as the great-est honor that they could render him; he saw himself smoked like meat," but gamely "said not a word." With Iberville on the Mississippi, Father Paul du Ru reported that, after puffing two or three times on a calumet, one of the Indians "came and blew smoke from his pipe into my nose as though to cense me." Du Ru may have come off better than the first French captain who sailed to the Men-ominees on Lake Michigan: he had tobacco ground into his forehead. One of the earliest Europeans to be honored with smoke was too ethnocentric to recognize his good fortune. When some Baffin Island Eskimos tried to place John Davis in the consecrating smoke of their fire, he pushed one of them into the smoke instead and testily had the fire stomped out and kicked into the sea.[26]

If being smoked connoted some kind of religious affir-mation, other ceremonies spelled political and social accep-tance of the newcomers. At least two European leaders had the honor of being "crowned" by their native counterparts, but the exact meaning of their coronation is still unclear. At the future site of La Navidad on Hispaniola, Columbus was fêted by the paramount chief Guacanagarí and five subordinate "kings," as the Admiral called them, "all with their crowns displaying their high rank." Guacanagarí led Columbus to a chair on a raised platform and "took off the crown from his own head and put it on the Admiral's. In return the grateful don dressed the chief in a collar of beautiful beads and agates, his own scarlet cloak, colored buskins, and a large silver ring. Probably the Indian got the better deal, as did the *Agouhanna* or head chief of Hoche-laga in 1535. When Jacques Cartier rubbed the chief's paralyzed arms and legs at his request, the grateful man took off the red hedgehog-skin band he wore as a crown and presented it to the Frenchman. Before he left, Cartier distributed an array of metal tools and jewelry to repay the

Hochelagans for their generous hospitality and political friendship.[27]

Cartier's education in native politics had begun even before he left his base near the future Quebec City. In an effort to dissuade Cartier from going upriver to visit the Hochelagans on Montreal Island, Donnacona, the chief of the rival Stadaconans, made him a present of three children, including the ten-year-old daughter of his own sister and the younger brother of Cartier's native interpreter. These human gifts, Cartier quickly learned, were meant as seals on a firm political alliance to prevent any trafficking with enemics. When the French persisted in their travel plans and threatened to give the children back, the Stadaconans relented and put the best face they could on the necessity of dealing with ignorant intruders who refused to play by the established rules of the diplomatic game. But Cartier had already learned enough to accept the eight-year-old daughter of the chief at Achelacy, some twenty-five leagues upriver, an alliance that paid dividends during French difficulties with Donnacona later that winter.[28]

More than a century and a half later, another French captain was given an Indian child to seal an alliance. In 1699 the chief of the Bayogoulas gave an adopted twelve-year-old slave boy to Jean Baptiste LeMoyne de Bienville, Iberville's younger brother and lieutenant in Louisiana. Perhaps realizing that he was slated to be shipped to France for training as an interpreter, the "poor boy regretted leaving the Indians so much that he cried incessantly without being able to stop." Sadly, he died of a throat ailment just after returning to his homeland "without getting to talk to any of his people."[29]

In native eyes, the integration of the European "others" was nearly complete. Yet one thing was missing. Although the strangers were religiously honored and politically allied, they were not bound by the gossamer ties of marriage or adoption as kinsmen. In the earliest sources, foreign observers seldom distinguished clearly between marriage *á la façon du pays* (according to native custom) and hospitable short-term companionship and even less seldom recognized adoption ceremonies when they occurred. So we have to rely on later evidence to interpret the faint signals left by the first Europeans, who seldom understood their hosts' language.

We know generally that in native society, an unattached person was *persona non grata*. To be accepted as a full member of a tribe or band was to be related—biologically or fictively—to other members. So a European trader, diplomat, missionary, or officer who wanted to exercise any sway over native life had to become part of an Indian family, either by adoption or marriage. More specifically, we know that throughout the sixteenth century the Indians of Florida readily adopted Spanish shipwreck victims, including several women who took native husbands and had *mestizo* children by them. We also know that all over eastern America in subsequent centuries, European war captives and runaways were adopted, married, and treated as if they had been born of Indian mothers. It is therefore likely that many of the chiefly "harangues," elaborate gift-givings, exchanges of official insignia, and bestowal of Indian names reported by European leaders marked the newcomers' adoption as fictive kin.[30]

By the same token, the bestowal of native women upon the strangers was probably meant not only to betoken temporary hospitality but often to pledge long-term fidelity in marriage, which in Indian society did not require banns, dowries, rings, or a church wedding. On the Mississippi in 1541, the caciques of Casqui and Pacaha offered Soto three of their close relatives as "testimonial[s] of love." Begging the Spaniard to take his daughter as his wife, one chief said that "his greatest desire was to unite his blood with that of so great a lord as he was." The other was willing to give up two of his pleasingly plump sisters, Macanoche and Mochila, to cement relations with the dangerous "children of the sun."[31]

William Hilton was similarly if somewhat more ambiguously propositioned on the Cape Fear River in 1663. After repulsing several minor attacks upriver, Hilton and his crew were called to shore by forty warriors crying "Bonny, Bonny." When the English landed, the natives threw beads into their boat, made a long, indecipherable speech, and presented the nonplussed crew with "two very handsom proper young Indian women, the tallest," Hilton wrote, "that we have seen in this Countrey; which we supposed to be the Kings Daughters, or persons of some great account amongst them. These young women were ready to come into our Boat." Indeed, he hurried to assure his sensitive English readers, "one of them crouding in, was hardly perswaded to go out again." Three years later, Henry Woodward discovered what such a gift entailed. Having been left with the Port Royal Indians to learn their language and to serve as hostage for the return of the chief's nephew, who was taken to Barbados for a similar purpose, the chief gave Woodward a large cornfield and his Indian counterpart's sister, "telling him that shee should tend him and dresse his victuals and be careful of him that soe her Brother might be the better used amongst [the English]."[32]

The sixty men who stopped with Iberville at the Bayogoula village in 1700 undoubtedly would have sold their honor cheap to share Woodward's fate. As the French arrived for the requisite three days of the calumet, the chiefs asked Iberville whether they "would require as many women as there were men in [their] party." Just as he, a non-smoker, was not eager to smoke the calumet, so Iberville "spoiled" what he perceived as his men's sport by showing his hand to his hosts and making them understand that "their skin—red and tanned—should not come close to that of the French, which was white."[33]

The attention and welcome generated among the Indians by the advent of the first Europeans was clearly exceptional; whether gods in human shape or rare mortals, these beings were quite unlike any of the "original peoples" of America. As such they deserved the most respectful treatment possible and required full incorporation into native society in order to harness their assets and to forestall any harm they might do. But what exactly was the source of the Europeans' fascination and power? What did the Indians see in the strangers that was not, or only dimly, seen in their own kind?

White Power

One difference was the whiteness of European skin. On Arthur Barlowe's reconnaissance of Roanoke Island in 1584, the natives "wondred mervelously when we were amongest them, at the whiteness of our skinnes, ever coveting to touch our breastes, and to view the same." Sixty years earlier, the natives of the Outer Banks had been equally astonished by the newcomers' whiteness. When one of Giovanni da Verrazzano's sailors was nearly drowned trying to swim with some small gifts to a group of Indians, they rescued him, took off his shoes, stockings, and shirt, built a large warming fire, "placed him on the ground in the sun . . . and made gestures of great admiration, looking at the whiteness of his flesh and examining him from head to foot." The Biloxi Indians, who first laid eyes on the French in 1699, also gaped at the "white-skinned people" in their midst. "Thus," noted André Pénicaut, the literate ship's carpenter, "we appeared to be quite different from them, who have very tawny skin."[34]

But the close examination that the Indians gave the explorers' chests, faces, and arms may have been focused on the skin's hairiness as well as its pallor. For Pénicaut went on to say that the Biloxis were also astonished by the heavy beards and bald heads among the French, for the Biloxis had "heavy black hair which they groom very carefully" and, like the other Mississippi tribes, "remove the hair from their faces as well as from other parts of the body . . . with shell ash and hot water as one would remove the hair from a suckling pig." Undiluted Indian genes still carry no chromosomes for baldness. Understandably, European beards and tufted chests held an ugly fascination for the smooth-skinned Americans. Before they actually saw a white man, the Potawatomis and Menominees around Green Bay believed the French to be a different species from other men, not because their skin was a shade or two lighter but because they were "covered with hair."[35]

The first Europeans were celebrated less because they were pale or hairy than because they were spiritually powerful "gods" (as the Europeans put it) or *manitous* (in Algonquian parlance), like Indian shamans and conjurers. There were two chief sources of their power. The first was their reputation among the Indians as purveyors or preventers of disease, exactly comparable to native shamans, who were also thought to wield powers of life and death. Jacques Cartier was asked to lay hands on all the sick and handicapped at Hochelaga as if, he said, "Christ had come down to earth to heal them." The three Spanish doctors in Cabeza de Vaca's traveling medicine show were thought to raise men from the dead as well as to cure a variety of ailments. They got into this profitable business—satisfied customers paid them fees of food and goods beyond their ability to consume—when their Texas captors forced them to practice traditional shamanic blowing and rubbing techniques for their keep, convinced that "we who were extraordinary men must possess power and efficacy over all other things." Not surprisingly, the cacique of Casqui thought it only sensible to ask the "son of the sun"—Soto—to restore sight to a number of his blind villagers.[36]

At the same time, the Indians believed that all spiritual power was double-edged: those who could cure could also kill. Only powerful "spirits" possessed the ability to bewitch or to counteract another's witchcraft. When the Roanoke colonists inadvertently carried deadly European diseases into the North Carolina coastal region, they were deified by their hosts for their ability to kill Indians at a distance and to remain unscathed themselves. "There could at no time happen any strange sicknesse, losses, hurtes, or any other crosse unto [the natives]," wrote Thomas Harriot, the expedition's Indian expert, "but that they would impute to us the cause or means therof for offending or not pleasing us." The Indians had extra cause to worry when four of five towns that had practiced some "subtle devise" against the English were ravaged by an unknown disease shortly after the colonists' departure. The English rivals under chief Wingina deduced that the havoc was wrought by "our God through our meanes, and that wee by him might kil and slaie whom wee would without weapons and not come neere them."[37]

The second and more important source of the white man's power in native America was his technological superiority. As native oral traditions suggest, European ships initially impressed the Americans who piloted nothing larger than dug-out canoes. Columbus attributed his divine reception largely to his clothes and his ships. Arthur Barlowe told Sir Walter Ralegh that the natives of Roanoke "had our shippes in marvelous admiration, and all things els was so strange unto them, as it appeared that none of them had ever seene the like." As late as 1700 many Mississippi Valley tribes had never seen a European sailing ship. So when Iberville returned to Louisiana with the French fleet, Sauvole took four native dignitaries to view the frigates. As predicted, they were "ecstatic to see such big contraptions." When they returned to Fort Biloxi they told waiting tribesmen that "they had been on the ships that went up to the clouds, that there were more than fifty villages on each one and crowds that one cannot pass through, and one made them climb down to a place where they did not see sun or moon." Then they all left for Choc-taw country upriver "to teach them these wonders."[38]

Another cause of wonderment was firearms, which Ver-razzano noted as early as 1524. On an "Arcadian" coast somewhere south of New York harbor, a handsome, naked Indian man approached a group of the French sailors and showed them a burning stick, "as if to offer [them] fire." But when the Europeans trumped his hospitality by firing a matchlock, "he trembled all over with fear" and "re-mained as if thunderstruck, and prayed, worshiping like a monk, pointing his finger to the sky; and indicating the sea and the ship, he appeared to bless us."[39]

Not without reason, European metal weapons continued to impress the natives who saw them in action for the first time. When chief Donnacona asked Cartier to demonstrate his artillery in 1535, of which two of the chief's men had given "great account," the Frenchman obliged by firing a dozen cannon into the nearby woods. The Stadaconans were "so much astonished as if the heavens had fallen upon them, and began to howl and to shriek in such a very loud manner that one would have thought hell had emp-tied itself there." When Pierre Radisson and Nicolas Perrot traveled among the Indians of Wisconsin in the 1650s and '60s, the natives literally worshipped their guns, knives, and hatchets by blowing sacred smoke over them "as if it were incense." Likewise, the woodland Sioux who captured the Recollect missionary Louis Hennepin in 1680 called a gun *Manza Ouckange*, "iron which has a spirit." Understandably, the gun's noise and smoke initially did as much to terrify the natives as did its lead balls, which everyone conceded did more crippling damage to internal organs and bones than did flint-tipped arrows.[40]

Weapons were of paramount importance to the feuding polities of North America, but metal objects of any kind, cloth goods, and cleverly designed or sizable wooden objects also drew their admiration. Thomas Harriot put his finger on the primary cause of the Indians' initially exalted opinion of the white strangers when he noted that

> most things they sawe with us, as Mathematicall instruments, sea compasses, the vertue of the loadstone in drawing iron, a perspective glasse whereby was shewed manie strange sightes, burning glasses, wildfire woorkes, gunnes, bookes, writing and reading, spring clocks that seeme to goe of themselves, and manie other thinges that wee had, were so straunge unto them, and so farre exceeded their capacities to comprehend the reason and meanes how they should be made and done, that they thought they were rather the works of gods than of men, or at the leastwise they had bin given and taught us of the gods.[41]

The Sioux, Illinois, and Seneca Indians, among whom Father Hennepin journeyed, frequently clapped their hands over their mouths in astonishment at such things as printed books, silver chalices, embroidered chasubles, and iron pots, all of which they designated as "spirits." In the 1630s the natives of southern New England considered a windmill "little less than the world's wonder" for the whisking motion of its long arms and its "sharp teeth biting the corn," and the first plowman little less than a "juggler" or shaman. Being shown the iron coulter and share of the plow, which could "tear up more ground in a day than their clamshells [hoes] could scrape up in a month," they told the plowman "he was almost Abamacho, almost as cunning as the Devil."[42]

In a very short time, the enterprising newcomers discovered how to turn the natives' awe of European technology to private advantage. Columbus's crewmen found that they could make a killing in a trade with the Taínos—over the Admiral's objections—for pieces of broken wine-barrel hoops, earthenware shards, scraps of broken glass, and lace tips. In the next century European colonists on the coasts of Florida and Georgia took advantage of the Indians' eagerness to swap decorative but otherwise useless gold and silver from Spanish shipwrecks for pieces of paper and playing cards. A Calusa man once gave a Spanish soldier 70 ducats of gold for an ace of diamonds. But Captain George Waymouth may have been the most calculating of all. In 1605 he used a magnetized sword to pick up a knife and a needle before a Maine band of potential fur-trading partners. "This we did," he confessed, "to cause them to imagine some great power in us: and for that to love and feare us."[43]

The white man's varied powers were celebrated in the generic names given to him by different native groups. The Narragansetts of Rhode Island called all Europeans "Coatmen" or "swordmen." The Mohawks of New York referred to the Dutch as "Iron-workers" or "Cloth makers," while the Hurons of southern Ontario called the French *Agnonha,* "Iron People." In northern New England the Pocumtucks knew the French as "Knife men," just as the Virginians, and later all white Americans, were known as "Longknives." The strong identification of the European "others" with their metal instruments of death seems sadly appropriate. After all, on the very first day the

Taínos met Columbus on the sands of Guanahaní in 1492, the Admiral "showed them swords and they took them by the edge and through ignorance cut themselves."[44]

The Domestication of Difference

The Taíno experience notwithstanding, European encounters with the North American Indians at the very beginning were predominantly peaceful and the natives generally welcomed the newcomers. The white explorers had too much curiosity about, and especially too much need for, the new peoples they had "discovered" to pick gratuitous fights; enough skirmishes would eventually break out through mutual misunderstanding and ham-handed tactics. The Europeans' immediate need was to learn enough about the natives and the land to be able to classify, utilize, and, ultimately, dominate both. In all these efforts they assumed that the American "others" were inferior—culturally and religiously, rather than racially—to themselves. So they began by trying to remake America in the images of the various Europes they had left behind, and to remake America's inhabitants less in their own European likenesses than according to a venerable set of normative stereotypes of aliens and "others."

Despite determined efforts, they foundered on the palpable reality of America. Although the various imperial competitors shared many goals and pursued them over several centuries, they were often stymied in the colonial period by the great number, variety, and determination of native societies living within equally stubborn and varied geographies. But the pattern of thought and activity laid down by these argonauts of empire allows us to glimpse the other side of America's post-Columbian encounters.

Taming the Land

In some ways, the "otherness" of the land was easier to domesticate, at least intellectually, than were the people. Usually before meeting any natives, the Europeans assimilated the land by relating it to familiar scenes at home or abroad, renaming its major features, and claiming it for their sovereigns to forestall competing European claims. The well-traveled Columbus established precedent once again by comparing the green of Antillian trees to those of his adopted Andalusia "in the month of May," and the cultivated fields of Tortuga to "the plain of Cordova." He also thought he recognized mastic like that grown on the Aegean island of Chios, noticed the difference between island palms and those of African Guinea, and believed (wrongly) that the mountains of Hispaniola were loftier than "Tenerife in the Canaries." By contrast, the best way a more sedentary Englishman could describe a large yellow-flowered meadow in South Carolina was "a pasture not inferior to any I have seene in England."[45]

Although the Indians had already endowed many prominent geographical features with names, the first Europeans signaled their imperial intentions by naming or renaming everything in sight. In choosing names they paid homage to their religions, homelands, social superiors, and, not least, their own egos. Catholic explorers were the most eager donors of religious names, such as 'San Salvador,' given "in remembrance of the Divine Majesty, Who had marvellously bestowed all this," said Columbus; "the Indians call it 'Guanahani.'" Other Spaniards dubbed two of their earliest towns 'St. Augustine' and 'Santa Fe.' Cartier baptized the majestic Canadian river 'St. Lawrence,' and wherever Christians came upon bone-covered sites of former epidemics or massacres they dubbed them 'Golgotha.' The hearth-hugging English, of course, were famous for transferring English place-names to the localities of *New* England,' but the French in sixteenth-century Florida also renamed eight rivers after well-known French ones. Flattery, too, had its place in the nominating process, as is proved by the existence of 'Virginia' (after Elizabeth I, the Virgin Queen), 'Montreal' (*mont Royal,* for King Francis I), 'Monterey' (for the viceroy of New Spain), and 'Lake Pontchartrain' (after the French minister of marine in 1699). And self-flattery was never far behind, as 'Lake Champlain,' 'Frobisher Bay,' and 'Pennsylvania' attest.[46]

Claiming the land was hardly more taxing than naming it: the "discoverers" simply stepped off the boat and performed a small number of symbolic acts, thereby accessioning whole islands, regions, and continents for their nation-states. On October 12, 1492, Columbus rowed to the beach at Guanahaní, unfurled the royal standard and two banners of the Green Cross (one for each sovereign), made legal proclamations of possession which his fleet secretary duly recorded and his captains witnessed, and transferred the island to Ferdinand and Isabella. As he continued through the Antilles, he wrote, "my intention was not to pass by any island of which I did not take possession, although if it is taken of one," he assumed, "it may be said that it is taken of all."[47]

Even more popular as symbols of possession were large wooden crosses, which also marked convenient harbors and landmarks for countrymen who followed. Simple crosses heralded the claims of Christians but did not specify their nationality unless coats of arms or other telltale insignia were attached. Thus when the Virginia colonists claimed Powhatan's empire for England, they insured against ambiguity by leaving a cross at the head of the newly renamed James River with the inscription "Jacobus Rex. 1607."[48]

More than one native leader, besides Powhatan, was sus-

European explorers began to rename—and thereby to claim—American places as early as Columbus's arrival on October 12, 1492. This woodcut from the Basel Latin edition of his first letter to Ferdinand and Isabella shows various Caribbean islands with the new names Columbus had given them. From *Carta de Colón* (Basel, 1493).

In the 1560s the French sought to lay claim to Florida by erecting tall stone columns on various river banks. In this engraving by Theodor de Bry (after the original painting by eye-witness Jacques Le Moyne), the local Timucuans worship one of the pillars as an idol with offerings of food, perfumed oils, and weapons. Other native groups received the columns with suspicion and much less reverence. From Theodor de Bry, *Brevis narratio eorum quae in Florida Americae* (Frankfurt, 1591).

picious of the meaning of these arrogrant constructions. When Cartier erected at the entrance of Gaspé Harbor a thirty-foot cross, complete with shield and plaque reading "VIVE LE ROY DE FRANCE" in bold Gothic letters, he got an argument from a Micmac chief. "Pointing to the cross," Cartier recalled, "he made us a long harangue, making the sign of the cross with two of his fingers; and then he pointed to the land all around about, as if he wished to say that all this region belonged to him, and that we ought not to have set up this cross without his permission."[49]

The French Huguenots who tried to preempt the Spanish in Florida may have gotten a similar message when they planted a white stone pillar on a riverbank. This was one of five man-sized columns they had brought to assert their claims, each inscribed with a royal shield, three fleurs-de-lis, the Queen Mother's initial, and the date '1561.' One of the local chiefs, however, was not amused by their audacity. When Jean Ribault, the French captain, went to visit him with gifts, the chief put on a grave face and only shook his head a little to show that "he was not well pleased" either with the column or the fact that the French had first planted one across the river in the domain of a rival. Before long the disgruntled chief was vindicated. When the French returned three years later to establish a military presence, they were gleefully taken to see the first pillar, which had been protected by the Indians and decorated with "crownes of Bay" and "little baskets of Mill [grain]." Within a year, however, the Spanish demolished the French fort, murdered the garrison, and carried off the offensive column to Havana.[50]

Situational Ethics

Claiming allegedly "virgin" land was one thing, mastering it and turning it to profit was quite another. The Europeans quickly found that the latter was impossible without the active aid of the natives, whom even the most contemptuous invaders realized had strong attachments, if not "legitimate" claims or "natural rights," to the land. The Indians also had unique knowledge of the land and its environmental limits, something European dreamers and schemers often sorely lacked. Before the newcomers could proceed to their larger goals of profiteering and domination, therefore, they had to learn enough about the American "others" to win their confidence and friendship, get them to supplement always-inadequate supplies, and induce them to reveal the sources of America's presumed wealth. Beginning with Columbus, European leaders initially instructed their men to avoid any behavior that would offend the numerically superior natives. "For if any rude and rigorous meanes shuldbe used towardes this people," Ribault predicted, "they would flye hither and thither through the woodes and forestes and abandon there habitations and cuntrye" or else, he did not have to say, they would turn and attack the offending parties.[51]

European Hospitality

So, on the ancient principle of 'When in Rome,' the Europeans tamed their haste for results and bent their initial efforts to reciprocating native hospitality as fully as possible. As they sought to earn reputations for generosity, perhaps the supreme virtue in communal Indian society, they also hoped to impress the natives with their superior technology, intelligence, and spiritual power, all of which they assumed gave them just claim to rule the new land and its people.

European hospitality was not much different from Indian, except that its spirit was more calculating, and the newcomers had no desire to reduce native difference and "inferiority" by incorporating them into their families, which were largely absent in any event. The staples of both welcomes were feasting, entertainment, and gift-giving, the essential lubricant of Indian social relations. For Indians, spending the night in a tarry, creaking ship was apparently considered a treat, perhaps more for the novel food and drink offered than for comfort or company. European-prepared meat, pease, beans, bread, and even ship's biscuits were eaten with gusto. A band of southern New England Indians liked everything Captain Bartholomew Gosnold served them but the mustard, "whereat they made many a sowre face." Alcoholic beverages got a mixed reception. A Timucua chief grew so fond of French wine—or company—that he broke a ban on daytime eating to request a cup in order to drink with Jean Ribault. Yet the Bayogoulas took "very little" of the wine and brandy Iberville offered them, being more stunned by the brandy he set on fire. In 1605 the Abenakis on St. George's River in Maine tasted English *aqua vitae* "but would by no meanes drinke." Sugar candy and raisins were more to their taste.[52]

What caught the attention of the European hosts was not the natives' palate but their unselfish sharing of everything they received. Columbus was the first to notice that when a Haitian cacique left his retinue on deck to go below to join the Admiral at dinner, he took only a small sample of each dish for tasting and "afterward sent the rest to his people, and all ate of it." A century later, Captain Waymouth similarly entertained two Abenakis, who, after eating a modest amount, characteristically "desired pease to carry a shore to their women, which we gave them, with fish and bread," wrote the ship's scribe, "and lent them pewter dishes, which they carefully brought [back] againe."[53]

Once the Indians had been wined and dined, they were serenaded by the European equivalents of native drums, flutes, and rattles. Most expeditions on land and sea carried a complement of martial drummers and trumpeters, who were often pressed into social service to entertain visiting natives. But some ships' crews included bona fide musicians: Sir Humphrey Gilbert had six, John Davis, four. Davis lured several Eskimo groups to trade by playing music and having his crew dance to it on shore. In 1603 some Massachusetts Algonquians were diverted by the "homely Music" of a young guitarist in Martin Pring's crew. After showering the musician with gifts, they danced around him "twentie in a Ring . . . using many Savage gestures [and] singing Io, Ia, Io, Ia, Ia, Io." In Louisiana a century later, the Colapissa villagers who hosted a dozen Frenchmen during one of their periodic supply shortages learned to dance the minuet and *la bourrée* to the fine fiddling of a violinist named Picard. His companions "nearly d[ied] of laughter" over their hosts' capers, but the natives obviously enjoyed themselves and even had the last laugh when Picard could not keep time with the intricate drumming at their traditional dances.[54]

European rituals of hospitality were brought to a close by the giving of gifts to the visiting natives. Fresh from the corrupt courts and countinghouses of Europe, the newcomers tended to see gifts as bribes, necessary palm-crossings to get a job done. In native America, by contrast, gifts were at once "words" in the rich metaphorical language of political councils and sureties for one's word. The potential conflict between these two meanings was largely avoided by the necessity of employing gifts in a native context. Since nothing could be done without them, the Europeans quickly learned that in using them they were bound by the promises made on each occasion. In such a setting, words could not be taken lightly and stark honesty was a necessity, particularly on formal or ceremonial occasions. If the Europeans wanted peace with the natives, reciprocal gift-giving was the only reliable way to secure it.[55]

As in Europe, gifts to leaders usually led to the best results. So it was chiefs and caciques who received an eye-catching drapery from Columbus's bed, red wool caps from Cartier, and "gownes of blewe clothe garnished with yellowe flowers de luce" from Ribault. Since Europe and

America were alike in generally adhering to social hierarchy, appropriate gifts were best given to the several ranks. When Cartier was ready to distribute gifts to the Hochelagans, he made the men, women, and children line up separately. "To the headmen he gave hatchets, to the others knives, and to the women, beads and other small trinkets. He then made the children scramble for little rings and tin *agnus Dei*, which afforded them great amusement."[56]

Taking the Americans' Measure

Having earned provisional reputations as "generous men," the explorers could then proceed to two final acts of preparation before attempting to impose their will on the land and the people. The first was to take the measure of the natives, for both intellectual and practical purposes. Attempting to make sense of the natives' novelty was natural to literate people whose culture relied heavily on encyclopedias and other compendia of knowledge to assimilate all that was known about their burgeoning world. And knowing the American "others" was the only way to beat them in the competition for their continent.

Like most people, Europeans tended to conceive of the new in terms of the old, to classify novelties according to conventional wisdom. Most explorers, therefore, began to cope with the shiny newness of the natives by putting them in mental pigeonholes constructed from ancient precedent and proximate experience. This had the added advantage of helping the homebound readers of their New World narratives learn by comparison with the known and the familiar.

When Europeans first sought to describe Indians and Indian culture, they slipped their often keen-eyed observations into interpretive slots marked 'Ancients,' 'Africans,' 'Wild Irish,' or, the most capacious and indefinite of all, 'Savages.' The people Verrazzano met in Narragansett Bay exhibited the "sweet and gentle . . . manner of the ancients." Arthur Barlowe found the natives of Roanoke "such as lived after the manner of the golden age." But other "ancient" analogies were less flattering to the Indians. When Theodor de Bry republished Harriot's account of Roanoke in 1590, he included many engravings of John White's paintings of "Virginia" Indians and life. After the index, he tucked in a section of five pictures of Picts and Ancient Britons "to showe how . . . the Inhabitants of the great Bretannie have bin in times past as sauvage as those of Virginia." Long-haired, naked, and tattooed from head to toe, a fierce Pict warrior is depicted wearing a deadly curved sword at his belt and holding a shield in one hand and the bloody head of a victim in the other.[57]

Since few other European colonizers had as much experience in Africa as the Portuguese had, the earliest comparisons of American Indians and Africans were limited largely to physical appearance, such as skin color, hair texture, and lip size. These comparisons tended to emphasize contrasts rather than similarities and to favor the Americans, who came closer to European norms of appearance and beauty.[58] The "wild Irish" and their culture, on the other hand, were quite familiar to many English adventurers in North America because the latter had served in Ireland trying to bring it under Elizabeth's royal wing. It was understandable that Captain John Smith likened the Virginians' deerskin robes to "Irish mantels," and Harriot compared their spear-fishing to "the maner as Irish men cast darts [short spears]."[59]

Any other native behavior or social custom that could not be easily classified was assigned to the 'Savage' category, an *omnium-gatherum* for temporarily isolating the un-

Theodor de Bry's engraving of an ancient Pict warrior served to remind the readers of Thomas Harriot's account of the Roanoke colony that the "Virginia" (actually North Carolina) Indians were not culturally inferior to the colonists' own ancestors. From Harriot, *A briefe and true report of the new found land of Virginia* (London, 1588).

familiar until it could be defused by myopic familiarity or accepted on its own terms as the stubborn reality of Indian life. In many ways, the first Europeans to meet America's natives were the most open to that reality, before the frustration of their dominating designs permanently warped their vision and judgment.[60]

Taming Tongues

The Europeans' final preparation for New World domination was to learn how to communicate with the Indians. For without the ability to plumb the nuances of their languages, their thoughts and feelings would remain dangerously hidden. The Indians faced the same task: the "other" must become intelligible in order to become predictable and, thereby, controllable. In the beginning the natives enjoyed numerical superiority and could dictate the terms of engagement. A Frenchman who made a grand tour of the Great Lakes in 1669 spoke for all European explorers when he realized early in his journey "how important it was not to engage one's self amongst the tribes of these countries without knowing their language or being sure of one's interpreter." "The lack of an interpreter under our own control," he lamented, "prevented the entire success of our expedition."[61]

Since the crude pantomimes of sign language were clearly not sufficient for reliable discourse, interpreters on both sides had to be trained. This generally entailed a voluntary program of student exchanges, at which the French both in Canada and later in Louisiana proved to be the most adept. Quick-witted children were sent to live with the "others" in order to learn not only their words but the social and cultural realities that lay behind them. It did not tarnish the exchange that the foreign students also served as hostages for the peaceful conduct of their people.[62]

Some interpreters, however, were not volunteers. A few European expeditions that arrived after the initial waves of invasion were fortunate to find countrymen who had been taken captive or saved from shipwrecks and adopted by the Indians and who were already fluent in the regional tongues. Soto's entrada would never have left the coast of Florida had he not redeemed Juan Ortiz, a survivor of the Narváez debacle in 1528 who had lived with the natives for twelve years. Fortunately, although he closely resembled the Indians, down to his arm tattooes and breechclout, Ortiz had not forgotten the Spanish he had learned in Seville. When he died somewhere west of the Mississippi in March 1542, the expedition began to unravel, for the only interpreter left was a young Indian slave acquired in northeastern Georgia, where different languages were spoken. "So great a misfortune was the death of . . . Ortiz . . . that to learn from the Indians what he stated in four words, with the youth the whole day was needed; and most of the time he understood just the opposite of what was asked."[63]

The need for interpreters among the early Europeans was so urgent that many ship captains endangered future relations with the natives by kidnapping tribesmen (never women) to take back to Europe for language instruction. Since it was nearly impossible for the Indians to distinguish the temporary "borrowing" of interpreters from the permanent kidnapping of slaves, which Europeans also snatched in alarming numbers, they could be forgiven a certain amount of violence toward the next ships to appear. Columbus inaugurated the sordid practice on his first voyage, but the pairs of interpreters taken by Jacques Cartier and Arthur Barlowe are the more famous because they were safely returned after a year abroad to play key roles in the colonial ventures of Canada and Roanoke respectively. Chief Donnacona's two sons, Domagaya and especially Taignoagny, did their best to foil French incursions into the St. Lawrence before they were shanghaied a second time, but Manteo and Wanchese from the Outer Banks left a mixed legacy. Wanchese, one of chief Wingina's warriors, was also hostile to European pretensions, but Manteo, a rival Croatoan, was instrumental in securing an English foothold, however briefly, in North Carolina. In 1587 he became the first native convert to the Church of England and was appointed chief of Roanoke Island by the last English governor.[64]

Second Encounters

But the fragile balance of power that characterized the protracted series of first encounters in North America all too quickly and inexorably tipped against the natives. Virtually in the wake of the European explorers sailed three battalions of powerful allies. The first consisted of microbic shock troops which swept unseen through defenseless Indian villages with lethal ruthlessness, reducing dramatically the natives' numerical superiority and exploding forever their mental equilibrium. Missionaries often accompanied these "shock troops" and practiced a new, aggressive faith, armed with self-righteous certitude, a seemingly omniscient culture of print, and the intolerant Truth of Holy Scripture. The third battalion was comprised of humbler clerks and colonial officials who nonetheless wielded with swashbuckling bravado the aggrandizing maps, charters, and long-term policies of Europe's emerging nation-states. The Indians were ultimately no match for these foes and their well-armed, technologically advantaged, and increasingly savvy predecessors. As soon as the invaders achieved a measure of political initiative or military superiority, they sought to realize their dreams of New World wealth, imperial hegemony, and propagation of the gospel, no matter what the cost in native lives, lands, or liberties.

Another casualty of these increasingly tragic encounters was the earliest image each side held of the "other." As the initial honeymoon of contact gave way to conflict and the eruption of irreconcilable differences, naive preconceptions gave way to more realistic notions, at once more complex and less optimistic. In Indian eyes, the strangers in their midst devolved fairly quickly from beneficent "gods" dropped from "the heavens," to dangerously powerful "spirits" or shamans, and finally to all-too-human or even sub-human "enemies" who deserved to be killed before they did irreparable harm.

Ironically, the Europeans' conception underwent a temporary *up*grading during their first encounters with the natives. Having arrived in America with largely negative notions of the "other" (particularly of those outside the cultural magnificence of China and Japan), the invaders were somewhat nonplussed to have their "savage" preconception undermined by the distinctly unsavage, even "civilized," behavior of their native hosts. It was simply difficult for the Europeans to find the hairy, godless, cruel, treacherous cannibals of their myths and fantasies in the smooth-skinned, simple people who appeared to worship them by fêting, feasting, housing, caressing, and showering them with gifts. Their discomfort continued spasmodically as missionaries and other pacific observers captured the benign aspect of native life in pictures and print, giving substance to Europe's self-critical image of the Noble Savage.

But the predestinate European drive for dominion in America ensured that the natives would be forced to defend their countries and cultures with arms, ferocity, and guile, thereby fulfilling the invaders' worst expectations. The history of first encounters, therefore, is a sad reminder that, in spite of the gentle and promising advent of European-Indian relations in many different places and on many different occasions, the intruders could not help but turn their genial hosts into stereotypical "Savages," whose "otherness" was as unfathomable as they were expendable. If we do nothing else in 1992 and beyond, we should work mightily to ensure that no citizens of our post-Columbian global village are ever regarded or treated like that again.

CHAPTER THREE

The Exploration of Norumbega: Native Perspectives

THE HISTORY OF INDIAN-EUROPEAN RELATIONS IN COLO-
nial North America encompasses a wide variety of native groups,
geographies, and contact situations, all evolving over time. Why
and how choose one group or situation over another? How and
why select one period over another? Answers will vary with historians because personal predilection—brewed from parentage,
education, experience, rational calculation, and inexplicable
likes and dislikes—plays a large role, not so much in historians'
interpretations or results (if they are well trained in their craft) as
in their choice of subject and general approach to it. Sometimes
the subject is chosen for them, as when a conference organizer,
publisher, or journal editor invites them to tackle a theme for a
special occasion.

In 1988 predilection and solicitation combined to induce me to
write the following essay for an NEH-sponsored conference on
"The Land of Norumbega: Maine in the Age of Exploration and
Settlement" in Portland. It is no coincidence that our favorite
summer vacation spot is Mt. Desert Island, Maine, which Samuel
de Champlain, one of my favorite colonists, explored and renamed in 1604. Portland in December admittedly is not Northeast Harbor in July, but the opportunity to enjoy a bona fide
seafood dinner out of season, to re-read closely the earliest records of contact in northern New England, and to hobnob with

several good friends and colleagues was too good to pass up. A splendid exhibition of maps, atlases, globes, and navigational equipment, mounted by Susan Danforth of the John Carter Brown Library and appearing simultaneously in the Portland Museum of Art, did nothing to lessen the weekend's attraction.

But as soon as I had delivered my paper on the second morning of the conference, I was roundly thumped for failing in my work to appreciate the value of native oral tradition in the re-creation of early contact history. The audience of several hundred, mostly secondary school, teachers and librarians was as befuddled as I by this intramural jousting because the opening, closing, and central concern of my paper was to demonstrate—after the criticism and assessment that any historical source must receive—the utility and validity of the oral tradition of Norumbega's natives on the eve of contact. Unfortunately, my critics—a non-native Mainer whose book on early French-Abenaki contact I had once reviewed with serious reservations and a young tribal historian from New Brunswick—had not read my paper in advance and instead took exception to my earlier book on conversion, which equally unfortunately begins with a chapter on native religion and worldview that likewise draws heavily on native oral traditions.* As I explained in my rebuttal, there are two kinds of oral traditions: one dealing with what Westerners would call the "mythological" world, the other dealing with "actual" or "historical" events. My interlocutors were at home in the former, I in the latter, and there our differences lay.

IN RE-CREATING THE STORY OF NORUMBEGA BEFORE the fateful advent of the Pilgrims in 1620, we should listen to—and really try to *hear*—some voices that are seldom even thought to have existed. These are the voices of the native Norumbegans who met and usually welcomed the seaborne strangers from Europe. Although the natives spoke tongues and dialects very different from those of

*James Axtell, *The Invasion Within: The Contest of Cultures in Colonial North America* (New York, 1985).

Elizabethan England and Henrician France, we are able in a few instances to eavesdrop on some of their interior and external dialogues, to catch glimpses of what they were thinking and how they were feeling about the novel visitors to their shores.

But why should we bother? Since the Indians could not write and therefore left us no collectible publications of their own, why should we go to the trouble of discovering their views on these Norumbegan events? Two reasons— better than affirmative action and historical fashion— suggest themselves. The first and more philosophical is that "society is an interweaving and interworking of mental selves. . . . The imaginations which people have of one another are the solid facts of society."[1] If we wish to recapture the historical essence of the meeting of past cultures on the rocky margins of Maine or anywhere else, we have to imagine the imaginations of all the participants, not just an easy or select few. For—and this is our second reason— people act on the basis of what they *think* is true, not necessarily on what *is* true. Indeed, in some sense, reality itself is socially constructed or imagined. When the Europeans and the Indians reacted to each other, they did so because of their respective ideas and feelings about each other, attitudes that drew their meaning and symbolic force from acquired and largely unconscious cultural contexts.[2]

If it is granted that we *must* seek the native perspective, or more accurately, native perspectives, is it actually *possible,* particularly when thoughts and feelings are not always best captured in words and when spoken words, by their very nature, vanish the instant they are voiced? Clearly, I and a great many other ethnohistorians would be out of work if it were *not* possible. Our sources are several, although each kind carries its own limitations. For pre-1620 Norumbega, there are only three sorts of major importance.

The first and most familiar sources are the written and

Through most of the 16th century, Norumbega was the name applied to an ill-defined region in New England and the Maritime provinces on European maps of North America. In this map of 1597 the name has been given to a fanciful Indian city as well as to the region in Maine around Penobscot Bay. From Cornelis van Wytfliet, *Norumbega et Virginia* (1597).

cartographic records literally manuscripted by the European explorers. While these seamen were interested more in Norumbega's natural and mineral resources than in its natives, they usually had to interact with the latter to learn about or gain access to the former. This entailed considerable "conversation" with the Indians, through ambiguous sign language, elementary trade pidgins, native interpreters who had spent time on European ships or in European ports, or, less frequently, sailors who had picked up some native phrases from Indian shipmates or trading partners. Even when the natives remained silent, their actions were often eloquent expressions of their attitudes toward the newcomers, if we but read them in cultural context.

Our second source consists not of evanescent and easily misinterpreted words but of subterranean shards, middens, and postmolds found in native sites. Because the members of a culture tend to pattern their behavior in similar ways, the artifacts they make and the ways they use and dispose of them tell us much about some of the values and ideals they cherish and about some of the events in their lives, which may not be documented in any other way.

Finally, a source with which traditionally bookish historians are distinctly uneasy is the recollection of native peoples who pass down through the generations oral accounts of "events" long in the past. Whether these events were "historical" or "mythical" (in a Western sense), oral traditions about them often give us unique insights into the emotional ambience and normative resonance of those occurrences from a native perspective. They may not tell us just *when* a particular event occurred, but they almost always convey how the native participants *felt* about it at the time, and often what kind of moral they drew from it.

If we bend our ears southwestward, toward Puritan Massachusetts, we might be able to catch a few faithful echoes of native responses to the earliest European men and ships in Norumbega's waters. This is the best resort we have because the lethal plague of 1616–18 and subsequent European irruptions seem to have left large patches of unhappy silence in the native oral record of coastal Maine. Fortunately, two early settlers of the Bay Colony listened carefully to Indian survivors of the plague in their area and recorded their tribal memories of the first Europeans. Since the conceptual worlds of the eastern Algonquians were essentially similar, we should be able to hear something of Abenaki and Etchemin responses to the first "Igrismañnak" (Englishmen) in their waters.[3]

During his four-year stay in Massachusetts, William Wood learned that the Indians had been "ravished with admiration" at the first European ship they saw. Like many of their brethren up and down the Atlantic coast, they took it for "a walking island, the mast to be a tree, the sail white clouds, and the discharging of ordnance for lightning and thunder, which did much trouble them." When the thunder stopped and the island dropped anchor, the natives hopped into their canoes to go pick strawberries there, which may place the incident in late May or early June. But when the ship gave them a friendly salvo in salute, they cried out (in the English pidgin common by the early 1630s) "What much hoggery [anger], so big walk, and so big speak, and by and by kill." Whereupon they beat a hasty retreat to shore, "not daring to approach" the ship again "till they were sent for" by the bearded "Coat-men" or "sword-men" (as their Narragansett neighbors called them).[4]

The version of this symbolic event heard by Edward Johnson, perhaps in 1630–31 when he traded on the Merrimack but probably after 1636 when he settled near the Bay, was richer in emotional and historical detail than Wood's. As Johnson understood it, the whole Massachusetts tribe was "affrighted" by the first ship in their bay. "Wondering what Creature it should be," they paddled from place to place "stiring up all their Countrymen to come forth, and behold this monstrous thing." "At this sudden news," Johnson noted, "the shores for many miles were filled with this naked Nation, gazing at this wonder, till some of the stoutest among them" decided to approach the creature by canoe. When they got within range, they "let fly" a shower of arrows at the becalmed ship. Some of their bone-tipped shafts bounced harmlessly off the hull, but others "stuck fast," causing the warriors to wonder why "it did not cry."

Their curiosity suddenly turned to terror when the captain ordered a cannon fired, "which stroke such feare into the poore Indians, that they hasted to shore, having their wonders exceedingly increased." Wrapped in amazement, the tribe huddled anxiously as the ship's crew furled the sails, manned the long-boat, and rowed to meet them. Upon which the natives fled into the woods, "although now they saw they were men," who signaled them to "stay their flight" in order to trade. When the sailors held out shiny copper kettles, the Indians gradually regained their composure and approached, "much delighted with the sound" of the kettles when struck and "much more astonished to see they would not breake, being so thin."

This encounter was fraught with more than ordinary significance for these southern Norumbegans because "not long" after—Kepler and Gassendi saw it in November 1618—a "bright blazing Comet" hung in the southwestern sky three hours every night for "thirty sleepes." Like most Europeans, educated and credulous alike, the natives beheld that "uncouth sight" in "great wonderment" and fully "expected some strange things to follow." The Massachusetts phase of the horrifying plague—which Johnson misdates in the summer of 1619—was the first. Then came the last straw: a numerous "Army of Christ" bent on supplanting native "paganism" and making southern New England a kinder, gentler place.[5]

J. Franklin Jameson, the editor of Johnson's *Wonder-Working Providence*, thought that the Massachusetts might have been remembering the well- (if self-) publicized visit of Captain John Smith in 1614. This is virtually impossible and underlines the danger of resorting to native folklore for historical specifics. Smith did sail into Massachusetts Bay early in the summer (around strawberry time), but his ship was attacked by only four bowmen from some rocks near a narrow passage. Moreover, he had been preceded that year by at least two French ships, which to his annoyance had garnered the best furs in six weeks of active trading.[6] But the French had also traded in Massachusetts waters for several years, perhaps decades, before Smith made his first and only voyage to New England. As both archaeological and written records make clear, copper kettles were a standard item in the French, not the English, trade kit in the late sixteenth and early seventeenth century. Smith touted the vendibility of coarse cloth, hatchets, beads, mirrors, and other "trash," but not relatively expensive kettles.[7]

Editor Jameson probably would not have made his venial mistake if he had read the extant literature of Norumbegan exploration. For no matter how early a European ship is known to have touched upon New England's shores, Indian reactions or possessions suggest that it had already been preceded by others. When Gaspar Corte-Real kidnapped fifty-some Indians in 1501 from what sounds like Maine, one man possessed "a piece of broken gilt sword," which to the Venetian ambassador in Lisbon "certainly seem[ed] to have been made in Italy." A native boy was wearing in his ears "two silver rings" made just as certainly in Venice.[8]

Twenty-three years later, Estevão Gomes, a Portuguese pilot in the Spanish service, filled his galleon with fifty-eight Indians "of both sexes," perhaps from islands at the mouth of the Penobscot River where the natives had come for summer fishing.[9] We have to ask how both of these Portuguese entrepreneurs managed to entice on board so many agile and normally suspicious natives. The likeliest answer (given the scattered and second-hand sources we have) is that many Norumbegans, as early as 1501 and certainly no later than 1524, were familiar with sea-going Europeans enough to swap "rare and valuable furs" for "merchandise" that pleased them.[10] Only by luring trade-minded and probably unarmed natives away from the wooded security of their encampments could the Iberians have shanghaied so many in large batches. Indeed, in light of the Indians' later reticence to expose their women to European ogling, we have to wonder how Corte-Real and Gomes were able to snatch any females at all. Perhaps these early successes *explain* the subsequent caution rather than being rendered problematical by it.

The more pertinent question we must ask is, can we tell anything about how the native victims felt toward their kidnappers? Since he had violated his sovereign's explicit instructions not to use violence against any natives, Gomes's Indians were "set at liberty" but were still in Toledo the following year. Whether they ever saw home again is unknown but not likely.[11] Corte-Real's human booty was "seen, touched and examined" by an Italian diplomat as soon as they disembarked at Lisbon in October 1501. After a quick four-week trip, these tall, tattooed, long-haired strangers, clothed in otter skins, seemed to have adjusted to their enslavement reasonably well (we have no idea how they were treated on shipboard or in port). Even while the curious Italian was discovering the "small breasts and most beautiful bodies" of the women and (correspondingly?) the "terribly harsh look of the men," the natives behaved "gentl[y]," "laugh[ed] considerably and manifest[ed] the greatest pleasure." Whether this was genuine emotion or the best face they could put on a frightening and desperate situation we will never know, but common sense points to the latter. The hopelessness of their predicament must have hit them with extra force when not one of their captors could understand their speech and, with equal result, they had been "spoken to in every possible language" known in that cosmopolitan port-city. Without communication, their very humanity was put in jeopardy, even as the Europeans acknowledged the humanness of their "form and image" and of their "not harsh" if indecipherable language.[12]

Giovanni da Verrazzano's leisurely and more peaceful visit to New England in 1524 discovered more about Norumbegan reactions to the bearded visitors than any voyage until the seventeenth century. When he tacked into Narragansett Bay in April, he was met by twenty canoes of painted locals "uttering various cries of wonderment" at the structure of the *Dauphine*, the French crew, and their manufactured clothes. But they kept their distance until the Frenchmen imitated their gestures and shouts of joy and threw them a few "trinkets." Then the natives, including two obvious chiefs, showed them where to anchor, brought them food, and "confidently came on board ship." Pointedly missing were their women who, although they were invited, waited in the canoes or, in the case of a curious "queen" and her attendants, withdrew to a nearby island to escape the "irksome clamor of the crowd of sailors." All of this behavior sounds like that of people who had had some experience in dealing with European ships and randy seamen. So does their courteous but not overly deferential treatment of the French, who were quick to assume that they were being regarded as minor or major divinities. That one chief asked about the ship's equipment, "imitated [French] manners," and "tasted [their] food" carried no such connotation.[13]

Yet other behavior seemed to belie any previous experience, or perhaps to suggest that their previous encounters were unusually benign. The first anomaly was their response to European trade goods and technology. If they *were* familiar with maritime traders, they certainly acted peculiarly toward known best-sellers. We can understand their preference for their own reddish copper to pale gold objects, but what do we make of their apparent disinterest in cloth of any kind, even their favorite reds and blues, and in "metals like steel and iron?" "For many times when we showed them some of our arms," wrote the astonished captain, "they did not admire them, nor ask for them, but merely examined the workmanship. They did the same with mirrors; they would look at them quickly, and then refuse them, laughing." The only items they really prized were decorative: "little bells, blue crystals, and other trinkets to put in the ear or around the neck." Furthermore, Verrazzano makes no mention of any furs being offered in trade; April would have been the right time for trade-minded hunters to dispose of their winter catch.[14]

Another piece of anomalous behavior (judged by later events in Norumbega) is that the Narragansetts allowed French excursions to penetrate inland five or six leagues to visit their largest fields and villages. The natives' "sweet and gentle" conduct throughout the explorers' two-week stay suggests either that previous European visitors had not bitten the hands that fed them or that the natives regarded the newcomers as traditional "spirits" or *manitous,* the extent of whose powers was still unknown and who therefore deserved respect and circumspection.[15]

Much less ambiguous was the behavior and attitudes of the Norumbegans whom Verrazzano found on the coast of Maine. These natives undoubtedly had had considerable experience with Europeans and had not found it particularly savory. Since Gomes arrived in Norumbega *after* Verrazzano, other voyagers must have given the Indians their first taste of Christian "civility." In stark contrast to the courteous denizens of "Refugio" (his name for Narragansett Bay), Verrazzano found the Mainers "full of crudity and vices," devoid of manners, "humanity," and agriculture, and "so barbarous that we could never make any communication with them, however many signs we made to them." They also made it clear that they did not want the sailors to land, even for trading. When twenty-five armed Frenchmen brazened their way inland and made several unwelcome visits to their houses, the natives "shot at

[them] with their bows and uttered loud cries before fleeing into the woods."[16]

If the French were in any doubt about the natives' attitudes toward them, it was quickly dispelled by the Indians'
trading etiquette. "If *we* wanted to trade with them for
some of *their* things," Verrazzano complained, "they would
come to the seashore on some rocks where the breakers
were most violent, while we remained in the little boat, and
they sent us what they wanted to give on a rope . . . ;
they gave us the barter quickly," he continued, "and would
take in exchange only knives, hooks for fishing, and sharp
metal." Then, in a priceless gesture of farewell, these reluctant, persnickety customers "made all the signs of scorn
and shame that any brute creature would make, such as
showing their buttocks and laughing."[17]

For half a century after Verrazzano's reconnaissance of
the Atlantic coast, we hear virtually nothing of European
activities in Norumbega. After Cartier's tactless kidnapping of chief Donnacona and several Stadaconans from
Quebec, the St. Lawrence was closed for more than forty
years to French traders, the likeliest sailors to make side
trips around Cape Breton and Nova Scotia to Maine's
promising shores. When they did return to the "River of
Canada" and Étienne Bellenger probably coasted as far
south as Penobscot Bay in search of furs, the English atypi-
cally had beaten them to the punch.[18] In 1580 John
Walker claimed to have discovered a silver mine nine
leagues up the "River of Norumbega" (probably the Penobscot) and, more to the point, an Indian lodge seven
miles upriver from which he liberated three hundred
dried moose skins, which he promptly sold in France for
£2 a hide.[19]

If Bruce Bourque and Ruth Whitehead are right (as I
think they are), this cache of Etchemin skins was probably
awaiting collection by a new force in Down-Eastern eco-

nomics: Micmac (and later Etchemin) middlemen who facilitated trade between French ships in the Gulf of St. Lawrence and the fur hunters of Norumbega, as far south as Massachusetts. These were the enterprising folks who met English explorers in the first decade of the seventeenth century, sailing (apparently stolen) French and Basque shallops of no mean size, sporting harlequin combinations of European clothes and native skins, and speaking trade pidgins of recognizable French and Basque elements. It seems very likely that they had sailed into the breach made by the exclusion of French traders before 1580 and were so successful that they could not be dislodged until the wholesale influx of European competitors in the next century.[20]

The first English ship of record to encounter one of these nativized craft was captained by Bartholomew Gosnold, who was headed for Verrazzano's "Refugio" to plant a winter trading post. As soon as he sighted the Maine or Massachusetts coast in May 1602, eight Micmacs in a "Biscay" shallop sailed out to greet him with "signes of peace, and a long speech." After "boldly" climbing aboard the English ship, they drew a chalk map of the local coasts and tried to talk the crew into staying to palaver and trade. But Gosnold had other fish to fry and sailed off to Cape Cod to catch them.[21]

Unable to find Narragansett Bay, he settled for wooded and well-watered Elisabeths Isle on Buzzard's Bay, which was "unpeopled" save by summer crabbers from the mainland. There and in trips to the main, the English had largely peaceful engagements with the trade-savvy natives, who "offered themselves . . . in great familiaritie" and plied their guests with food and anything they happened to be wearing or carrying. The usual exception, of course, was the women, whose menfolk paid "heedfull attendance" on any who sidled too near the sailors and who themselves "would not admit of any immodest touch." A handful of natives helped the English dig sassafras, and a large group traded furs after due deference was paid to their chief. He received as gifts a straw hat, which he wore, and two knives, whose shiny sharpness he "beheld with great marvelling." The same party was feasted with ship's beer and dried cod, but the mustard condiment "nipp[ed]" their noses, "whereat they made many a sowre face."[22]

We would like to know how the proud natives responded to the Englishmen's obvious "sport" at their discomfort and perhaps anxiety (not knowing whether they had been poisoned). For relations soured before the food-short English pulled out after one month. Two or three incidents may have contributed to the Indians' change of heart. The first was Gosnold's stealing a canoe that four men had temporarily abandoned in fear. Another was his disingenuous handling of the theft of an English shield, which he had connived at "onely to trie whether they were in subjection" to their chief. The English got their jollies when, "with feare and great trembling," the natives restored it, thinking (no doubt correctly) that the well-armed intruders "would have beene revenged for it." Perhaps even a humorous incident carried darker meaning for the Indians. When one man offered to swap an artificial beard of animal hair for the apparently unnatural red beard of a sailor, he was of course rejected and probably laughed at in the bargain. Whatever stuck in their craw, less than two weeks into the strangers' stay, four natives attacked two crewmen who had been sent to collect seafood. One sailor took an arrow in the side and the other escaped injury or death only by leaping after his assailants and cutting their bowstrings.[23]

The following year (1603) an English voyage under Martin Pring spent seven weeks digging sassafras at a barricaded post on the tip of Cape Cod. They, too, began on a jolly note with the Indians but had clearly outstayed their

This somewhat fanciful European engraving of Martin Pring's "barri-cado" on Cape Cod depicts the temporary cessation of hostilities be-tween local Indian warriors and English sassafras hunters. The two English mastiffs can be seen in their houses beside the front gate, while the guitar-playing seaman entertains the dancing Indians in the fore-ground. From Pieter van der Aa, *De Aanmerkenswaardigste en alom beroemde zee-en landreizen* (Leyden, 1706).

welcome by the end. Like Gosnold's group, Pring's party played host to large sorties of curious natives, whom they entertained with small gifts, food, and the homely melo-dies of a young guitarist. But they also purloined a large birchbark canoe, a rarity in southern New England. Worse yet, when they tired of the natives' eager company, they let loose their two great mastiffs, Fool and Gallant, one of whom carried a half-pike in his mouth to show that he meant business. Understandably, the Nausets were more afraid of the huge-jawed dogs than of twenty Englishmen, and must have resented mightily such "savage" treatment. Accordingly, on the eve of the Englishmen's departure, they set fire to the woods where the English were working, having been foiled in an earlier attempt to surprise the lightly guarded post and the napping workmen with 140 warriors.[24]

For the next five years, English investors turned their attention toward the cold heart of Norumbega, what was now called "North Virginia." Because of the active French and Micmac presence in Maine's waters, English relations with the Indians there were trickier and more complex than they had been around Cape Cod, and were made more so by English actions. Captain George Waymouth's trading expedition in the summer of 1605 provided the inspiration for the more ambitious Sagadahoc colony two years later, but inadvertently may also have contributed to its premature demise.

Waymouth's crew encountered their first Abenakis in Georges Harbor when three canoes made for a neighboring island. Responding to a hat-waving invitation from the English, one canoe approached and a sagamore began to speak "very lowd and very boldly . . . as though," the intruders felt, "he would know why we were there," and by pointing with his paddle towards the sea, "we conjectured he meant we should be gone." But a brave show of trade goods and how they were used seemed to change the natives' tune, even though most of the items—except peacock feathers and clay pipes—must have been familiar fare. To new eyes, the natives "seemed all very civill and merrie: shewing tokens of much thankefulnesse, for those things we gave them."[25]

During the next few days Waymouth consolidated his good fortune with more openhandedness and a little technological wizardry. He feasted visitors below deck where they "marvelled much" at the construction of the cook's kettle and metal can (which may indicate this particular group's lack of direct experience with European ships). When the crew set their seine net, they gave most of the catch to the "marvell[ing]" and no doubt grateful spectators, who in turn impressed the English by their careful sharing of all food with their absent women and mates and by their prompt return of pewter dishes lent to carry it. To entice the locals to trade, Waymouth left trade goods in a conspicuous path and bestowed upon their sagamore a shirt (apparently a true novelty), a large knife, necklace, comb and mirror, "whereat they laughed and," unlike Verrazzano's Narragansetts, "tooke gladly." The Indians were also offered *aqua vitae,* but they would not drink it after having a taste; they much preferred small beer or cider, sugar candy, and raisins.[26]

English technology also played a role in securing the natives' attention and initial respect if not long-term affection. They were "most fearefull" of firearms and "would fall flat downe at the report of them," a tactic that suggests some acquaintance with Europeans.[27] When James Rosier, the *Archangel*'s scribe and cape merchant, began to collect Abenaki vocabulary, the natives brought him natural specimens just to see him make his magical black marks on the thinner-than-birchbark paper, the silent import of which other Englishmen could fathom more easily than their own shamans could read native minds at a distance.[28] The finale was Waymouth's plucking up a knife and needle with his magnetized sword, all "to cause [the Indians] to imagine some great power in us," Rosier admitted, "and for that to love and feare us."[29]

During this moment of good feelings, the natives and the English swapped guests for the night. The English emissary was Owen Griffin, one of the two crewmen the voyage's sponsors planned to leave with the Indians over the winter; he happily stood hostage for three natives who slept on deck in an old sail. (Avoiding Pring's gaff in etiquette, Waymouth tied his dogs up whenever any Indians visited the ship.) The natives ashore treated Griffin to a two-hour religious dance, in which he participated by singing and "looking and lifting up his hands to heaven." As we might expect, the Indians were as unsuccessful in interpreting his gestures as he was theirs. By turn, they pointed to the moon, the rising sun, and the stars to ask what he worshipped, but each time he signaled his denial and they ended up "laughing one to another."[30]

Other aspects of English behavior must have been equally puzzling. One morning after two days of brisk trade, the ship suddenly closed shop and sent all canoes home because "it was the Sabbath day," although that evening, after the official end of the day, half a dozen crewmen went ashore to see if they could raise any truck with the ship's biscuits the natives inexplicably fancied. There the cape merchant refused certain local foods in trade and drove a hard bargain for four goslings because, he said, he wanted "always [to] make the greatest esteeme I could of our commodities whatsoever." Such close-fisted conduct, contrasted with Waymouth's liberality aboard ship, cannot have pleased the natives, to whom generosity was the prime social virtue.[31]

But relations took a nose-dive on the fifth day when the English seized five Abenaki warriors by the hair (the only option given their near-nudity) as future interpreters and informants for their sponsors. Two of the men were below deck at the cook's fire; the other three had to be lured away from their numerous companions (Griffin counted 283 during the dance). All were inhabitants of the nearby Pemaquid village, including Nahaneda, its sagamore. The English added insult to injury during the next few days by planting a cross up the St. George River, marching around the interior on a "parching hot" day in armor, refusing to meet with Bashabes, the supreme sagamore of the region, and pestering a sagamore who had come to redeem his neighbors to sell his official red roach coronet. Although the captives were treated kindly and were ready students (and teachers) of language, they may have exacted small but keen revenge when, after seeing English cattle, they told their captors "how they make butter and cheese of the milke they have of the Rain-Deere and Fallo-Deere, which they have tame as we have Cowes."[32]

After a year's immersion in things English, Nahaneda and his "brother," Amooret, were returned to native life at Pemaquid. In 1607 a third captive, Skidwarres, shipped out with the Popham colony headed for Sagadahoc. After two years abroad, he was intended to serve as a trusted interpreter-liaison with his tribesmen. But as soon as he introduced the colonists to Nahaneda's armed and wary people at Pemaquid, he slipped into the native crowd and never again cast his lot with the newcomers.

During the Sagadahoc colony's brief existence, Skidwarres and Nahaneda made only two documentary appearances, but they clearly played a key role in defeating its economic ends. Early in October they and three others showed up at the heavily armed fort to join the hundred colonists at table and, as it turned out, church services. For their timing they had to endure public prayers both morning and evening; one witness thought they attended with "great reverence & sylence," another that they "seemed affected with our mens devotions." Having learned the art of flattery from English adepts, they told their hosts that "King James is a good King, his God a good God, and Tanto [their own evil deity] naught." Yet they also let slip, not without purpose, that Tanto had "commanded them not to dwell neere, or come among the English, threatning to kill some and inflict sicknesse on others, beginning with two of [Nahaneda's] children, saying he had power, and would doe the like to the English the next Moone. . . ." This potent prophecy did not stop one native visitor from staying behind, trading the beaver coat off his back, and expressing a wish to visit England.[33]

A month earlier, the two Anglo-Indians had also promised to take the English to Bashabes on the Penobscot to open a profitable trade, which in September was highly improbable. More likely the Indians knew that Bashabes, the overlord of Mawooshen, a nine-river region of some ten thousand people, expected that "all strangers should have their addresse to him, not he to them." But at the appointed time the guides vamoosed into the interior and the English could not find their way alone, and so returned empty-handed. To judge from the report of a ship captain who returned from Sagadahoc in mid-December with a number of frozen settlers, the colony's anticipated fur trade was likely never to materialize. One reason was the ubiquitous French: four ships that year had combed the coast as far south as Massachusetts. Another was the fractured leadership of the colony: the president and people "devid[ed] themselves into factions, each disgracing the other, even to the Savages, the on[e] emulatinge the others reputation amongst those brutish people." A rumor circulating in England, probably on the tongues of the returnees, spelled out some of the settlers' shenanigans. The English, reported Sir Ferdinando Gorges, a man with a keen interest in that part of the world, were "worse than the very Savages, impudently and openly lying with their Women, teaching their Men to drinke drunke, to swear and blaspheme the name of GOD, and in their drunken humour to fall together by the eares."[34]

The chief obstacle to a successful fur trade, however, seemed to be the former captives. Not only were the local natives "exceedingly subtill and conninge" in concealing the source of all the commodities the English wanted, but if by chance any Indians appeared ready to reveal those sources, the turncoats were hustled off by Nahaneda and Skidwarres and prohibited—probably on pain of death or of offending Tanto—from showing their faces near the fort.[35]

A key player in this tug-of-war was Sabenoa, the local sagamore of the lower and middle Kennebec. After the colonists began construction of Fort St. George without his permission, he and four men canoed down to inform them, in "broken English," that he was "Lord of the River of Sachadehoc." He then invited a delegation to visit his village upriver, which one did after an exchange of hostages. When they arrived, they were met by "50 able menn very strong and tall . . . all new[ly] paynted & armed with their bowes and arrowes." Apparently without any gift-giving to dissolve the tension, and only a teasing show of trade goods for the future, the English headed home in their shallop. Predictably, they were soon intercepted by sixteen warriors in three canoes, who said they wanted to trade. When the English disdained their tobacco and small skins, the pursuers' true motives became clear: one Indian stepped into the shallop and, pretending to light his pipe, seized the firebrand used to ignite the English matchlocks and threw it into the river. His comrades then grabbed the boat rope and prevented a soldier from landing to secure another brand. Fortunately, the combatants came to a Mexican stand-off and departed with no casualties except their trust.[36]

But sometime during the following year the natives and newcomers came to blows. The English record is silent on the matter, but Indian traditions give two different, perhaps congruent, explanations. The one closest to the event was collected by "an Ancient [Maine] Marriner" before 1660 from an old Kennebec Indian who, as a youth, had seen the English build their fort at Sagadahoc. He reported that "upon some Quarrel that fell out betwixt the Indians and them, the English were some of them killed by the said Indians and the rest all driven out of the Fort, where there was left much of their Provisions and Ammunition; amongst which there were some barrels of Powder; but after they had opened them not knowing what to do therewith, they left the Barrels carelessly open, and scattered the Powder about, so as accidently it took Fire; and blew up all that was within the Fort, burnt and destroyed many of the Indians, upon which they conceived their God was angry with them for doing hurt to the English."[37]

A much later tradition, published in 1792 from Norridgewalk testimony, may point to the causes of the initial "Quarrel" that led to the natives' reprisal. When a number of natives went to the fort to trade, the Norridgewalks remembered, the planters asked them to haul a small cannon by a rope. "When they were arranged on a line in this process, the white people discharged the piece, and thereby killed and wounded several of them. . . . The story is, that the resentment of the natives, consequent to this treacherous murder, obliged the Europeans to re-embark the next summer" and return to England in disgrace. Obviously, the Abenakis did not lament their departure, particularly when the French supplied their needs better and did not stay long enough to spoil the neighborhood.[38]

But the Norumbegans would get no peace. Maine's waters and then rivers soon became a wild international frontier of cutthroat competition and cultural domination. And the plague-weakened natives bore the brunt, as they did everywhere in North America, the victims of a geopolitical reality they could not foresee and only partially fashion.[39]

CHAPTER FOUR

Native Reactions to the Invasion of America

PERHAPS THE GREATEST DIFFERENCE BETWEEN THE COL-umbian observances of 1892 and 1992 is that the American na-tives were virtually absent a century ago whereas today they are clearly at the center of attention. Indian voices loudly and clearly present their own views on the meaning of their ancestors' dis-covery of Columbus and its deadly aftermath, while even non-native academics ensure that the "Admiral of the Ocean Sea" no longer enjoys the limelight.

The reason is simple: since the late 1960s and the concatena-tion of Vietnam, the American Indian Movement, the rise of Black Power, the civil rights movement, the woman's movement, and the hothouse growth of a new brand of social history, Ameri-can society, the media, and the historical profession have redis-covered history's forgotten peoples—natives, women, and mi-norities—the allegedly "inarticulate" who left relatively few traces in the written records so favored by traditional historians. At a time of social upheaval, the nation's and the profession's focus and sympathy shifted from the newscatching movers and shakers of the past to its anonymous victims, the hewers of wood and drawers of water who swelled the ranks and made the elites and their successes possible. Indeed, "success" was redefined to include sheer survival, particularly when the deck was stacked and the odds were overwhelming.

The shift of focus is particularly salutary for students of colonial North America because its history is simply inexplicable without the active inclusion of its Indian (and black) inhabitants.* The dual perspective of ethnohistory also requires us to attend with equal care and skill to both sides of the colonial frontier. For all these reasons I was glad to be asked to open the interdisciplinary conference "Transatlantic Encounters: The Discovery of the Old World and the New" at Vanderbilt University in October 1992. For the session "Native Americans: 'Vision of the Vanquished'" I wrote the following essay in an effort to anatomize the surprising variety of ways Indians responded to the Europeans who invaded their lands in the wake of Columbus.

In 1492 Columbus inaugurated what we in this historical generation are choosing to call the "Columbian Encounter" between the cultures and peoples of *two* old worlds—the Americas and the rest of the world known to Western Europeans. The term "encounter" is largely apt because it suggests that the so-called discovery was mutual: the American natives discovered, laid fresh eyes on, the swarthy Spanish sailors as surely and as importantly as the sailors discovered them for the first time.

But "encounter" is not a perfect fit: it is slightly misleading because it implies true parity of initiation and participation. Certainly the natives were involved up to their necks in America's rapidly evolving history from the moment Columbus and his crew stepped off the boats, not just in relatively segregated "Indian affairs," where we would expect to find them, but in many, perhaps most, aspects of colonial life for literally hundreds of years, where historians and ethnohistorians are increasingly discovering

---

* James Axtell, "Colonial America Without the Indians," *After Columbus: Essays in the Ethnohistory of Colonial North America* (New York, 1988), ch. 11.

them (and where native people knew them to be all along). But the interaction between Indians and Europeans (and their unwilling African partners) occurred almost exclusively in the Americas, not in the other "Old World." And the Indians spent most of the conquest and colonial periods reacting and responding *to* the European strangers and invaders. Thus, the human encounter that we are commemorating and reflecting on before and after 1992 was largely initiated by the Europeans but took place locally, on the Indians' turf, which forced the natives primarily into a defensive mode.

If there is any doubt about these elemental points, we have only to consider 1492 counterfactually and what the Indians did *not* do. They did not launch a fleet of dug-out canoes in hopes of attending a family reunion with their Mongoloid relatives in northern China. They did not run into the Iberian coast en route and immediately lay claim to it and its odd, overdressed, hirsute peoples for the Taíno Empire. They did not make their way by spear, blood, and bow to Seville and Rome in order to liberate the Spanish people from the despotism of Ferdinand and Isabella or the European masses from their pagan thraldom to Alexander VI. Fortunately for the course of civilization, they did not plunder Europe's royal courts and treasure houses of blue glass beads, lace points, peacock feathers, and courtesans' rouge. And most important, they did not wreak havoc upon Europe's loins, lungs, and numbers by sharing the pleasures of syphilitic sex followed by a good cigar.

Although the Indians were put on the defensive by the European incursion, they remained so only in a general sense. In the three hundred years after 1492, they had plenty of room and ability to respond to the European challenge, not as Pavlovian automata acting in a few predictable ways, but as infinitely various, creative shapers of their own destinies. Like the actions of their new rivals, native responses were fashioned from experience, expectations, and situational calculations of self-interest and odds of success. They also varied according to native interest groups, to the perceived nature, power, and stance of the European challengers, and to the timing or stage of contact. Except in the scenarios of generalizing historians, the Columbian encounters were never between generic "Indians" and "Europeans" but always between segments or factions of native groups (which we call "tribes" for convenience) and similar, equally interested subgroups of European nationalities. Both sets of factions were grounded in differences of age, gender, social status, kinship, history, and perception of the problem and its potential solution.

In the fluid conditions of contact, the American natives understandably sought to maintain the *status quo ante* as much and as long as possible. In the face of new challenges from a people and a world they had never before known or even imagined, the various Indian groups worked mightily and often cleverly to maximize their political sovereignty, cultural autonomy, territorial integrity, power of self-identification, and physical mobility. In one way or another, of course, the European colonists over time sought to or effectively did minimize the natives' freedoms in order to reduce the natives' "otherness" to familiarity, predictability, and control.[1] To counter this offensive, the natives resorted to five basic strategies, which were not always sequential or mutually exclusive: initially, they tried to *incorporate* the newcomers; when that failed, they tried at various times to *beat* them, to *join* them, to *copy* enough of their ways to beat them at their own game, and to *avoid* them altogether.

In the inaugural stage of exploration, natives and newcomers enjoyed a relatively short "honeymoon," a peaceful period of feeling each other out. Because the technologically stronger Europeans were greatly outnumbered and found themselves in the dangerous unknown of someone else's country, they kept their weapons sheathed and put on their most accommodating behavior until they could get the lay of the land and probe the weaknesses of its peoples. But they were extremely wary the whole time because they brought to America prefabricated images of the "savage," occasionally noble but mostly ignoble, from their experiences in Africa and Asia and from their reading of ancient, biblical, and Renaissance travel literature.[2] They expected the worst and, in their ignorance or ham-handedness, often provoked the natives into fulfilling their expectations.

Likewise, the Indians based their initial behavior upon their own preconceptions and expectations. But unlike the Europeans, the natives expected novel strangers to be either equal or superior to themselves, either powerful and potentially dangerous "persons," animated by living "souls" like their own, or "gods," "spirits" from the heavens whose powers were of a higher order.[3] The strangers' skin color was less noticeable than their hairiness; to the smooth-skinned natives, European beards and tufted chests and limbs were simply uncouth, signs of unintelligence and unmanliness.[4] It was largely the items the newcomers wore, carried, and made that marked them as "spirits" of extraordinary ability and power. European cloth, metal, glass, and especially objects that seemed to "speak," such as clocks, books, and guns, all impressed the Indians as worthy of respect if not worship, as were their makers.[5]

In order to harness or at least neutralize these unusual powers, the natives tried to incorporate the Europeans as honorary Indians or "true men," just as they adopted native strangers and even enemies captured in battle. They greeted them in friendly fashion by clapping them on their

chests, rubbing their arms, or painting their faces. They
seated them on their best mats or furs and feasted them on
their tastiest dishes. They showered them with presents,
offered them the calumet pipe or wampum belt of peace,
and made long speeches of welcome and adoption. They
then bestowed Indian names upon them, the ultimate sign
of acceptance. On occasion, they offered their young women as partners for the night or forever.[6]

But even native groups who did not immediately offer
the strangers full acceptance extended help, advice, and
friendship. When European ships skirted the Atlantic or
the Gulf coast after several weeks at sea, Indians usually
guided them to safe anchorages, helped their crews collect
firewood, food, and fresh water, and opened a small trade,
sometimes giving the lonely sailors sexual favors or decorated fur pouches for hometown girls in exchange for durable (if weevilly) hardtack, rum, or movable pieces of
ship's equipment. Natives often rained loaves of cornbread
or freshly caught fish into the visitors' longboats; one
crew of rowers in North Carolina also found themselves
crowded with two tall, beautiful young women, the "gift"
of native leaders who sought to win the strangers' alliance
through marriage, American-style.[7]

Communication quickly became a problem, once the an-
tic pantomime of sign language ventured beyond simple
counting and exchange of visible objects. As the numerically dominant party on their home ground, the natives
sought to make the gibbering newcomers learn the language of the country. Assuming that the hairy incompe-
tents were the equivalent of Indian children, the natives
quickly devised simplified pidgin languages for them, featuring elemental vocabularies and truncated grammars
and syntax. A few European words might be thrown in to
designate newly introduced objects, but the linguistic base
remained American. When the explorers caught on as fast

as Indian toddlers, they prided themselves on their linguistic skills and unwittingly bequeathed the childish pidgins to future generations as full-blown adult languages.[8]

Spanish and English explorers, however, were usually too ethnocentric to do in Rome as the Romans did, so they sought to turn the linguistic tables by making the natives learn their national languages or regional dialects instead. Some Indians were eager and able to put their tongues to a new school and quickly became indispensable as interpreters and brokers between the two cultures. A few young adventurers must have volunteered to sail away with the departing ships in order to see the touted miracles of the strangers' "new world" and to participate in the earliest American exchange programs for language immersion. But when volunteers could not be found, the Europeans did not hesitate to shanghai candidates for a year or more before returning them to America to serve as bilingual guides and go-betweens.[9]

Those who were well treated and did not suffer unduly from the curiosity or contempt of their European hosts sometimes returned to be helpful to the invaders; Manteo at Roanoke and Squanto in Plymouth exercised considerable influence among their countrymen by virtue of their command of the English language and apparent possession of the secrets of English power.[10] Others, however, quickly reverted to native ways and used their new skills against their teachers. Domagaya and Taignoagny, the two sons of chief Donnacona who were kidnapped by Jacques Cartier in 1534, taught their kinsmen at Stadacona (present-day Quebec City) to offer much lower prices for French knives and hatchets, presumably because they had seen how cheaply they could be made in Brittany.[11] And when an Indian renamed Don Luis was returned to his native Virginia in 1571 after several years of involuntary education in Spanish hands, he immediately ran away, took several wives Indian-style, and led the killing of the Jesuit missionaries sent to pacify his tribesmen.[12]

Don Luis's behavior marks a transition from the wary but peaceful human explorations of initial contact to the often hostile reaction of natives upon what might be called "second contact." Second contacts are easily confused with truly first contacts because they are the initial encounters described in several famous documents by European colonizers. But, in fact, we know from other sources and even the same documents that the natives had been provoked into bellicosity by previous European insults or injuries. When, for example, the English landed at Cape Henry in Virginia in 1607, Chesapeake warriors crept up on all fours "like Bears, with their Bowes in their mouthes" and charged the newcomers "very desperately in the faces," wounding a captain and a sailor with arrows "very dangerous[ly]."[13] In the winter of 1620 the Plymouth Pilgrims had a similar "First Encounter," for which they (re-)named the Cape Cod location where it occurred. Apparently for no reason, a number of Wampanoag warriors suddenly emerged from the woods and let fly several volleys of arrows at an English exploring party. The English expected the worst from the American "savages," but we can easily see that the Indians' response was not some atavistic bloodlust vented upon innocent white men. They had had plenty of contact with and provocation from Europeans before the Pilgrims stumbled into their midst. Some of the arrows they shot were tipped with European brass. Only six years earlier, Thomas Hunt of Virginia, the leader of a fishing party left behind when Captain John Smith sailed back to England, had, under the pretense of trade, kidnapped twenty-seven natives from the Cape and sold them as slaves in Spain. And to add insult to injury, the curious Pilgrims had rifled temporarily abandoned houses, corn caches, and graves of the local Indians while looking for a suitable site for settlement.[14] It is small wonder that the natives were not prone to regard the latest wave of bearded seafarers simply as peace-loving pilgrims seeking religious toleration, as our textbooks have led generations of American schoolchildren to regard the Pilgrims.

The advent of large-scale parties of permanent settlers drastically recast the Indian-European equation, demanding from the increasingly beleaguered natives a set of responses as creative as they were crucial. The first major challenge posed by European settlers was inadvertent and only indirectly personal, namely, the importation of epidemic diseases that killed with added virulence in the "virgin soil" populations of the Americas. Ancient European scourges such as smallpox, diphtheria, and influenza and childhood diseases such as measles and mumps alike snuffed out the lives of astonishing numbers of defenseless Indian adults and children, leaving wide rents in the social fabric of native life. The biggest killer, smallpox, was capable of striking down 50–90 percent of an Indian village or tribe, partly because everyone fell sick at the same time, leaving no one to provide fires, food, and especially water for the fever-ravaged victims, partly because the natives initially had no immunities from previous exposure to the disease.[15] And native responses to the diseases, which were spread largely by human touch and breath, only increased their deadly reach and exacerbated their effects. It was native custom to crowd around the bunk of an ailing relative to lend comfort and a sense of solidarity; in the new disease environment, such behavior was as far from quarantine as it was possible to get. Moreover, the preferred native cure for most ailments was a stint in a steaming sweatlodge, followed by a naked plunge into the nearest snowbank or body of cold water. Particularly for the deadly fevers of smallpox, this was the worst course the Indians could have taken. Only when compassionate colonists in the eighteenth century persuaded them to forsake this traditional remedy did native mortality rates deaccelerate to some extent.[16]

Although the natives remained helpless before the onslaught of foreign microbes all through the colonial period, they did respond flexibly to the demographic devastation wrought by them. As disease left yawning gaps in their social structures, technological repertoires, and communal memories, the Indians made three adaptations to cope with their losses. First, many tribes, the Iroquois nations of New York in particular, resorted increasingly to warfare with both native and colonial enemies to replenish their lodges. In traditional "mourning wars," native clans that suffered losses from disease or battle sent their menfolk on the warpath to capture prisoners as replacements. Once captured and brought home, prisoners were treated well, ritually separated from their former allegiances, and adopted fully and faithfully into the suffering clan in the precise place of the deceased. This process served the dual purpose of healing the losses of the grieving group while removing kith and kin from the ranks of the enemy.[17]

Two other strategies were also variations on age-old schemes. One was to intermarry with black Africans and white Europeans. This practice did not differ much from inter-tribal marriages resulting from the adoption of native prisoners. To the culturally "colorblind" Indians, taking spouses of a different hue was a much less "racial" act than it appeared to the increasingly race-conscious colonists. Nor was it confined to one sex, as intermarriage and sexual relations tended to be in patriarchal colonial societies. Indian women felt as free to move in with European traders, hunters, and soldiers as Indian men did to take captive or runaway Europeans to wife.[18]

Like the first and second, the third strategy was a sensible response not only to epidemic mortality but to all forms of depopulation and dislocation caused by colonization. When tribal or village populations approached unviable levels, the survivors sought cultural and military refuge with more populous neighbors or with linguistically related kin even at a distance. The handful of Patuxets who survived a deadly sea-borne plague just before the Pilgrims arrived abandoned their village site overlooking Plymouth Harbor and threw in their lot with their Narragansett and other inland neighbors, who had been relatively unscathed.[19] After the Tuscaroras rose up against the encroaching North Carolinians in 1711 and were beaten back by larger and better-armed English forces, the Iroquoian-speaking natives slowly made their way to western New York, where they were adopted in 1722 by the Iroquois confederacy and given their own homeland in which to live, plant, and hunt.[20] And in the first half of the eighteenth century, the amalgamated Catawba Nation earned a place as one of the four "most considerable" Indian peoples in the Southeast, more than filling the vacuum created by the removal of the Tuscaroras. Along the gentle Catawba River in the Carolina piedmont, the nation was formed by the confluence of a host of small, Siouan-speaking tribes—Sugaree, Esaw, Shutaree, Cheraw, Pedee, Nassaw, Weyaline—who were buffeted by disease, war, dislocation, and pressure from English settlers and northern Iroquois enemies. The Catawbas chose not to become emasculated Settlement or "Parched Corn" Indians, like some of the coastal tribes, but to remain masters of their own fate in their own territory. Even when ripped by further epidemics, the nation's attractiveness to southeastern remnant groups ensured their autonomy nearly until the nineteenth century.[21]

Geographical relocation was a prominent native response to colonization all over North America. But it was not, contrary to popular opinion, then and now, easy for the semi-sedentary—not nomadic—natives to pull up stakes and leave their ancestral homelands. Nor was the direction of movement always predictable. Many groups, such as the Western Abenakis in northern New England and the Powhatans in Virginia after the 1622 uprising, responded to the European incursion by quietly drifting away from the new settlements and their corn-loving cattle and melting into the forgotten corners of the land.[22] To maintain the hunting and gathering facets of their economies, native groups in the East had to put wide swaths of woodland between themselves and the spreading fields and unfettered herds of the colonists.

But some colonial establishments were not as intrusive as English farms and towns, and several native groups actually moved toward them to take advantage of their economic, military, or religious services. French trading posts and settlements in Canada and Louisiana were the most obvious beneficiaries of native relocations. After the founding of Quebec in 1608, nomadic hunters north of the St. Lawrence shifted their summer encampments along the river closer to the new town in order to receive presents and preferential rates from the French traders there.[23] Beginning in the 1640s, natives from all over the Northeast moved to the vicinity of Montreal and Quebec to occupy *reserves* where missionary Catholicism, sedentary farming, and marginally frenchified living prevailed. Only *reserve* Indians who converted to Christianity were allowed to buy guns, with which they often defended the underpopulated French outpost of empire from the grasp of its Dutch and particularly English neighbors until 1760.[24]

Native movements on the St. Lawrence were nothing compared with the French-sponsored resettlements in Louisiana, which resembled a high-speed chess game. The other European player in the early eighteenth century was the frail Spanish garrison at Pensacola. Because the Spanish were militarily weak and poorly provisioned, they could not give adequate protection or guarantee a steady supply of trade goods to their Indian neighbors and allies. When the French arrived in 1699, therefore, several small tribes moved to the new French capital at Mobile, around which French officers allotted them tribal domains. One such tribe was the Tawasas, who arrived in 1705. "They had deserted the Spaniards . . . ," wrote André Pénicaut, a literate ship's carpenter and chronicler, "because they had been daily exposed to raids of the Alibamon [Indians], and the Spanish had not stood by them." But they were certainly no drag on the French economy, for they were "good hunters," Pénicaut testified, "and every day they brought us much game of all kinds." They also brought a "great deal of corn" to plant the fields they were allotted. Some Apalachees who came the same year were regarded as "excellent Catholics" to boot; they had been well catechized by Spanish priests at Pensacola and were easily put under the wing of a French missionary.[25]

As soon as the French moved up the Mississippi, local native villages leapt into a merry minuet, to an old French tune. In 1709 the Houmas "departed their settlement" and went to live on the west bank of the Mississippi near the river of the Chitimachas, while the Tunicas shifted to the Houmas' old site, closer to the French. A few years later, the pugnacious Chitimachas made peace with the French and were persuaded to "leave their homes on the river where they were and . . . settle on the bank of the Missicipy . . . in a place that was marked off for them." Their move in turn "caused other native [*sauvage*] nations to make several changes of dwelling place," most of them to the banks of the river that served as the French lifeline to the rich Illinois country and upper Great Lakes. "All these nations are highly industrious," noted an appreciative Frenchman, "and all are quite helpful in furnishing food to the French, to the troops as well as to the people on the concessions."[26] He did not have to say that the natives also furnished the deerskin staple of the French trade and the crucial military difference between life and death.[27]

Virtually everywhere the Europeans went, disease, depopulation, and dislocation followed close on their heels. As favorite hunting and planting grounds were lost and traditional economic activities constricted, native individuals and tribes adjusted to the best of their abilities to the new order. For tribes blessed with access to the fur- and skin-bearing animals craved by colonial traders, initial efforts were directed toward harvesting those supposedly inexhaustible resources with just enough energy to supply their everyday needs, leaving intact their cultural and political autonomy. But these needs increasingly included imported European objects, made of superior materials or available in preferable colors and styles, such as woven cloth, glass beads, metal tools, ceramic tableware, and guns and ammunition. Over time, even the most abstemious natives became dependent on European manufacturers and distributors and the credit system that oiled the nascent "world system" in which they were all enmeshed.[28] They also depleted their animal resources in their accelerating quest to supply colonial demand and their own, newly awakened wants and needs.[29]

The advent of this predicament typically drew three related responses from the Indians. The first was to accelerate their search for rival Europeans as economic and political partners. By playing off at least two of their French, English, Dutch, and Spanish competitors, native tribes tried to augment their leverage as allies and customers, on the principle that two fighting foxes might ignore the vulnerable henhouse. If a tribe was not located conveniently between two European colonies or outposts, they might move to such a place, invite a colonial post or garrison to locate near them to complete the desired triangle, or carry their furs and skins long distances to another supplier to show their more proximate partner their independence. Since virtually all colonies needed Indian neutrality or allies to succeed, the natives were usually assured of success in obtaining better prices, more gifts, and some increase in services, justice, and respect for their sovereignty. Only after the English drove the French from Canada and Louisiana and the Spanish relinquished Florida did the Indians find themselves between a rock and hard place.[30]

A second Indian response to increased debt and scarcity of marketable game was to sell land to eager English farmers, cattlemen, and governments. Between 1650 and 1670, the natives of the upper Connecticut River valley were largely forced by mounting debts at John Pynchon's stores, reduced colonial markets for surplus native food, and the overhunting of fur-bearing animals to sell major portions of their tribal estates along the river. But this remedy was not universally approved by the natives because they, like their English competitors, were riven by political factions. They knew, as Peter Thomas has reminded us, that "Indian leaders were no less guilty than some English of pursuing self-aggrandizement at the ultimate expense of other members of their own society."[31] At a similar though later stage of development, the western Massachusetts Indians who had been settled by the English in a reserve town at Stockbridge on the Housatonic River chose to sell the land surrounding the town proper to satisfy English creditors. In 1765 these creditors persuaded the Massachusetts General Court to allow the natives to reduce their debts—accumulated largely in purchasing farm and household equipment to make them more like their English neighbors—by alienating land. Within three years, the English had acquired sixty-five native plots, usually at greatly discounted prices; by 1788 the Stockbridges had moved to Oneida territory in New York for a clean start.[32]

The Cherokees and Muskogees or Creeks resorted to similar tactics to unburden themselves of trading debts. In 1771 the Cherokees ceded sixty square miles of prime farmland on the Savannah River to a group of English traders who had advanced them considerable sums on credit both before and after the Cherokee-English war of 1760–61. Although the British Superintendent of Indian Affairs was disconcerted that the deal was closed behind his back, he acknowledged the justice of compensating the traders because they had lost all their goods and skins at the sudden outbreak of war, and after it had entrusted the destitute Cherokees for all their purchases, including high-priced woolens. But the fly in the ointment was the Creeks, who claimed the ceded land as their own by right of conquest in the war, when they fought beside the English. Understandably, they wished to use the contested land to erase their own trading debts, which had mounted even though they were "good hunters" and owned "the most extensive hunting-ground of any nation" in the Southeast.[33]

The Creeks and Cherokees were unusual in still having large territories at their disposal well into the eighteenth century and in being able to lop off sizable chunks of unessential land to appease their creditors. Until the 1760s they also felt only modest pressure from South Carolina and Georgia settlers, cattlemen, and government officials, who needed their friendship, labor, and trade more than their land. But smaller, less insulated groups closer to European settlements felt the pressure to sell much earlier and more forcefully. If we may generalize from the behavior of the Delawares in northern New Jersey, these natives alienated their real estate in ways that prolonged their tenure on ancestral lands far longer than anyone could reasonably expect, given the growing hegemony of the colonists. The Delawares retained their autonomy for a century and a half by selling land slowly and methodically and by extracting as many concessions from the buyers as possible. "At no time were lands sold in a scattered or random fashion." Only parcels that abutted already alienated tracts were sold by native proprietors. In order to ingratiate themselves with their more powerful colonial neighbors and to forestall more drastic forms of aggrandizement, the natives sold cheaply. Low sale prices helped them retain use of the land until the colonists actually fenced, plowed, and built upon it. By deeds of sale, Indians all over the English colonies were permitted to hunt, trap, fish, plant, cut wood, or gather natural resources for the foreseeable future.[34] And finally, native sellers were sometimes quite choosey about their buyers, preferring honest, peace-loving, non-speculative neighbors such as Quakers, Labadists, and members of other minority groups seeking their own fruits of toleration.[35]

When the constriction of their land base and traditional sources of livelihood began to pinch the natives, they turned to a third strategy to ensure a future: they went to work in the colonial economy, usually on its margins but occasionally in major industries. Most of these jobs were part-time and compatible with traditional skills and occupations. The fur and skin trades required not only expert Indian hunters and trappers but guides, packhorsemen, canoemen, interpreters, and sometimes factors.[36] Government officers in New England and elsewhere relied on swift Indian messengers and couriers.[37] Particularly in the early eighteenth century, white southern planters and slave-dealers needed native hunters and trackers to capture Indian slaves from Spanish missions in Florida and to return African runaways.[38] Virtually every colonial army needed the keen eyes and ears of native scouts and flankers and the daunting ferocity of guerilla warriors.[39] On Long Island, Cape Cod, and Nantucket, experienced natives earned good salaries on English whaling vessels, especially as harpooners.[40] Early explorers in New England and later entrepreneurs in Canada and New York relied on the practiced native eye for fugitive sassafras and ginseng, which enjoyed short boom periods on European markets.[41] And colonial tables were often supplied by Indian hunters, who occasionally passed off sides of the colonists' own cattle as "venison" or "moose" and tough eagle meat as tender turkey.[42] The only role that native men found totally distasteful and inconsonant with their dignity was that of farm laborer. In the Eastern Woodlands, particularly in patrilineal New England, Indian men were not accustomed to the backbreaking drudgery of planting, weeding, chopping, and harvesting, which was women's work, nor the repetitious round of chores required on a colonial farm. They were certainly not used to having their independence curtailed, which many experienced for the first time when they sold themselves as indentured servants to make ends meet.[43]

But these were jobs filled mostly by men. Native women were equally industrious in adjusting to the new economic order. They, too, hired out their services as farm and household servants, but more often they opted for work that guaranteed better pay and more freedom. They grew crops to feed European garrisons, where some of them had white or black husbands on duty.[44] They handcrafted baskets, brooms, birchbark containers, porcupine-quill-decorated pouches, multi-colored reed mats and hangings, and finger-woven wool sashes for urban and country customers. They married colonial traders, taught them their language and cultural protocols, and finessed their access to the native hierarchy. Other "trading girls" only leased their charms for short periods and ample amounts of trade

Indians assisted European whalers in North Atlantic waters from the 16th century. Many natives were excellent harpooners, like Queequeg in Herman Melville's *Moby-Dick*. From Theodor de Bry, *Americae*, Part IX (Frankfurt, 1602).

goods.[45] Perhaps the most resourceful entrepreneurs of all were the women who controlled the alcohol trade among their tribesmen. Iroquois and Creek women obtained much of the rum and brandy from colonial suppliers and conveyed it in wooden rundlets and kegs to their villages, sometimes stopping to top off less-than-full containers with water. These may have been the same women who, when offered swigs of the fiery liquids by generous party-throwers, surreptitiously spit the contents into a bottle hidden beneath their blankets for later resale to the men.[46]

Becoming a part of the colonial economy was one step away from autonomy. Still, other Indians chose to move even farther by becoming Christian converts and cultural neophytes in European "praying towns," missions, or *reserves*. In Spanish Florida and Georgia, French Canada, and Puritan New England, native individuals and families, and sometimes whole villages and tribes, placed themselves under the spiritual and cultural guidance of Christian missionaries, who eagerly worked to exorcise their traditional "paganism," convert them to "one, holy, and apostolic faith," and acculturate them to an idealized brand of domesticated agriculture and behavior known as "civility." Frequently, commitment to the new cultural programs entailed movement away from ancestral villages and homelands and amalgamation with members of other tribes, even ancient or recent enemies. Enlisting invariably put white foreigners over them in positions of highest authority, although native leaders might still play familiar roles in secular affairs.[47] At the same time and for many of the same reasons, some Indian parents placed their children under the cultural tutelage of white schoolmasters, usually far from home. Although colonial officials frankly regarded the native children as "hostages" for the good behavior of their tribal adults, Indian leaders willingly sent their sons—seldom their daughters—to learn the white men's ways.[48]

From certain modern perspectives, Indians who turned to European schools and praying towns seem to have been committing cultural suicide. In submitting themselves to European institutions, values, and authorities, they appear to have abandoned their struggle for autonomy and opted to live under the heavy colonial thumb. A few individuals may indeed have acted out of cowardice or weakness, but the majority of Indian neophytes turned to the invaders' cultures and religions for empowerment, knowledge, and skills with which to sustain native identities and values in other guises. They threw in their lot with the blackrobes for three major reasons.

First, villages and tribes that reconstituted themselves in praying towns, particularly in New England and Florida, had been so badly crippled by disease, dislocation, and depopulation that their only other alternatives were to amalgamate with other groups in a similar condition or to place themselves at the mercy of ancient enemies, neither of which seemed calculated to promote a long or happy life. They were in such danger of extinction as distinct peoples that only the distasteful but powerful remedy offered by the colonists held out any hope of long-term survival. So they swallowed the bitter prescriptions that sought to turn them into tawny replicas of "civilized" European farmers and housewives, knowing that beneath their new fitted clothes and short hair they would still be "true people" (as they identified themselves in tribal name).[49] They would still enjoy communal property (guaranteed to some extent by colonial law) and native leaders chosen from traditional ranks of authority. In time of need, they might count on military and material assistance from their colonial sponsors. And despite the missionary idealization of farming as the only "civilized" way of life, they could in fact pursue most aspects of their tradition economies, at least part-time. In other words, accepting the circumscribed life of "praying Indians" gave them the time and protective coloration to adjust to the worst stresses of living in a dangerous new world.[50]

Individual Indians sought in the invaders' religions and customs two other ways to cope with that world. One was to acquire some of the white men's "power" or *manitou* (as Algonquian-speakers called it) by learning to call upon their god through prayer. Although the missionaries warned that their God was supreme, all-sufficient, and intolerant of rivals, many converts reasonably added Him to their traditional pantheons in hopes of increasing their spiritual odds. For them, Christianity and its cultural attendants offered answers to serious and disturbing questions posed by the strange and sudden advent of white and black people, epidemic diseases, enlarged cosmologies and geographies, and technological wonders. The people who sailed into and shattered the natives' old world seemed most able to reassemble the old and the new pieces with some coherence and meaning.[51]

Secondly, native neophytes sought practical as well as intellectual skills for contending with their new world. While colonial schoolmasters aimed ultimately at giving their pupils the cultural luxury of Latin and Greek, native parents sent their beloved children primarily to learn to read, write, and count—skills that would protect their people from fraudulent deeds, inflated debts, and selectively enforced laws. If they and their praying elders also learned to manage a colonial-style farm and household, to sew, knit, weave, cobble, hammer, and saw, and to manipulate the machinery of colonial courts, so much the better.[52]

While the praying Indians were forging survival tactics in the midst of the enemy, other, more fortunate tribes armed themselves at home for the inevitable assaults upon their independence, lands, and ways of life. Of course, even in the most embattled tribes, factional divisions prevented united responses. Some parties wanted to sell out fast and relocate to avoid colonial aggression; others complained loudly and often to colonial governors and imperial officials about the criminal activities and trespassing of white hunters, traders, and cattlemen on Indian land. Most tribes made concerted efforts to play the competing European powers against each other, yet strong factions invariably pulled for each competitor as well as for strict neutrality in what they considered white men's wars. Members of pro-colonial factions sometimes risked transatlantic journeys to the dazzling courts of Europe in order to plead for more aid, effort, or justice.[53]

Sooner or later, the strongest tribes with seductive acreage felt they had to defend their domains with force: the Powhatans in 1622 and 1644, the Pequots in 1636–37, the Wampanoags and Narragansetts in 1675, the Tuscaroras in 1711, the Yamasees and Creeks in 1715, the Cherokees in 1760, and the Ottawas and other Great Lakes tribes in 1764, to mention but a few. Typically, they did not fight alone. They either made peace with a former rival or two to coordinate action against the interlopers or to buy space for their own, or, more rarely, they concocted larger pan-Indian alliances to eradicate the foreign menace. In 1770 the British Superintendent of Indian Affairs warned the governor of Virginia that "at this very time there are in the Creek nation deputies from the Shawnese, Delawares, and other Northern tribes, accompanied by some Cherokees, endeavouring to form a general confederacy on the principle of defending their lands from our daily encroachments."[54]

The natives of southern New England had perceived a similar threat as early as 1641. In the summer of that year, a Narragansett chief from Rhode Island had secretly approached the Montauks on Long Island with plans for a coordinated attack upon all the English settlements of the region. To the Montauks he argued:

So are we all Indians as the English are, and say brother to one another; so must we be one as they are, otherwise we shall be all gone shortly, for you know our fathers had plenty of deer and skins, our plains were full of deer, as also our woods, and of turkies, and our coves full of fish and fowl. But these English having gotten our land, they with scythes cut down the grass, and with axes fell the trees; their cows and horses eat the grass, and their hogs spoil our clam banks, and we shall all be starved.

Therefore, he concluded, forty-one days hence they should "fall on and kill men, women, and children, but no cows, for they will serve to eat till our deer be increased again."[55]

As colonial goods and values infiltrated native life, and settlers, farms, and cattle chewed up tribal lands, many Indians found themselves on the brink of despair. When none of the options we have been discussing seemed feasible, these natives faced two final alternatives. One was to lose themselves in alcoholic stupor, to forget the frightening prospect around them in the amnesia of drunkenness.[56] The other option arose largely in the late eighteenth century, when a new breed of native prophets began to preach salvation through the purification and revitalization of Indian culture. Neolin among the Delawares and Great Lakes tribes and later Handsome Lake among the Iroquois sought to infuse native culture with new life by persuading the Indians to purge themselves of all dependence on whites, particularly by ridding themselves of trade goods and alcohol. If they returned to the "old ways" of their pre-Columbian ancestors, the invaders would be powerless to harm them and the path to the Spirit World would be open and bright.[57]

Fortunately, very few natives enjoyed regular access to, or commanded the resources to purchase, sufficient firewater to wash away their troubles effectively. But unfortunately, alcohol was more plentiful than prophets or hope, and too many troubled Indians found relief only in the bottom of a bottle. At the end of the colonial period, the native population of Eastern America was a small fraction of what it had been before 1492, and their landbase was comparably constricted.[58]

It would be all too easy in the current climate of opinion to attribute the native predicament wholly to Columbus or to the European explorers and colonists who followed him to America, who were certainly responsible for a good share of it. While that might be emotionally satisfying, it would not advance our moral understanding of the past or prepare us—Indians and non-Indians alike—to face the future with equanimity, courage, and imagination. Because it would reduce the Indians to passive victims and deny them an active role in the making of history, theirs and ours together. If we wish to rectify the colonists' worst mistake—their failure to regard the natives as not only humanly *different* from but *equal* to themselves—we must acknowledge that the Indians, in large measure, fashioned their own new world.[59] Within certain cultural and physical constraints, which were always changing, partly by their own actions, they chose their own directions and fates. They had plenty of options, as I have tried to show, and when those ran out, they invented more, like other creative cultures who have found themselves in a bind. Perhaps the best measure of their inventive strength is that, after five hundred years of stiff competition, nearly two million Americans are proud to call themselves "Natives."[60]

Encounters Light
and Dark

CHAPTER FIVE

The First Consumer
Revolution

IN THE PAST TWENTY YEARS, ONE OF MY SCHOLARLY GOALS
has been to demonstrate that Indian history cannot be separated
without violence or chicanery from the history of European-
Americans, either in broad outline or in many cultural specifics.
I have sought to remind students and readers that acculturation
is always and everywhere a two-way street, that all the inhabitants
of North America's cultural frontiers were affected and changed
by each other, without exception. The sea-changes and revolutions that rocked one group were always felt in some degree by
the others.*

When I was invited to participate in the lecture series "The
Chippendale Wigwam: European and Oriental Styles Invade
America" at Mary Washington College in March 1990, my first
impulse was to turn tail and run. What could I, an ethnohistorian, possibly have to say to a decorative-artsy audience in
preservation-minded Fredericksburg, Virginia? When the other
five speakers were slated to discuss various colonial adaptations
in style, how could I bring the Indians into the European stylistic
orbit without fabricating evidence, succumbing to ethnocentrism, or lowering the tone?

*James Axtell, *The European and the Indian: Essays in the Ethnohistory of Colonial
North America* (New York, 1981), esp. chs. 9–10.

My answer to these and other troubling questions was the following essay, which was profusely illustrated with slides, in good art history fashion. When the polite and puzzled applause of the audience died away, my old friend and tutor in things consumer, Tim Breen, submitted my argument to his keen eye and illegible pen, pushing me to clarify and reinforce it in several places. If it does not convince, the fault is none of his.

W<small>E HAVE CELEBRATED TWO IMPORTANT REVOLU</small>-tions in recent years, the American and the French, and we are in the midst of observing another event of revolutionary proportions, the Columbus Quincentenary. Each of these revolutions has a publicly accepted inaugural date—July 4, 1776, July 14, 1789, October 12, 1492—which enables us to fill our calendars with commemorative events. But the latest addition to the revolutionary pantheon comes without a birth certificate or scholarly consensus about its credentials and pedigree. I refer to the English "consumer revolution," which claims no kinship to the more famous English revolutions of Tudor government, civil war, or 1688.

It's small wonder that scholars cannot agree about the causes, timing, effects, and long-range importance of this latest revolution because they discovered it only within the last ten years or so. Another reason for the lack of consensus owes to its nature: this is one of the first "revolutions" to be discovered by the Early Modern practitioners of the "new" social history, rather than by political historians of a conventional stripe. Given the scope of their questions and the quicksilver quality of their evidence, social historians seldom agree about anything, and the consumer revolution is no exception. Yet the outlines of the phenomenon are becoming clearer with each passing article.

It seems that sometime between 1690 and 1740, first in England and Scotland and soon in England's mainland American colonies, consumers of the gentle and particularly "middling" classes began to purchase an unprecedented number and variety of manufactured goods and to use many of them in conspicuous displays of leisure, social ritual, and status affirmation (or arrogation). Thanks to a pronounced increase in per capita wealth and disposable income, consumers not only upgraded their necessities, such as bedding, eating utensils, and clothing, but chose from a veritable Sears catalogue of competitively priced luxury goods and amenities, which reached the remotest corners of the land in peddlers' packs and the inventories of myriad country stores. Often patterned after the latest of the ever-changing fashions of Paris and London and vigorously promoted by window displays, newspaper advertisements, and word-of-mouth, these goods quickly spread from responsive English manufactories across regions and classes in a wide but standardized repertoire. This had the effect of forging strong material bonds between mother country and colonies, even as political fissures were beginning to appear in their union, some the result of mounting debts incurred by colonial shoppers anxious to keep up with the Carters and the Schuylers.[1]

One might legitimately ask, Why is the purchase—even the widespread, cross-class purchase—of satin waistcoats, looking glasses, japaned dressing tables, Wedgwood china, forks, and matching tea services considered "revolutionary"? The experts offer a number of answers. The first is that, unlike the later Industrial Revolution, the consumer revolution was made, less by increased, more efficient, and more competitive productivity on the supply side, than by unprecedented and particular consumer demand, which called forth the supply and inspired many of the technological and organizational advances of the Industrial Revolution. This demand, in turn, was moulded by new techniques of mass marketing and the conscious creation of "imaginary necessities." "As wealth and population increased," explained an English visitor to colonial Baltimore, "wants were created, and many considerable demands, in consequence, took place for the various elegancies as well as the necessaries of life."[2]

Enjoying for the first time so many economic choices, consumers, especially women, were empowered by a heady sense of personal independence and the ability to fashion themselves with the material trappings of "gentility." In the American colonies, however, this heavy dependence on the credit extended by English merchants and manufacturers led to fears of economic enslavement. These fears, in turn, exacerbated fears of political tyranny from the Stamp Act on and gave rise to such consumer boycotts as the Association to halt importation of the "effeminating" and enervating "Baubles of Britain." In other words, when the British government injected coercion into its relations with the colonies, the ties of loyalty that bound the colonists to an empire of free-flowing goods quickly came undone. "A constitutional crisis transformed private consumer acts into public political statements" and many Americans "discovered political ideology through a discussion of the meaning of goods."[3]

In sketching the outlines of this eighteenth-century British revolution, I have a strong sense of *déjà vu*. Where have I seen this before? The answer, as might be expected from an ethnohistorian of colonial North America, is in the Indian communities of seventeenth-century North America. Such an answer will undoubtedly be greeted with a certain amount of reasonable skepticism. After all, don't we all know that the American Indians were poor and spiritual people who lived from hand-to-mouth in a precarious environment and put their faith in strange gods and spirits rather than earthly things? Don't we know that their "no-madic" lifestyle and their communal ethic of sharing mili-tated against the senseless acquisition of material com-forts? Perhaps unlikelier candidates for a *consumer* revo-lution could not be found, certainly not fifty or seventy-five years before their "civilized" and admittedly mate-rialistic English counterparts experienced one.

Such skepticism is unwarranted. The Indians of the Eastern Woodlands experienced a consumer revolution every bit as revolutionary as that experienced by their Eu-ropean suppliers, though not identical in every respect, and they did so many years earlier, usually as soon as the commercial colonists founded trading posts, *comptoirs*, and nascent settlements. How, if the natives lived in penury, was this possible? Without gold or silver mines like those in Mexico and Peru, how did native North Americans across the social spectrum (which was not wide in any case) find the purchase price of any European goods, much less goods in sufficient quantity and variety to warrant a "revo-lutionary" denomination?

The per capita wealth of Indian America, though it can-not be measured in native currencies, increased dramati-cally from the earliest stages of contact because European traders were willing and eager to pay top pound, franc, and florin for American animal pelts and skins, which the Indians were adept in curing and procuring for their own domestic uses. Three kinds of pelts were the most lucrative for the Indians. Beaver, for which the natives had little use before the trade, became the best seller because its soft, microscopically barbed underfur was in great demand for the manufacture of broad-brimmed felt hats for Europe's gentlemen. A ready market also existed for rare and luxu-rious "small furs," such as marten, otter, and black fox, which were used to trim the rich gowns of the high-born. And beginning in the last quarter of the seventeenth cen-

This engraved cartouche from an English map of Canada in 1777 shows a typical trading scene between Indians and Europeans. The barrel may have held metal goods packed in sawdust to prevent breakage, and the bale probably contained blanket cloth or duffels. The two pipes suggest the amicable, semi-ceremonial nature of the occasion. From William Faden, *Map of the Inhabited Part of Canada, from the French Surveys* (1777).

tury, the Indians of the Southeast could sell any number of humbler but larger deerskins, which provided scarce leather for Continental breeches, saddlebags, bookbindings, and workingmen's aprons. The European demand for skins the natives regarded as commonplace was seemingly insatiable and enabled all male hunters of a tribe to participate in the search for income-producing pelts if they wished.

To judge by the traders' export figures, a substantial majority of native hunters did quite well in the new European market. The Mahicans and eastern Iroquois brought about 8,000 beaver and otter skins to the Dutch posts at Fort Orange and New Amsterdam in 1626. Nine years later they had doubled their take. By the late 1650s, 46,000 pelts were pouring into Fort Orange alone.[4] The French in Canada were even better supplied by their native partners.

In 1614, only six years after the founding of Quebec, 25,000 skins, mostly beaver, were shipped to France's hatters. By the 1620s the Montagnais on the north shore of the St. Lawrence were trading 12–15,000 pelts at Tadoussac every year. In flotillas of 60–70 canoes, some 200 Huron traders from southern Ontario brought 10,000 skins a year to Quebec. Twenty years later, even as their population was cut in half by disease and intertribal warfare, the Hurons produced 30,000 beaver pelts annually.[5] In New England, the Plymouth colony was able to pay off its English creditors only because Abenaki hunters on the Kennebec River in Maine kept them supplied with animal skins: about 8,000 beavers and 1,156 otters between 1631 and 1636 alone. Even then the lion's share of Abenaki pelts went to French traders from Acadia.[6]

To the south, the natives of the interior supplied Charleston's outgoing ships with 54,000 deerskins a year between 1700 and 1715. Between 1740 and 1762 the take was up to 152,000 skins a year. The best hunters were the Muskogees or Creeks of Alabama and Georgia. In 1720 they traded more than 80,000 skins to South Carolina and French Mobile. Forty years later, with a new market in Savannah, they were killing 140,000 deer every season.[7] In the 1750s the Cherokees took 25,000 skins annually from the mountains of North Carolina, Georgia, and Tennessee, an average of 12 deer for each of 2,000 warriors. In the twenty years between 1739 and 1759, Cherokee hunters alone reduced the southeastern deer population by 1.25 million.[8]

Clearly, the natives of eastern America controlled resources that were in great demand in Europe. But did they realize their profit potential? Or did they kill all those animals for a few cheap trinkets and a swot or two of rot-gut rum, leaving themselves no better off than they were before the advent of the white man? British traders in particular knew that the natives, whose simple lives required few necessities, had to be given a sense of personal "Property" if their American business was ever to thrive. For a notion of material accumulation, "though it would not increase their real Necessities, yet it would furnish them with imaginary Wants."[9] By 1679, Indians from Hudson Bay to the Carolinas had discovered that "many Things which they wanted not before because they never had them are by . . . means [of the trade] become necessary both for their use & ornament."[10] They had been, in a stay-at-home European's words, "cosoned by a desire of new-fangled novelties."[11]

But had they? To hear both native hunters and knowledgeable Europeans tell it, the Indian was nobody's fool and certainly felt that he made out like a bandit in his dealings with the rubes from the Old World. For ordinary skins "which cost them almost nothing," the Indians received novel trade goods superior to their own artifacts of skin, bone, stone, and wood.[12] A Montagnais hunter once exclaimed that "'The Beaver does everything perfectly well, it makes kettles, hatchets, swords, knives, bread, in short it makes everything.' He was making sport of us Europeans," explained his Jesuit guest, "who have such a fondness for the skin of this animal and who fight to see who will give the most to these Barbarians, to get it." Some while later, the same Indian said to the Frenchman, holding out a very beautiful knife, "'The English have no sense; they give us twenty knives like this for one Beaver skin.'"[13]

While the natives didn't easily understand price fluctuations obedient to Western laws of supply and demand, they were shrewd enough to advance their own bargaining position by playing European competitors against each other, by avoiding superfluities that had no place in their own culture, and by being extremely finicky about the quality and style of goods they would accept. In 1642 Roger Williams noted how the Narragansetts of Rhode Island "will beate all markets and try all places, and runne twenty, thirty, yea, forty mile[s] and more, and lodge in the Woods, to save six pence."[14] Likewise, testified a Recollect priest who knew them well, the Iroquois and natives of the Great Lakes "are rather shrewd and let no one outwit them easily. They examine everything carefully and train themselves to know goods."[15] A Virginia trader in Chesapeake Bay in 1630 complained, to no avail, that his Indian customers were "very long and teadeous" in viewing his array of trade goods and did "tumble it and tosse it and mingle it a hundred times over."[16] Four years later, a trader on the coast of Maine groused to his English boss that "The Indians ar[e] now so well seen Into our tradinge Commodities, that heare is litle to be got by yt." Not only did the competing French and English traders undersell one another in a frenzy to acquire furs, but the Indians refused to buy short English coats, coverlets that were not "soft & warme," or unlined hats without bands.[17] A half-century later, in the mountains of Virginia and North Carolina, William Byrd's Indian customers would have no truck with large white beads (instead of small ones), porous kettles, light (instead of dark) blue blankets, guns with weak locks, or small (instead of large) hoes.[18] "They are not delighted in baubles," Thomas Morton had observed as early as 1632, "but in usefull things."[19] As European trader after trader quickly learned, in native America the customer was always right.

The customer was not only right, he held the upper hand in the struggle over payment. Because his necessities and even his acquired tastes were so few and relatively inelastic, in the establishment of trade the Indians needed the European trader less than he needed them. The sharp competition between company traders, *coureurs de bois*, and government factors for most Indian customers, even

those in the *pays d'en haut,* only increased the natives' leverage. So they quickly demanded and received credit
from the traders.

In late summer or early fall, the trader advanced the
Indians on account the goods, arms, ammunition, and
food they needed for the winter hunt. When the hunters
returned in the late spring or early summer with their
catch, the trader cancelled their debts and, if they had a
surplus, furnished them with supplies and luxuries. If the
hunters had a poor season, they often escaped the consequences of their growing debts by simply moving to new
hunting grounds and striking up business with a new
trader, who was only too happy to purchase their pelts and
to extend them a line of credit. As a Swedish governor
complained of his native trading partners in 1655, "If they
buy anything here, they wish to get half on credit, and
then pay with difficulty."[20] Traders in Hudson Bay, New
France, New England, New Amsterdam, and the Carolinas
felt the same crunch early in their relations with the fur-
toting natives.

If we are going to declare these new Indian purchases a
"consumer revolution," similar to the later English one, we
should also analyze in some detail the kind and quantity of
trade goods the Indians preferred. We have two major
ways to learn about native preferences. One is from the
work of archaeologists, whose excavations of Indian villages and burials turn up the broken and discarded material of native life as well as the most treasured possessions
buried with the dead. The second way is from the hand of
traders' clerks and government officials, who made detailed lists of trade items and diplomatic gifts to be shipped
to Indian villages by canoe or packtrain. These two sources
can be supplemented to some extent by the findings of
underwater archaeologists at the feet of cold northern
river rapids, where French canoes overturned with all

their bright new cargoes headed for Indian country.[21] These beautifully preserved objects can tell us what in the peddlers' packs may have attracted the Indians, but they do not necessarily tell us whether the natives purchased them or used them in ways that Europeans would expect.

According to all our sources, the *nouveaux-riches* natives bought five kinds of European goods: tools, clothing, decorations, novelties, and occasionally food. Even before they had direct and regular access to European traders, the Indians acquired a variety of utilitarian and decorative items from sea-going traders, abandoned colonial facilities, shipwrecks, or natives who had access to these sources. Many native communities met their first European objects in the sixteenth century, long before the English or the French established lasting colonies in North America. When Gaspar Corte-Real sailed to Newfoundland or a nearby coast in 1501, for example, he met one Indian man clutching a piece of an Italian gilt sword and another sporting a pair of Venetian silver earrings.[22]

The earliest items favored by both native men and women were metal tools to make their work go easier and faster. Since the natives were already fully equipped with the requisite tools to manage their environment, they purchased the same kinds of European implements made of superior materials. Processed metal was brighter, more durable, and held an edge longer than annealed native copper, bone, fired clay, stone, or wood. So the natives sensibly spent their first fur paychecks on iron axes (to save the time involved in burning large trees down), hatchets (to gather firewood and crack enemy skulls), awls (to punch leather and drill shell beads), ice chisels (to break-open beaver lodges), butcher knives (to replace more breakable and costly flint knives), swords (to point spears and arrows with pieces of broken blade), fishhooks (to replace unbarbed bone hooks), wide hoes (to replace deer scapula or

These hoes were excavated from a Narragansett cemetery on Conanicut Island, Jamestown, Rhode Island, by Professor William Simmons in 1966–67. They were buried with an elderly woman as grave offerings between 1620 and 1660. From William Scranton Simmons, *Cautantowwit's House: An Indian Burial Ground on the Island of Conanicut in Narragansett Bay* (Providence: Brown University Press, 1970); it is reproduced with the kind permission of University Press of New England.

short digging sticks), and brass or copper kettles (to replace heavier, thicker, and more fragile clay pots).

We know a good deal about the metal goods the Indians purchased because they survive well in the ground and frequently end up in caring museums. But their numbers are somewhat deceiving, for the best-selling item in native (as in English and colonial) markets from the seventeenth century on was cloth of all kinds.[23] Unfortunately, cloth does not fare well in the ground over centuries unless it happens to be parked next to some copper or brass, whose salts during oxidation preserve vegetable matter. We do have a few archaeological cloth remnants, but most of our

This Revolutionary-era engraving of Theyanoquin or "King Hendrick" (c. 1680–1755), chief, diplomat, and orator of the Mohawks, demonstrates the native adaptation of European trade cloth. His shirt is linen or calico, and his mantle and breechclout are made of English wool duffels. Hendrick had visited England in 1710 and again in 1740, when he received a blue coat with gold lace and a cocked hat from King George II. The 39 notches on the tree indicate the number of men Hendrick, a Protestant convert, had killed or captured on the warpath against the French and their native allies. From an anonymous engraving, c. 1776, in the Library of Congress, Washington, D.C.

knowledge of the Indian appetite and stylistic preferences for cloth comes from lead seals used to certify cloth at its source (which turn up in archaeological contexts) and from the letterbooks and inventories of traders. They make it clear why most of the early Indian names for Europeans meant "Cloth makers" or "Coat-men" when they were not called "Iron-Workers" or "Swordmen."[24]

Why would the natives spend their fur proceeds on European cloth when they already had perfectly adaptable fur and skin clothing? Woolen blanketing or duffels was the single biggest seller for several reasons: it was lighter than and as warm as a fur mantle or *matchcoat*, it dried faster and remained softer and suppler than wet skins and was even warm when wet, it came in bright colors which natural berry and root dyes could not duplicate (though most Indians preferred "sad" hues of red and blue), and, with metal knives and scissors, it could quickly be fashioned into leggings, breechclouts, tie-on sleeves, or mantles by women who no longer had to laboriously cure and dress several skins. Another potential advantage was seldom realized because the Indians almost never washed their clothes and literally wore them off their backs.[25] Soap was not in the trader's kit until the more fastidious nineteenth century, and since the dead were always buried in their best clothes, cloth heirlooms and hand-me-downs were rare. With the "bargains" offered by the European traders, the natives found it easier to buy new threads than to slave over a soapy stream.

While cloth was in great demand in Indian country, a few items were unpopular. There was almost no market for tight or fitted clothing, for example. Until the genteel eighteenth century, no native man would have been caught dead in a pair of European breeches: they impeded running and other natural functions (southern men, at least, squatted to urinate). Elaborate military-style coats with braid, buttons, and capacious cuffs were worn only by a handful of favored chiefs and head warriors on ceremonial occasions. The only fitted pieces of clothing that sold relatively well were brightly patterned calico shirts, which the men wore open at the neck and flapping in the breeze.

We can be very brief about the food trade because it was rare. In the seventeenth century the native hunters of eastern Canada occasionally bartered a beaver for some durable ship's biscuit or bread when they couldn't find Indian corn among their agricultural neighbors. But prunes and raisins never caught on except as gifts, and sugar, flour, and tea made their way very slowly into native larders, and then only if colonial settlements were close by.[27]

From the earliest indirect contact with Europeans, the Indians sought to enhance their beauty and status with decorations of foreign material or manufacture. Chinese vermilion, sold in tea-bag-sized paper packets, gradually supplanted native red ochre, and verdigris added a brand new color to harlequin faces. As the Portuguese explorer Corte-Real discovered, silver earrings found a male as well as female market. Copper and brass bracelets, tin finger rings (particularly engraved Jesuit rings with religious motifs, initials, and hearts), bangles or jingling cones made from sheet brass, necklaces of Venetian glass beads in both solid colors and stripes, mostly red, white, and blue, corkscrew wire ear dangles, and, in the eighteenth century, German silver brooches, pins, and gorgets custom-made for the Indian trade were among the most popular European jewelry. While several of these items were new in form and function, the natives made more familiar jewelry from thimbles (by attaching a leather thong through a hole cut in the bottom to make jinglers), scraps of kettle or sheet copper (cut into pendants, gorgets, and even sweat scrapers in the Deep South), and gold and silver coins (perforated and worn around the neck as pendants).[28] With

Among the novelties traded by Europeans to Indians were mouth or Jew's harps. These examples from a 17th-century Seneca site are missing their flexible brass "twangers," which gave the mouth-held instrument its rhythmic resonance. From the collections of the Rochester Museum and Science Center, Rochester, N.Y., by whose courtesy it is reproduced.

jewelry as with most things, the Indians used, adapted, and interpreted Europe's introductions in traditional ways.

This is less but still true of the final category of Indian trade goods, what we must call novelties because they had no native counterparts. Part of the revolutionary character of native consumerism is attributable to the effects some of these material innovations had on native life. Mouth harps, bells, and clothing fasteners (buttons, buckles, and lace points) played only bit parts in transforming Indian culture in the seventeenth and early eighteenth centuries. But guns, alcohol, and even mirrors were center stage.

An arquebus or flintlock was, in one sense, only a noisy bow and arrow. It was also heavier, harder to make and

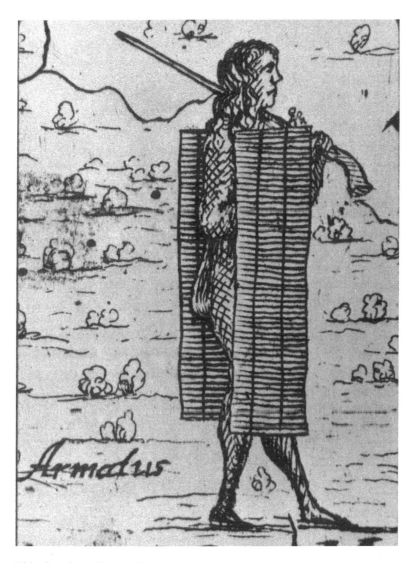

This drawing of a northeastern Indian warrior (Huron?), probably by Jesuit missionary Francesco Bressani, juxtaposes a European gun with the ancient wooden slat armor made obsolete by the advent of firearms. From *Novae Franciae Accurata Delineatio* (1657).

repair, more expensive, less reliable in wet weather, much slower, and incapable of surprise after the first round. Despite the many deficiencies of firearms, however, the Indians rushed to acquire them as soon as they had seen them in action. For guns drove fear into enemy breasts as often as balls, smashed bones and did more internal damage than razor-sharp arrowheads, and heralded the status of their owners in ways that traditional weapons never could. Against traditional wooden slat armor and old-time massed armies, the gun won hands down.[29] One major effect of the advent of firearms, therefore, was the natives' sole reliance on dispersed guerilla tactics executed behind trees or from ambush. Sir William Johnson, the Superintendent of Indian Affairs for the British northern department, was of the opinion that the authority of chiefs had also declined since the introduction of firearms because, he said, "They no longer fight in close bodies but every Man is his own General."[30]

The effects of alcohol upon Indian society were nearly as destructive. Cadwallader Colden, an expert on the Iroquois, thought that drunkenness among the American tribes "has destroyed greater Numbers, than all their Wars and Diseases put together."[31] He was wrong about the magnitude but right about the seriousness of the problem which the advent of brandy kegs, rundlets of rum, and case bottles of wine posed for native communities. Although— or perhaps because—the Woodland Indians had no previous experience with intoxicating beverages or hallucinogens, they took to liquid spirits with frightening abandon. And they drank only to become fully inebriated, in which state they felt invincible, capable of making antisocial mayhem with a perfect excuse, and perhaps (though the evidence is weak) more susceptible to the dreams in which "guardian spirits" conveyed their sacred secrets for success.[32] When the "water-that-burns" arrived in sufficient quantity in a village, the place was soon turned into the very "image of hell." Drunken "frolics" lasting several days often produced several victims of shootings, stabbings, brawls, burning, biting, and bawdry. Neither resident missionaries nor native leaders were very successful in persuading the traders to halt the profitable flow, although they used two compelling arguments: the Indians were dying in excessive numbers from drink-related murders (and, we know also, from exposure and increased susceptibility to colds, pneumonia, and other diseases), and the temperance issue "produce[d] all Evil and Contention between man and wife, between the Young Indians and the Sachims."[33] Alcohol was clearly one trade good the natives could well have done without.

By contrast, mirrors seem terribly tame as novelties go. But the first "looking-glasses" and mirror boxes, which reached the remote Senecas of western New York by the 1620s, may have promoted a preoccupation with personal fashion as much as full-length hanging mirrors did among the genteel colonists. Among the Indians, however, "the men, upon the whole, [were] more fond of dressing than the women" and carried their mirrors with them on all their journeys, which the women did not.[34] As a vehicle of vainglory, the mirror was a necessity, especially for young warriors who now had more income to spend on imported face paints, jewelry, and other finery. Before the advent of mirrors, a native coxcomb had to have his face painted "by some woman or girl," which curtailed his independence and let some of the air out of his vanity.[35] With his own mirror, which he wore constantly around his wrist or over his shoulder, he could arrange his hair, refurbish his scalplock, and paint his face to his heart's content in the privacy of his own toilette. One unfoppish Frenchman who knew the Great Lakes tribes well believed that "if they had a mirror before their eyes they would change their appear-

The effects of the trade mirror on personal grooming and vanity are
suggested by this painting of a Flathead Indian "dandy" by a Jesuit
missionary in the 1840s. From *Wilderness Kingdom: Indian Life in the
Rocky Mountains: 1840–1847. The Journals & Paintings of Nicholas
Point, S.J.*, trans. Joseph P. Donnelly, S.J. (New York, 1967). Reproduced with the kind permission of Loyola University Press.

ance every quarter of an hour."[36] But the tell-tale object, like all spiritual power, was capable of bringing bad news as well. During the great smallpox epidemic of 1738, which killed half of the Cherokee population, "a great many" Indians "killed themselves" by shooting, cutting their throats, stabbing, and throwing themselves into fires because they had seen themselves disfigured by the pox in their ubiquitous mirrors and, "being naturally proud," could not stand the literal loss of face.[37]

We can now appreciate the amazing variety of European goods that reached Indian customers in the seventeenth and eighteenth centuries. To constitute a revolution comparable to the later English one, however, these material products had to arrive in native villages in such quantities that tribesmen and women up and down the social scale had their lives altered by the pursuit, purchase, and use of them. There are basically two ways to establish these quantities. The indirect way is to look at the substantial leap in exports from England to the American colonies in the seventeenth century. It is surely no coincidence that exports of woolens and metalwares doubled between the 1660s and 1700, and miscellaneous manufactures, including tableware and sewing accoutrements, increased threefold.[38] Most of those items were the mainstays of the Indian trade, which we know was burgeoning, even as the native population was declining from disease, wars, and dislocation.

The more direct way is to register the changes in Indian villages, either above or below ground, at the time or later. Obviously, we don't have comparable evidence for every tribe in every region. But what we do have is strongly suggestive. For example, on both Seneca and Onondaga Iroquois sites from 1600 to 1620, only 10–15 percent of the artifacts found by archaeologists are European in origin. From sites dated 1650–55, fully 75 percent of the assemblages are European (and this, remember, grossly underestimates the amount of cloth used).[39] Small wonder, then, that in 1768 Eleazar Wheelock, the master of an Indian school in Connecticut, conducted a frustrated search among the eastern Iroquois nations for a native artifact that was "perfectly Simple, and without the least Mixture of any foreign Merchandise" to send as a gift to the Earl of Dartmouth, the benefactor of his future college. A "small specimen" was all he could find because, he apologized, "our Traders have penetrated so far into their Country." Only "some articles which were defaced by Use" were crafted from the traditional materials he sought. Perhaps he shouldn't have been so surprised, for two years earlier one of his English missionary-teachers had written that the Iroquois were "in some measure like those in New England much degenerated, both as to their Customs, their Dress and their Impliments."[40]

"Degeneration" is the wrong term to describe any cultural change, unless, of course, we believe that the only bona fide Indian looks and acts like his pre-Columbian ancestors. But New England's native population, largely converted to Christianity and settled in "praying towns," had indeed felt the forces of acculturation in the century since the Reverend John Eliot began to proselytize them. Many lived in English frame houses complete with standard colonial furniture, plowed their fields with horses or oxen, kept cattle, dressed in English garb, cooked in iron kettles and skillets, and ate off glazed earthenware with spoons and forks. Even those who still lived in wigwams, such as Phebe and Elizabeth Moheege of Niantic, Connecticut, cooked in an iron pot suspended from a trammel, drank at a tea table, ate at another table in a chair (presumably not at the same time), stored their cups and plates in a wall cupboard and their prized possessions in two wooden chests.[41]

Another symbol of the revolutionary changes in the lives

of virtually all eastern American natives lived just down the road from the Moheeges, across the Rhode Island line. There in a house or "palace" lived "King George Ninigret," the chief of the once-mighty Narragansetts. When Dr. Alexander Hamilton of Annapolis rode by in 1744, King George owned 20–30,000 acres of "very fine level land" upon which he had "many tennants" and "a good stock of horses and other cattle." "This King," Hamilton noted with evident approval, "lives after the English mode. His subjects have lost their own goverment [*sic*] policy and laws and are servants or vassals to the English here. His queen goes in a high modish dress in her silks, hoops, stays, and dresses like an English woman. He educates his children to the belles lettres and is himself a very complaisant mannerly man. We pay'd him a visit, and he treated us with a glass of good wine."[42]

King George, of course, was atypical of his American brethren in the degree of his apparent success. He was, after all, a chief. But he was a new kind of chief, one who sold his tribal lands to white men and pocketed most of the proceeds, rather than consulting the will of his people and distributing the revenues among them. Nor did he share his personal property as a traditional chief would have a century earlier. This Indian looked out for Number One in good capitalist fashion: he gave many thoughts to his own family's future but far fewer to that of his "subjects" who labored menially for his English models and neighbors.[43]

But most Indians in colonial America were unable to ride the crest of change like King George and were caught instead in the undertow and dragged into dependence and debt. In their initial rush to acquire the material marvels of Europe, they gave no thought to the future and hunted out the game that gave them access to foreign markets. When the beaver and whitetail deer disappeared, the na-

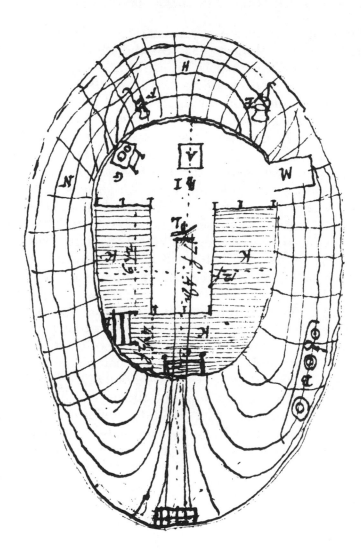

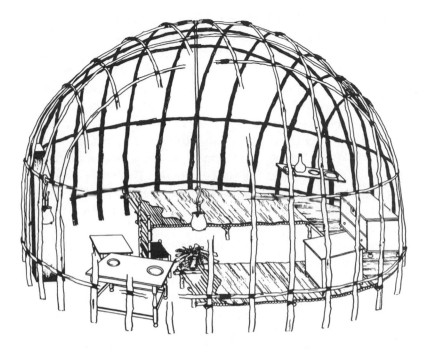

Ezra Stiles, later president of Yale College, drew this plan of Phebe and Elizabeth Moheege's wigwam in Niantic, Connecticut, in 1761. Its acculturated owners had furnished this ancient Indian dwelling with many English colonial items, such as a tea table, chests, a table and chair, and a dresser. Edward G. Schumaker has artistically reconstructed the Moheege's lodge with period furnishings from the Smithsonian Institution's Museum of History and Technology. From William C. Sturtevant, "Two 1761 Wigwams at Niantic, Connecticut," *American Antiquity*, 40:4 (1975), 437–44. Reproduced with the kind permission of Yale University Library, Edward Schumaker, and William Sturtevant.

tives were left with nothing to sell but their land, their labor, or their military services, which the proliferating colonists were only too glad to buy at bargain rates. Those prices, paid always in desirable trade goods, were low because, with the game diminished, the Indians had little leverage left and had become dangerously dependent on their European suppliers for an ever-growing list of "necessities." In 1705 Robert Beverley noticed that "The *English* have taken away great part of their Country, and consequently made everything less plenty amongst them. They have introduc'd Drunkenness and Luxury amongst them, which have multiply'd their Wants and put them upon desiring a thousand things they never dreamt of before."[44] These "artificial Wants," as Ben Franklin called them, were so numerous that even the Indians admitted, particularly in the early eighteenth century, that "they could not live without the English" and that they would "always be ruled by them."[45]

Yet, like their colonial neighbors who later formed the Association to rid themselves of foreign debt and debilitating "luxury," many tribesmen in the eighteenth century sought to recapture their autonomous aboriginal past by participating in what anthropologists call "revitalization movements."[46] In 1715 the Yamasees and several Muskogee groups resorted to all-out, purifying war with the South Carolinians because they had accumulated tribal debts of 100,000 deerskins, which, in the face of greatly diminished herds in the increasingly settled coastal region, they had little hope of ever paying off.[47]

But the most famous revitalization took place among the Delawares of western Pennsylvania and the Ohio Valley, where in the early 1760s they were called to action by several messianic prophets. Their message was much the same: if the Indians wished to get to their own heaven and to make life on earth bearable in the meantime, they had to revive their "old" ceremonies and to make several sacrifices. The most onerous but the most purifying was to "learn to live without any trade or connections with the white people, clothing and supporting themselves as their forefathers did."[48]

Such a message was particularly welcome in the camps of the Great Lakes Indians who followed Pontiac into major "rebellion" against the British in 1763. The major cause of their discontent was material: once the French competitors of the British were driven from North America, the British felt free to raise the prices of their trade goods, drastically cut the number of goods (including ammunition) distributed as gifts in the long-standing protocol of diplomacy, and prohibited the sale of liquor, all in a spirit of unmasked contempt for native life and values. No longer able to live without the "Baubles of Britain," Pontiac's warriors decided on a course of action every bit as revolutionary as that followed by the colonists themselves thirteen years later.[49]

CHAPTER SIX

Agents of Change:
Jesuits in the Post-Columbian
World

SOME INVITATIONS TO GIVE LECTURES OR WRITE ARTICLES feel just right: the desired topics seem comfortably within one's intellectual range or reach. If my teaching, family, and unsolicited writing obligations permit, I usually succumb to such enticements, particularly if the proffered audience, location, or honorarium is congenial. Outside offers serve as antidotes to our natural torpor and spurs to purposeful activity; if we're publishing, we're usually not perishing. But a few invitations come as a surprise, apparently based on a false or skewed impression of one's scholarly depth, breadth, or interests. These I don't hesitate to decline, in order to save everyone future embarrassment.

In the spring of 1989, Loyola University of Chicago asked me to deliver the keynote address to a power-packed, three-day conference on "Agents of Change: The Jesuits and Encounters of Two Worlds" on the weekend before Columbus Day 1992. Having lived happily in the Chicago area for two years, having a number of friends there, and having lectured at Loyola once before predisposed me to accept. But I took some persuading because I was uncertain about the reasons I was asked. Clearly, the organizers of this Jesuit conference at a Jesuit university lighted on me because I had written a comparative history of conversion in colonial North America in which the Jesuits of New France came off the better of the two major European contenders.* If I had been chosen because I was deemed "pro-Jesuit," I wanted no part of it because I have always been extremely skeptical of the missionary impulse in general, particularly when it is directed against native or tribal peoples. My admiration for the Jesuits of seventeenth-century Canada was strictly scholarly, the product of an historical assessment of their efficiency compared with the record of their English Protestant rivals—a point that a few, otherwise friendly, Canadian reviewers failed to perceive when they bodychecked me for saying anything favorable about their current *bêtes* (*robes*) *noires*.

Happily, I was reassured that I was not chosen for my biases, so I wrote the following essay in the demi-glow of flattery, ever-conscious of the unknown future response of a hallowed hall-full of true Jesuit experts.

WE WHO HAVE GROWN UP IN THE SLURRY OF TUMUL-tuous change known as the twentieth century are hard pressed to appreciate the revolutionary nature and speed of the effects wrought in America's native societies by the advent of Columbus and his European successors. Having become inured to the rapid pace of change powered by the automobile, radio, television, computers, jet planes, communication satellites, and golden arches, we find it difficult to imagine life in our hemisphere that once danced to the familiar, unrushed rhythms of nature, all but deaf to the frenzied tunes of technology.

Contrary to the misleading and ethnocentric connotations of the word "prehistory," Columbus did not intrude upon a static, stagnant Indian order and give it a salutary goose into a vital and vibrant occidental future. The natives of the Americas certainly had bona fide histories be-

---

*James Axtell, *The Invasion Within: The Contest of Cultures in Colonial North America* (New York, 1985); "Were Indian Conversions *Bona Fide*?" *After Columbus: Essays in the Ethnohistory of Colonial North America* (New York, 1988), ch. 7.

fore Europeans brought their books, writing, and libraries to the hemisphere; there was nothing "pre-" about them.[1] Native histories lived in the oral memories of the people, in ritual, and in myth, and they served the same uses that written history served in Europe. They bound peoples together in common cause, endowed their social forms with reason and meaning, and defined their place in the world of the seen and unseen. They were the ligaments of cultural continuity, resistant to the wasting assaults of communal amnesia.

The natives also knew change, albeit slower paced, and revolutionary largely when nature deemed. Droughts, floods, earthquakes, and storms might suddenly raze villages, topple empires, realign power, test faith, and erase memory. But major change also came with the slow domestication of plants and animals and the sporadic evolution of new cults, new modes or instruments of warfare, new forms of government. On the eve of contact with Europeans, native Americans everywhere were in the inexorable process of adapting to changes in their environment, natural and man-made, as they had been for thousands of years.[2]

But the unforeseen arrival of Columbus *accelerated* change in both of the ancient worlds he effectively yoked together, particularly in that world he came to regard as new. For the Admiral and his successors carried in their holds powerful catalysts of change, the likes of which the natives had never known. Epidemic disease was the most powerful and the most terrible because it killed and maimed without warning and apparently without reason. It could be spread at will by those possessed of its maleficent secrets, but never stopped until it had run its deadly course through the "virgin soil" populations of the Americas. It attacked with indiscriminate and lethal efficiency, claiming as its victims young and old, men and women, shamans, kings, and commoners alike, leaving only the pale newcomers unmarked and standing. Smallpox or pneumonic plague could easily erase 50–90 percent of a native community or tribe in one terrifying visitation, forcing the dazed and battered survivors to alter their lives in ways scarcely experienced or imagined before 1492.[3]

Another force for change was equally new and audacious, but it appeared less dangerous because it wore a human face, however disfigured by unsightly hair. If diseases were the shock troops of the invasion of America, Christian missionaries were its commandoes, disguised in feminine black robes as members of a Peace Corps. Although they came bearing a message from a "Prince of Peace," they unconsciously bore a whole civilization that would not tolerate the America they had found. In its claim to universality and adamantine truth, evangelical Christianity had no room for "false gods," strange rituals, and local beliefs. It sought to bend the "pagan" and "infidel" worlds to its own will and vision of the good, true, and beautiful. In America as in China, "Christianity was a religion that changed customs, called into question accepted ideas and, above all, threatened to undermine existing situations."[4] In countless instances, it not only threatened, it did so. As agents of change, missionaries in post-Columbian America had no human equals and only one strain of superiors.

Perhaps the best agents of all were the Jesuits. By history and design, the Society of Jesus was destined to change the American world. It was a fraternity designed for war, the greatest human engine of social change. Its founder was a stubborn Spanish-Basque courtier-soldier, much taken with the "exercise of arms" in young manhood. The Society he founded was sanctioned by the pope in 1540 in a bull entitled *Regimini militantis Ecclesiae*, which accurately reflected its pugnacious stance toward the Protestant Reformation and international "paganism." The *Spiritual Exercises* that Loyola devised for his recruits sought to dissolve their individual wills in Christ's, which, they were reminded, was to "conquer the whole world," particularly "all the lands of the infidel."[5]

The *Constitutions* of the Society also cast it in a military mould. Jesuits were regarded as "soldier[s] of God beneath the banner of the cross," enlistees in the "militia of Christ," "clad for battle day and night." Studiously "detached from the world and determined to serve God totally," they were "ready at any hour to go to some or other parts of the world where they may be sent" because they had taken vows of "special obedience to the sovereign pontiff in regard to the missions." To the pope, their own aptly named General, and all superiors in their strict hierarchy of command, their obedience was complete and unquestioning, as if their orders came from Christ himself. Needless to say, Jesuit houses were "dedicated to [active] labor in His vineyard" and not to contemplation, singing, and prayer as in the reclusive choirs of other orders.[6]

Yet the Jesuits were unusual soldiers in that they were strictly forbidden to carry weapons of any kind; even the General could be cashiered for "the infliction of a wound."[7] Their armaments were of a different sort: weapons of will, intellect, and persuasion rather than arquebuses and Toledo swords. Doctrinal uniformity was one weapon against divided or less-than-adamant enemies; Jesuits were taught to "think alike and speak alike, in conformity with the Apostle's teaching."[8] Another weapon was a formidable education in logic, languages, and the arts of verbal argument and persuasion. Man for man, the Jesuits were the best and most rigorously trained minds in Europe, who prepared for the mission field by applying their bookish learning to the teaching of noisy adolescents in Jesuit schools and the pastoral care of European pagans in noisome hospitals, slums, and jails.[9] And finally, while the Jesuits were morally and doctrinally unbending, their anthropology in the field was consciously flexible and, to a point, culturally relative. They followed the apostle Paul who felt it necessary to "become all things to all men, in order to win all to Jesus Christ." "As God made himself man in order to make men God's," one of them remarked, "a Missionary does not fear to make himself a Savage, so to speak, in order to make them Christians."[10]

While the Jesuits were exceptionally well prepared to change the native worlds they found in the Americas, we should resist the temptation, particularly in the stormy Quincentenary climate, to *pre*judge the nature or quality of the changes they wrought. Because the Jesuits were white, European males, often from advantaged social classes, they are an easy target for dismissive or condemnatory treatment at the hands of a variety of modern critics. Many critics, on the left and the right, operate from a romantic assumption that social and cultural change is usually deleterious, that the "old days" were better, happier, and healthier than the new. Accordingly, they view the Jesuit-induced changes in Indian America as wholly unfortunate for the native peoples and worthy of summary censure.

They may very well be right. But if we are interested in the past more for historical understanding than for the ammunition it can provide us for modern moral or political in-fighting, we should not rush to judgment before we have thoroughly done our homework. We should remind ourselves that, in and of itself, change is normal, natural, and neutral. In human societies as in the natural world, change is the universal norm. Without change, there would be no history. In retrospect, of course, change can be interpreted as "good" or "bad," adaptive or dysfunctional, for the societies that experienced it. And change can be generated from within or without, by spontaneous invention or by foreign agents and stimuli. Yet it is our historical task not to decide in advance whether change itself is good or bad or whether induced change is worse than internal change, but to accurately determine the engines of change and to assess short- and long-range consequences, for both the immediate society and the wider world. Our major task is less to praise or condemn the past according to modern standards than to understand the past in its own terms. We will have opportunity enough at the completion of our task to draw moral conclusions and lessons for the future.[11]

In order to convert the American natives to Catholic Christianity, the Jesuits first had to supplant the natives' traditional religious leaders. This was not easy because Indian shamans or priests performed a number of functions, both secular and religious, that made them all-but-indispensable to their people. They used a wide and sometimes secret variety of local plants and herbs to cure internal and external ailments; the current *U.S. Pharmacopaeia,* used by druggists to compound medicines, contains 170 ingredients whose medicinal properties were discovered and used by native Americans.[12] Shamans also cured or alleviated the symptoms of mental and psychosomatic illness. Since their personal "spirit" or "soul" power was believed to be greater than that of ordinary humans, only they were thought capable of interpreting dreams, the important "wishes of the soul," and of detecting the source and symptoms of witchcraft. In many groups, the ability of shamans' souls to leave their bodies in dream or induced trance and to fly in time and space was thought to enable shamans or conjurers to find lost objects and to predict the future. For native groups living in precarious environments and subsistence economies, as most of them did, the shaman's ability to predict the advent of rain or snow or the success of war or hunting parties was often regarded as a matter of

life-and-death, little different from his ability to cure illness or to expose the life-threatening maleficence of
witches and other evil-minded persons.[13]

After the Jesuits carefully infiltrated native life, they
sought, first, to dislodge these religious practitioners from
their social and cultural niches, and then to insert themselves in their places and in the regard and fear of the
natives. The methods they used for the first task were ridi-
cule, the questioning of habit, and audacity, none of which
the natives expected from friends. Like most inhabitants of
small, face-to-face societies, the Indians of eastern Canada,
for example, while being talkative and "ready jesters," took
pains to "cultivate peace at home" and to avoid public
anger, quarrels, and direct insults. Understandably, they
"at first were greatly surprised when the [Jesuit] Fathers
censured their faults"—as the Jesuits described them—
"before the assembly; they thought that the Fathers were
madmen, because among peaceful hearers and friends
they displayed such vehemence." "To jest in the victim's
presence," confessed a Jesuit historian, "or to make a verbal attack, face to face," was "characteristic of religion," not
of native etiquette.[14]

In attacking native habits and traditions, the Jesuits enjoyed two advantages. The first was that the Blackrobes
were on the offensive. Habits, by definition, are unex-
amined, largely unconscious facets of behavior. They are
easily undermined by scrutiny or questioning. When Jesuit
missionaries sought to expose shamanic beliefs and practices as "mere nonsense and child's play," therefore, they
enjoyed the dual advantage of surprise and attack.[15]

The Jesuit arsenal contained another double-barreled
weapon of great effectiveness. Among the predominantly
oral peoples of the Americas, the missionaries' printed
books and literacy allowed them to undercut native traditions and knowledge and to argue that their own religion

of The Book was much more certain and reliable. Visible words and illustrations on paper, the Jesuits argued, with no little success, were more credible than mere mental images, which were easily manipulated by the Devil, or than oral words, which vanished as soon as they were spoken. By the same token, the Christian religion was more believable than native religion because the true, capital-w Word of the Christian God was preserved unaltered in a book, open to all readers rather than the private preserve of a mercenary priesthood. Even more impressive was the ability of the Blackrobes to read minds at a distance, that is, to know the thoughts of distant correspondents by reading their handwriting. Since only shamans were thought to exercise such a skill, the Jesuits moved one step closer to their goal of supplanting them in native society.[16]

The Jesuits also sought to displace their religious rivals by superior displays of prediction, healing, and worldly knowledge. With an almanac and some simple math, the Jesuits could accurately predict—and thereby seem to control—solar and lunar eclipses, which fascinated and often frightened the natives. The Jesuits' timely administration of some sugar or raisins or some elementary nursing might save the lives of natives suffering from infectious disease, apparently without jeopardizing their own health. When the Jesuits told the natives that native susceptibility to disease was directly attributable to pagan ignorance of Christianity and sinful ways, the natives had another powerful reason to convert.[17]

Certainly, the Jesuits' confident knowledge of a vast new geography, cosmology, ethnology, and technology diminished the Indians' sense of self-worth and rocked the foundations of their conventional wisdom. The Blackrobes' ability to explain the action of the moon upon the tides, to predict the hourly chime of a clock, to magnetize a sword with a lodestone, to infallibly chart a path through the woods with a compass, even to enlarge a flea with a magnifying glass—all impressed and often "amazed" the natives as manifestations of extraordinary spiritual power, greater than that possessed by their traditional shamans.[18]

People who wielded such power had to be treated with a certain respect and circumspection, for in the native mind, all power was double-edged: it could injure as well as impress, kill as well as cure. Initially, at least, no sensible Indian would knowingly offend such powerful *manitous* (as the Algonquians called them); and more than a few natives threw in their lot with the new, blackrobed shamans, hoping to enlist their strength and to avoid their wrath.

The Jesuits did their best to nurture these neophytes and to enlarge their numbers in native communities. Their chief targets of conversion, however, were native leaders— chiefs, sachems, and caciques. The Society's *Constitutions* advised that "preference ought to be given to those persons and places, which, through their own improvement, become a cause which can spread the good accomplished to many others who are under their influence or take guidance from them."[19] If public leaders could be persuaded to adopt the strangers into their own families, to make them fictive kin, the missionaries' task would be considerably advanced.

The conversion of native individuals, groups, and villages invariably split communities and tribes into hostile factions of "pagans" and "Christians." Some of these divisions undoubtedly occurred along ancient faultlines in the native body politic. But many were new, the products of calculated efforts by the Jesuits to conquer by dividing. The Christian wedge in native unity set son against father, sister against brother, village against village, thereby weakening the natives for European and Christian assaults on other fronts.[20]

A Jesuit missionary, wearing a distinctive Catholic biretta, baptizing a Canadian Indian. From the cartouche on Guillaume de l'Isle, *Carte du Canada ou de la Nouvelle France* (Paris, 1703).

If the Jesuits could not convert a whole village within a reasonable period, they often encouraged their neophytes to move to a more conducive environment, one that could be carefully controlled by the priests. The removal of converts and neophytes from the sins and temptations of "pagan" life was an important motive, but the Jesuits also wanted to institute a number of social and cultural changes that had more to do with European assumptions about "civilized" life than with Christian preparation for salvation. Only in French Canadian *reserves,* northern Mexican *doctrinas,* or Paraguayan *reducciones* were the Jesuits able to impose major reforms of native life with relative impunity, free from cosmopolitan interference or colonial contamination.

The changes entailed for the natives simply by subscribing to the new Catholic faith were substantial, enough to give any native pause and many natives cause to decline the Blackrobes' invitation. As culturally flexible as the Jesuits often were, they followed a strict construction of the Ten Commandments and the seven sacraments, and were nearly as adamant about the seven Deadly Sins. This meant that polygynous native husbands had to give up all but their first wives, unhappy spouses were stuck together for life, warriors could not kill enemies for revenge without a great deal of soul-searching, and worshippers had to forsake their former "idols," amulets, and rituals, which served as added insurance against an increasingly hostile and unpredictable world.[21]

On top of these quasi-religious changes, the Jesuits often demanded that their native flocks adopt European institutions, economies, and domestic styles, as if the Indians could not be trusted to believe and pray like Christians until they looked and ate like the Christians from whom the missionaries derived. By identifying faith with a particular cultural construct, the Jesuits ensured that their missions would become powerful agencies of directed change in native America.

In northwestern New Spain, for example, native neophytes were taught to cover their partial, adaptive nakedness with European peasant clothes—skirts and shifts for the women, shirts and trousers for the men. Men were forbidden to wear their hair long. Families were encouraged and taught to build substantial Spanish-style houses of timber, adobe, or stone, which also served to anchor them in the missions. Semi-sedentary maize-growers were taught to raise wheat (for communion wafers, if not acculturated native palates), and mobile hunter-gatherers were enticed to settle down to raise maize. Many groups, particularly those suffering the economic disruptions of epidemics, were sold on the idea of raising livestock in order to have a supply of "fast food" on hand should hunting or planting become impossible.[22]

To rationalize the division of labor in the missions, which often contained 500–1,000 people, the Jesuits trained local natives or imported from the south specialists in blacksmithing, woodworking, and weaving, and trained local herdsmen, plowmen, and adobe-makers. Orchards were planted (albeit with little success on the sere Pacific slopes of the Sierras) and irrigation systems dug to water the new crops. Most of the natives worked three days a week in the mission fields, the rest in their own. Surpluses, primarily of maize and cattle, were used to attract new natives to mission life and to succor neighboring missions during droughts and epidemics.[23]

After supplanting or sidestepping the native *hechiceros* or shamans, the Blackrobes also assumed many functions of the traditional caciques. Since the missions after conquest were considered part of the Spanish empire, secular officials delegated native leaders to administer justice, labor, and the church, but the missionaries usually had the largest voice in their selection. Former caciques were often given the formal title of *gobernador* (governor), a cane of office, and a fancy suit of clothes to ensure their continued cooperation with the Jesuit program. Other native leaders might fill the offices of *alcalde* (justice of the peace) and *fiscal* (church superintendent). Yet every morning after Mass, the missionary typically directed the life and work of the mission from the front door of his adobe residence.[24]

In the Jesuit *reserves* of New France, the natives experienced other alterations in their traditional ways of living and thinking, some the result of religious prescriptions, others because of the Jesuits' cultural preferences. All Jesuit neophytes had to acquire a new sense of time and, to some extent, space. Catholic time was very different from the natural rhythms of the seasons by which the Indians kept time. Rather than the migrations of geese, the sprouting of green corn, or the break-up of river ice, the missions marked time by ecclesiastical calendars, mechanical clocks, and church bells. One day a week was set aside as a holy day of rest; 165 days (the equivalent of 5½ months) a year were supposed to be meatless (although the benign pragmatism of the Sorbonne faculty enabled Canadians to regard the beaver as a fish).[25] Bells called worshippers to Mass twice a day, and special holy days, dedicated to the lives of Christian saints from a strange and distant world, punctuated the church calendar.

Although most Indian groups regarded certain locations as sacred and endowed with special power, Catholic spaces were more numerous and regarded by the priests, at least, as more sacred. Only the faithful could be buried in the consecrated ground of the church cemetery, just as the afterlife was rigidly divided between Heaven and Hell, the land of eternal life and the land of death. Processions sanctified particular places en route. The church, of course, was the holiest turf of all. Male worshippers were segregated from female, the confessional cast a giant shadow, the choir enjoyed a place of honor, and the altar was railed and approached only by the holy fathers.

The advent of mission life also affected relations between the sexes. As a patriarchal church, with God as a Father-King, Christ as a Prince-Son, and pope and priests as holy fathers, the Roman Catholic version of Christianity did not treat men and women equally, a lesson the natives could not fail to learn. While native women had spiritual role models in the Virgin Mary and the few nuns who came to the Americas, the Church and the imperial state worked in tandem to promote or sustain the supremacy of men in secular and religious affairs.

Among egalitarian native groups in Canada, for instance, where men and women divided work equally and enjoyed roughly equal statuses, and particularly where women controlled major sources of production, rights of distribution, and property, the Jesuits and French officials sought to realign the balance of authority by making native men supreme. Male heads of household, particularly Christians, were encouraged to assume the lion's share of food production and distribution and an uncharacteristic physical domination over their wives and children. Indian "captains," elected with the approval of the missionaries, resorted to corporal punishment and even imprisonment to keep their liberty-loving families in line.

The daughters of converts probably felt the loss of their customary freedom most keenly. Because the new converts believed that Eve tempted Adam with the fruit and brought sin upon mankind, her descendants were held liable for the sexual straying of his; and in the Catholic Church at this time, sexual sin was considered more dangerous than pride, the original transgression. Accordingly, the patriarchal priesthood and newly patriarchal native families were charged with bridling the dangerous "license" of Indian girls, most of whom traditionally enjoyed the sexual and behavioral freedom of their brothers.[26]

The Jesuits did not neglect Indian boys by any means. All over the Americas, the well-educated priests sought to remould the minds and bodies of native boys by educating the most promising of them in local and metropolitan schools. After rudimentary training in a European language in their native villages, the brightest boys were sent

Two Huron women converted by Jesuit missionaries, worshipping their new Christian God instead of (or perhaps in addition to) their ancient deity, the sun. From *Novae Franciae Accurata Delineatio* (1657), probably by Francesco Bressani, S.J., who worked among the Hurons in the 1640s.

off to boarding schools in a colonial capital or even a Jesuit college in Europe. There they acquired as best they could the three European R's, a Westernized world-view, a firm grasp of catechism, loyalty to their surrogate fathers and the Church, and a well-founded fear of corporal punishment. They were probably unaware of their effective status as hostages for the good behavior of their parents and tribesmen. When they had proven themselves, they returned to their communities to serve the missionaries as interpreters, acolytes, catechists, and spies, a veritable fifth column in the den of the Devil.[27]

Although native women and children were the initial
targets of Jesuit control, their husbands and fathers were
never far behind. They soon discovered that even grown
men were not exempt from the lash of Christian discipline.
No one who was whipped for running away from Spanish
missions or for some venial sin in Canada could miss the
Jesuit's hand behind the sting administered by garrison
soldiers or by native *gobernadores, fiscales,* and *dogiques.*[28]
Nor could they fail to notice the loss of independence in
their lives, nor how they had to answer to a new hierarchy
of authorities, with precious little voice in their selection.
In the Indians' new world, colonial—particularly Jesuit—
rule meant an acute loss of autonomy in virtually every
facet of life. For many natives, the Jesuit priest wa the most
visible and vocal symbol of their predicament. To an extent
unimaginable before Columbus, blackrobed foreigners
now decided for many natives what to eat, how to live,
when to work, whom to obey, and even their fate after
death.

On the other hand, it is obvious that those Indians who
survived the dislocations and devastation of imported diseases also benefitted from the Jesuit regimes. In the face of
inexplicable epidemics, expanded geographies and new
heavens, and the advent of dangerously unpredictable
black and white peoples possessed of miraculous technologies, the natives received from the Jesuits and their missions crucial new intellectual powers of explanation and
control for coping with those novelties. In increasingly
constricted fields of maneuver, many converts found more
secure livelihoods in the agricultural and stock-raising missions. And in a colonial world of often unfettered aggrandizement, mission Indians gained at least a temporary
measure of safety and protection from grasping miners,
debauching traders, and trigger-happy settlers. In tough
situations that were spinning further out of the natives'

control, the Jesuit missions offered a new lease on life for many Indians who were willing to tolerate a significant loss of autonomy. Some gave up their freedom prematurely, perhaps, but most derived substantial benefits, which we, from this distance, should be very careful not to deny.[29]

The Jesuits played a number of important roles in the conquest and colonization of the Americas. They were explorers and geographers who captured American space within Ptolemaic coordinates and helped replace America's native names with European ones on power-giving maps. They wrote and published evocative descriptions of the New World and its human, floral, and faunal inhabitants which did much to draw settlers and entrepreneurs to its golden possibilities. The Jesuits' noble depictions of many native groups and practices contributed importantly to Europe's search for better social forms and philosophical enlightenment in the seventeenth and eighteenth centuries. And the Jesuits built and staffed some of the earliest and most successful schools and colleges in the hemisphere, where native and colonial leaders alike received their intellectual and moral foundations.

Yet the Jesuits were most effective as missionaries to the Indians, the landlords of the soil. In finding ways to breach the cultural defenses of the natives, who understandably sought to keep all invaders at bay and to maintain the lives they had known, the Blackrobes surpassed their Christian and secular rivals by virtue of education, apprenticeship at home, organization, discipline, and tactical shrewdness. Although they could not control the ravages of disease, the seduction of trade goods, or the wars and whims of secular factions, at every opportunity they took advantage of them to advance their spiritual and cultural objectives. In so doing, these unarmed missionaries became some of the most powerful agents of colonialism and change in native Amer-

ica. The quincentenary of the ongoing "encounter" between Europeans and Americans is a perfect time to probe
the legacy of the Jesuits in more depth, but also with
greater attention and sensitivity to their impact on the native peoples and cultures of the Americas.

CHAPTER SEVEN

Humor in Ethnohistory

THE OCCASIONS WHEN A SCHOLAR CAN PUBLICLY "LET IT all hang out," can write about the subjects closest to his heart with relative disregard for the niceties and proscriptions of scholarly discourse, are rare. We simply don't expect our button-down scholars to operate with the abandon of poets, novelists, and satirists, to drop the mask of cool, dispassionate reason to reveal the warm or silly humanness beneath. I can think of only three places where scholarly writing is allowed such latitude (and then only after the granting of tenure): book acknowledgments (where purple prose is tolerated if not expected), inaugural lectures of endowed chairs (when it is too late to retract the prize), and presidential addresses (preferably at the end of one's tenure rather than the beginning).

When I was elected president of the American Society for Ethnohistory for 1988–89, I felt so comfortable and familiar with our relatively small membership that I decided to throw caution to the winds and to deliver the kind of post-banquet address I have always wanted to hear. As it turned out, our convention hotel in Chicago had not laid on enough desserts for the buffet banqueteers, so my address had to provide the only "light confection" many of the audience got that windy afternoon in November 1989.

Initially, I had entertained the notion of speaking, in a

typically pedantic vein, on "Ethnohistory as a Liberal Art."
Thankfully I did not because I was richly rewarded by the audience response to my risky attempt to laugh at ethnohistory, both
the discipline and the subject matter. After the talk, which had to
be given with laughably little help from a faulty public address
system, colleagues gave or sent me numerous incidents to add to
my album of humorous ethnohistory. These have been added
gratefully to the text below, which editor and friend Shepard
Krech was obliged by corporate by-law to publish in *Ethnohistory*
the following spring.*

LIKE A GOOD PURITAN PREACHER, EVERY PRESIDEN-
tial addresser should have a text. I take mine from a character in Charles Dickens's *Hard Times* who once lisped,
"People mutht be amuthed. They can't be alwayth a learning, nor yet they can't be alwayth a working. They an't
made for it." Hard-working students such as ourselves
should take such sage advice to heart, especially after several long sessions of opiniatry and a full meal. So I propose
to spend a blessedly few minutes considering a subject of
light confection, a *jeu d'esprit* which also has, I hope, some
serious import for practitioners of ethnohistory. My topic
is humor in ethnohistory, which, I assure you, won out
only after an exceedingly close race with three other subjects: morbidity in ethnohistory, the irrelevance of Der-
ridadaism, and fieldwork among the Toyotas.

But seriously, folks, consider the humorous side of ethnohistory. Since the characters of the past were fully human, they were downright funny some of the time, at least
as often as we and our elected officials are. They found
each other funny, and we find them funny. As historians,
we also find some of their mutual predicaments funny,

particularly those resulting from cultural misunderstandings. So we have at least three subjects ready for analysis
and the engorgement of dissertations: what past actors
found funny in each other, which necessarily involves the
relative standards of their respective cultures; what we,
individually and personally, find funny about the actors of
the past, which involves our own culturally relative standards; and what we, as humane scholars, find funny about
the situations and predicaments they got themselves into,
which calls for, not an Olympian objective standard of
judgment, but a dry, disinterested, finely honed sense of
irony and of the ridiculous.

But hark, I hear someone asking, "Why, as a professional obligation rather than mere presidential preroga-
tive, should we laugh with and sometimes at the past?
Don't we demean our historical subjects and render our
discipline a laughingstock in the mouths of our more seriously disciplined sisters and brethren?" To which I have,
like a good Puritan preacher, three answers of weight and
substance. We all ought to take humor seriously, first, because not to do so is to skew the history of humanity, the
complex reality of human actors, past and present. Only
those who have never laughed at themselves in embarrassment or at others in nervous empathy have earned the
right to wear stony faces while teaching, reading, or writing ethnohistory.

Second, a light touch and a keen eye for the ridiculous
can lighten our heavy load of moral awareness of past iniq-
uities and tragedies, especially those that fell most heavily
on the native side of cross-cultural encounters, where most
of us work. A sense of humor can lift our spirits when our
historical news gets too depressing and, conversely, inocu-
late us against an epidemic of "the smugs," to which we are
all susceptible by virtue of birth in the ethnographic present. Moreover, as I have argued on other occasions, irony

and wit are two of the sharpest tools we have for deciphering the cultural codes on both, or all, sides of past frontiers, and especially for puncturing the pretensions and self-deceit of imperial bigwigs and eventual winners, whose technologies have given them a substantial archival and therefore historiographical advantage.[1]

Finally, humor, as mode and subject matter, serves as an effective antidote to the solemn navel-gazing all academics are prone to much of the time. Why do we work so hard to exorcise any trace of wit or laughter from our scholarship? Graduate schools should not confer degrees of terminal solemnity or entail upon their recipients a leaden legacy of lugubriousness. Of course, all adults, particularly bookish ones, are afraid of appearing lightweight and insubstantial. And Lord knows, the joyless scramble for publish-or-perish promotions leaves little time to savor the wit and whimsy of the past and even less to cultivate a lightness of touch in our re-creations of it. There *is* a real danger in flippancy and misplaced irreverence toward sacred subjects; both can lead to partiality and unfairness, every scholar's, especially the ethnohistorian's, deadliest sins. But if we take our subjects rather than ourselves seriously, we will recognize, as children and sensible parents do, that play is serious work and that intentional humor usually and situational humor always carry a serious message. It behooves us to pay attention to it, and to the spirit in which it was conveyed.

Like most academic discourse, ethnohistory as we practice it could use a general purging of self-indulgence and claptrap, and the implantation of a funny bone. After six years on the editorial board of *Ethnohistory*, and after having read more than fifty manuscripts for the *William and Mary Quarterly*, the great majority of which treated ethnohistorical subjects, I am continually dismayed by the obtrusive jargon, rampant reification, and ponderous prose of most submissions, sliced and diced by parentheses of anthropological-style citations. The only thing we do that is more ridiculous is to use the ethnological singular to indicate plural members of native tribes. To write sentences such as "The Huron *were* such and such" is no laughing matter and ought to be a source of deep humiliation. *Amerindians* and, worse yet, *Amerinds,* while superfluous and annoying, are at least grammatical.

But you did not invite me here to poke fun at hallowed tribal customs. Now that we've established the moral seriousness and professional utility of humor, let's cut right to the funny business of the past. Our first order is to look at Indian-white relations in colonial North America for examples of what natives and newcomers found particularly funny about each other. Of course, at various times they found each other frightening, contemptible, or barbaric, but we're looking for, not the snicker or the sneer, but the good old-fashioned belly laugh or chuckle emanating from sheer, unhegemonic amusement at the human comedy.

Because they were newcomers in a strange land, and greatly outnumbered at first, Europeans tended less to laugh at the natives than to worry about their unpredictability or to look down their noses at their novel behavior. They got their jollies only in small doses, largely from observing selected pieces of native etiquette, hearing the natives try to speak European (usually pidginized) languages, and seeing their reactions to a variety of European material introductions.

Like children of all ages, the Europeans must have cracked a smile over the Indians' uninhibited airings of digestive opinion. Unfortunately, most of our testimony on this flatulent subject comes from the pens of supposedly offended missionaries. But beneath their upturned noses it is not difficult to imagine the priests' unstarched amusement at this all but universal custom. Given to greasy and often leguminous diets, natives north and south, it was said, "belch continually" and "break Wind backwards" "before everyone regardless" and "laugh heartily at it, it being accounted no ill Manners amongst [them]."[2] During a long eat-all feast, such comic relief must have been welcome, even by blackrobes. Gabriel Sagard only "sometimes" and "very gently" reproved his Huron hosts on this score, "and then they would laugh," as he was probably forced to himself. Paul Le Jeune, a more worldly Jesuit, obviously took such expressions of relief in stride. "God knows what kind of music follows this banquet," he quipped. "As to the odors that are then exhaled in their Cabins, they are stronger than the perfume of roses, but not so sweet."[3]

As guardedly humorous (though for different reasons) was the greeting accorded the seven survivors of La Salle's abortive Texas colony. As they neared an Indian village somewhere on the Plains in 1687, several villagers came to carry them piggyback the rest of the way as a token of hospitality. At first, the whole idea put the French (who were already supplied with horses) "much out of Countenance," but their frowns quickly melted when they mounted their native stallions. Henri Joutel, the expedition's most reliable chronicler, seems to have enjoyed himself the most. "Being of a pretty large Size," he allowed,

> and loaded with Cloaths, a Firelock, a Case of Pistols, Powder and Ball, a Kettle and other Implements, there is no Doubt but I made a sufficient Burden for him that carry'd me, and because I was taller than he and my Feet would have hung upon the Ground, two other *Indians* held them up for me; so that I had three to carry me. Other *Indians* took hold of our Horses to lead them, and in that ridiculous Equipage we arriv'd at the Village.

Having staggered a "long Quarter of a League," the porters were all too happy to lay their foreign burden down. The French were equally grateful to be let down so they

could, in Joutel's words, "laugh in private, for it behov'd us
to take Care not to do it before them."[4]

Another source of European amusement was native attempts to speak Europeanized pidgins. To judge by the
number of examples they left, the English in New England
got the biggest kick out of "savage" attempts to imitate
"civilized" speech. The colonists' interest in recording native jargon probably fed their legendary superiority complex, but some of it was disinterested and grounded
in simple amusement at the natives' grammatical high
jinks. Even during King Philip's War, Puritan chroniclers
couldn't resist a well-turned pidgin phrase during a light
moment in the hostilities. When an English captain and
sixty men hauled into sight of three hundred warriors
drawn up for battle across an open field, he plucked off his
expensive wig and stuffed it into his breeches for safekeep-
ing. Upon seeing this bizarre act, the Indians "fell a Howl-
ing and Yelling most hideously," and their leader cried,
"Umh, Umh me no stawmerre [understand?] fight Engismon, Engismon got two Hed, Engismon got two Hed; if
me cut off un Hed, he got noder, a[nd] put on beder as
dis." Whereupon the consternated natives beat a hasty retreat into the forest rather than face their two-headed, and
no doubt relieved, nemeses.[5]

On the rough coast of Maine a half-century earlier,
trader Christopher Levett revealed an obvious soft spot for
the colorful speech of his Indian customers. He especially
enjoyed himself when they called his English rival a
"Jacknape"—"the most disgracefull word that may be in
their conceite"—and dubbed *him* a "foure fathom" sagamore, likening him to wampum of maximal value. When
Levett told them that he was returning to England to fetch
his wife, who would not make the crossing without him,
"they bid a pox on her hounds," a sailor's phrase they had
learned and used when they wanted to curse, and urged

him to beat her, Indian-style. Native New Englanders, it seems, were forever "condemn[ing] the English for their folly in spoiling good working creatures" with soft rule and misplaced respect.[6]

But Europeans got their biggest laughs from watching natives react to the food, fauna, and other freight from the Old World. The response to mustard was always good for a guffaw. Bartholomew Gosnold served dried cod, mustard, and beer to native Cape Codders in 1602. "But the Mustard nipping them in their noses they could not indure," a crewman reported. "It was a sport to behold their faces made being bitten therewith." In 1658 a Jesuit described with no solemnity how an Indian at a French table gulped down a heaping spoonful of mustard in the spirit of culinary discovery. While the native strove manfully to put a good face on it, his brimming eyes "betrayed him, although he set his teeth and compressed his lips to the utmost." When his comical stoicism finally deserted him, he marveled at the strength of the Frenchmen's "yellow porridge." A century later, at Fort Toulouse in Alabama, the French commander offered the curious servant of the Coweta "Emperor" a spoonful of "very strong mustard." Predictably, the servant went through "all kinds of ridiculous contortions," which tickled his master and the French no end. But the victim thought he had been "poisoned" until a swig of brandy effected a miraculous cure.[7]

In 1699 the French had gotten an equal kick from the kick the Biloxi Indians got from making the acquaintance of a gun. At first, the Indians shrank in fear from the flashing powder and noise of a French demonstration. But one brave fellow signaled that he wanted to try his hand at the new "thunderstick." You can guess the rest. As André Pénicaut told it, "The Frenchman who loaded for him— out of mischief or for some other reason—put too heavy a charge of powder in the gun; and the Indian, in his eagerness to shoot, leaned backward instead of forward as one ordinarily does. The recoil of the gun knocked him down, the Indian in one direction, the gun in another. This accident caused the natives to go more than two weeks without wishing to touch a gun."[8]

The Biloxi response to French gifts was no less ludicrous in the eyes of the donors. When Pierre LeMoyne d'Iberville distributed a number of gifts from the king's warehouse, the natives divided them and "examin[ed] them with astonishment." Several items were so strange that the Indians could not figure out how to use them, even though some, such as long woolen breechclouts and two-piece leggings, were staples of the trade in Canada, where Iberville and many of his men had served. Needless to say, the men took "keen pleasure" in watching the natives' "bewilderment," nor could Iberville keep from laughing. At least he had the grace to order his men to demonstrate the use of each article. So the French decked the Indians out in their new shirts, hats, and breechclouts, stitched their leggings together and pulled them on their legs, and carved handles for their axes and picks.[9]

For similar reasons, acculturated Delawares in the eighteenth century were able to smile over their innocent ancestors who had met the first Dutch ship early in the previous century. According to an oral tradition collected by John Heckewelder, the Dutch captain distributed gifts of beads, axes, hoes, and stockings to the hospitable natives and promised to return the following year with more to trade. When the Dutch kept their promise, they landed to find the Indians wearing the axe and hoe blades around their necks as laughably heavy gorgets and using the stockings as tobacco pouches. The crew then "put handles to the former for them, and cut trees down before their eyes, hoed up the ground, and put the stockings on their legs." At which, it was remembered, the grateful but sheepish

Delawares erupted in "general laughter" at their own naïveté.[10]

Since Europeans could seldom predict how the natives
would react to any novel item or experience, the sources
and occasions of their amusement were legion. Take the
first meeting of Canadian Indian and European ass. When
the Recollect friars of Quebec imported a pair of donkeys,
the beasts brayed enthusiastically upon landing and smell-
ing the coniferous shore. To the great amusement of the
French, all the native onlookers "were seized with such
terror that they fled helter-skelter into the woods for defense against these demons, and none looked behind him.
'O what furious beasts have these Frenchmen brought us,'
they said, 'either to devour us or to delight us with their
musical songs.'"[11]

Even after the natives of western Virginia had long been
acquainted with English mounts, they too were apt to look
a gift horse in the mouth. At least that was the response of
a Saponi chief who accompanied acting governor Alexander Spotswood and his entourage from Fort Christanna
to the English settlements in 1716. Since the chief was prepared to walk the whole way, Spotswood lent him a fine
horse. But the Indian was not accustomed to riding, as
quickly became obvious to the amused colonists. When the
party crossed a deep river, the English by swimming their
mounts from the saddle, the chief stripped to his breechclout and considerately led his horse across. His kindness
was ill-rewarded, however, for before they had ridden two
miles, the horse threw him. In a burst of courage, the bare-
legged chief remounted, but before another mile had
passed, he was so terribly chafed that he was forced to
dismount voluntarily. He promptly returned the horse to
the governor and told His Excellency that he "could not
imagine what good [horses] were for, if it was not to cripple
the Indians."[12]

Lest you think that Europeans found humor only in Indian attempts to be serious or dignified, we should eavesdrop on the Louisiana Frenchmen who lived temporarily with the Colapissas and Nassitoches around Lake Pontchartrain in 1706. Among them was a violinist named Picard, who "could play . . . well enough to have the natives [*sauvages*] do some figure-dancing in step." When the whole village gathered around him and began to dance to his foreign beat, wrote an eyewitness, "they had us nearly dying of laughter . . . ; it was the most comical sight in the world to see them open their eyes in amazement and every now and then cut the most comical capers ever seen." For his labors, Picard the next day received a big kiss from the Nassitoches chief's daughter. But he also met his match when the Indians put on their own dance to a drum accompaniment. Despite a "painful" attempt to keep time with the native drum and singers, Picard caused everyone to "laugh out loud" because "he never was able to approximate their rhythm." "He made amends by teaching many of the girls in the village to dance the minuet and *la bourrée*." One of his companions got his fun from teaching the chief's daughters to speak French. "They made me die of laughing," he said, "with their savage pronunciation, which comes entirely from the throat."[13]

Although the written record is heavily skewed toward the Europeans, American humor was very much a two-way street. When the moccasin was on the other foot, Indians found plenty in white appearance and behavior to laugh about. The Stadaconans who introduced Jacques Cartier and his crew to harsh Quebec tobacco cannot have failed to see the humor in their facial gyrations. "When [the smoke] is in one's mouth," Cartier admitted, "one would think one had taken powdered pepper, it is so hot." The Crees who met the first Hudson's Baymen in 1670 also found the Europeans' handling of native heat a source of amusement. After the crew of the *Nonsuch* spent a steamy session in a native sweatlodge, rather than follow their hosts into the nearest snowbank or river to close their pores, they "rubbed and dried" themselves off "with cloths," which sent the hardy Crees into peals of laughter.[14]

Catholic missionaries were often good for a laugh. Their haloed tonsures, effeminate dress, and lack of interest in women all touched the Huron funny bone. To judge from Gabriel Sagard's confessed discomfort, the "continual importunity and requests" of Huron women and girls to bed and wed the Recollect friars must have been a source of good fun on cold evenings around the fire.[15] We know that teaching the Jesuits to speak a decent—or indecent—sentence was. Micmac informants "often ridiculed, instead of teaching us," the Blackrobes complained, "and sometimes palmed off on us indecent words, which we went about innocently preaching for beautiful sentences from the Gospels." When the wintering Montagnais wanted entertainment at a feast in 1634, they asked Father Le Jeune to make a speech in their language because, he admitted, he pronounced Montagnais "as a German pronounces French." When he began to stammer, "they burst out laughing, well pleased to make sport" of him.[16]

After many years in Canada, Le Jeune, as one might expect, developed a sensitive ear for native humor at French expense. In 1658 he described for the polite readers of the Jesuit *Relations* the Indian opinion of French handkerchiefs. "Politeness and propriety have taught us to carry [them]," he said. But the natives "charge us with filthiness: because, they say, we place what is unclean in a fine white piece of linen, and put it away in our pockets as something very precious, while they throw it upon the ground." One day, when an Indian "saw a Frenchman fold up his handkerchief after wiping his nose, he said to him laughingly,

'If you like that filth, give me your handkerchief and I will soon fill it.'"[17]

The French were not the only newcomers to have their legs pulled by native jokesters. The five Abenakis kidnapped in 1605 by George Waymouth had some fun at their captors' expense by describing "how they make butter and cheese of the milke they have of the Rain-Deere and Fallo-Deere, which they have tame as we have Cowes."[18] English gullibility was also the target when a Massachusett Indian sold to the steward of Harvard College a side of "moose" which, it was soon discovered, had formerly masqueraded as a cow in a local pasture. Probably only the prankish students and the perpetrator saw the humor in his crime.[19]

Even at this remove, we can appreciate the humor in most of the things that caught the fancy of both Indians and Europeans. But some native efforts to get a laugh simply do not, and did not, translate well across time and culture. I'm thinking of an incident in 1754 when a returning war party of Catawbas allegedly tried to kidnap an English child from a North Carolina farm. At a council with colonial officials, King Hagler, their chief, denied the charge by explaining that "it was Only done by way of a joke by one of our wild Young men in Order to Surprize the People that were the parents of the Child, to have a Laugh at the Joke." In the context of related complaints about thefts of food, cattle, and clothes, English parents and officials understandably failed to find anything funny about the Catawba sense of humor.[20]

Not only did the Indians and Europeans laugh at each other, but some evidence, admittedly rare, remains of Europeans laughing at themselves for their comic handling of Indian affairs. William Byrd II of Virginia had a keen eye and a bawdy wit, the best of which comes out in his "Secret

History" of an expedition he led in 1728 to survey a dividing line between North Carolina and Virginia. Thrown into unlikely company were seven gentlemen, three surveyors, two servants, a chaplain, and "15 able Woodsmen, most of which had been Indian Traders." After a womanless month in the woods, the party stopped for the night at a Nottoway town on the way home. Although the village elders failed to offer the weary travelers "she-bedfellows" for the night "according to the good Indian fashion," a few gents decided to pursue ethnographic studies on their own. The most important item on their research agenda, it seems, was to discover, as Byrd put it, "the difference between [Indian] and other Women." This turns out to have been a sly euphemism for checking to see if native women had no "furr." While the frontier scientists knew little or nothing about shovel incisors or epicanthic eyefolds, they had become fascinated by the Indians' Asiatic hairlessness. But despite the natives' relative nakedness, they couldn't satisfy themselves on this point by casual observation because, as Byrd noticed with some regret, the women put on their "aprons" or miniskirts "with so much art, that the most impertinent curiosity can't in the Negligentist of their Motions or Postures make the least discovery." In the short time they had, participant observation was their only recourse. In the morning, however, the group's spiritual adviser "observ'd with concern, that the Ruffles of Some of our Fellow Travellers were a little discolour'd with pochoon [puccoon, a reddish vegetable dye], wherewith the good Man had been told those Ladies us'd to improve their invisible charms." Unhappily for science, neither Byrd nor his mates ever published the results of their research.[21]

Occasionally, the Europeans even laughed at the Indian handling of a comic affair. In the spring of 1797 Louis-Philippe, the future "King of the French," traveled through Cherokee country at the suggestion of George

Washington. On the Tennessee River near Tellico, the French party visited several Indian families to observe their manners and mores. With them to interpret went an Irishman named Carey, who had lived among the Cherokees for thirty or forty years. Carey's familiarity with the natives seems to have known no bounds. "When the husbands or fathers were distracted," noticed Louis-Philippe, "he made no effort to disguise his little *games* with the wives or daughters; and they were so little embarrassed that one of them who was lying on a bed put her hand on his trousers before my very eyes and said scornfully, *Ah, sick.*" With understandable chauvinism, His Grace showed his appreciation for the women's beauty, flirtatiousness, and spirit by confessing that "no Frenchwoman could teach them a thing."[22]

That's enough scholarly detachment for the moment. We've attended to the culturally relative norms of past humor long enough and should move on to our second level of analysis. It's time now to explore briefly my own personal and, needless to say, culturally relative sense of humor by sharing some of my favorite episodes from North America's ethno-comic-history. There is absolutely no evidence that any of the participants found any of these events funny or even mildly amusing. As a precedent-loving historian, I'm a bit nervous about this. But on this occasion I'm willing to throw scholarly caution to the wind if you will lower your own high standards of professional probity and emotional detachment. With one fair warning: My wife told me to tell you that my sense of humor ranges from the malign to the ridiculous. And she ought to know: she's a cultural relative.

Let's start at the beginning, with Columbus. As you know, the Admiral of the Ocean Sea *thought* he saw many strange peoples on his first voyage to the West Indies, Amazons and cannibals among them. My favorite apparition

was the "three sirens" he saw at the mouth of a river in
Hispaniola. These "rose very high from the sea," reported
his first biographer, "but they were not as beautiful as they
are depicted, for somehow their faces had the appearance
of a man." Even though Columbus claimed to have seen
others earlier on the African coast, he failed to recognize
his sirens as manatees or sea cows, either by their un-
feminine beauty or their less-than-seductive songs.[23]

As the Spanish made imperial forays into North America, *entradas* often played havoc with Indian communities
and cultures. As an inveterate champion of underdogs,
I'm always delighted when a conquistador gets his just de-
serts in one of those lopsided encounters. Having sponged
off the villagers of Chicaça for three long months, Soto's
entrada suddenly found itself engulfed by a furious "rebellion" in 1541. The Indians caught the Spanish garrison
unawares and set fire to the men's lodges and the stables,
causing widespread panic. Only Soto and one soldier managed to mount their horses for a counterattack. But when
the governor thrust his lance at his first victim, he and his
saddle went flying through the air and ended up on the
ground, "for in [his] haste he had badly fastened the girth
and fell from his horse." Unfortunately for the "rebels,"
only his hidalgo pride was wounded.[24]

Another hapless invader, this time an Englishman, got a
literal comeuppance on Cape Cod in 1620. Afer violating a
number of Wampanoag graves and corn caches, a Pilgrim
exploration party came upon a native deer snare in the
woods, which they stopped to examine with considerable
interest. But when William Bradford, bringing up the
rear, passed by the device, "it gave a sudden jerk up, and
he was immediately caught by the leg." After His Eminence was cut down, undoubtedly to the good-natured
hoots of his companions, they captured the offending rope
and noose as souvenirs because they were made as artfully

"as any roper in English can make, and as like ours as can be."[25]

I couldn't go home if I didn't show a little chauvinism toward my comic Virginia ancestors, so let me extract three vignettes from the hoary tale of Captain John Smith and the Powhatans. Smith, we know, was a little guy much given to braggadocio and displays of machismo, and he had virtually no sense of the ridiculous, particularly where he was involved. Thus I cherish the deadpan portrait he painted of himself fishing from a barge on Chesapeake Bay. Since the English had no nets with them and the fish were "lying . . . thicke with their heads above the water," said the landlubbing soldier, "we attempted to catch them with a frying pan: but we found it a bad instrument to catch fish with."[26]

A few months later, a one-armed, one-time pirate named Christopher Newport arrived from London with orders to crown Powhatan, momentarily peaceful, as a vassal of James I. So Smith and four men trooped overland to Powhatan's capital at Werowocomoco to set a date for him to come to Jamestown to receive his crown and royal gifts. On the way, however, the party was waylaid by the pubescent Pocahontas and thirty "naked" women, "onely covered behind and before with a few greene leaves, their bodies all painted." With "hellish shouts and cryes," they seated the messengers at a fire and proceeded to sing and dance around them for nearly an hour in a wild masque of "infernall passions," as Smith described it, probably with a *frisson* of remembered delight. For when the entertainment ended, the "Nymphes" invited Smith to their lodging, where they "tormented" him with "crowding, pressing, and hanging about him, most tediously crying," he recalled, "Love you not me? love you not me?" Fortunately for the awkward bachelor, a feast intervened and saved whatever it was he was trying to save.[27]

Powhatan refused to go to Jamestown under any circumstances, saying that "if your King have sent me Presents, I also am a King, and this is my Land." So his presents were shipped a hundred roundabout miles by water
and fifty Virginians marched overland to perform his coronation. When his new basin and ewer and canopy bed and
hangings were set up in the village square and he was
attired in his scarlet cloak and regalia, it was time to crown
him. But "a foule trouble there was to make him kneele to
receive his Crowne, he neither knowing the majesty nor
meaning of a Crowne, nor bending of a knee. . . . At last
by leaning hard on his shoulders," Smith wrote, without so
much as a smile, "he a little stooped, and three having the
crowne in their hands put it on his head." To express his
gratitude for this great honor, Powhatan gave Captain
Newport "his old shooes and . . . mantell."[28]

Before we leave the Chesapeake, I want to honor the
good-humored wit of Colonel Henry Norwood, a well-
educated Royalist who washed up on the shores of Maryland in the winter of 1649. After ten days of piercing cold,
the English castaways were rescued by the local natives
and cosseted with warm fires, abundant food, and touching hospitality. Totally unable to communicate with each
other, Norwood and the Kickotank chief signed and
wagged at each other for days in endless frustration, until
they erupted in relieved laughter at their mutual predicament. Only the chance arrival of an English trader and his
Indian guide released the English from their comfortable
prison of silence. When Norwood reached the "civilized"
settlements on Virginia's Eastern Shore, he gladly honored
the chief's request to have his camlet coat glittering with
gold and silver lace. The reason, the resolute Royalist
quipped, was that the Indian was "the first king I could call
to mind that ever shew'd any inclination to wear my old
cloaths."[29]

But my all-time favorite episode occurred on the barren coast of Maine in 1524 as Giovanni da Verrazzano sailed up to trade with a cluster of Indians on the rocks. Unlike the friendly natives who had entertained him and his crew in Narragansett Bay a few days before, these people seemed "full of crudity and vices" and totally uninterested in communication, even by sign. At best, when the crew attempted to trade with them, they warned the boat not to land and would only exchange goods on a rope. And then, after they had disdained gewgaws and accepted only knives, fishhooks, and sharp metal for their furs, from their granite promontory they saluted the armed intruders with a magnificent gesture of human defiance: they "made all the signs of scorn and shame that any brute creature would make," the captain complained, "such as showing their buttocks and laughing."[30] If I am not mistaken, this was the inspiration behind that golden oldie, "Moon over Monhegan."

Surely that's enough ribaldry for one day. We need to move on to our third and final category of ethnohumor, namely intercultural predicaments or encounters which give rise less to raucous laughter than to knowing smiles at the inherent irony or cunning of the situation. In the winter of 1607–8, for example, Powhatan's warriors captured John Smith in a swamp. After submitting him to shamanic scrutiny to determine his intentions, they fed and fêted him before sending him back to Jamestown loaded with loaves of cornbread. But they kept his bag of gunpowder until the following spring, he said, "to plant as they did their corne; because they would be acquainted with the nature of that seede."[31]

In the nineteenth century a comic anecdote circulated that may have taken a kernel of truth from the Powhatan incident. It seems that a trader once sold a packet of gunpowder to a gullible Indian as a fine, wheatlike grain. So the native planted and weeded his crop with great care, but to no avail. Some time later, the trader tried to collect from the farmer a large, overdue debt he had accumulated at the trader's store. Now wiser by half, the Indian told his creditor, "Me pay you when my powder grow."[32]

But the natives were not always on the winning end of such contests of cunning. A French captive once had a dream duel with his Iroquois master, who with his tribesmen believed that dreams were wishes of the soul that must be fulfilled to prevent misfortune. Noticing that the captive had a "rather good blanket, better than his own," the Indian

> promptly dreamed of it and asked him for it. The Frenchman, who was not stupid, gave it to him willingly, counting on having his revenge. A few days later he went into his man's lodge and, seeing a good buffalo robe, claimed that he had dreamed of it. The Indian gave it to him without being begged. These alternating daydreams went on for some time. . . . Finally the Indian grew tired first. He went to find the Frenchman and made him agree that they would no longer dream of one another's possessions.[33]

According to the eighteenth-century Canadian trader John Long, Chief Hendrick of the Mohawks found himself similarly outfoxed by the wily Sir William Johnson. At a council meeting, Hendrick told Sir William that the previous night he had dreamed that Johnson had given him a fine laced coat, the very one Johnson was wearing. "Well then," said Johnson, "you must have it," and instantly pulled it off and helped Hendrick into it. When the council broke up, Hendrick left crying "Who-ah" in great good humor. At the next council, Johnson "told the chief that he was not accustomed to dream, but that since he met him at the [last] council he had dreamed a very surprising dream." With some trepidation, Hendrick asked what it was. Whereupon Sir William told him, with as straight a face as he could put on, that

> he had dreamed that [Hendrick] had given him a tract of land on the Mohawk River to build a house on and make a settlement, extending about nine miles in length along the banks. The chief smiled and, looking very cheerfully at Sir William, told him if he really dreamed it he should have it; but that he would never dream again with him for he had only got a laced coat, whereas Sir William was now entitled to a large bed, on which his ancestors had frequently slept.[34]

I shouldn't like to leave you with the impression that only native religion was open to manipulation. Consider the case of the "theological fish." In New France, Lent fell at the hungriest time of year, between the snowy take of winter hunting and the dicier offerings of spring gathering and fishing. To ask Indian neophytes and French woodsmen to go without meat of any kind was simply not feasible. One potential solution was the beaver, which was relatively available year-round. But according to contemporary zoologists (though not the ancients), the beaver was classified as an animal and so could not be eaten on the 165 meatless days of the Catholic calendar.

With the professoriate's infinite capacity for rationalization, the faculty of the Sorbonne solved Canada's problem with two strokes of the pen: the faculty of medicine juridically declared that, by virtue of its webbed feet, scaly tail, and aquatic life, the beaver was a fish; and the faculty of theology decided that, since it was a fish, "it might be lawfully eaten on [so-called] meagre days." As the wry Baron de Lahontan put it, "Those who love Meat are indebted to the Doctors, who perswaded the Popes to Metamorphose these terrestrial Animals into Fish." Religious purists in France took no such liberties with their abnegations. A noble friend of Frère Sagard once killed a beaver during

Lent near Nancy, "but," marveled the former Canadian, "we ate only the tail and hind feet, which were considered to be fish and the rest meat."[35]

All good Puritan preachers, once they had established their text and parsed its spiritual or moral meaning, sought to carry their message home by leaving their audience with a few concrete "applications," the more graphic the better. For the same reason, I would like to leave you with three visually striking illustrations of the discovery I hope we have made today: that ethnohistorical truth is stranger, and a good deal funnier, than fiction.

The first picture is of a hundred Virginia soldiers cutting a deadly swath through Nansemond country in the humid summer of 1611. Since the Indians were nonplussed by English armor, their conjurers began a series of "exorcismes, conjuracyons, and charmes, throweinge fyer upp into the skyes, Runneinge up and downe wth Rattles, and makeing many dyabolicall gestures" in an effort, said an unsympathetic observer, "to cawse Raine to fall from the Clowdes to extinguishe and putt owtt our mens matches and to wett and spoyle their powder." Had they but known what rust could do to a suit of armor, they might have conjured harder.[36]

The second picture is actually a triptych on tobacco. In native America, as you know, tobacco was sacred and on its smoke prayers were lifted to heaven. The best way to honor great-spirited beings, such as the first Europeans were thought to be, was to offer them tobacco or smoke. In the Great Lakes, Nicolas Perrot had smoke blown directly into his face "as the greatest honor that they could render him; he saw himself smoked like meat" but gamely "said not a word." With Iberville on the Mississippi, Father Paul du Ru reported that, after puffing two or three times on a calumet, one of the Indians "came and blew smoke from his pipe into my nose as though to cense me." Du Ru may have come off better than the first French captain who sailed to the Menominees on Lake Michigan: he had tobacco ground into his forehead, as if it were an ashtray.[37]

My final illustration really belongs in Ripley's *Believe It or Not,* but I assure you that I have it on good authority. While serving among the Hurons in the 1620s, our old friend Gabriel Sagard could not but notice their proclivity for stealing from strangers with both their hands and their feet, which they used "like a second pair of hands." The object, of course, was not to get caught in the act, for that would have meant loss of face in that proud face-to-face society. According to Sagard—and he always had one hand on the Bible—a Huron man, "having robbed the French of a silver spoon, concealed it cunningly in the most private part of his body, preferring to suffer the pain of it than the shame of being considered clumsy."[38]

And on that metallic note, this talk is behind me.

1492 and Beyond

CHAPTER EIGHT

Europeans, Indians, and the Age of Discovery in American History Textbooks

SCHOLARS SOMETIMES WIND UP IN HOT WATER INADVERtently; occasionally they dive in headfirst. At the December 1986 meeting of the American Historical Association, I took the plunge on behalf of the Columbus Quincentenary Committee. We had decided to pave the way for a sensible, reflective commemoration of 1492 by taking stock of what educated Americans were apt to know about Columbus and the age of mutual discovery he launched in the Americas. College textbooks seemed the likeliest source of public knowledge because they dominated introductory history courses in most universities, and the Admiral and his age were not the stuff of the mass media except every fifty years. So I undertook a one-man survey of the leading textbooks, with the following results.

When the report was published in the *American Historical Review* the following June, it caused a brief but audible rustling in the dovecotes of academe and publishing.[1] Two historians at the University of California-Santa Barbara separately wrote letters to the editor of the *AHR,* who published them in the February 1988 issue with my reply. Wilbur Jacobs argued that "the Black Legend is in many respects an accurate *interpretation* of history," which I continue to deny. Robert Kelley, the author of one of the textbooks I critiqued, sought largely to defend the status quo by pointing to the "iron laws" of textbook publishing, which I regard only as timeworn habits based on unfounded assumptions.[2]

On the positive side, three publishers asked me to critique the early draft chapters of their new texts and other publishers resorted to fellow scholars of the "Encounter" period for the same services. The article also caught the attention of several textbook authors, to judge by subsequent conversations at historical conventions.

If I thought that my critique had had a durable or widespread impact on the textbook industry or on the teaching of early American history, I would not include it in this volume. But it is painfully obvious that very little has changed in the six years since I forced myself to read those sixteen texts. As someone wise in the ways of academe once said, it is easier to move a cemetery than a college faculty to change its curricular habits. I can only hope that history students in the near future will be served much better than I was in 1986.

IT WOULD BE DIFFICULT TO OVERESTIMATE THE ROLE played by textbooks in the teaching of American history. Yet, for some peculiar reason, textbooks are the only products of historical scholarship that do not receive regular critical review by acknowledged experts in the various subfields of American history. Publishers frequently hire pedagogical consultants or teachers from large institutions to critique textbook manuscripts, in order to ensure that the complexity of content and prose style do not overshoot their targeted audiences. But they seldom ask the best scholars to review the books before publication and only occasionally do so for subsequent editions. More to the point, perhaps, the leading historical journals, both general and specialized, do not deign to review textbooks. Only *The History Teacher* regularly extends itself in this direction; even *History: Reviews of New Books* overlooks the survey text in favor of the occasional specialized text and the usual monographs. Fortunately, the new face of the *Journal of American History* at last smiles on review essays of American history textbooks.

It was this state of affairs—and the forthcoming Columbian hoopla, of course—that prompted the AHA's Columbus Quincentenary Committee to launch this modest, one-person inquiry into what American college students were reading about, not so much Columbus's daring (and ever-controversial) voyages, as important as those were, but the earth-making changes that followed in his wake over the next century and a half. What, if anything, were students learning about the Columbian legacy, the shaping of a new Atlantic (and later global) world that linked the destinies of several continents and myriad peoples? What were they reading about the native peoples of the Americas and Africa who were so suddenly yanked into the European orbit? Were they still being shown the Spanish empire through the distorting lens of the "Black Legend"? Did they ever see the French and other non-English colonizers arrive in the Americas and, if so, with what result? And, perhaps most important, could they, from what they were reading, understand what motivated Columbus, his European successors, and the natives, and what caused the tangle of events to which Americans are collateral if not direct heirs? With these questions in mind, I have read the first chapter or two of sixteen of the most popular college textbooks currently being used.[3] A few texts were written by one person, but most were collaborative products, whose first sections were authored by specialists in Anglo-American colonial history. Some texts had been around a long time and had seen multiple editions and sometimes revisions; several others were virtually hot off the press.

The similarity of content and treatment is striking. The contents of the sixteen "discovery" chapters are almost interchangeable, especially in the older texts. The standard scenario includes: the native societies of the New World after the Asian migration; European society on the eve of colonization, usually in transition from medieval to early modern; Christopher Columbus and explorers of other nationalities; the Spanish conquest and the establishment of empire; Spain's colonial competitors—the Dutch, French, and English; and the background of English colonization, including the Reformation, the Armada, and joint-stock companies. Some of these topics receive only a column or two (only three texts treat the reader to full book pages), but most texts touch on them all in some fashion.[4] A few of the newer texts go considerably beyond the standard treatment by adding new topics or by fleshing out some of the traditional topics in greater detail. Gary Nash and Mary Beth Norton have added substantial sections on western Africa in describing America as the commingling of three peoples, while James Henretta has given extensive attention to the social and economic preconditions of European settlement.

All of the texts share two other similarities. The new maritime roads all lead to the new Rome—the founding of the United States via the thirteen English mainland colonies. Although this focus is appropriate for later phases of the subject, it distorts the reality of America's origins. The Spanish and French empires are introduced only to provide strong contrasts with the emerging Protestant democracy sandwiched between them and never to help explain why the English colonies evolved as they did. The rich island colonies of the West Indies might as well not have existed, for all the reader learns of them. Only the regions of North America north of the Rio Grande and south of the 49th parallel are of interest, except when "foreign" wars inconveniently spill over the borders. The fluid possibilities of North America in the sixteenth and early seventeenth centuries are simply ignored in the face of the eventual *fait accompli,* and readers can only regard Anglo-America's imperial rivals as paper tigers.

The textbooks are also stingy with historical time. On the average, they devote only 4 percent of their first-semester pages to the crowded and formative century of discovery, which accounts for some 30 percent of the time between Columbus's celebrated landing and Reconstruction. The challenge of explaining some of the most complex, important, and interesting events in human history—the discovery of a new continent, the religious upheavals of the sixteenth century, the forging of the Spanish empire, the Columbian biological exchange, the African diaspora—all in twenty or twenty-five pages is one that few, if any, textbook authors have met or are likely to meet. The results thus far are not encouraging.

Even though some authors have treated some subjects better than others have, together, the group of sixteen has committed enough sins of commission and omission to give one serious pause about the possibility of the enterprise as presently conceived. The sins of commission encompass not only an alarming density of factual errors but also ineffective visual material, insensitive characterizations, and insidious half-truths. Virtually no parts of the discovery text are immune to errors of fact. But some subjects seem especially susceptible, particularly those that demand acquaintance with an extensive and active historiography. Among the subjects most vulnerable are Indians, the Spanish empire, and the French colony in Canada (Louisiana and the Illinois country being virtually unheard of until the Anglo-Americans "discover" them late in the eighteenth century). Indians come in for trouble as soon as they decide to leave Asia. Three texts, including that of the renowned sailor Samuel Eliot Morison have the first immigrants crossing an unfrozen Bering Strait in boats, in search of political and religious liberty, no doubt, rather than hot meals on the hoof.[5] Another migration occurred, according to two other texts, during or just before the sixteenth century, when the five Iroquois tribes moved from the Southwest—or the Mississippi Valley—into New York State.[6] As it turns out, since at least the 1950s, archaeologists have known that the northern Iroquoian cultures developed *in situ* over many centuries, probably from before the birth of Christ.[7]

Tribal names and linguistic families are additional sticking points. Many texts, especially on their vague, continent-sized maps of native cultures, mangle tribal names, misplace tribal territories, and confuse individual tribes with linguistic groups. Probably because of James Fenimore Cooper, "Mohegans" are forever usurping the land of the "Mahicans" on the upper Hudson; the Hurons, who spoke an Iroquo*ian* language but were the arch-rivals of the New York Iroquo*ois,* are seldom placed in their homeland on Georgian Bay in southern Ontario; and the Algonqu*in* tribe on the Ottawa River west of Montreal is too frequently mistaken for the language family of Algonqu*ian* speakers, who inhabited much of the northeastern woodlands.[8]

Three other common errors creep into discussions of Indians. Several texts assert that the concepts of "private property" and "landownership" were virtually unknown to Indians.[9] On the contrary, although the woodland tribes owned land communally, individuals owned any objects they made and food they procured. House sites, garden plots, fishing spots, and hunting territories were often assigned to families by tribal leaders and were then regarded as "private" as any modern property that is subject to confiscation by a sovereign state. Other texts charge that native government was not truly "organized," particularly in contrast to the empires of Mexico and Peru, and therefore

doomed Indians to "disunity" before the European onslaught.[10] This point of view overlooks the proven effectiveness of noncoercive government in face-to-face societies and of the Creek, Powhatan, Iroquois, and Huron
confederacies, which bedeviled various invaders for as
long as two centuries. The textbooks characterize native
religion as some kind of "primitive" or "pagan" "pantheism" because Indians allegedly believed that everything in
nature—"the land, trees, rocks, and animals"—contained
living spirits or souls.[11] Scholars today believe that the natives respected the "souls" or animating "spirits" only of
living things, not rocks or land *per se,* and normally suppli-
cated and thanked not individual plants and animals but
rather the "boss-spirits" or representatives of species.

The half-truths about Indians are perhaps worse than the
errors. Despite native population estimates ranging from
one to twelve million, several older male authors persist in
characterizing the "vast and lonely North American continent" as a "virgin" land, which "like all virgins, inspired
conflicting feelings in men's hearts."[12] What happened
next varies from text to text. Younger authors invariably
describe it as rape; at least one of their chivalrous elders
preferred to think that "the New World gracefully yielded
her virginity" to the conquerors.[13] Another gentleman was
obviously relieved that this "vast and virgin continent
. . . was so sparsely peopled by Indians that they could be
eliminated or shouldered aside. Such a magnificent opportunity for a great democratic experiment," he chirped with
unintended irony, "may never come again." (This from the
same historian who thinks it relevant that Sir Walter
Ralegh seduced one of Elizabeth's maids of honor and
Louis XIV had numerous mistresses.)[14]
  Equally misleading is Bernard Bailyn's statistical apology
for English colonization, much in the manner of John Win-

throp's argument from *vacuum domicilium*. In 1600, Bailyn wrote, the 362,000 square miles of the eastern seaboard were "largely uncultivated" by the Indians (as indeed they still are today). Somehow, he knew that "nowhere was more than 1 per cent of all the land available for cultivation being farmed." East of the Appalachians, the average population density, he tells us without interpretive comment, was thirty-four persons per hundred square miles. In New England, the average density was between four and five persons per square mile, as if the student knew whether that was sparsely or densely settled for a semi-hunting-and-gathering society. Consequently, although Bailyn acknowledged that the natives sensibly concentrated their semi-permanent settlements in "the fertile coastal plain and the broad river valleys," he concluded, as did the Puritans, that "the Indians' hold upon the land was light."[15]

Other misleading assertions abound. The (illiterate) chief Powhatan "signed" a peace treaty with the Virginians in 1614 and "sealed the deal in traditional fashion by marrying his daughter Pocahontas to John Rolfe."[16] Not only was no treaty ever signed but Powhatan ceased his efforts to evict the English trespassers only after Sir Thomas Dale's troops had pummeled his villages relentlessly for two years, and Pocahontas had been kidnapped by the English as a hostage for peace, converted (when her father refused to come up with the ransom), and married (which Powhatan did not witness, for fear of his life).[17]

For some of the same reasons, the French and Spanish do not fare much better at the hands of Anglo-American historians. Sad to say, the "Black Legend" and others still warp the treatments of the Spanish empire. Typical is Bailyn's, which, despite its careful attention to Spanish administrative successes over a vast area, leaves no doubt that the Spanish story is primarily a "tale of slaughter and con-

The unwitting architect of the "Black Legend" of Spanish cruelty toward the Indians was Bartolomé de Las Casas, former conquistador of Cuba-turned-Dominican friar who became bishop of Chiapas in Mexico and acknowledged "Defender of the Indians." His graphic histories of the Spanish conquest, written to obtain justice for the natives in Spanish law, were widely republished in translation by Spain's Protestant enemies for political purposes, often with lurid engravings to illustrate the heinousness of the conquistadors and, by extension, of the Spanish national character. This picture by publisher-engraver Theodor de Bry accompanied the first Latin translation of Las Casas's *Very Brief Relation of the Destruction of the Indies* (1552). From *Narratio Regionum Indicarum Per Hispanos* (Frankfurt, 1598).

quest" with "no heroes." "Half-mad with greed," *conquistadores* were "unbelievably determined," "courageous," "fierce," "brutal," and "ruthless," characterizations echoed in most of the other texts without Bailyn's compensatory treatment of Spanish achievements after the conquest.[18]

Under the spell of the legend, truth gives way to fiction. One text asserts that Spain claimed all of the New World "except for a chunk of it (Brazil) that they"—not Pope Alexander VI—"left to the Portuguese."[19] Another text vows that Cortés burned—not scuttled—his ships in Veracruz harbor. The same text says, without indicating the period, that some 750,000 Spaniards emigrated to the New World, another that "few" were "able or willing to emigrate."[20] The latest estimates suggest less than 250,000 in the sixteenth century, another 200,000 in the first half of the seventeenth.[21] Perhaps the most common misunderstanding about Hispanic America is the equation of the *encomienda* system with simple land grants.[22] On the contrary, land was plentiful but worthless without native labor. The Spanish colonists therefore requested grants of specified Indian villages, which would supply them, landholders who lived elsewhere, with tributary goods and labor to work their farms and industries.

If possible, the French suffer more misunderstandings and errors than do either Indians or Spaniards. Considering the relatively small cast of characters on the Canadian stage, one would think that the skimpy program notes offered by these authors would be more accurate. More than one text has Giovanni da Verrazzano (usually spelled incorrectly, with only one 'z') sailing in 1523 instead of 1524, and Jacques Cartier exploring the St. Lawrence "as far inland as present-day Montreal" on his first voyage in 1534 rather than a year later on his second voyage.[23] Cartier did not winter "near the mouth of the Saguenay," as Morison inexplicably asserted, but much farther upstream on the St. Charles River at today's Quebec City.[24] His famous complaint about "the land God gave to Cain" referred to Labrador, not Newfoundland.[25] And the statement that Cartier's voyages "did not lead immediately to colonizing efforts" is incorrect.[26] In 1541–42, a third expedition, to-

The only contemporary portrait of Samuel de Champlain is his own depiction of his famous battle with the Iroquois on (renamed) Lake Champlain in 1609. With his frightening arquebus, Champlain leads his Algonquin and Montagnais allies from the north shore of the St. Lawrence against an Iroquois (probably Mohawk) war-party not far from the Mohawk homeland in eastern New York. Since the Canadian tribes and the Iroquois were ancient enemies, Champlain had no choice but to ally the beaver-dependent French with the Canadians who controlled the prime hunting grounds of the north. From Champlain's *Voyages* (Paris, 1620).

taling eight ships under Cartier and le sieur de Roberval took several hundred colonists of both sexes to the St. Lawrence, along with livestock and farm equipment. When the colonists scampered home after one winter, the French did not, as Edmund Morgan suggested, "forget" North America "for the rest of the century."[27] In 1562, they established an ill-fated colony of Huguenots in Florida, and, in the 1580s, merchant ships returned to the St. Lawrence in number to reestablish a lucrative fur trade.

The next textbook star of Canadian history, Samuel de Champlain, is equally tarnished by myth and error. Champlain was an intrepid traveler, but his explorations could never have extended French claims "as far inland as Wisconsin," as Thomas Bailey alleged they did, because Champlain never got farther west than Georgian Bay on Lake Huron.[28] Nor was he personally responsible for earning New France "the lasting enmity of the Iroquois tribes" in 1609 by his actions at the battle of Lake Champlain.[29] If he wished to procure the rich fur trade of the north for his employers, he had no choice but to ally the French with the Montagnais and Algonquin hunters on the north shore of the St. Lawrence and with their traditional friends, the Hurons (who were not, as Bailey suggested, "nearby" but several hundred river miles away).[30] Long before Champlain and his men fired on the Iroquois at Lake Champlain, the French had cast their lot with ancient enemies of the Iroquois.

Most textbooks do not extend themselves beyond the founding of Quebec, but those that do continue to pattern the French story after the dusty scenarios of Francis Parkman and George Wrong. This is puzzling because most chapter bibliographies—which obviously change much faster than the texts themselves—contain the corrective works of William Eccles.[31] It is a mystery how anyone, after reading Eccles, can write that the French *habitants* were "serfs" or "peasants," that New France was a "feudal" society under an "almost completely autocratic regime," that the French colonies "never prospered," that the French population was only 2,000 when the crown took over in 1660 (it was 1663), that French *coureurs de bois* brought packs of "deerskins" to Montreal on "packhorse," that the Jesuit missionaries "made few permanent converts," and that "the natives were folded into the French Canadians," in Morison's half-baked simile, "as a pastry-cook folds butter into pie-crust dough."[32] Anyone who can write, as Bailey did, that "the lasting effect" of French influence, "ex-

cept in Canada [!], was not great" has obviously never visited Louisiana, the Great Lakes states, northern New England, or the old Illinois country around Ste. Genevieve
and Kaskaskia.³³

More than errors and misconceptions mar the average
textbook account of the Age of Discovery. Most alarming
to the ethnohistorian are ethnocentric or inaccurate characterizations of Indians. Authors who still use words and
phrases like "red man," "superstitious," "primitive," "half-
breeds," "massacre," "French and Indian wars," "war-
whooping," "feathered foes, " "painted allies," and "tawny-
skinned pagan aborigines" need a crash course in cultural
relativism and ethnic sensitivity.³⁴

Of greater concern, perhaps, is the ineffective, misleading, often distracting use of visual materials. It is difficult
not to share Jacques Barzun's recent regret that the heavy
use of visuals encourages the unfortunate habit of hop,
skip, and jump in "the most continuous [and] integrated of
all subjects." "Each double spread in quarto size," he has
written, "is filled with pictures, maps, charts, and diagrams
in four colors. Among these islands of attraction there is a
black and white river of printed text meandering irregularly and looking as superfluous as the prose of a good
display ad. Picture and caption do all the work."³⁵ There is
no doubt that publishers go too far in this glitzy direction.
Whole-page pictures, particularly of simple portraits, are
unnecessary, especially when detailed maps and engravings often cry out for enlargement. When the portrait features an anonymous child pointing to a contemporary
Latin map of the Chesapeake, both obviously without
historical importance or relevance to the text, you know
that Madison Avenue has invaded the offices of the pub-
lisher.³⁶

Worse yet is the use of fictionalized, nineteenth-century

engraved portraits from the Bettmann Archive and pictures that do not teach. Indian baskets and bowls, no matter how beautifully wrought, are boring and pedagogically
useless, as are John White's drawing of an Indian couple
eating, an unfocused, ultra-linear rendition of Tenochtitlán from *National Geographic*, a Massachusetts Bay Colony seal on which the Indians' alleged request "Come over
and help us" is illegible, and an engraving of the ordinary
exterior of the great silver mountain at Potosí.[37] Poor captions only compound the injury inflicted by ill-chosen illustrations. The use of Theodor de Bry's engraving of a Florida Indian farming scene to illustrate the sexual division of
native labor is misleading if the caption does not also point
out that the artist depicted the fields as plowed European-
style rather than hilled Indian-style and the horseshoe-
crab hoes as one-piece monstrosities.[38]

As someone who uses hundreds of slides in his teaching,
I applaud the judicious use of visual materials in history
books of all kinds. Despite some exceptions, the sixteen
textbooks under study contain some excellent illustrations.
Among the most evocative and useful are new maps of
western African cultures and slaving ports, the world
known to Europeans in 1492, and a satellite view of North
America in 1650 looking west from Europe; Indian smallpox victims from an Aztec codex and a syphilitic man by
Dürer; engravings of Luther in the pulpit overlooking
Catholic officials in the mouth of hell and of an eighteenth-
century western African village beside a field of Indian
corn; a fancy German box of Oriental spices displayed like
jewels; and a colorful painting of Canadian *voyageurs* pulling canoes on sledges over a frozen river.[39] These illustrations are keyed to the text and served by ample captions
that highlight their historical (rather than aesthetic) value.
Although they do interrupt the flow of the printed page, as

Barzun lamented, they are capable of teaching video-bred students about novel subjects in ways that prose alone can seldom match. When they are chosen and captioned well, they have the power to reify and reinforce the imaginative word.

In reading the sixteen texts, I was most struck not by misinformation and misconceptions, as plentiful as those were, but by lost opportunities. The authors' sins of omission seemed then, and seem now, much more serious than the venial sins of commission to which historians are all more or less prey. The things I missed in most of these textbooks are any hints of lively prose, evocative details, and an occasional quotation from contemporaries to relieve the tedium of arid generalizations and omniscient paraphrase. Unfortunately, when five or six of the most momentous events in Western history are crammed into twenty-five pages, nearly half of which are consumed by illustrations, liveliness and detail are the first victims.

As for missing contents, the list is rather long. Acceptable treatments are beginning to appear of the Irish precedents for English colonization, the African diaspora, disease, and various facets of mutual acculturation.[40] Two textbooks, those of Stephen Nissenbaum and Samuel Eliot Morison, even do justice to Columbus himself.[11] Yet the Age of Discovery is not fully explicable without attention to at least nine other subjects.

First, we textbook writers and teachers have to explain *why* Europeans needed spices, silks, furs, and fish; young, twentieth-century Americans simply do not know the sixteenth-century uses of such things. Second, Columbus's voyages to America are more faithfully rendered when put in the context of the crusading mentality of the Spanish *Reconquista* and of the Iberian experience in colonizing the

islands of the eastern Atlantic. The Spanish expulsion of
the Moors and Jews and the conquest of the Canaries led
directly to the reduction of the West Indies.

Third, since so much of the sixteenth century was devoted to maritime enterprise, we need to evoke for our
landlubbing students the smells, noises, and colors of the
sea, the volatile forces of wind and water, the constraints
and opportunities of nautical technology and navigation,
and the living conditions and jobs aboard various kinds of
sailing ships. We also need to make them regard the Atlantic as a highway rather than a moat. Fourth, we need to
evoke the changing geographies of our historical settings.
As Captain John Smith warned in 1624, "History without
Geography wandreth as a Vagrant without a certaine habi-
tation."[42] Richard Current was the only textbook author
who paid the least attention to the geography of colonial
North America and then only in a separate, generalized
section.[43]

Fifth, although texts are offering somewhat more accurate generalizations about Indians, we also need to portray
more accurately their politics, religions, economies, and
warfare (which usually appears only as a noisy, hair-raising
melee). To understand the making of Anglo-America is
impossible without close and sustained attention to its indigenous predecessors, allies, and nemeses.[44] A sixth need
is to describe at some length post-conquest society in the
Spanish empire and the nature of nonmilitary Indian relations, lest the Black Legend continue to skew our perspective and feed our WASPish delusions. Perhaps we could
begin to remedy the myth of Nordic superiority, as Salvador de Madariaga once suggested, by hanging our maps
with the South up and the North down.[45]

Seventh, it is time to integrate the Caribbean colonies
into the history of North America, rather than relegating

them to some warm-watery limbo. They were never far from the thoughts of colonial administrators and investors, and they should be as close to ours. In treating the West Indies, we should certainly describe the economic and political importance of privateering, which helped underwrite several mainland colonies. Eight, since American history textbooks dwell on the evolution of the United States, we would do well to pay much closer attention to the Spanish borderlands in the Southeast and Southwest. We need more than the obligatory bow to St. Augustine and Coronado if we are to explain the nation's evolving history and the enduring Hispanic legacy in those regions. How refreshing it would be to find a textbook that began on the West Coast before treating the traditional eastern colonies and then worked in opposite directions toward a late eighteenth-century meeting at the Mississippi.

To make it work, we need to fill the ninth and, to my mind, largest gap—the full story of French experience, not only in Canada but also in the Great Lakes and the Ohio, Mississippi, and Missouri valleys. Textbooks must explain why, suddenly in 1689, the French set upon the hapless English colonies, as well as what the French had been doing in Canada since Quebec was founded and how they procured their Indian allies. In a battle for pages, I would argue that the French affected the course of North American history much more than did the Spanish and therefore deserve considerably more coverage than they are currently getting, which is an error-ridden pittance. If we could address all of these important omissions, our students might have a fighting chance to grasp the deep significance of the sixteenth century, not only for American history but for the history of the world. As it is now, they are bound by the vital omissions from and gagged by the stylistic aridity of our textbooks.

Why are the opening chapters of our textbooks so inadequate? The task of explaining the Age of Discovery is made largely impossible by the way we divide our survey courses at Reconstruction. This arbitrary division forces us to cover nearly 400 years in the first semester and little more than a fourth as much time in the second. Not only is this pedagogical nonsense but it smacks of egregious whiggism as well: the closer we get to the present, the more important events become. It also ignores the origins of American society, which, like all origins, contain the seeds, roots, and even stems of later developments.[46]

Another unfortunate constraint on the first chapters is the textbooks' national focus. If we enter the New World in 1492 blinkered by the future boundaries of the United States, we are unlikely to do justice to the complex relations between geography, history, and culture on that vast hemispheric stage or to the non-English colonizers and natives who played their own important parts on it. To these reasons, we should add the peculiar pressures on academic publishers, who are often forced by politics and mass-market economics to pitch their products to the lowest common denominator. Thus, language, explanation, organization, and controversy are oversimplified. As the "lightning rods of American society," textbooks frequently attract too much social static to allow them to present the full and complicated truth about the past.[47]

Closer to home, many of our failures in writing textbooks are attributable to the authors' relative lack of preparation. The writers of single-authored texts are seldom trained in colonial history, and the colonial experts of multi-authored texts are seldom familiar with the sixteenth century. Since the Boltonian generation, American colonial historians have virtually neglected the histories of non-English empires—the Spanish, Dutch, and Portuguese but particularly the French. Because more colonialists were trained in New England and the Northeast, they absorbed the residual Black and Black Robe legends of their mentors, who were nursed on William H. Prescott and Francis Parkman. The result is a regrettable if understandable ignorance of the historiographies of Hispanic and Franco-America, not to mention maritime history and ethnohistory. If the bibliographies of the textbook chapters are any indication, their authors are not reading the latest or best literature, or, if they are, their notes are not making it to the text. Of course, some acquaintance with the primary sources of the period would serve as a firm rudder in the shoals of a vast and turbulent historiography. With the publication of David Quinn's five-volume *New American World* and John Parry's and Robert Keith's *New Iberian World,* authors no longer have an excuse to procrastinate.[48]

It behooves me to end on a more positive note and to offer some concrete suggestions to the authors, publishers, and users of textbooks. As a bare minimum, we need to double the space allocated to the Age of Discovery. Even if no one else had written a word, Quinn's twenty-four books should force American historians to take seriously the sixteenth century and its colonial legacies. It follows that multi-author textbook teams should include a comparative colonialist to handle the first 200 years, roughly from the 1480s to 1689. It is simply unreasonable to expect one person to master the first 300 years of American history, including the American Revolution, when two, often three, people are needed to cover the last 125 years. And, although a broad knowledge of the colonial Americas is required, no one should be hired to write a textbook who does not possess enough imagination and stylistic punch to capture and hold the fractured attention of TV-teethed and Walkman-weaned teenagers.

My advice to these scholarly paragons is to buck tradition

and insist on two freedoms: first, total responsibility for choosing illustrations, drafting maps, and writing captions, so as to integrate all three with the text; second, the right to restore to the text page a modicum of historical concreteness and fuller explanations of causation, even at the risk of sacrificing some topical coverage or visual material. To their publishers, I offer two related suggestions: give authors more conceptual and stylistic rein, and, when the manuscript is submitted, ask experts on exploration, Indians, European empires, and African history to critique it with as much rigor as an honorarium can buy.

Finally, for the adopters and readers of textbooks, I have two suggestions. Stop adopting textbooks that are hopelessly outdated, stylistically painful, and cratered with crucial omissions. By exercising your options in the free market, you can eventually secure the pulping of the worst books and initiate the writing of better ones. Second, pressure the better journals into the regular reviewing of textbooks. Specialized journals such as the *William and Mary Quarterly, Journal of the Early Republic, Ethnohistory,* and *Labor History* should be encouraged to commission periodic review essays of the treatment of their specialties by the current crop of textbooks, similar to this initiative. Such a strategy would do much more for the future quality of our textbooks than would the generalized overviews offered by *The History Teacher*. If our goal is to capture new audiences for history, we must first ensure that we do not alienate the one captive audience we have.

CHAPTER NINE

The Columbian Mosaic
in Colonial America

NATIONAL ANNIVERSARIES CALL FORTH RELATIVELY CIR-
cumscribed efforts from historians. The centennial and sesqui-
centennial celebrations of revolutions, constitutions, and wars
are largely bounded by those events—short in duration, narrow
in geography, and often limited in global significance. The quincentenary of the Columbian Encounter, however, is very different. It commemorates rather than celebrates the forging of a
single world from hitherto isolated continental and insular fragments, not by a single sailor in a single year but by the mutual
action of the inhabitants of all those lands over half a millen
nium. Historians called upon to treat that expansive theme have
their work cut out for them.

Early in March 1989 the New Jersey Historical Commission
invited me and three other historians to address their annual
public meeting in December of the following year on the social
impact of the Age of Discovery on Africa, America, and Europe.
My assignment was the (to me) daunting one of concluding the
conference with a forty-five-minute discussion of "the general
nature of colonial North American society resulting from an
amalgamation of western European, Native American, and West
African societies." Since the conference was to be held in Princeton, where several friends live, I accepted the assignment with
some alacrity but no little dread.

Although I conjured up a generic title within a month, I had no clear idea about how or where to proceed until the summer of 1990, when several looming deadlines made me apply pants to chair and mind to matter. I chose *mosaic* as the key concept because the notion of "melting pot" was inaccurate even for the late nineteenth and twentieth century which it was supposed to describe. There was little *mixing* of cultures in colonial America and even less *amalgamation*, so I took my cue from John Porter's sociological description of modern Canada, *The Vertical Mosaic*.*

Given my time limit and audience, I also felt obliged to restrict my focus to British North America, what became the future United States, and to only glance at New Spain and New France for notable contrasts. Finally, "covering" with anything like responsibility three hundred years of complicated social history was out of the question. At best, I could only hope to suggest the nature and magnitude of change between 1492 and 1790 by juxtaposing two snapshots of North America, taken at each end of the period, and hinting at some of the causes of difference.

An abbreviated version of this essay, *sans* footnotes, was published in *Humanities* [National Endowment for the Humanities], 12:5 (Sept./Oct. 1991), 12–18.

AFTER THE REVOLUTION, THE NEW UNITED STATES were a source of great curiosity to citizens of the Old World. Not only had the American upstarts pulled off the biggest small-r republican coup in recent memory, they had beaten the greatest empire in the modern world in the process. Who were these brash new giant-killers? What kind of societies had they fashioned in the American wilderness? How did they manage to wrest their new country from its aboriginal inhabitants? Where did their wealth—and audacity—come from? What manner of folks were

*(Toronto, 1965).

they and how did they differ from their European cousins?

To find the answers to these and similar questions, a veritable host of European travelers and sightseers struck off on tours of America in the 1780s and '90s, usually in a north-south direction. Men of every major nation in Europe made the grand tour from New England to South Carolina, often in the company of countrymen or servants. Sometimes they combined their trips with other business— military, scientific, political, or mercantile. But each visitor sought to encompass the regional and human diversity of the former colonies, as if their letters and journals would give Europe its only true and accurate portrait of the new nation.

In their uneven progress through the land, the visitors, like all tourists, tended to generalize from the small range of details they had seen with their own eyes and from the accumulated lore of new, often chance, acquaintances. When, for instance, Francisco de Miranda, the gifted Venezuelan revolutionary, toured Connecticut in 1783, he inferred from tombstones in a Norwich churchyard that "this place is highly salutary, for the age dates are quite high, and among them I counted more than twelve between eighty and ninety years of life."[1] Similarly, Louis-Philippe, the future king of France, noticed that in the Shenandoah Valley of Virginia, the young people reached "notable heights." Most of them, he said, "seem taller than their elders" and are "increasing still."[2] These and other observations on the bounty of American farms suggested that the great white middling population, at least, was experiencing exceptional health and an enviable amount of prosperity. The most prosperous colony of all, Pennsylvania, had had on the eve of revolution a population of 350,000, some 275,000 of whom Moreau de St. Méry estimated to have been "Foreigners, all bought" as indentured servants or redemptioners. Twenty years later, they, too, were enjoying the salubrity of the state's economy and climate and reproducing like rabbits.[3]

But for everyone who prospered, there were many who suffered, usually those of a darker complexion. Johann David Schoepf, a learned scientist stationed in America with the Hessian troops until 1783, noted that even German and Irish indentured servants were unwilling to be sold in Carolina and Virginia because "they are too proud to work with and among the negroes who . . . are almost the only working people" in those states. "Any [white] man whatever, if he can afford so much as 2–3 negroes, becomes ashamed of work and goes about in idleness, supported by his slaves." Most visitors choked on the blatant disparity between a republic founded on the philosophical freedom of man and the actual bondage of men who happened not to be white. Schoepf could not decide to laugh or cry over a North Carolina slave sale where the auctioneer talked up the slaves' qualities while the "merchandise" sassily downgraded themselves from the platform "because they knew well that the dearer their cost, the more work will be required of them."[4] Having fled the excesses of the French Revolution in 1793, the West Indian-born Moreau de St. Méry was appalled that white American children "beat little slaves and if grown-up slaves try to interfere, adult whites beat them in turn."[5] Virtually every visitor agreed that slaves were treated more harshly in the South than in the North. The Italian naturalist Luigi Castiglioni heard a South Carolina planter "justify his vicious behavior toward negroes" by declaring "without blushing that they were a kind of animal closer to monkeys than to man."[6]

By contrast with the imported Africans and Europeans, the most American group of all received hardly any notice from the travelers unless they happened to venture into the still-dangerous "back-country." For in the settled portions of the new states, native Americans were in very short supply, restricted largely to tiny reservations. In his discussion of the racial composition of Philadelphia, Moreau de St. Méry felt no need to speak of Indians, he said, because "they inhabit only such places as are set apart for them; and if they appear in cities . . . it is always for some political reason."[7] In South Carolina the Catawbas called twelve square miles home, while in spacious New York, said Chateaubriand, "the remains of the [once-mighty] five Iroquois nations [are] enclaved in the English and American possessions."[8] When a young Oneida Iroquois returned to Boston in 1788 after three years of French education, testified a fellow passenger, Brissot de Warville, "he caused as much surprise as he had in Paris, for Indians are never seen there. They have been gone from Massachusetts for so long that people have forgotten what one looks like."[9] The outlook for their western cousins was no brighter, according to the French general, the marquis de Chastellux. In 1780 he had predicted with uncanny but sad accuracy that "a necessary consequence of a peace, if favorable to Congress, will be their total destruction, or at least their exclusion from all the country this side of the [Great] lakes."[10]

For all their perspicacity, acquired knowledge, and luck, those traveling ethnographers invariably missed the big picture of New America. Like all tourists, they suffered from the myopia of personal experience. How could it have been otherwise? They were virtually all white, male, foreign, insulated by wealth, class, or connections, and traveling low to the ground. While they could read about the conventional histories of some of their destinations, before or after leaving, and could pick up assorted facts and gossip en route, they were essentially prisoners of their own eyes and expectations. Since they were short of time, they took only one road, usually well worn, through a region, leaving 99 percent of its byways and precincts un-explored. Understandably, they gravitated to towns and great houses, where they could obtain bugless bedding, clean laundry, credit, and a soupçon of society, but in the process they missed much of the country, in both senses.

One source they might have used to trace the social pro-file of the new America, had it been available to them, was the first Federal census of 1790. In addition to the un-counted and undercounted, the new United States of nearly 900,000 square miles was populated by almost 4 million people, black and white. A few over 3 million were white, three-quarters of a million—19 percent—were black. Ninety-five percent of these folks still lived in the country; only 24 towns could count more than 2500 inhab-itants. More than a third of America's households con-tained seven or more persons, though the average was not quite six. Predictably, the white population was predomi-nantly British in origin: nearly 80 percent had English, Scottish, or Irish surnames.[11]

But one group was conspicuous by its absence from the census figures: according to the new U.S. Constitution, Indians who were "not taxed" were excluded from the count, and that meant virtually all Indians, who were ei-ther too poor or too inaccessible to fall prey to the tax collector. Therefore, the social portrait the census paints is strictly chiaroscuro; we don't really know how much burnt umber ought to be added to America's features. In one large region, however, we have a good idea. Historian Pe-ter Wood's detailed demography of the colonial Southeast shows that Indians in 1790 numbered about 56,000, or 3 percent of the population. More than a third of all south-erners were black, more than a million were white.[12] But that was the South, and the complexion of other regions was much paler. In Massachusetts, for instance, the black population was only 5000, less than $1\frac{1}{2}$ percent of the total; Indians numbered only a few hundred.[13] In 1790, tourists and census-takers alike saw mostly white faces in the new Republic.

Whatever the regional proportions, newly independent America was a triracial, multicultural society. It was a "mosaic" rather than a "melting pot," a huge, constantly changing, imperfect amalgamation of biologies, histories, and anthropologies. Perhaps the best way to view such a restless and complex organism is to look at it over time by twisting the eyepiece of an historical kaleidoscope. For each twist in time will tumble the multicolored human fragments in space, throwing them into strikingly new patterns of American density and destiny.

We might well call America a *Columbian* mosaic because it was the Italian admiral who effectively bound together all of the world's continents with the shipping lanes of one continuous ocean sea. When Columbus bumped into America en route to Asia after a maritime apprenticeship in Europe and Africa, he made it likely—indeed, inevitable—that the peoples of the world's insular continents would no longer live in splendid isolation but would soon become a single "global village," due largely to European colonialism, technology, and communications. Although he never set foot on the North American continent, he was personally responsible for introducing Europeans to America, and Americans—albeit in chains— to Europe. It was left to Nicolás de Ovando, his successor as governor of the Indies, to introduce African slaves in 1502, just as Columbus set sail on his fourth and final voyage.[14] The paternity of triracial America is not in doubt; the only question is, how did the new American mosaic of 1790 come about?

One short but hardly sweet answer, which is increasingly heard as we enter 1992, is that Columbus and his European successors found a "virgin" paradise of innocence and harmony and proceeded to rape the land, kill the natives, and pillage Africa to replace the American victims of their "genocide."[15] There is, of course, some truth to that, but not enough to be morally useful or historically truthful. If we can take our itchy fingers off the trigger of moral outrage for a spell, we might be able to view the human phase of what is being called the "Columbian Encounter" less as an excuse for passing judgment than as a vehicle for understanding. For in the ideological climate of the 1990s, where our collective skin is paper-thin and intolerance has been raised to an art form, we stand in sore need of some critical distance from the irreproducible problems of the past. Instead of picking through the bone heaps of history for skeletons to line the closets of our current nemeses, we might better cultivate a little disinterestedness toward both the failings *and* successes of our predecessors, in hopes of taking courage and counsels of prudence from their struggles and solutions. Since their circumstances, their field of experiences, opportunities, and limitations, are never the same as ours, we cannot draw universal *laws* from their example, good or ill. We can only try to emulate their good example and to avoid their worst mistakes by paying close attention to the historical circumstances in which they acted, by recognizing that their time is not our time, and that we must be equally alert to the complexity and uniqueness of our own circumstances as we strive to thread a moral path through the present.[16] Perhaps then we can recognize that the social mosaic of the 1990s is the lineal descendant of the 1790s, and that, although in one sense we cannot change the *facts* of history, we can, through a critical and disinterested examination of its *causes,* suggest a few ways to improve the personal and group relations we continue to fashion in the modern American mosaic.

A test of our moral mettle and patience arises as soon as we begin to discuss the influx of Europeans or "white" people into monochromatic Indian America. On the simplest level, what do we *call* the process and the participants? Since all language is loaded with value judgments, it makes quite a difference whether we refer to the process as *colonization, imperialism, settlement, emigration,* or *invasion.* (For reasons both historical and moral, my major lecture course at William and Mary is called "The Invasion of North America.") By the same token, were the newcomers *imperialists, conquistadors, invaders, trespassers,* and *killers,* or were they, on balance, only *Europeans, whites, colonists, strangers,* and *settlers?* If modern Indians ought to have their wishes respected as to the generic names by which historians refer to their native ancestors, surely the descendants of European colonists should be accorded the same courtesy (recognizing, of course, that there may be stylistic or other reasons for not fully granting either group's wishes).[17] It has long been one of the cardinal rules of the historical canon—one I see no reason to lay aside—that the parties of the past deserve equal treatment from historians—equal respect and empathy but also equal criticism and justice. As judge, jury, prosecutor, and counsel for the defense of people who can no longer testify on their own behalf, the historian cannot be any less than impartial in his or her judicial review of the past. For that reason, I suggest, we should avoid language that is inflammatory or pre-prejudicial to any historical person or party. Which is *not* to say that, once we have *proven* our case, we may not call a spade a spade, an imperialist tool, or a killer of innocent worms. If we have presented the pertinent evidence on all sides of the issue with fairness and accuracy, our audience can make up their own minds about the judiciousness of our verdicts.

How, then, did the face of America become so blanched when only three hundred years earlier it had been uniformly brown? The short answer is that Europeans emigrated in great numbers to the Americas and, when they got there, reproduced themselves with unprecedented success. But a somewhat fuller explanation must take account of regional and national variations.

The first emigrants, of course, were Spanish, not merely the infamous conquistadors, whose bloody feats greatly belied their small numbers, but Catholic priests and missionaries, paper-pushing clerks and officials who manned the far-flung bureaucracy of empire, and ordinary settlers: peasants, artisans, merchants, and not a few hidalgos, largely from the cities and towns of central and southwestern Spain. Since permission to emigrate was royally regulated, "undesirables" such as Moors, Jews, gypsies, and those condemned by the Inquisition reached the New World only in small, furtive numbers. In the sixteenth century perhaps 240,000 Spaniards slipped into American ports. They were joined by 450,000 more in the next century. The great majority were young men; only in the late sixteenth century did the proportion of women reach one-third. This meant that many men had to marry, or at least cohabit with, Indian women, which in turn gave rise to a large *mestizo* or mixed population. The relative unhealthiness of Latin America's subtropical islands and coasts also contributed to a slow and modest increase in Spanish population. When the mature population finally doubled by 1628, it had taken more than fifty years and only half the increase was due to biology; the other half was contributed by emigrants from home.[18]

In sharp contrast to the Spanish were the French in Canada, which Voltaire dismissed as "a few acres of snow." In a century and a half, Mother France sent only 30,000 emigrants to the Laurentian colony, the majority of them against their will. Only a few hundred paid their own way, many of them merchants eager to cash in on the fur and import trade. The rest were reluctant *engagés* (indentured servants), soldiers, convicts (primarily salt smugglers), and *filles du roi* or "King's girls," sent to supply the colony's superabundant, shorthanded, and lonely bachelors with wives. Not until 1710 were the Canadian genders balanced. But even in the seventeenth century, Canadiennes married young and produced often, doubling the population at least every thirty years. Fortunately for their Indian hosts and English neighbors, this high rate of natural increase was wasted on a minuscule base population. When Wolfe climbed to the Plains of Abraham in 1759, New France had only 75,000 Frenchmen, a deficit of colonial population on the order of 30 to 1.[19]

The biggest source of white faces in North America was Great Britain. In the seventeenth century she sent more than 150,000 of her sons and daughters to the mainland colonies and at least 350,000 more in the next. In 1690, white folks numbered around 194,000; a hundred years later they teemed at 3 million-plus.[20] Emigration obviously accounted for some of this astounding growth. In the eighteenth century, 150,000 Scotch-Irish, 100,000 Germans (many of them "redemptioners" from the Palatinate), 50,000 British convicts, and 2000–3000 Sephardic Jews made their way to English lands of opportunity.[21] But the proliferation of pale faces was predominantly a function of natural increase by which the colonial population doubled every twenty-five years, to that time the highest rate of increase known to demographers. After an initial period of "gate mortality," when food shortages, new diseases, and climatic "seasoning" might exact a high toll, white couples in most of the English colonies began to produce an average of four children who lived to become parents themselves.[22]

The reasons for their success were mainly two: in the words of Ben Franklin, "marriages in *America* are more general, and more generally early, than in *Europe*."[23] Colonial women married at the age of 21 or 22, about four or five years sooner than their European sisters, and they remarried quickly if their helpmates died, both in part because men tended to outnumber women. When their children were born (at the normal European rate), fewer died in infancy and childhood (before the ages of one and ten, respectively) and fewer mothers died in childbed. Women continued to have babies every two years, in the absence of Catholic prohibitions (as in Latin America and Canada) and birth control (except that partially provided by breast-feeding). But American mothers were healthier and lived longer than European mothers, thanks to sparser settlements, larger farms, more fertile land, fuller larders of nutritious food, and less virulent diseases. They therefore produced larger, taller, and healthier families, who in turn did the same.[24]

The results of all this fecundity were impressive to imperial administrators, catastrophic for the Indians. The Powhatans of Virginia could not have been too alarmed by the initial wave of English settlers and soldiers because 80 percent of them died of their own ineptitude and disease. But by 1640 the pale-faced population had recovered from the deadly uprising of 1622 to reach some 10,000, largely through persistent supplies from England. By 1680 the contest for the colony had been decisively won by the tobacco-planting English, who now outnumbered the natives about 20 to 1.[25]

Massachusetts, the other pole of archetypal Anglo-America, grew even faster. From only 9000 Puritans in 1640, the commonwealth of the cod spurted to 150,000 within a century, owing largely to unpuritanical bedroom behavior; Boston alone housed over 15,000 people.[26] But the fastest growing region, both by emigration and nature, was eighteenth-century Pennsylvania. Between 1690 and 1790, "the best poor man's country" (as its fans liked to describe it) saw its white population increase 38-fold. On the eve of independence, Philadelphia was the largest and most diverse city in North America, filled with religious denominations, ethnic groups, and social strata of every imaginable stripe. The Iroquois and Delaware chiefs who came to be wooed to neutrality or the rebel cause in the imminent war cannot have failed to be daunted by its 25,000 crowded inhabitants.[27]

Yet numbers alone do not allow us to draw a moral bead on the early American story. We must not only know *how many* Europeans emigrated to—or invaded—Indian America but *why*. For without an understanding of their motives, we cannot treat them as moral agents with choices to make or hold them accountable for the foreseen and foreseeable consequences of their actions. The one thing we can be sure of is that they came for a wide and usually mixed variety of reasons. At the beginning of the "Great Migration" to Massachusetts, even a Puritan promoter harbored no illusions about the exclusivity or purity of the migrants' motives. "As it were absurd to conceive they have all one motive," wrote John White in *The Planter's Plea,* "so were it more ridiculous to imagine they have all one scope. . . . It may be private interests may prevail with some. One brother may draw over another, a son the father, and perhaps some man his inward acquaintance. . . . Necessity may press some, novelty draw on others, hopes of gain in time to come may prevail with a third sort."[28]

For many, but by no means all, settlers of New England, religion played a key role in their decision to uproot their families and move to America. But religious motives did not always guarantee the health, sovereignty, or well-being of the American natives. Believers who wished simply to practice their own faiths without persecution, real or imagined, may be let off the hook, unless, of course, like the

Puritans, their own intolerance and desire for a state monopoly led them to proscribe the natives' worship of their own gods. On the other hand, French nuns and missionaries were sent to Canada by visions of transforming the "pagan" wilderness into a "new Jerusalem," where nomadic native souls "washed white in the blood of the [paschal] lamb" would join good French Catholics to form "one [sedentary] people." New English missionaries not only reduced the native landbase by resettling the Indians in smaller, anglicized "praying towns" but inadvertently increased their neophytes' risk of contagious disease. In other words, good intentions alone are not sufficient to exempt historical actors from criticism, and history, unlike the law, has no statute of limitations.[29]

Other motives are equally hard to condemn wholesale. Can we blame ordinary European farmers, craftsmen, and merchants for wanting to forge a better life for their families, even if they wound up on land that once belonged to America's native inhabitants? The vast majority of immigrants hardly, if ever, *saw* the original owners, much less cheated or forced them from their land. Even male freeholders seldom knew about the backroom chicanery of their elected representatives who speculated with ill-gotten Indian lands. Much less could the voters control the machinations of imperial officials and army officers who wheeled and dealed for the same sorts of native property. If we blame ordinary colonists for wanting lower taxes, less crowding, more land, higher wages, healthier climates, more and better food, and family harmony, we will have to include ourselves in the blame—and most of the human race, for that matter. Collective guilt of such magnitude doesn't seem very productive.

On the other hand, immigrants were not only drawn to America but pushed out of Europe. Many shipped out because they were trying to run away from something:

death sentences, debtor's prison, bishop's courts, oppressive seigneurial dues, recruiting sergeants. We may have little sympathy for those who chose to evade their civil responsibilities and the law, but what about the scrupulous avoiders of sin and immorality, who ran from drinking, gambling, and wanton women as if from the plague? Should we cut no slack for poor henpecked husbands who fled from shrews and harridans, or young women who could not wait an extra four or five years to marry and start a family? How hardened do we have to become to withhold our empathy from young servants who escaped abusive masters or young lovers kept apart by flinty or tight-fisted patriarchs?

If we want to take a hardnosed stance on the spoiling, illegitimate, or immoral character of white immigration, we would do better to focus on those who came solely to highjack America's wealth to Europe, often with the help, witting or unwitting, of its native owners and trustees, or those who carried war and destruction to Indian country, directly or indirectly in pursuit of geopolitical objectives of a European sort. Obviously it is easier to pillory the designers, and to some extent the agents, of military and economic imperialism than it is the run-of-the-mill emigrant who carried no conscious intent to defraud, harm, or dispossess anyone. Oppressive Spanish mine owners, freebooting pirates, absentee owners of West Indian sugar plantations, and fork-tongued traders who swindled Indians of their furs and skins with watered rum and false measures undoubtedly deserve our censure, mostly because they contravened the moral standards of their own day, less, perhaps, because those standards resemble our own.

At the same time, we should recognize that to condemn every aggressive military, religious, or economic action in the past is to question some of the fundaments of Western society, past *and present*. If everything associated with mercantilism, capitalism, evangelical religion, and armed force is beyond the moral pale, we may find it difficult, if not impossible, to approach our past—or the histories of most of the world's cultures—with the requisite empathy, understanding, and disinterestedness.

Another topic that requires an abundance of all three qualities but allows ample room for moral judgment is slavery. Nineteen percent of the human shards in the social mosaic of the new United States were black, the result of a legal, culturally sanctioned, but heinous trade in African slaves.[30] The slave trade was already ancient by the time America was brought into the European orbit in 1492. But the discovery of gold, the development of sugar plantations, and the founding of cities in Spanish and Portuguese America created a vast new market for the human chattels brought from the African interior by rival African kings, merchants, and war chiefs.[31]

Before independence, the Spanish alone transported 1.5 million blacks to their colonies, perhaps 200,000 before 1650. In the Caribbean the blacks replaced Indian laborers, who died in massive numbers from oppression, dislocation, and imported diseases. By the seventeenth century, the native populations of Mexico and coastal Peru were also seriously depleted, so black slaves were substituted as panners of gold (they died too easily in the cold damp of the mines), cutters of sugar cane, sailors, shipwrights, and particularly domestic servants in urban households. They did their work so well that by the eighteenth century the majority of blacks were free, especially the women and children of the cities who were manumitted by their owners at death or by purchase.[32]

In Canada the French preferred Indian slaves from the eastern Plains and Great Lakes called *panis* (after the Pawnees of modern-day Nebraska). In 125 years they imported only 1,132 Africans (fewer than ten a year), mostly as household servants in Quebec and Montreal. Since they were expensive and relatively rare, their lot was not onerous and, contrary to expectations, they adjusted to the Canadian winters with little difficulty.[33]

But their brethren in French Louisiana had a much harder row to hoe, to judge from the mortality rates. Between 1719 and 1735, royal and company administrators imported some 7000 Africans, mostly "Bambaras," or acculturated slave soldiers, from Senegal. Yet in 1735 only 3400 remained to be counted. The same loss of life must have occurred during the next fifty years: over 20,000 arrived but the black population in 1785 was only 16,500. Even immigration could not keep pace with Louisiana's morbid climate and the physical demands of plantation labor.[34]

The English demand for black labor grew much more slowly than did the Spanish, largely because the supply of indentured servants from the British Isles was adequate until the late seventeenth century. With the renewal of tobacco prices in Europe and the development of rice culture in South Carolina, however, English planters in the tidewater and the piedmont alike had a need for hands that could not be fully met with white workmen, who in any event often proved troublesome to the colonial elite upon gaining their freedom. So the planters turned primarily to "seasoned" slaves from the West Indies to fill the gap. Thanks to an increase in the African traffic in colonial and British bottoms, the price of a strong male slave remained a bargain when amortized over a lifetime. But after 1720, demand for acculturated West Indian slaves outstripped the supply and 80 percent of the slaves for English plantations came directly from Africa.[35]

Black talent and energy were never equally distributed in time or space. In 1690, for example, both Maryland and

Connecticut had white populations of 21,000, but the New England colony had only 200 blacks to Maryland's nearly 2200. With double the white inhabitants, Virginia had more than four times the number of Maryland's blacks. Overall, the English mainland colonies could count fewer than 17,000 blacks, or 8 percent of the intrusive population. A hundred years later, more than three-quarters of a million blacks had moved into Indian America with their white masters.[36]

After 1680 the proliferation of black faces was especially noticeable in the South from the Chesapeake to South Carolina. In 1680, Virginia's social complexion had been only 7 percent black; by 1720 it was 30 percent. The proportion of blacks in South Carolina went from 17 to 70 percent in the same forty years, making it the only mainland colony with a black majority. And that was just the beginning: between 1730 and 1770, Anglo-America imported between 4000 and 7000 Africans every year. Strangely enough, even this influx did not amount to much on an international scale: only 4.5 percent of the 10 million slaves who survived capture and the horrendous "Middle Passage" to the New World were landed in the English mainland colonies. The vast majority went to the Caribbean, where their chances for living long were very slim, and to Latin America, where they were somewhat better. Although the condition of perpetual bondage was never easy, life on English farms and plantations—for economic more than humanitarian reasons—was tolerable enough to allow the black population to increase naturally as well as by constant infusions of new or "outlandish" Africans.[37]

Despite the uninvited presence of some four million Europeans and Africans, it could be argued—and was—that America in 1790 had plenty of elbow room for both natives and strangers. Even if the natives had been at full, pre-Columbian strength, some said, a slight change in their economy would have freed up enough land for all the newcomers without any noticeable pinch. By giving up the wild, nomadic life of the hunter for the taming, sedentary life of the farmer, the Indians (by which was meant male Indians) would require only a fraction of their former real estate and would be happy to swap the residue to their white neighbors for the more valuable blessings of civilization, such as Christianity, short hair, and long pants. And if for some perverse reason they did not like the sound of foreign neighbors, they could always move west, beyond the Mississippi where the white man would never think of moving.[38]

But of course the natives were *not* at full strength in 1790 and their room for maneuvering was greatly circumscribed by nearly three hundred years of cultural crowding and numerical decline. In the South, where they were at their strongest, they had suffered a 72 percent drop in population since 1685, while the white settlers had multiplied 21 times and the blacks nearly 18 times. The hardest hit were the natives of eastern South Carolina, who went from 10,000 to 300 in a century, a loss of 97 percent. The Natchez and other Indians of the lower Mississippi were not far behind at 90 percent: at 4000 they were actually experiencing a slight rebound from a nadir of 3600 in 1760, but they had irretrievably lost 38,000 relatives since the seventeenth century. The Choctaws and Chickasaws, who had been able to play off the Louisiana French and the Carolina English before 1763, had lost only half their people, but the Cherokees, located closer to the English colonies, suffered a 75 percent decline.[39] The story in New England, Pennsylvania, and Virginia was no different: everywhere, the original inhabitants had been reduced to a fragile fraction of their former selves and an even smaller minority of the states' new citizens. How had this come about?

Contemporaries who wishfully asserted that eastern America was big enough for everyone made one large, erroneous assumption about the Indian economy: they assumed that the natives were primarily hunters who chased wild game over the whole map. In fact, the Indians in the huge area claimed by the kings of England subsisted primarily on vegetables—corn, beans, and squash—cultivated by the women in the most fertile soils available. Among these three-season fields they lived in semipermanent towns and villages ranging from several hundred to a couple of thousand inhabitants. Although the women provided 50–75 percent of the annual diet, native men did have to range far and wide for the rest. Until the men could be persuaded by white reason or necessity to obtain their protein from domestic cattle and pigs rather than fish and game, the natives were forced to guard their extensive hunting and fishing grounds as jealously as they defended their villages and fields.

The advent of European farmers in search of those same cleared and fertile fields put them on a predestinate collision course with the Indians. Initially, there was no question of sharing the best soils because in most areas the native population pressed hard against the carrying capacity of the environment and fully occupied most of the prime farm land. The issue that was to be decided over the next three centuries was whether one intrusive group of farmers (and land speculators) would replace another, indigenous group of farmers. How this was in fact done varied from colony to colony. But in general the English (and their reluctant black helpers) prevailed by out-reproducing the natives and bringing about their precipitous decline as independent peoples.

The Indians could not reproduce themselves because their mortality rates far outstripped their birth rates. The single greatest cause of native deaths was epidemic diseases imported from Europe without malice aforethought. In the "virgin soil" populations of the Americas, European afflictions such as smallpox, typhus, diphtheria, measles, mumps, and whooping cough—many of them childhood diseases—turned adult killers because the natives had acquired no immunities to them. Ignorant of their causes, the Indians treated them like familiar ailments by immersing patients in a sweatlodge and then into the nearest body of cold water. If this did not kill them, lack of fire, water, and elementary nursing usually did because, in the absence of quarantine, virtually everyone contracted the disease at the same time.[40] In a shipborne plague of 1616, for example, the natives of coastal New England "died on heapes, as they lay in their houses." "The livinge being . . . not able to bury the dead, they were left for Crowes, Kites, and vermin to pray upon." One of the earlier English settlers compared the bone-strewn landscape to "a new found Golgatha."[41] And that was before either Pilgrim or Puritan stepped off the boat.

Throughout the colonies from the beginning of contact, Old World pathogens served as the shock troops of the European invasion, softening up the enemy before the battalions of busy farmers waded ashore. From the English standpoint, these were "preparative Stroakes" of divine providence. As a South Carolina governor put it so succinctly, "the Hand of God was eminently seen in thin[n]ing the Indians, to make room for the English."[42] And thin them He—or the diseases—did.

Smallpox was the worst scourge. In 1699 it typically swept away a whole nation in coastal South Carolina, "all [but] 5 or 6 which ran away and left their dead unburied, lying upon the ground for the vultures to devour."[43] Forty years later the Cherokees were cut in half by a contagion which had been "conveyed into Charlestown by the Guinea-men," as James Adair called African slaves, "and soon after among them, by . . . infected goods" carried on packtrain by English traders. The Cherokee medicine men attributed the epidemic to a polluting outbreak of "unlawful copulation" by young marrieds who "violated their ancient laws of marriage in every thicket" and bean-plot "in the night dews." A "great many" of those who survived the onslaught horribly killed themselves, not out of shame for their sacrilegious actions, but because they literally could not bear to live with the pock-marked faces they saw in their recently acquired hand mirrors.[44]

The second major horseman of the Indian apocalypse was war and the dislocation, starvation, and exposure that accompanied it. Most of the Anglo-Indian wars were named after the Indians involved: the "Powhatan Uprising"—or "Massacre"—of 1622, the "Pequot War" of 1637, "King Philip's War" of 1675 (named for the Wampanoag chief Metacomet who was dubbed King Philip by the English), the "Tuscarora War" of 1711, the "Yamasee War" of 1715, the ever-popular "French and Indian War" of 1754–63, and "Pontiac's Rebellion" of 1763. This should not surprise us because the victors have always written the histories and blamed the losers for instigating war in the first place. But in every "Indian" war in colonial America, the warring Indians invariably *reacted* to European provocations, usurpations, or desecrations, arrogations much more specific and serious than mere trespassing on Indian soil. Because quickly outnumbered by the prolific and technologically superior newcomers, the warring tribes or confederacy had to have their collective back to the wall or their stoical patience exhausted before they would risk armed conflict.

Their caution and forbearance were well placed, for once the aggressing colonists felt the sting of attack, they became in their own minds aggrieved victims with holy vengeance for their cause. Their retaliations were usually savage, if not particularly swift: their lack of defensive preparation was predicated on their disbelief that anyone could doubt their innocence. So the Indians suffered doubly. To take but one example, of some 11,600 natives in southern New England in 1675, King Philip's War claimed almost 7900 victims, or 68 percent of the belligerent population, in little more than a year: perhaps 1250 died in battle, 625 later died of wounds, 3000 succumbed to exposure and disease, 1000 were sold as slaves and transported out of the country, and 2000 became permanent refugees from their native land.[45]

In every English colony, native people found themselves regarded as environmental impediments to colonial "improvement," not unlike awkwardly placed swamps or undiscriminating wolves. If the crowding of the English did not kill them through war or contagion, the colonists developed an arsenal of tactics to wrest the land from them or to dispirit them enough to move "voluntarily." One way was to incite "civil" war between rival tribes and to reward one side for producing Indian slaves, who were then sold to the West Indies, often for more biddable black slaves.[46] Another was to play on the reasonable native regard for European trade goods, particularly cloth, metal tools, guns, and addictive alcohol. By extending credit, the English traders got the Indians into deep debt, which could not be settled without selling real estate or hunting the local fur-bearing fauna to extinction.[47]

But for effortless cunning, the third ploy took the cake. English farmers simply released their corn-loving cattle and swine into the natives' unfenced fields. The Indian plea on this score to the Maryland legislature in 1666 speaks eloquently for the plight of most coastal Algonquians in the seventeenth century. "Your hogs & Cattle injure Us, You come too near Us to live & drive Us from place to place," Mattagund complained matter of factly.

"We can fly no farther; let us know where to live & how to be secured for the future from the Hogs & Cattle."[48]

But of course the honorable assemblymen of Maryland had nothing to say. Like their successors in the national Congress of 1790, they sat on their hands as Indian America was slowly but inexorably transmuted into a lopsided mosaic—predominantly white and significantly black, with only a fading margin and a few shrinking islands of native brown.

CHAPTER TEN

Moral Reflections on the Columbian Legacy

THE IMPETUS GIVEN BY OUTSIDE INVITATIONS TO PUT one's thoughts on paper cannot be overvalued. Although invitations often arrive at inopportune moments (during final exams, the extraction of wisdom teeth, the arrival of a new baby), they almost always allow enough lead time to research, outline, and write the masterwork while ignoring only two other commitments and a trio of best laid plans. Occasionally, the results seem worth all the angst and you silently thank your persistent benefactors for providing both a text and a pretext for exercising your latent literary inclinations.

For this reason especially I am grateful to the Mead-Swing Lectureship Committee at Oberlin College for inviting me to talk about "the moral dimensions of the interaction of European and native American peoples in the wake of Columbus's voyages" in September 1990. I had just taught a course "The World of Columbus" and was eager to see what I thought about the whole messy "Encounter" by writing it down. I was also happy to accept because an old Yale and Cambridge friend, Fred Starr, was president and my younger son had attended the college not long before.

Having fulfilled my obligations to Oberlin, I was free to take the lecture on the road whenever a university or group wanted an unconventional slant on the Quincentenary, which happened frequently. And in December 1991 I gave an abbreviated version to a plenary session of the American Historical Association in Chicago. As a student and teacher of both "The Age of Exploration" and "The Invasion of North America" (my major courses at William and Mary), I regard "Moral Reflections" as my most generally useful contribution to the public and academic debate generated by the Quincentenary. If it does no more than make us extremely careful with the words we use to talk about 1492 and its aftermath, it will have served its purpose.*

AS WE HAVE SEEN IN RECENT YEARS, THERE ARE MANY ways to *celebrate* or *commemorate* or *observe* an historical anniversary; the mere choice of verbs gives some clue to the possibilities. We can manufacture and hawk T-shirts, bumperstickers, and Frisbees with official or unofficial logos of the event prominently displayed, preferably in red, white, and blue. We can appoint national commissions of tycoons, politicians, judges, and a token scholar or two to design the logos, subcontract the souvenirs, and bless if not coordinate the myriad public and private activities surrounding the anniversary. We can have our legislators read into the *Congressional Record* moving (if misleading) resolutions to recognize the historical importance of the occasion and even set aside a national holiday to honor it, if the business community will go along.

We can also mount a thousand parades on a declared day, give a thousand speeches, and sponsor a million grade-school essays on the theme. We can watch thirty-second "public service" spots on TV and certainly a tendentious talk-show or mendacious "made-for-TV" movie about the great event. We can let ourselves be cozened by

*See also James Axtell, "Forked Tongues: Moral Judgments in Indian History," *After Columbus: Essays in the Ethnohistory of Colonial North America* (New York, 1988), ch. 2.

the clever advertisements for new and used cars, toddler clothing, or hamburgers that stereotype, romanticize, lampoon, or otherwise trade on the celebrated event or hero. We might even buy a well-advertised biography or "historical" novel about our hero or a collector's set of commemorative coins from the Franklin Mint.

All of these commemorative acts and objects have one thing in common: they serve as icons or talismans of our touching (if fleeting) faith in the public resonance of past events, or, at the very least, in the corporate and national usefulness of recognizably "great" events. But the problem with public genuflection toward selected events in the past is threefold. First, we accept the meaning and importance of those events on *faith*, rather than constantly rediscovering and arguing about them. We *assume* what should be *proven*. Second, the public nature of our worship of the past—and the mass quality of our media coverage of it— numbs us to the need for *private* reflection. We assume that a congressional resolution or a docudramatic one-night-stand absolves us of any personal responsibility for interpreting and internalizing the meaning of the past, of making it a functional part of our own lives. And finally, the form in which our celebrated events are typically presented—drastically simplified, neatly packaged, and attractively wrapped, usually in the flag of national chauvinism or corporate altruism—prevents us from recognizing the events as they actually occurred, in all their manifold complexity and meaningful contextuality. Perhaps worst of all, such tidy presentations prevent us from confronting and grappling with the humanistic, the *moral*, meanings and implications which all of the large, messy, real events of the past hold for the present.

Certainly it would be a great pity if we were blinded by all the public hoopla and private hucksterism to the moral immensity of what we in the United States are calling the

244   BEYOND 1492

"Columbian Encounter." What we are commemorating five centuries after 1492 is not the textbook-simple event known as "the discovery of America," but the much more complicated, longer-range legacy of Columbus and the Europeans who sailed in his wake. For what Columbus set in motion was the creative recognition of a unified world, its continents and islands bound together in rounded space by a single navigable sea. In less abstract terms, Columbus and his nautical successors brought together, not an Old and a New World, but two ancient worlds whose former unity was irretrievably lost in geological time.[1]

In moral terms, the Columbian legacy was to bring into contact and often conflict not only the human populations of Asia, Africa, Europe, and the Americas but their plants, animals, and organisms, their institutions, values, and ideas. Inevitably, this global encounter of peoples and cultures raised a host of moral questions for contemporaries. It raises still more for us because we are the often direct legatees of those momentous encounters, many of whose consequences are unfolding fully only in our own time. Whether we have benefitted or suffered, the Columbian legacy can be calculated more accurately today, I think, because we have also inherited a goodly share of hindsight. The farther we stand from the events of the past, all things considered, the better chance we have of seeing the event whole—its causes, forms, and outcomes—and of putting some emotional distance between us and the historical participants on all sides.

A degree of critical disinterestedness—a studied lack of *personal* interest in the evolution and dénouement of past events—may be our most valuable piece of equipment on this moral excursion because the "Columbian Encounter" did not then and does not now mean only one thing to all people. It speaks to us in many tongues with many voices, each filled with passion and urgency. Its moral meanings resonate with the vocal accumulations of the past and the interested polyphony of the present. If we have any hope of making moral sense of that great and ongoing event, we must listen carefully to all the voices, not just a favorite one or few, from the past as well as the present. Even when they are weak or altogether silent, *especially* then, we must strain our empathy and imagination to hear them.

The Columbian colloquy features four main sets of voices. The first set belongs to the Spanish explorers and conquistadors who sought to explain, legitimate, and rationalize their extraordinary actions in what they regarded as a "New World."

"We men of Castile and Aragon (they might have said) were the first to discover the New World and to incorporate most of it into the Spanish empire, an empire greater than Rome's, an empire upon which the sun literally never set. And we did so according to the laws of God and of nations. As loyal soldiers of Christ, we sought to extend God's earthly kingdom, first, over our own peninsula and its Muslim invaders in the glorious 800-year *Reconquista,* and then over the millions of pagan inhabitants of the Americas. Our voyages to the New World were little more than extensions of the Crusades to free Jerusalem from the scimitared hand of the Infidel. Moreover, His Excellency Pope Alexander VI gave us exclusive right to bring the New World into Christ's fold in a papal bull issued immediately after Columbus's return in 1493."

"When our Christian brethren in Portugal confirmed our papal privilege in the Treaty of Tordesillas the following year, we added the force of international law to the acknowledged right—indeed *duty*—of all civilized nations to convert and to reduce barbarous peoples to civility. It was incumbent upon us to wean the West Indians from their shameless nakedness, lasciviousness, and cannibalism and the Aztecs from their insufferably proud despots and their bloodthirsty priests, who cut out the beating hearts of thousands of captives annually as offerings to their false gods and idols. In turn, we brought them the priceless blessings of the one holy Catholic Church, the legal and military protection of the greatest empire on earth, and the comforts of European technology, society, and values."

"We did all this with scrupulous regard for law. After an unfortunate initial period of weak leadership, we abolished the enslavement of peaceful Indians, prohibited their cruel and unfair treatment in a series of laws passed in 1512 and 1542, and established a hierarchy of judges and courts to oversee the colonies, including a special court for Indian cases. Moreover, we prohibited our conquistadors from making unjust war on the natives by requiring them to read to every Indian group encountered a brief history of the Catholic Church and of the Spanish crown's rights to the New World and to offer them a clear choice between stubborn resistance and peaceful acquiescence. If the natives resisted the gentle yoke of civilized law and true religion, their wives and children would be enslaved, their property forfeit, and just war waged against them. Even a notary was required to witness the reading of the *Requerimiento* and to affix his signature and the date to it. Who among our European imitators has paid as much attention to the protection and incorporation of strange and unpredictable peoples?"[2]

But the Spanish colonists did not speak with one voice. Particularly critical of the Hispanic party line in the Americas was a relatively small but vocal group of clergymen and judges who felt that the conquistadors and *encomenderos*—those who received grants of Indian labor and tribute from the local Spanish governors—were literally getting away with murder. From his pulpit in Santo Domingo in 1511, Fray Antonio de Montesinos told the assembled citizens and officials that he and his Dominican brethren henceforth refused to confess or absolve anyone who continued to oppress or enslave the Indians of Hispaniola, at that time the major Spanish island. With "choleric" but "efficient" sternness, he harangued his audience:

"You are living in deadly sin for the atrocities you tyrannically impose on these innocent people. Tell me, what right have you to enslave them? What authority did you use to make war against them who lived at peace on their territories, killing them cruelly with methods never before heard of? How can you oppress them and not care to feed or cure them, and work them to death to satisfy your greed? And why don't you look after their spiritual health, so that they should come to know God, that they should be baptized, and that they should hear Mass and keep the holy days? Aren't they human beings? Have they no rational soul? Aren't you obliged to love them as you love yourselves? . . . You may rest assured that you are in no better state of salvation than the Moors or the Turks who reject the Christian Faith."[3]

The Dominicans raised their fiery voices in protest during the lawless "boom" period of colonization on Hispaniola, before the royal reforms and the *Requerimiento* of 1512. Yet the Spanish treatment of the Indians in the rest of the Caribbean and on the mainland did not noticeably improve, to judge from later Spanish voices. The Franciscan friar Toribio de Motolinía, one of the twelve "apostles" who began Mexico's conversion in 1524, likened the advent of the Spanish to the ten plagues of Egypt. The Mexicans were devastated, he said, by deadly outbreaks of imported diseases; by famine; by overwork in the gold and silver mines, during the demolition of Tenochtitlán, the majestic Aztec capital, and in the building of Mexico City upon its pagan ruins; by the cruelty of Negro and native overseers; and by the deadly chain gangs that provisioned the mines and cities.[4]

The principled investigating judge for the vast Audiencia (the supreme royal court) of Mexico, Alonso de Zorita,
added impressive weight to the friars' accusations. Risking
the universal opprobrium of his countrymen, who gave
"not a rap whether [the] poor and miserable Indians live[d]
or die[d]," he reported to the king that the Mexicans were
much better off before the Spanish liberators arrived, even
under the allegedly despotic rule of Montezuma. "Because
of the sufferings and cruelties the Spaniards inflicted on
the Indians, and because of the plagues that have vexed
them, there is not one third the number there used to be."
Nor could the natives expect relief from the Spanish judici-
ary, "for the Spanish judges either are blind to [the oppressive nature of the colonial labor system] or wink at it, and
some actually approve of it and even coerce the Indians to
do the Spaniards' bidding." Under the *encomienda* system,
Zorita lamented, the tribute demanded of the natives was
so excessive, particularly as the population declined, that
many Indians "sold their land at a low price, and their
children as slaves." Many others were enslaved in "just
wars" and sent to the mines or to the chain gangs, where
they perished in appalling numbers from "hunger and
cold or extreme heat." When an Indian porter, "man or
woman, was worn out from the burden he was carrying,
the Spaniards cut off his head so as not to have to stop to
unchain him. . . ." As for the royal laws to protect the
Indians, the judge explained, they are "obeyed but not
enforced"—in the classically evasive formula of colonial
governors—"wherefore there is no end to the destruction
of the Indians."[5]

By the time Bartolomé de Las Casas, former conquis-
tador-turned-Dominican friar and bishop of Chiapas,
penned his chilling *Very Brief Relation of the Destruction of
the Indies* in 1542, the native populations were plunging
toward oblivion. Of the American territories then under

Spanish rule, Las Casas thundered, "the inhumane and abominable villainies of the Spaniards have made a wilderness." "Over twelve million souls innocently perished, women and children included. . . . Moreover," he continued, "I truly believe that I should be speaking within the truth if I were to say that over fifteen millions were consumed in this massacre."[6]

In the face of such massive destruction and loss of life, it is a minor miracle that the native voice was not completely silenced. But the human spirit is unquenchable and natives have raised their voices in grief, in protest, and in pride ever since Columbus set foot on the warm sands of Guanahaní. Their descendants have certainly not been quiet about the Quincentenary and what it means to them.

As the victims of the earliest encounters, the non-literate natives sought the motives of their invaders, not in the Europeans' paper rationalizations or propaganda, but in their unvarnished actions and behavior. The Aztecs of Tenochtitlán had no difficulty discerning what brought the Spanish in 1519 to their beautiful lakebound city, far from the Gulf coast and the islands of the Caribbean. When Montezuma sent to Cortés's approaching army a gift of gold ensigns and necklaces, Aztec oral sources well remembered after the conquest that "the Spaniards burst into smiles; their eyes shone with pleasure. . . . They picked up the gold and fingered it like monkeys. . . . The truth is that they longed and lusted for gold. Their bodies swelled with greed, and their hunger was ravenous; they hungered like pigs for that gold."[7]

By the beginning of the nineteenth century, the Iroquois of New York State had acquired a somewhat subtler understanding of the white man's motives. This they conveyed in an oral tradition about "How the White Race Came to America and Why the Gaiwiio"—the revitalizing message of the prophet Handsome Lake—"Became a Necessity" for the downtrodden Iroquois. It seems that the Devil cozened a young Jesus-like preacher into sending a bundle of "five things that men and women enjoy" to the native peoples of the New World in order to "make them as white people are." The young preacher then found Columbus to do his bidding and to convey the bundle to the far shores. Which he and his successors in great number did until they had spread the Devil's gifts to "all the men of the great earth island" (as the natives called North America).

Then the Devil laughed and revealed to the gullible preacher the contents of the bundle and their purposes: the pack of playing cards, he said, "will make them gamble away their wealth and idle their time"; the handful of coins "will make them dishonest and covetous and they will forget their old laws"; the violin "will make them dance with their arms about their wives and bring about a time of tattling and idle gossip"; the flask of rum "will turn their minds to foolishness and they will barter their country for baubles"; then will the secret poison from the decayed leg bone "eat the life from their blood and crumble their bones."[8]

Contemporary Indian assessments of the white man's motives do not differ much from those of their ancestors and inform most native attitudes toward the Quincentenary. Wendy Rose, a Hopi/Me-wuk and Coordinator of American Indian Studies at Fresno City College in California, writes that "my people and my land have been obstacles to the maximization of profit for five hundred years . . . I must remember that all of this death was for money. . . . I must remember that exploration and genocide have always just been business as usual. Neither scientific nor strictly political, those brave trekkers whose names frost the pages of every American child's schoolbooks carried their banners not for kings, but for companies, for traders, for miners, for every kind of coinage, for the freedom not to worship or walk or speak or elect, but to profit beyond the reach of the king."⁹

Given the near-harmony of native voices about their past encounters with the invaders, it is small wonder that few Indians are disposed to celebrate anything about 1492, much less the "discovery of America." The favorite bumpersticker in Indian country for some time has been "Americans Discovered Columbus," with the (correct) implication that he was lost. "How can it be a discovery," asked an Abenaki man, "if we were already here?" For a Mohawk elder, "October 12, 1492 is the date when the Dark Ages descended on the Indians of America." Nearly three-quarters of the natives from North, Central, and South America who responded to a Cornell University American Indian Program survey about the Quincentenary viewed it either as "500 years of Native People's resistance to colonization, or as an anniversary of a holocaust."¹⁰ The Assembly of First Nations, a national Canadian Indian organization, felt the same way. "For the First Nations to celebrate the near destruction of our culture and identity would be insane." "We are talking about 500 years of genocide and we don't want to see another 500 years of that."¹¹

The last but not least act of important voices contributing to the Columbian colloquy belongs to black Africans. When the Reverend Jeremy Belknap of New Hampshire pondered in 1784 whether the discovery of America had been "useful or hurtful to mankind," he may have surprised many of his readers by arguing that "The NEGROES OF AFRICA have experienced the most fatal DISADVANTAGES" by the discovery.¹² Although he could not have known, as modern historians do, that nearly twelve million African men, women, and children would be ripped from their homelands by both African and European merchants before the slave trade ended in the nineteenth century, he had correctly gauged the moral enormity of enslavement, transportation to utterly strange lands, and a debased and often short existence in harsh and perpetual bondage.[13]

For a long time the voices of the slaves themselves were unintelligible to their white buyers and sellers, although the cries and moans of human hurt needed no translation. By the eighteenth century, however, a number of slaves and former slaves had learned to turn their native thoughts into European idioms. One of the most articulate Africans was Ottobah Cugoano, who had been kidnapped as a child from the Gold Coast, shipped to Grenada in the West Indies, and eventually carried to England, where he obtained his freedom and a singular education. In 1787 he published his *Thoughts and Sentiments on the Evil and Wicked Traffic of Slavery,* which accurately linked the European treatment of Indians and of Africans, historically and morally.

"The Spaniards began their settlements in the West Indies and America," he wrote, without any mincing of words, "by depredations of rapine, injustice, treachery and murder. . . . This guiltful method of colonization . . . led them on from one degree of barbarity and cruelty to another" until "they had destroyed, wasted and desolated the native inhabitants" who performed all their labor. To replace the Indians they resorted to the slave trade, "that base traffic of kid-napping and stealing men . . . begun by the Portuguese on the coast of Africa."

And what were Cugoano's conclusions about the morality of those Columbian encounters? "None but men of the most brutish and depraved nature, led on by the invidious influence of infernal wickedness, could have made their settlements in the different parts of the world discovered by them, and have treated the various Indian nations, in the manner that the barbarous inhuman Europeans have done; and their establishing and carrying on that most dishonest, unjust and diabolical traffic of buying and selling, and of enslaving men, is such a monstrous, audacious and unparalleled wickedness, that the very idea of it is shocking, and the whole nature of it is horrible and infernal. It may be said with confidence," he concluded, ". . . that all their foreign settlements and colonies were founded on murders and devastations, and that they have continued their depredations in cruel slavery and oppression to this day."[14]

Given the international magnitude of the Columbian encounters, it should not surprise us that there are many other voices from the past and the present that we could add to the moral dialogue of '92. Those of the Sephardic Jews expelled from Spain in 1492 by the aggressively "Catholic kings" Ferdinand and Isabella are perhaps the next most important voices associated with the Quincentenary. Less than three months after the final surrender of the Moors at Granada and less than three weeks before Columbus signed on with Spain to sail west to the Far East, perhaps 50,000 practising Jews and half-hearted *conversos* (Jews who had converted to Christianity) fled the country and fanned out around the Mediterranean, where many continue to speak a form of Renaissance Spanish.[15] Although they were officially barred, some made their way to the New World, where the Inquisition did its best to ferret them out.

Only in 1990, some 498 years later, did the Spanish government officially welcome them back and give Judaism the same official status that Catholicism enjoys. The famous Jewish Quarter of Toledo, with its Synagogue of the Transito and its "School of Translators" where Jewish, Christian, and Muslim scholars worked in concert to transmit classical culture to Western Europe in the thirteenth and fourteenth centuries, is being extensively reconstructed as one of Spain's many Quincentenary projects.[16]

While some international Jewish groups are understandably ambivalent about the Quincentenary, most are participating under the aegis of Sepharad (the Hebrew word for Spain) '92. A spokesman for the Jewish communities of Spain acknowledged his satisfaction with "this reparation for the injustice done our ancestors 500 years ago. But," he added, "it is also a tribute that Spain is paying itself. It's a re-encounter with its own past, its own identity." An American organizer for Sepharad '92 made the moral point even more clearly. "People think it's a celebration," he said. "It's not. You can't celebrate something as traumatic as an eviction. But you can commemorate it, like the Holocaust. Part of our experience is never to forget."[17]

An even quieter set of voices has given the moral debate a new twist in recent decades. Beginning as long ago as the 1930s with the work of cultural geographer Carl Sauer, a number of scholars who might be called "ecological historians" have charted, explained, and usually lamented the extensive changes in the biological world that resulted from Columbus's maritime union of the "ecological islands" of Asia, Africa, Europe, and the Americas. While as good ecologists they invariably go about their work whistling the measured tunes of value-free science, the conclusions they draw as good humanistic historians often scat up but mostly down the moral scales. The listener is left with the distinct feeling that while ecological change should be seen as inexorable, inevitable, and normal, Columbus and his human successors may be regarded as the serpents in the American garden of Eden.

Sample some of these voices:

William McNeill believes that "the unification of the globe inaugurated by Columbus . . . damaged and sometimes destroyed many local forms of life—human as well as nonhuman. . . . Germs, weeds, and pests, transported by accident, together with plants and animals brought in deliberately, invaded new lands and soon created sharp ecological crises for themselves and for the older life forms. . . . No one planned it that way. No one intended it to happen. . . . [But] the ecological vanguard of European expansion regularly prepared the way for, and often made possible, political conquest and settlement."[18]

In his nuanced ecological history of colonial New England, *Changes in the Land,* William Cronon concluded that "Capitalism and environmental degradation went hand in hand . . . Economic and ecological imperialism reinforced each other."[19]

The major student of the "Columbian exchange" is Alfred Crosby, a scholar with the mind of a scientist and the heart of a humanist. He writes that "the major initial effect of the Columbian voyages was the transformation of America into a charnel house." The cataclysmic loss of native life, largely to imported diseases, "was surely the greatest tragedy in the history of the human species." "The positive result [of the biological transfers from the eastern to the western hemisphere] has been an enormous increase in food production and, thereby, human population. The negative results have been the destruction of ecological stability over enormous areas and an increase of erosion that is so great that it amounts to a crime against posterity." "It is possible that [European man] and the plants and animals he [brought] with him have caused the extinction of more species of life forms in the last four hundred years than the usual processes of evolution might kill off in a million. . . . The Columbian exchange," he concluded in 1972 and reaffirmed in 1989, "has left us with not a richer but a more impoverished genetic pool. We, all of the life on this planet, are the less for Columbus, and the impoverishment will increase."[20]

As bleak a scenario as that is, one final set of voices is

even more pessimistic and certainly more strident. An ad hoc group of "progressive" educators, students, ecologists, and community activists, known collectively as "The Columbus in Context Clearinghouse," proposes to prevent the official U.S. observances from being exclusively an "extravaganza of Nationalism, Patriotism, and self-congratulatory media messages reinforcing current-day Western mythology." Their first brain-storming session in New York led to a newsletter entitled *What's to Celebrate?* and a number of provocative suggestions for activities to "raise debate about the historical meaning of Columbus's 'discovery,'" particularly for "Native Americans, Africans, women and working people." Some of the suggestions were to:

—"Celebrate the resistance of Native Americans to 500 Years of genocide . . ."
—"Plan a die-in to coincide with the appearance of the Tall Ships (yes, again!) in New York"
—"Create a 'truth squad' to respond to official pronouncements"
—"Demonstrate the real impacts of 'discovery': Imperialism & Colonialism, Racism and Oppression"
—"Make connections with modern struggles, e.g., Wisconsin Native fishing rights, Puerto Rican independence, Bensonhurst."[21]

If nothing else, the moral stance of the "progressives" is unambiguous.

Any of the prevailing moral attitudes toward the Columbian encounter that we have sampled—or several at once—may strike a responsive chord in a modern audience. Nothing is unusual about that because the present is always involving itself in the moral conflicts of the past, usually wily, sometimes nilly. Even when those conflicts have no direct pertinence to us or our own dilemmas, we cannot resist the temptation to strike a moral pose. Indeed, it often seems that our moral reflexes (like the proverbial knee-jerk) tend to occur faster the less we know about the facts of the matter. In the absence of knowledge, it is easier to *judge* than to *understand,* for understanding in some depth usually undermines the rocky grounds of rectitude, often obviates the need for judgment, and sometimes leads to forgiveness, that most unfashionable virtue.

While "natural" in the sense of both frequent and unthinking, the human propensity to jump on moral bandwagons, to make snap judgments about human behavior in other times and places, causes a lot of mischief in our current lives and affairs. Our moral standards and behavior are confused, uncertain, and inconsistent because we commit too many elementary sins against straight moral thinking.

First, we hang simplistic, abstract labels when we should unpack and probe more deeply the complexity of past events, social conditions, and human motivations. To declare the Columbian legacy as nothing more than "Imperialism & Colonialism, Racism and Oppression," as the New York "progressives" have done in capital letters, is to *close* discussion, not to open it. To call a man (or woman) "sexist," a government (or college administration) "oppressive," or a person of European (or African) descent "racist" is to dismiss their views on *all* subjects and *in advance* as worthless and beneath contempt. Essentially, labeling is a form of name-calling, with just as few benefits. It might fulfill some atavistic need for visceral vocalization, but it does no justice to the object of reproach and leads to no reforms.

Our second mistake is to stereotype people according to one or a few characteristics—usually the only ones we have bothered to learn about—when we should continue to search for their full and individual humanity and withhold judgment until we know much more of it. We are experts at lumping people into racial, national, political, and other cultural categories, particularly people with whom we have no personal acquaintance; we should work much harder at splitting the human race into its individual components, at recognizing many more human faces in our mental crowds, just as we would like to be recognized by others.

Take, as just one of many possible examples, the conquistadors of New Spain, who have gotten almost as much bad press as the Nazis of the Third Reich. We learn very little about a sixteenth-century Spaniard by calling him a "conquistador," except that probably he received a share of captured native wealth or an *encomienda* of Indian tributaries for his investment of prowess and sometimes equipment in an initial "discovery" and search of an American region. For the Spanish root of *conquest* is simply "to seek."[22] And that's exactly what the very diverse Spaniards who made up the rag-tag forces of "discovery" were doing—seeking their fortunes in any form possible: land, treasure, servants, or business. The great majority were anything but stereotypical "conquistadors," lean and hungry-looking in morion and breastplate, brandishing thin Toledo swords while spurring foaming steeds into habitual and genocidal war. Horses were relatively scarce; a *caballero* received double shares of booty for his enhanced contribution. Cortés's army of nearly 600 had only 16 horses; Pizarro's was better equipped with 62 mounts for 168 men. As for martial prowess, nearly every contemporary Spanish male knew how to wield a weapon of some sort, but very few made a career of it, either in Europe or the Americas. Of the 91 conquerors of Panama, 41 had no military experience whatsoever: 20 were craftsmen, 11 farmers, 13 sailors, and 10 were members of the professional or urban middle class. Pizarro's *entrada* contained the same cross-section of Spanish colonial society: notaries and clerks, merchants and managers, artisans, lower hidalgos, and upper plebeians. Most of them were single men in their twenties, in search of the main chance. Professional killers were few and far between.[23]

Yet even if we know that many conquistadors were ruthless Indian fighters, particularly when they were badly outnumbered (as they invariably were), we should remember that they might also have been—all in the same person and at the same time—doting fathers and unfaithful husbands, devout Catholics and poor scholars, dutiful sons and headstrong servants, ardent gardeners and heavy drinkers, gentle lovers and gouging businessmen—bundles of human contradictions, in other words, just like the Indians and the Africans they often mistreated. Before we hang them or any other historical actors from a label, we should try to imagine how we would feel if we could be known to posterity by only a single negative characteristic or action from our relatively long and constantly evolving lives.

Imagination is the key to moral understanding. Lack of it blinds us as seriously as it did the European colonists who savagely killed Indians and enslaved Africans. For as Margaret Atwood reminds us, "Oppression involves a failure of the imagination: the failure to imagine the full humanity of other human beings."[24] When Columbus unified the world, it lost its center. Europe no longer occupied a privileged position; Jerusalem no longer appeared in the middle of the maps. In such a plural world of places and peoples, any person, any subject, was conceivably the center. But Europeans, even those who moved to the new worlds, remained incapable of recognizing "the others" they met as both *different* from and *equal* to themselves. They could not acknowledge the validity of plural paradigms for seeing and interpreting the world, nor would they relinquish their stubborn will to dominate inherent in their ethnocentric world-views. The "other" remained for them an *object,* never a *subject* in his own right, and therefore the constant victim of intellectual and physical oppression.[25]

Winner or loser, conqueror or victim, the flesh of any human being turns to cardboard as soon as we substitute stereotypes and labels for imagination and empathy.

The third error we make in our moral judgments of the past is to constitute ourselves one-or-more-person "truth squads," clad in the armor of self-righteousness and armed with an infallible divining rod for the secrets of dead men's hearts. Unfortunately, "the truth" is never simpler than it seems to the simpleminded, for whom the only colors are black and white; it is never clearer than it appears to the steely eyed, whose icy glare betrays an advanced case of myopia. When we reflect on how very difficult it is to obtain even half-truths about our own contemporaries, their thoughts, or their activities, we should be doubly humble about our ability to plumb the depths of the irreproducible past. Any historian who thinks he has grasped "the whole truth and nothing but the truth" about his subject, particularly given the accidental, fragmentary nature of our documentation, is a person given to delusions and a good candidate to join the next crusade of righteousness.

We are also impeded in our moral thinking by our sloppy handling of moral vocabulary, which is nearly as large as the language itself and for the most part unspecialized. Most of the words we use in history and everyday speech are like mental depth charges. When heard or read they quickly sink into our consciousness and explode, sending off cognitive shrapnel in all directions. On the surface they may look harmless enough, or resemble something equally benign. But as they descend and detonate, their resonant power is unleashed, showering our understanding with fragments of accumulated meaning and association. It therefore behooves us to use words—not just the moral-*sounding* ones but *all* of them—with extreme care and precision because they are powerful instruments of judgment, capable of maiming heedless handlers.[26]

To take but one example, consider the use of "genocide" to describe the loss of Indian life during the colonial period. There are three major problems with employing such a highly charged word. The first is that "genocide" is too loosely employed whenever an historical European kills or even contributes to the death of an Indian, in total disregard of the accepted definition of the word. As you know, the word was coined in 1944 to describe the infamous Nazi attempts to annihilate the Jews, a religious and cultural group they chose to classify as a biological sub-species or race. The latest and most inclusive definition of *genocide* is simply "a form of one-sided *mass* killing in which a *state* or other authority *intends* to destroy a group, as that group and membership in it are defined by the *perpetrator*."[27] Such a definition excludes from consideration victims, civilian or military, of two-sided *war,* of any natural or unintended disaster, and of any individuals or "loose cannons" acting outside the orders of the state or political authority. If the word is to retain any meaning or moral impact at all, we must not apply it wholesale to every Indian death in the colonial period. To do so is to dilute our moral vocabulary to insipidity and to squander its intellectual and emotional force.

The second reason to use "genocide" with extreme care is that it is historically inaccurate as a description of the vast majority of encounters between Europeans and Indians. Certainly no European colonial government ever tried to exterminate all of the Indians as Indians, as a race, and you can count on one hand the authorized colonial attempts to annihilate even single tribes. The (unsuccessful) Puritan assault upon the Pequots of Connecticut in 1637 and the French smashing of the Mississippi River Natchez and Wisconsin Foxes in the 1730s are the most notable, and even they do not differ much in method or result from the Iroquois destruction of the Hurons in 1649.[28] For the rest, only the rare, certifiable, homicidal maniac sought to commit "genocide" upon the Indians. The vast majority of settlers had no interest in killing Indians—who were much too valuable for trade and labor—and those who did took careful aim at temporary political or military enemies. We should cleanly erase from our minds that much-misunderstood remark of a post-*Civil War*—not colonial—general who said that "the only good Indians I ever saw were dead."[29] By which he meant, *not* that all Indians should be shot on sight, but that none of the dangerous Indian warriors he was fighting on the Plains were to be trusted. That quotation, always taken out of context, has done more harm to straight thinking about Indian-white relations than any number of Sand Creeks or Wounded Knees.

The final problem with "genocide" as a description of, or even analogy to, the post-Columbian loss of Indian life is that the moral onus it tries to place on the European colonists, equating them with the Nazi S.S, is largely misdirected and inappropriate. As Edmund Burke warned us in the late eighteenth century and as we have come to realize in the late twentieth, "you cannot"—or rather, *should* not—"indict a whole nation" for the misdeeds and crimes of a few.[30] A relatively small and pernicious cadre of Nazis *was* guilty for all six million Jewish deaths; the colonists were personally and directly guilty for only a fraction of the Indians who died in the two or three centuries after contact. Even the Spanish of the "Black Legend" were not directly responsible for most of the native deaths in Latin America. In North and South America, the vast majority of Indians succumbed, not to colonial oppression or conquistador cruelty—as real and pervasive as those *were*—but to new and lethal epidemic diseases imported *inadvertently* by the settlers. In only one or two verifiable instances late in the colonial period did the colonists—British officers rather than Spanish, incidentally—deliberately spread smallpox among an Indian group in hopes of diminishing their formidable armed resistance.[31] Genocide, as distinguished from *other* forms of cruelty, oppression, and death, played a very small role in the European conquest of the New World.

Finally, we make a hash of our historical judgments because we continue to feel guilty about the real or imagined sins of our fathers and forefathers and people to whom we have no relation whatever. The dirtiness of their business somehow keeps rubbing off on us. This is perhaps understandable but it is also unnecessary and unproductive. We carry all the moral weight we can bear from our own dilemmas and conflicts; we do not need any excess baggage. Only when we perpetuate the immoral actions and attitudes of our predecessors should they be of *personal* (as opposed to historical or heuristic) concern to us. Despite the resort to universalizing labels such as "Imperialism" and "Colonialism," most of the moral battles of the sixteenth and seventeenth centuries are behind us. Unless the United States militarily invades Quebec or Mexico in the near future and makes it the 51st state, we can stop flogging ourselves with our "imperialistic" origins and tarring ourselves with the broad brush of "genocide." As a huge nation of law and order and increasingly refined sensibility, we are not guilty of murdering Indian women and babies, of branding slaves on the forehead, or of claiming and confiscating any real estate in the world we happen to fancy. We have a related but quite different set of moral problems: personal and institutional racism toward people of all colors; Indian reservations and urban ghettoes of hopeless poverty and disease; leveraged buy-outs and junk bonds; predominantly black and Indian prison populations; military interventions in Latin America and the Middle East; immigration quotas; abortion policies; and campus intolerance, to name just a few.

None of these criticisms should be construed as an argument against the legitimacy and utility of judging the past. We do it all the time, we are incapable of *not* doing it, and we *should* do it. But we should do it *well* and we should do it for valid reasons, not because our knees or trigger fingers twitch every time we open a history book.

It seems clear that we judge the past for three important reasons. The first is to appraise action, an intrinsic part of historical thinking. Not to make such judgments is to abandon the past to itself, rendering it unintelligible, untranslatable, to the present. The second reason for judging the past is to do justice to it. But rendering a judgment is not the same as passing sentence. As historians, professional or amateur, we are too involved in both the prosecution and the defense; the words and reputations of the dead on *all* sides are in our hands. Moreover, historical justice is retrospective; its goal is not to punish or rehabilitate historical malefactors—who are all mortally incorrigible in any event—but to set the record straight for future appeals to precedent.

Finally, we also judge the past to advance our own moral education, to learn from and, in effect, to be judged by the past. Since we think and speak historically for our own generation, we can have judgmental effect only on ourselves. Consequently, history becomes, in Lord Bolingbroke's famous phrase, "philosophy teaching by example," a "preceptor of prudence, not of principles."[32] After bearing witness to the past with all the disinterestedness and human empathy we can muster, we should let ourselves be judged by the past as much as, or more than, we judge it. For the past is filled with the lives and struggles of countless "others," from whom we may learn to extend the possibilities of our own limited humanity. And as we learn about what it is like to be other than ourselves, we are better able to do justice to the past. The best way to learn to make discerning moral judgments is to practice making them. To judge is human, and to judge according to the highest standards of moral judgment is humanizing.

But what standards should those be? One of the firmest canons of the historical discipline is that a past society must be judged first and foremost by its own values and norms. We judge the conduct of people by their success in acting in accordance with the ideals they have chosen. While an individual event or action should be evaluated in terms of the practices and conventions of its time, we may also measure it comparatively against similar events in other times and places and, less effectively perhaps, against our personal scales of values. Whichever standard we choose, our judgments should be made only *after* we have thoroughly done our homework. "To advance and defend our view of how things were, and why, and what this meant to the people of the time, and what it means"—or should mean—"to people of today" is, as Gordon Wright said, a *final* step, not one to be taken prematurely or lightly.[33]

When cultures, societies, and groups clash, as they frequently did during the Columbian "Encounter," however, how do we assess or resolve the moral conflict involved while honoring the values of each side? I suggest that after making a special effort to achieve parity of understanding, we simply let the conflicting societies judge each other, as much as possible in their own words. "Contemporary moral judgements enable us to enter the lives of the [people] of the past. We begin to see 'heroes' and 'villains' in their terms, and thus to appreciate more fully not just their circumstances, but the moral choices and judgements that they themselves made."[34] If the surviving documentation of their respective positions is lopsided, as it usually is in Indian-white relations, we may sensitively apply our imagination and empathy to a mastery of the slim sources on the native side to establish a culturally valid standard of judgment, and we may make a light use of irony or gentle iconoclasm to prick the pretensions and self-righteousness of the advantaged society on the other. If more comment or moral criticism is called for by the complexity, abnormality, or enormity of the conflict situation, we may use the standards of other contemporary societies, preferably neighbors who found themselves in similar circumstances. Beyond this kind of concrete, contextual treatment most of us will not need or want to go.[35]

As we drift into 1992 and beyond, I hope we will hear not only the certain noises of the national chauvinists, professional celebrants, and salesmen, but will make a public and private effort to listen carefully to the variety of authentic voices speaking from the post-Columbian past. Opportunities to hear those voices are or will be abundant. The educational fallout from this anniversary in the form of accessible scholarship, museum exhibits, and radio and TV productions is already greater than that produced by the '76 Bicentennial. If we still believe that we can learn from the past, the quincentenary of the unification of the world—the fabrication of the "global village"—contains all the moral counsels and cautions we could possibly want. Perhaps our *re*-encounter with each other and our pasts will prevent us from making such a sad mess of it this time around.

CHAPTER ELEVEN

Beyond 1992

THE COLUMBIAN QUINCENTENARY HAS GENERATED AN abundance of public and academic scholarship, most of it of high quality. Perhaps quixotically, I have attempted to keep up with the flow for the sake of my teaching, my writing, and the American Historical Association's Columbus Quincentenary Committee, which I chaired for its last two years. I also made the attempt out of sheer interest in the rare phenomenon of an international (rather than mere national) observance, and because this book needed a concluding chapter that looked beyond 1992.

The following essay seeks to survey the recent productions of individual scholars, museums, and film and television companies that promise to have a durable and salutary impact on future thinking, teaching, and scholarship about the "Columbian Encounter." It concludes by suggesting several ways we can incorporate these advances into our textbooks, classrooms, and public media. If we have been able to see more clearly the complex, controversial, and often tragic post-Columbian world than did previous generations, it is due largely, I think, to the serious, ethnically sensitive, commemorative (rather than celebratory) spirit with which we approached the five hundredth anniversary. My only regret is that I will probably not be around to experience the Sexcentenary.

The essay has benefitted from the editorial offices of Michael

McGiffert, who published an abbreviated version in the special
Quincentenary issue of the *William and Mary Quarterly* in April
1992.

AMERICA HAS PROFITED ECONOMICALLY MORE
than educationally from its major historical anniversaries.
Typical was 1976 when popular and scholastic understanding of America's revolutionary heritage and distinctive political origins was advanced much less than were the
profits of corporate hucksters who cashed in on what Jesse
Lemisch aptly called "Bicentennial Schlock."[1] Despite the
considerable array of scholarship spawned by the Bicentennial, one of every three high school juniors in the late
1980s could not place the Declaration of Independence in
its correct half-century, did not know that it signaled the
colonists' break from England, and did not recognize its
best-known passage about "Life, Liberty and the pursuit of
Happiness." Even one in four college seniors could not
distinguish the ideas of Karl Marx from those of the U.S.
Constitution or explain the purpose of the *Federalist* papers.[2] While patriotism sells, it doesn't always educate.

The quincentenary of Columbus's voyage of discovery
has a much better chance of realizing its educational potential. Certainly the challenge exists. In the 1988 National
Assessment of Educational Progress, 56 percent of fourth
graders could name Columbus's ships, but only 36 percent
understood why he sailed to the Americas. Nearly a third
of the seventeen-year-olds thought that Columbus reached
the New World after 1750. Only 60 percent knew that the
American Southwest was explored and settled by Spain,
the same number who knew that the eastern seaboard was
settled mainly by England.[3]

The Columbian Quincentenary is likely to make a

deeper public and pedagogical impact for five reasons. First, in the United States at least, we are choosing to commemorate rather than celebrate the event, with a concomitantly greater degree of serious reflection on its much more mixed results. Second, the event we commemorate is less a single sea voyage by an Italian-born captain than the five-centuries-long "Encounter" of human and biological populations, institutions, and ideas from all of the world's continents that followed upon his fortuitous voyage. Third, since the event belongs to the world and not exclusively to the United States, patriotism and huckster-ism are much less likely to steal the show. Fourth, unlike the American Revolution, which for much of this century has been intensively studied by scholars and widely if not universally taught in American schools and colleges, the concept of the Columbian Encounter is quite new and provides myriad opportunities for scholars, teachers, and educational institutions. And finally, thanks largely to the advance planning, economic sponsorship, and scholarly oversight of the National Endowment for the Humanities, the community of serious history-makers and -interpreters has been able to take advantage of those opportunities and thereby to dominate the proceedings.

So prolific have been the historical and interpretive results of the Quincentenary, in Latin America and much of Europe as well as the United States, that it has been a challenge just to keep track of them, much less to take full stock of their contributions. Fortunately, beginning in the fall of 1984, three newsletters tried valiantly to publicize the great variety of serious undertakings aimed at 1992.

First off the press was *1992: A Columbus Newsletter*, edited by Foster Provost for the John Carter Brown Library. *1992* specialized in scholarly news: conferences, learned society meetings, reviews of foreign and domestic books about Columbus. Then came the more comprehensive quarterly *Encuentro,* published in English by the Latin American Institute at the University of New Mexico until the winter of 1988, when a glossier, less focused magazine called *Encounter* took its place with new support from the Spain '92 Foundation. *Encuentro* was quickly joined by an even more inclusive Spanish-English newsletter sponsored by the Organization of American States and Ohio State University, *Quincentennial of the Discovery of America: Encounter of Two Worlds,* which appeared irregularly up to six times a year. Appropriately, it covered many activities in Latin America, some scholarly, most official, which the other newsletters underreported. These publications, supplemented by regular announcements of Quincentenary-related grants by the NEH, comprise a reasonably complete record of the rich educational dividends we can expect from the Columbian anniversary. For they describe literally hundreds of projects, the majority of them capable of making serious and lasting contributions to scholarship and public understanding.

What have we learned from all this productivity? How can we most fruitfully incorporate the new history of Encounter into our teaching and scholarship, both academic and public? What, in other words, remains to be done beyond 1992, after the replicas of the *Niña, Pinta,* and *Santa Maria* have sailed home?

For better or worse, the center of attention is still Cristoforo Colombo, the Admiral of the Ocean Sea. While the scholarly community in the Western Hemisphere has largely shifted its focus away from the serendipitous "discoverer" of America to the ongoing Encounter he inaugurated, public attention remains fixated on Columbus himself. So do a number of European scholars and American Indians and activists, though for different reasons. Spain and Italy remain the centers of serious Columbus scholarship. But a few American scholars, most with activist bents, and a large number of native Americans also dwell on Columbus, as the anti-heroic First Cause of the Encounter's dark legacy of death, despoilation, and dispossession. The result is an immensely blurred image of Columbus, which oscillates between candidate for canonization and genocidal maniac.[4]

Whatever their purposes, students of Columbus will have more and better scholarly aid after 1992 than ever before. Foster Provost has pointed the way by surveying the past in an invaluable annotated guide to 780 items of the most pertinent Columbian scholarship in all languages.[5] He has also prepared A Columbus Dictionary, a 140-page work of reference to the people, places, and events associated with Columbus and his four voyages.[6] On a grander scale, Simon and Schuster and editor Silvio Bedini enlisted the international expertise of nearly 150 scholars for a two-volume, 350-article Christopher Columbus Encyclopedia. With articles as long as 10,000 words, up-to-date bibliographies, and 400 illustrations, this work establishes the state of the Columbian art at the Quincentenary.[7]

The basis for any reassessment of Columbus, of course, must be textually precise, annotated editions of his writings and correspondence. The first critical edition, Raccolta di documenti e studi, published by an Italian commission for the fourth centenary, has more than held its own.[8] Indeed, the Nuova Raccolta Colombiana, for which twenty-seven volumes are planned, is largely a re-editing and amplification of the original Raccolta for more popular consumption.[9] Although Consuelo Varela omits textual notes and discussion of her choice of copy-texts, her Cristóbal Colón: textos y documentos completos comes close to a fully critical edition of the Admiral's journals, maps, and memorials.[10]

Two American projects will soon give English-speaking

readers access to the Columbian corpus, and one of them may establish a new standard of critical editing as well. Ohio State University plans to translate twelve key volumes of the *Nuova Raccolta*. UCLA's projected fifteen-volume *Repertorium Columbianum* will establish new texts, fully annotate them, and translate them on facing pages. Only two volumes will duplicate Ohio State's titles.

But two of the most important works of Columbus have already received definitive textual and scholarly treatment in *en face* editions. The more widely used but also more problematic is Columbus's *diario* or journal of his epochal first voyage, which has been lost. What we have instead is part copy–part paraphrase of a now-lost copy of the original, in other words, the Admiral's words thrice removed. Oliver Dunn and James E. Kelley, Jr., have painstakingly reconstructed Bartolomé de Las Casas's text of the *diario* from the surviving manuscript, including all marginalia, insertions, and canceled text, and have added notes on textual variations and differing translations and a concordance of Spanish words. On facing pages they have translated the Spanish text fairly literally. The precision of their text and the completeness of their concordance will prove very useful to students not only of Columbus's language but of his navigational skills, native relations, and the hoary landfall question.[11]

By comparison, the second work has been virtually ignored because it seemed uncharacteristic of the forward-looking Modern Man of the Renaissance conjured up by earlier historians. The *Libro de la profecías*, compiled by Columbus in the winter and spring of 1501–2, is not a discursive work of original composition but a notebook with learned commentary of carefully chosen biblical passages, particularly prophecies, on "the recovery of God's holy city and mountain of Zion and on the discovery and evangelization of the islands of the Indies and of all other peoples and nations." The notes were to have served as the basis of a long apocalyptical poem to be presented to Ferdinand and Isabella, proving that the discovery of the new world was "simply the fulfillment" of biblical prophecy and a foretaste of divine things to come. This extraordinary text, now edited and translated by Delno West and the late August Kling, shows that the man who was then signing his name *Christum ferens* (Christ-bearer) was at heart a backward-looking providentialist-millenarian. His considerable confidence and tenacity of purpose came not from Renaissance science and innovation but from Scripture, classical texts, and medieval commentaries. Moreover, the editors present evidence that his plan of prophetic discovery was essentially laid by 1481, eleven years before his famous voyage. This would seem to render irrelevant Juan Gil's recent argument that Columbus did not read or annotate Marco Polo's *Travels* until *after* the first voyage, in 1497.[12] If Columbus's primary motivation came from the Bible, which spoke "prophetically" of "gold, and silver" and other riches collected regularly by naval fleets, he did not need to read Polo to inspire him westward.[13]

Columbus scholarship in English will receive an additional boost from the translation of Juan Gil and Consuelo Varela's editions of *Newly Discovered Letters of Christopher Columbus to King Ferdinand, The Complete Texts and Manu scripts of Christopher Columbus,* and *Contemporary Letters Written to and about Christopher Columbus* by the University Presses of Florida. We have already had a taste of the discoveries to be made in the 400-page *Libro de Armadas* (*Book of the Armadas*), which Eugene Lyons rediscovered in Seville's Archive of the Indies and is editing and translating for Florida. The *Libro* describes the ships, cargoes, and crews of several Spanish fleets sent to the New World between 1495 and 1500. From it we learn that the *Niña* ("Little Girl," the nickname of the *Santa Clara*), Columbus's favorite ship, was an unsinkable, *four*-masted, largely square-rigged caravel of 67 feet that weathered his first three voyages and several hurricanes, only to be sold in 1499 to help pay his debts in the Indies. On her third voyage to Hispaniola in 1498, she carried 3 anchors, a small boat, 10 swivel guns, 74 lances, and a passenger contingent of farmers, crossbowmen, and female murderers freed on the condition that they emigrate.[14]

New documentary discoveries like the *Libro de Armadas* will tell us a good deal about life aboard Columbus's ships. The excavated remains of certain wrecks may tell us even more. An interdisciplinary team of scientists and underwater archaeologists known as CCAP (Columbus Caravel Archaeological Project), masterminded by Texas A&M's Institute of Nautical Archaeology, has been closing in on several of the Admiral's ill-fated ships. The *Santa Maria,* which broke up off the northern coast of Haiti on the maiden American voyage, has proven the most elusive, even though its general whereabouts are well known. Of greater potential as historical sources are the *Capitana* and the *Santiago,* which Columbus was forced to beach in St. Ann's Bay, Jamaica, on his fourth and final voyage in 1503–4. Because Columbus and his crew of 115 lived in huts aboard the worm-eaten hulks for more than a year and were fed by local natives, the site should reveal much about Taíno life at early contact and the acculturation of the Spanish.[15] The third CCAP target is the *Gallega,* embedded somewhere in the sand and silt of the Río Belén on the northern coast of Panama. The caravel and a garrison of eighty men were left to their own devices in the winter of 1503. If it can be found, its carcass and contents should reveal many missing details about sixteenth-century naval architecture and lading.[16]

A nautical footnote that may prove especially interesting to Americans comes from a recent three-volume study of the Pinzón brothers, the mariners from Palos who captained the *Niña* and the *Pinta*. Against the hagiographical grain, its Spanish authors conclude that Martín Alonso Pinzón may well have died at home almost immediately from syphilis contracted in Hispaniola after he had deserted Columbus's fleet in November 1492. If so, his truancy was costly. But he was clearly not alone in fraternizing with the natives; a major epidemic of syphilis broke out in Barcelona the same year (1493).[17]

Archaeology is also giving us major new glimpses of Columbus's landside life in the Caribbean. When his second fleet disgorged its 1200 passengers in 1494, the settlers founded La Isabela on the northern coast of the Dominican Republic. In accordance with the cultural code they carried in their heads, they built a familiar grid-town around a plaza fronting on the sea, surrounded by a church, hospital, 120-foot-long warehouse, stone fort, 200 thatch huts for themselves and a *palacio real* for Columbus. A large kiln produced traditional fifteenth-century *mudejar* (Iberian Christian-Muslim) pottery, as if the settlers had never left Spain. The cemetery, when opened, revealed traditional Christian burials: bodies extended on their backs, heads to the west, hands crossed on their chests, shrouds rather than coffins. One skeleton spoke plainly of the harsh treatment meted out to deserters and mutineers: a Caucasian male was buried face down with his hands behind his back. An interesting find at the warehouse site suggests why such a man might have run into the hills: thousands of unruly drops of mercury used to separate gold from its mineral matrix.

The remains of Columbus's *palacio* may be the most spectacular discovery. The thirteen-by-twenty-foot structure rested on a limestone foundation and was roofed with timbers and dull-red tiles. The front wall was made from solid blocks of limestone, quarried nearby; the others were of packed mud, whitewashed on the inside. That the house and yard were surrounded by a stone wall hints that the Governor may have needed protection from his own restless colonists as much as from the local Taínos. Shards of a large, unglazed chamberpot also remind us that the history of even the great can often be reconstructed from the bottom up.[18]

As the biography of Columbus is revised by scholars from a variety of disciplines and countries, we might reasonably expect a new synthesis to emerge. But the man's complexity, the remaining gaps in our knowledge, and the disagreement about the nature of his legacy, particularly in the Americas, make unlikely the appearance of a sanguine successor to S. E. Morison's admiring *Admiral of the Ocean Sea.*[19] Paolo Emilio Taviani's *Christopher Columbus: The Grand Design* is a scholarly though not a literary tour de force and covers the Admiral's life to the eve of discovery. *The Voyages of Columbus: The Great Discovery* is a handsome, heavily illustrated, two-volume treatment of the rest of Columbus's life, also for scholars primarily; the second volume is devoted entirely to Taviani's latest thinking on various aspects of the problematical historiography. Having examined all of the sites that Columbus explored with greater attention than even Morison's, he is an unusually reliable guide through the thickets of controversy. His *Columbus: The Great Adventure,* a severe and unadorned abridgment of his four-volume Italian biography, is less helpful on the context and long-range significance of Columbus's achievement than on the ascertainable facts.[20]

Kirkpatrick Sale's *The Conquest of Paradise: Christopher Columbus and the Columbian Legacy* is well researched and powerfully argued. But Sale is so remorseless in his indictment of Columbus and Western culture, both of which he caricatures, that most readers will not be persuaded. The polemical quality of this tract-for-the-times by an environmental activist will unfortunately prevent its hardheaded accounting of the debit side of the Columbian ledger from reaching the wide audience it deserves.[21]

Fortunately, two better alternatives exist. John Noble Wilford's *The Mysterious History of Columbus* is a sprightly "story of the story of Columbus," not a full-scale biography. It is aimed at the general or non-scholarly reader who knows little about the man and wants a quick course in what we know about him and his achievements, how we know what we know, and how much we do not know, even from the latest archival and archaeological findings. Its sound research, disinterested balance, and clear writing distinguish it as popular history and journalism of a high order.[22]

Felipe Fernández-Armesto's even briefer *Columbus* is more scholarly and designed to give busy readers "unadorned facts about Columbus." But it is strong on the contexts in which Columbus thought and moved: the Genoese world of the late fifteenth century, the partly Genoese Lisbon and Andalusia to which he moved at a critical period of his career, the Spanish royal court, the mapping and exploration of the Atlantic in his day, the world of geographical speculation which surrounded him, and the slow shift of the center of gravity of Western culture from the Mediterranean to the Atlantic. Fernández-Armesto's Columbus is a sailor and explorer of very great achievements, but also a "socially ambitious, socially awkward parvenu," an "autodidact, intellectually aggressive but easily cowed," an "embittered escapee from distressing realities," and an "adventurer inhibited by fear of failure." Like most recent biographers, he finds Columbus an elusive man of paradox and contradiction.[23]

Although no major museum has tackled Columbus's life, the New-York Historical Society in the winter of 1991–92 mounted a sizable exhibition on "Imagining the New

World: Columbian Iconography," featuring images of Old World monsters, New World flora, fauna, natives, and towns, and Columbus himself (none of which were made during his lifetime). The exhibition catalogue is introduced by four essays; Pauline Moffitt Watts's on evangelizing sixteenth-century Mexico and Michael Mathes's on the first century of printing in the Americas are fresh contributions to Encounter scholarship.[24]

The only other media capable of bringing Columbus's life and times into focus are television and film (and their videotaped offspring). Predictably, several "blockbusters" and a few less ambitious (and perhaps more useful) efforts were made for mass audiences. A Dutch company and a French company each produced Hollywood-sized films originally called *Christopher Columbus* (and fought over rights to the title, which could not be copyrighted). Alexander and Ilya Salkind, the producers of *Superman: The Movie*, hired bestselling author Mario Puzo to script the Dutch film, which had its premier as *Christopher Columbus: The Discovery* in Columbus, Ohio, in the summer of 1992. In *1492*, the Paris-based company counterpunched with Gerard Depardieu as the Italian explorer and Ridley Scott, the director of *Alien* (from an Indian perspective, an apt precedent).[25]

In the fall of 1991, WGBH-TV (Boston) launched seven carefully researched but somewhat distended hour shows, "Columbus and the Age of Discovery." Much of that research and 336 well-chosen illustrations went into a companion volume of the same title by executive producer Zvi Dor-Ner. Among other questions, it asks—and answers— why other advanced societies, such as China in the fourteenth century, did not effectively discover the Americas first.[26] Omnigraphics, Inc. of Detroit used on-site visits and interviews with experts to fashion six videotapes, available in 15- and 30-minute versions, "Christopher Columbus: Admiral of the Ocean Sea." In 1988 Swiss National TV broadcast a show in five languages, "The Internal Route of Christopher Columbus" from La Isabela across the mountains with 400 men to subjugate the natives of Hispaniola. And for those who could not get enough of the celluloid explorer, the Library of Congress presented a series of old Columbus films, made, on average, every five years. The student who manages to take in all of these visions, new and old, will come away with an image of Columbus more blurred than even print can produce.[27]

One reason it is difficult to take full measure of the "discoverer" of America is that we tend to ignore his European background and his previous experience in the Mediterranean and the Atlantic, where his secular plans for exploration and colonization were laid. The Quincentenary has provided several excellent remedies for our myopia. Taviani administered the first treatment in his learned but undigested study of the pre-American Columbus.[28] In a now-published lecture at the James Ford Bell Library, Stuart Schwartz reminded us that Columbus received his maritime and mercantile education by working the long-established Italian and Portuguese trading routes to Chios in the Aegean and to England, Ireland, Madeira, and the African Gold Coast in the eastern Atlantic. In search of sugar, slaves, and gold, he took as his economic model the Portuguese *feitoria* or "factory" at São Jorge da Mina, where a small garrison of soldiers and traders bartered European manufactures for black slaves, ivory, and gold from the African interior. He also witnessed the enslavement and transportation of the Guanche natives of the Spanish Canaries, a precedent that would influence his treatment of the natives he encountered in the Caribbean. By 1497, however, Columbus had shifted to a plan for full-fledged settlement by Spanish women and farmers as well as treasure-seeking conquistadors. Unlike the *feitoria* model, his revised plan more closely resembled the *Reconquista* of the Iberian peninsula from the Moors, whose last stage he had also witnessed in Granada in 1492. Schwartz concludes that "Columbus was in many ways the last man of the Fifteenth century and his image of a new society was molded by what he had seen and experienced in the Mediterranean and in the Atlantic."[29]

In *The Worlds of Christopher Columbus,* the best biography for classroom use and the most contextual, William and Carla Rahn Phillips remind us that from ancient times Asia was the center of the "Old World's" attention. Even before the Polos, Western merchants and missionaries sought to penetrate the vast markets and populations of the East. Columbus followed a long line of Italian traders and bankers into the eastern Mediterranean. Only as the Portuguese monopoly tightened on the sea routes around Africa did he concoct his improbable scheme of reaching the East by sailing west from the Canaries. When he accidentally ran into the Western Hemisphere, he precipitated not only the Spanish empire but the unification of the globe, with all their momentous consequences for world trade, demography, and politics.[30]

While the Phillipses scan the whole world before and after 1492, Franco Cardini's sumptuous coffee-table portrait narrows the focus to life among the great and small in *Europe 1492.*[31] His richly and freshly illustrated tour of Columbus's Europe visually undermines Sale's denigrating caricature, even as it fully acknowledges the underbelly of fifteenth-century life. Equally sumptuous is a book that serves as a striking visual complement to the Phillipses' literate survey of Columbus's worlds. *Circa 1492: Art in the Age of Exploration,* the byproduct of a major exhibition at the National Gallery of Art in Washington, is a 450-page catalogue of learned essays and illustrations, 500 in color.

The world covered is Columbus's, minus Africa and the Atlantic islands: the Mediterranean from Portugal to Turkey, the Far East and Cathay, and the great empires and chiefdoms of the Americas.[32] The visual feast laid by these two volumes greatly helps to supplement the monotonous diet of words served up by chroniclers and scholars.

So do two other historical media. For those who prefer their history in a tube, Wisconsin PBS-TV has produced six one-hour shows, "The Story of Spanish," comparable to Robert MacNeil's popular series on the evolution of the English language. Spanish TV's entry in the six-hour sweepstakes is a humanized portrait of "Isabel and Ferdinand," directed by the Oscar-winning American director James Goldman. The Catholic Monarchs not only sent Columbus off to the west in 1492, but sent as many as 50,000 Jews and *conversos* packing in order to purify the land newly reconquered from the Moors. Since the Spanish government acknowledged its historical fault in 1990 and welcomed Judaism into the official fold, Spain's Jewish heritage has received considerable attention. Among Spain's official Quincentenary projects is the restoration of the famous medieval Jewish quarters of Toledo, Seville, Barcelona, and Gerona. Although it is generally accepted by experts that Columbus had no Jewish heritage as far back as anyone can trace, the important Jewish contribution to Spanish culture and the not-unrelated departures of Columbus and of the Jewish deportees within weeks of each other in 1492 make these restorations of honor and buildings apt examples of contemporary benefits to be had from the Quincentenary.[33]

Since the appearance of Morison's biography in 1942, we have learned much more about Columbus's pre-American experiences and Spanish precedents. Philip Argenti has described the role of Genoese Chios in the Mediterranean economy.[34] John Vogt has vividly analyzed what Columbus saw at Saõ Jorge da Mina.[35] And David Quinn has scrutinized the available evidence on Columbus's probable visit to England and Ireland and his possible voyage to Iceland.[36] But the region that played the greatest role in Columbus's and Spanish colonial thinking was the Atlantic islands, particularly the Canaries.

The Canaries were the only Atlantic archipelago with human inhabitants, the cave-dwelling Guanches. French, Portuguese, and Spanish invaders fought off and on throughout the fourteenth and fifteenth centuries to subdue the islands and their native defenders, who were enslaved and transported to Iberia and Portuguese Madeira in peace and war. Not until the treaty of Alcáçovas in 1479 did the Spanish gain exclusive right to the seven Canaries, the last of which was not subdued until 1496. Though lacking metal, cloth, boats, horses, bread, cattle, and bows, the Guanches held out against great odds in their mountainous domains with only stone slings, a strange whistling war language, mobile herds of sheep and goats, and clever stratagems based on their superior knowledge of the terrain. Eventually succumbing to factionalism and foreign horses, ships, and disease, they became "the first people to be driven over the cliff of extinction by modern imperialism."[37]

Drawn by the Canaries' native dyestuffs, hides, beeswax, and slaves and later-introduced wheat, wine, and sugar, the Spanish dispossessed the natives, distributed their land, and resettled the islands largely with Iberian peasants according to "just war" concepts drawn from the *Reconquista* of Castille and Granada. But the novelty of conquering "savage" people on a set of islands some two weeks' sail from Cadiz forced the Spanish to modify their peninsular practices and institutions and to experiment with new forms of colonization. In the Canaries, natives who, after a preliminary warning, peacefully submitted to the Church and the Crown were juridically treated as citizens and given land in the post-conquest divisions; in the Indies, this warning became the famous *Requerimiento* ridiculed by Las Casas. In the protean state of Hispano-native relations, the many-hued Canarians were treated not as a racial problem but as a challenge of class and culture; Spanish colonists had no qualms about marrying "noble" native women. As in the Indies, which were being explored and colonized at the same time the Canaries were being effectively colonized under royal auspices, later conquests were financed largely by ad hoc companies of Genoese financiers and Spanish conquistadors. The ranking officials in the islands were first called "governors" in the Canaries, and each one received a rigorous *residencia* or judicial audit at his departure from office, even in mid-career in the Canaries. And an *Audiencia* or supreme court of oversight and appeal was created in the Canaries and in Santo Domingo in the same year (1526), symbolizing the linked trajectories of Spain's eastern and western Atlantic possessions. Only the greatly reduced native populations in the Canaries prevented the transplantation of a *repartimiento* system of spoils that included jurisdiction over the indigenous peoples in the apportionments of land, the *Reconquista* practice that became the *encomienda* system in the Indies. Otherwise, the Canaries served as a "conceptual half-way house" between the feudal *Reconquista* of the Iberian peninsula and the fully articulated imperialism of the Americas.[38] It is therefore historically important as well as symbolically fitting that in 1492 Columbus sailed to Gomera in the western Canaries for supplies and refitting before catching the northeast trade winds to the Indies of the West.

The most striking difference between the fourth and fifth Columbian centenaries is that the American natives in 1892 were relegated to footnotes while today they not only dominate the text but have begun to rewrite it. The

Columbian Expositions in Chicago and Madrid in 1892–93 were brash celebrations of Euro-American cultural superiority and "progress," in which the Indians were visible only as glass-cased souvenirs of "primitive life" or as well-scrubbed models of Western education and "civilization."[39] Today, nearly every Quincentenary planning group, conference panel, museum design staff, and film advisory board includes native American members. The reason is less affirmative action or political correctness than a marked shift of focus from the benefits of Columbus's discovery to its costs, particularly for the victims of European colonialism. As older historiographical trends shifted our viewpoint from Seville, Paris, and London to Santo Domingo, Quebec, and Jamestown, the Indians who surrounded those capitals have also moved toward the center of our attention, just as they occupied the schemes, dreams, and fears of European colonists for much of the colonial period. Not surprisingly, much of the best scholarship generated by the Quincentenary is devoted to the Indian side of the Encounter story.

Because native scholars are still too few, and fewer still specialize in the earliest stages of contact, published native perspectives on the Columbian Encounter have not been numerous. Native activists and organizers have been heard more than native scholars. Indian organizations have made it clear that either they wish to mourn the Quincentenary as the anniversary of a holocaust and the descent of the Dark Ages upon America, or they wish to celebrate it in their own ways as "500 years of Native People's resistance to colonization." Or they want nothing to do with it because they anticipate another self-congratulatory media circus like those in 1892 and 1976.[40]

The only sustained scholarly discussions of the "discovery" from an Indian perspective have appeared in *Seeds of Change,* the catalogue accompanying a major Smithsonian exhibition, and in a special issue of the *Northeast Indian Quarterly* entitled "View from the Shore: American Indian Perspectives on the Quincentenary."[41] In the former, George Horse Capture, a Gros Ventre museologist and historian, gives an eloquent personal reading of post-Columbian America, looking backward and forward from the daring Indian occupation of Alcatraz Island in 1969. In the latter, John Mohawk, a Seneca professor of Native American Studies at the State University of New York-Buffalo, skillfully debunks some of the mythology surrounding Columbus's voyages of "discovery" by placing them in their pre-American context, and José Barreiro, the journal's editor, contributes a long and thoughtful "Note on Tainos: Whither Progress?" Shorter pieces sample native views of the mutual discovery, the five-hundred-year Encounter, and the Quincentenary itself.

Early Quincentenary issues of the *Northeast Indian Quarterly* were devoted to "Indian Roots of American Democracy" and "Indian Corn of the Americas: Gift to the World."[42] These subjects are typical of the "contributions" approach that has been a dominant theme of Native American Studies since their inception in the late '60s, a phase that all minority studies tend to go through on their way to cultural assurance and self-definition.[43] By concentrating on the (usually material) contributions that native cultures have made to the dominant Euro-American cultures, minority students marginalize their own group by making it conform or "contribute" to the dominant culture and its standards of importance, rather than assert the integrity and value of their own cultures and histories. The addition of nonmaterial contributions has broadened the discussion, without really transcending the limitations of the genre. Thus far the discussion of the native contribution to American democracy has been limited to the alleged Iroquois influence on the Founding Fathers, though in *Indian*

Givers and *Native Roots* anthropologist Jack Weatherford seeks to describe, in the words of his subtitles, *How the Indians of the Americas Transformed the World* and *How the Indians Enriched America.*[44]

Although native scholars are not contributing to the Quincentenary in large numbers, their colleagues and a number of museums and publishers are seeing that the Indian story is memorably told in words, maps, and images. Archaeologists Michael Coe, Dean Snow, and Elizabeth Benson have encompassed the whole hemisphere in their *Atlas of Ancient America,* which contains 56 maps and 329 illustrations.[45] The substantial scholarly text takes the reader from the Bering Strait to Tierra del Fuego, through all aspects of culture from housing to religion, and ends with the living cultures of today. Philip Kopper's popularization, *The Smithsonian Book of North American Indians Before the Coming of the Europeans,* adds an interesting section on scholars of native life and how they investigate the past to a visually striking if traditional survey of American culture areas.[46] *America in 1492,* edited by Alvin Josephy, treats in a readable way the latest scholarship on the native cultures of all the Americas on the eve of colonization, augmented by more than two hundred illustrations.[47] Introductory scenes that focus on representative individuals give geographically and culturally diverse chapters a common human thread.

America 1492: Portrait of a Continent 500 Years Ago, by Spanish historian Manuel Lucena Salmoral, is a densely illustrated coffeetable-sized depiction of America's various Indian cultures on the eve of European colonization.[48] Its text and illustrations cleverly describe native religions, arts, and everyday customs, such as sexuality, child care, and coming of age; it is particularly good on the lives of women, as depicted in effigy pottery. In a smaller format, Brian M. Fagan's *Kingdoms of Gold, Kingdoms of Jade: The*

Americas Before Columbus is briefer, more historical, and less personalized in describing the evolution primarily of the urban civilizations of South and Central America.[49]

Two major exhibitions that resulted in important books focus on America north of the forty-ninth parallel. More than most museum catalogues, both highlight their scholarship as much as their objects and illustrations. *The Spirit Sings: Artistic Traditions of Canada's First Peoples* opened at the Glenbow Museum in Calgary during the 1986 Winter Olympics. Unhappily, the appearance of this extraordinary assemblage of native artifacts—665 lent by 90 institutions in 20 countries—met with protests stemming from an ongoing land grievance of the Lubicon Lake Cree in northern Alberta.[50] It is ironic that one of the show's main goals was to stress the continuity and resilience of native culture in spite of overwhelming European influence, oppression, and suppression."[51] But the protests could not tarnish the visual and interpretive integrity of the exhibition and catalogue.

The second exhibition, *Crossroads of Continents: Cultures of Siberia and Alaska,* encountered no protests when it was mounted in 1988 by the National Museum of Natural History during the heyday of *glasnost.* To produce a companion volume, William Fitzhugh and Aron Crowell assembled twenty eight Russian and American scholars to write essays on the history and cultures of the international circumpolar region.[52] These essays, modestly but well illustrated with maps, objects, drawings, and photographs, formed a substantial book of 350 triple-columned pages. The wide similarities between the native peoples of the North Pacific revealed by this book should stimulate thinking about the Asian origins of the original Americans perhaps thirty thousand years before Columbus discovered his long-sought "Asians" in America.

Another set of books will appeal to those who like their

history straight, without much visual adornment. A Cambridge University Press trilogy will survey all of the Americas and focus on the evolving histories of the natives in relation to their Euro-American invaders and neighbors. Bruce Trigger and Wilcomb Washburn are editing the North American volume of *The Cambridge History of the Native Peoples of the Americas*, the first attempt to encompass the complex ethnohistory of the hemisphere.[53] That such a broad synthesis can now be made signals the maturity of both ethnohistory and the history of Indian-white relations and augurs well for the continued centrality of the Indians in the history of the Encounter.[54]

In a more accessible medium, Robin Maw's Media Resource Associates is producing a ten-hour series of television documentaries, "Indian America: A History." This series is distinguished by its unusual coast-to-coast locations and its imaginative use of native speakers as the on-screen authorities and narrators of their own history. The Newberry Library also has plans to produce a four-hour series, "Tales from the Center of the Universe," in which four native authors from different regions will describe the beliefs and tell the stories of their respective people. Another visual presentation seeks to re-create history in three dimensions. A four-hundred-acre site in Columbus, Ohio, is being transformed into Three Rivers Reserve, a c. 1792 Indian settlement that will be peopled by native interpreters. The portrayal of viable native life in the East on the eve of the nineteenth century will be salutary for Americans misled by loose Quincentenary talk of Columbian "genocide" into thinking that only the post-Independence West had—and has—Indian inhabitants.

A prominent feature of the Ohio reserve will be its ample fields of corn, beans, and squash. Two of the more unusual projects of the Quincentenary revolve around the productive processes and exportable products of native agriculture. In October 1991 the National Museum of Natural History opened a major if flawed exhibition called "Seeds of Change" and published a lavish and intellectually challenging catalogue of the same title.[55] The theme of exhibition and book is the transformation of the globe by flora, fauna, and microbes exchanged between continents after 1492, particularly sugar, maize, the potato, the horse, and epidemic diseases. Instead of the products of native agriculture, *Indian Agriculture in the Americas*, a projected three-volume study edited by William Denevan, concentrates on its technology.[56] Denevan notes that without draft animals or wheeled vehicles, native farmers before 1492 had developed techniques far in advance of those used by contemporary farmers in the other Old World and obtained crop yields not equaled until the present century.[57]

Unlike the ethnocentric justifications of European colonialism found in the 1892 celebrations, the dominant theme of the quincentenary is Encounter. It has much to recommend it. Encounters are mutual, reciprocal—two-way rather than one-way streets. Encounters are generically capacious: there are encounters of people but also of ideas, institutions, habits, values, plants, animals, and microorganisms. Encounters are temporally and spatially fluid; they can occur at any time in any place, before or after 1492, around the globe. And, while natives, critics, and activists may not approve, encounters are morally neutral; the term does not prejudge the nature of the contact or its outcome. In sum, *encounter* is a spacious description that jettisons normative baggage to make room for disinterestness and parity. It is a salutary word for our conflicted postmodern commemoration of a conflicted protomodern event.

What brought the peoples of two hitherto isolated worlds together was European imperialism. Europeans left their own countries to invade, conquer, and resettle the Indians' lands. Understandably, the invaders felt compelled to justify and rationalize their actions abroad, often before they launched their fleets. The compound of ancient and humanist philosophy, church doctrine, "international" law, and colonial precedent used to carve out new empires in the Americas is the subject of two thorough and largely overlapping books, *The Law of Nations and the New World* by L. C. Green and Olive Dickason, and *The American Indian in Western Legal Thought* by Robert A. Williams, Jr. They are a useful reminder that while the colonization of America was in part an armed invasion, those with might also wanted right on their side in the eyes of (Western) world opinion. Both books drive home the conclusion that "a will to empire proceeds most effectively under a rule of law."[58]

As we think of law as the blind lady holding the impartial scales of justice, so we tend to view cartography as the scientific representation of geographical space. The late Brian Harley tried to rid us of our naïveté by demonstrating that maps were and still are "active instruments of power," particularly in the hands of those with power who aspire to more. In a traveling exhibition and catalogue called *Maps and the Columbian Encounter*, Harley persuasively argued that for European imperialists maps were, like laws, essential because the invaders knew that "to catalogue the world is to appropriate it." "The map was an instrument with which European power and values could be reproduced along the most distant shore." In the face of the Ptolemaic grid, abstract coordinates, and print, the Indians were at a severe disadvantage. It was too easy for European map-makers simply to leave native names (and therefore claims) off the maps or to rename them, thereby reifying the myth of the empty frontier, the *vacuum domicilium* so dear to the New England Puritans.[59] Harley made a bold, productive contribution to Quincentenary scholarship. His scrutiny of the English mapping of New England was arguably the high point of the interdisciplinary conference "The Land of Norumbega: Maine in the Age of Exploration and Settlement" in 1988, for which Susan Danforth mounted an excellent exhibition of maps, books, prints, and instruments.[60]

The Atlas of Columbus and the Great Discoveries by Kenneth Nebenzahl is a more conventional aesthetic and positivist tracing of the explorers' attempts to chart the newfound lands; it ignores altogether the native Americans, who supplied many of the details on early maps.[61] A new project at the University of Wisconsin-Milwaukee, which sponsored Harley's exhibition, will fill that large lacuna by treating native maps and mapping in North America in an ambitious exhibition and catalogue. The effort to describe the geographical encounter of natives and newcomers has already begun in a major way with the production of *The Exploration of North America: A Comprehensive History*, edited in three volumes by John Allen.[62] Virtually all of its essays emphasize the indispensable role of native guides, interpreters, and impromptu map-makers in helping the Euro-American explorers of every century find their way around the continent, ultimately to the Indians' own loss.

Literary scholars as well as cartographers and legal historians have analyzed the European thrust for empire. In *Marvelous Possessions: The Wonder of the New World*, a short but "thick" book of lectures, Stephen Greenblatt perceptively dissects the European use of kidnapped natives, acculturated go-betweens, and a rich discourse of wonder to take possession of the Americas. Representations of wonder, "the central figure in the initial European response to New World," Greenblatt argues, were used primarily to "supplement legally flawed territorial claims." Only a few Europeans such as Montaigne, who met his Indians in Europe, recognized themselves in the "other" and reclaimed the power of wonder "for decency as well as domination."[63]

Judging by the titles of conferences and books, the most popular encounters took place between cultures, a term seldom employed with ethnological precision but useful as a kind of historical *omnium gatherum*. One good result is that the best Encounter conferences have been multi- and, at their best, interdisciplinary, with wide representation of North and Latin American historians, anthropologists, archaeologists, geographers, students of literature and language, and a variety of other scientists and social scientists of historical bent. Perhaps the earliest conference of this nature occurred at Ohio State University in October 1986, under the title "Early European Encounters with the Americas: Reciprocal Influences of Cultures in Contact." A smaller and equally stimulating conference, "Rethinking the Encounter: New Perspectives on Conquest and Colonization, 1450–1550," was sponsored by the Institute of Early Contact Period Studies (a Quincentenary foundation) at the University of Florida two years later. Neither conference published its heterogeneous proceedings, but thenceforward the organizers of nearly every conference incorporated publication plans in their budgets and took greater care to achieve balance of coverage and uniformity of quality in their programs to justify the expense and risk of publication.[64]

The most ambitious conference to date occurred in three parts, two in Trujillo, Spain, and the third in Albany, New York, and involved sixty scholars, mostly Latin American experts. Sponsored by a Spanish foundation and the State University of New York-Albany between 1988 and 1990, "In Word and Deed: Interethnic Encounters and Cultural Developments in the New World" will result in three bilingual volumes of revised proceedings. The first volume, *Interethnic Images: Discourse and Practice in the New World,* appeared in 1992.[65]

At least four other Encounter conferences will publish—or have already published—their proceedings. William B. Taylor and Franklin Pease Y have edited the results of a joint Smithsonian–University of Maryland 1989 conference called *Violence and Resistance in the Americas: The Legacy of Conquest,* which focuses primarily on Latin America.[66] The Center for Early Modern History at the University of Minnesota will publish the papers from its innovative international conference "Implicit Ethnographies: Encounters Between Europeans and Other Peoples in the Wake of Columbus," which took place in October 1990. And on the weekend before Columbus Day 1992, two ambitious symposia will generate hefty books of proceedings: Vanderbilt University will host a discussion "Transatlantic Encounters: The Discovery of the Old World and the New"; Loyola University of Chicago will set Church scholars and ethnohistorians upon the topic "Agents of Change: Jesuits and Encounters of Two Worlds."[67]

The geographical and generic flexibility of the Encounter theme is apparent not only in individual papers at conferences but in the regional and topical focus of several conferences, exhibitions, and books. All these venues show the benefits of applying the larger questions of cultural contact generated by the Spanish experience in the Caribbean and southern America to other parts of the continent. In July 1992 the National Museum of American History opened a show and published a substantial companion volume called *American Encounters,* an invocation of the polyglot and intersecting lifeways of the Indian, Spanish, African, and Anglo Americans in the upper Rio Grande valley of New Mexico.[68] Farther afield, *Russian America: The Forgotten Frontier,* the catalogue of a traveling exhibition sponsored by the Washington State Historical Society and the Anchorage (Alaska) Museum of History and Art, serves to check the southern and eastern biases of the Quincentenary. Consisting of over six hundred artifacts, documents, and artworks from American, Finnish, and Soviet repositories, the exhibition and its black-and-white guide demonstrate that "Russian America offers a variation on the colonial pattern familiar elsewhere in North America."[69] Like their American rivals in the sea otter trade, the employees of the early Russian companies initially exploited the native populations and natural resources. But particularly after 1818, when the imperial navy assumed the management of the Russian-American Company, the few hundred Russians who inhabited the North Pacific began to encourage native languages and customs, support widespread education and employment of natives and *métis* in responsible positions, and conserve marine resources. At the same time, the Orthodox Church produced devout native adherents and dedicated missionaries, including several of native parentage—a legacy that persists in present-day Alaska.

Scholarly discoveries have come thick and fast during the Quincentenary. None have been more satisfying, both visually and intellectually, than those made by Jacqueline Peterson Swagerty, the organizer of a traveling exhibition entitled "Sacred Encounters: Jesuit Missionaries and the Indians of the Rocky Mountains West," scheduled to open in St. Louis in 1993. The exhibition is based on the discovery at Washington State University of a remarkable collection of watercolors and pencil and ink drawings by missionary-artist Nicolas Point, which rivals the works of Carl Bodmer and George Catlin in ethnographic detail and artistic significance; a new collection of early maps of the trans-Mississippi West drawn by Father Pierre Jean De Smet, fur traders, and Indians, which was found in the

Jesuit Missouri Province archives; and a rare assemblage of liturgical and ethnographic objects discovered in a trunk in a Belgian chateau near De Smet's birthplace. The hundreds of Point drawings in particular vividly depict the spiritual odyssey of the Flathead Indians who recruited the Jesuits in St. Louis, helped them establish the St. Mary Mission in 1841, and syncretized Christianity with their own religion to cope with the changes in their no-longer-isolated world. The catalogue accompanying the drawings will feature curators' and invited experts' essays, with lavish, full-color illustrations; the show will use Roman chants, European band music (which the Jesuits introduced to America), and the sacred smells of incense, sage, and tobacco to evoke the religious life of the mission, from both native and missionary perspectives.

The publication of substantial catalogues will ensure that the educational impact of Encounter exhibitions does not end with the closing of their tours. One museum will see that the post-Columbian story of seventeenth-century Virginia has a much longer run: in 1990 Jamestown Settlement (formerly Jamestown Festival Park, a state facility) opened a renovated 30,000 sq. ft. museum built explicitly around the Encounter theme. The first gallery introduces England on the eve of colonization and the European arts and goals of discovery in the new-found lands. In the second gallery visitors meet Powhatan Indian culture as it had evolved over hundreds of years in the distinctive ecological niche of the tidewater. In the third gallery they see how the conjunction of these cultures and peoples, joined reluctantly by African slaves after 1619, created the rural world of great and small planters, representative institutions, two catastrophic Indian uprisings, civil war, and the social tensions of economic and racial divisions. Authentic reconstructions of early Jamestown and its fort, a Powhatan village, and the three ships of 1607, including a new *Susan*

Constant, lend credence to the museum's historical message.

One happy result of the Quincentenary is renewed attention to the global extent of cultural encounters and to the value of studying them comparatively. Such comparisons are capable of generating not only social scientific typologies but, perhaps more broadly useful, newly angled questions to ask of our own familiar subjects. We invariably gain by comparing Europe's American encounters with each other and with colonial encounters that occurred in other parts of the world.

Several books exist to put us in a comparative mode. Anthropologist Brian Fagan provides a set of detailed case studies in *Clash of Cultures,* which ranges from Aztecs and Hurons in North America to Tahitians and Maoris in the Pacific.[70] Urs Bitterli studies the "cultural history" of contact in *Cultures in Conflict: Encounters Between European and Non-European Cultures, 1492–1800.* Using a typology of fleeting *contacts,* major *collisions,* and long-term *relationships,* he devotes chapters to the Portuguese in Africa and Asia, the Spanish in Hispaniola, the French in Canada, the English in Pennsylvania, Europeans in China, and English and French in the South Seas. Though his details are occasionally unreliable and his generalizations sometimes suspect, Bitterli's effort to bring major post-Columbian encounters into comparative focus, like Fagan's, is imaginative and salutary.

The benefits of having a single intelligence compare multiple encounters are partially realized in William Fitzhugh's introduction to and four-part commentary in *Cultures in Contact: The Impact of European Contacts on Native American Cultural Institutions, A.D. 1000–1800,* a collection of papers originally presented to the Anthropological Society of Washington by historians and archaeologists.[72] The unifying topic was the effects of European contact, not only on material culture and technology, but on the institutions that organized native societies. The papers dealt with four regions: Greenland and the Eastern Arctic, New England and New York, the Chesapeake, and Florida and Hispaniola. In the Arctic, fairly uniform natural resources, geographical features, and native lifeways, when combined with sporadic European contacts of a mostly economic nature, produced similar effects on the native cultures. But in the other regions, the diversity of native cultures, geographies, and European goals, methods, and societies made for a variety of institutional effects, within as well as between regions. These kinds of case studies remind us that comparative history is as likely to find salient differences of process and outcome as it is striking similarities, and that we must work equally hard to explain both. Cultural contacts were and are extremely complex, and we should scrutinize carefully easy or ideologically tempting monocausal explanations such as disease, imperialism, racism, or sexism.

All encounters had a beginning, a flashpoint of contact where the histories, goals, and feelings of the parties intersected to form a new entity, which in turn refashioned their image of their individual pasts. The study of truly first contacts is only beginning. My American Historical Association booklet, *Imagining the Others First Contacts in North America,* looks at the process from both sides of several encounters, from Guanahaní in 1492 to the Lower Mississippi in the early eighteenth century.[73] I emphasize the expectations that each side had of the other, how both defined the other in cosmological or ethnological terms, and how power relationships maintained or altered initial perceptions. Bruce Trigger argues from somewhat different premises that, after a short period of contact, Indians shifted from an idiosyncratic, relativist, romantic, *religious* view of the newcomers to an objective, naturalistic, pragmatic view based on "the *rational* component inherent in the mental processes of every human being." Trigger's strong argument for the possibility of "an objective understanding of human behavior" shaped mainly by "calculations of individual self-interest that are uniform from one culture to another" is weakened by his failure to define key terms such as "rationality," "self-interest," and "practical reason."[74] Yet his bold outline of interpretive choices, however dichotomized he makes them, should prove useful in encounter studies.

Theories of behavior would not loom so large if we had better access to the thoughts and feelings—even the facial expressions—of the natives at first contact. We do have a few oral traditions, some personal testimony mediated by European informants, a few reliable drawings and paintings, and a few handsful of archaeological evidence that speak to initial Indian responses. These we have to cobble together and fill in the remaining gaps with philosophical assumptions. We would give a great deal for sustained and full diaries by European participant-observers, photographs, and film footage of any initial encounter in the Americas.

Happily, we have the next best thing: a book and film that describe in fascinating detail the mutual discovery of white men and the hitherto isolated Highland peoples of Papua, New Guinea, whose cultures bear a striking resemblance to those of many groups of American Indians. *First Contact*, the book and the film by Australian film-makers Bob Connolly and Robin Anderson, tells the story of a pair of diary-keeping, camera-carrying Australian gold prospectors who stumbled on the Stone Age Highlanders in the early 1930s.[75] The raw evidence of their mutual encounter and of their mutual responses to it was preserved by one prospector's unusual diaries, still and moving pictures, and the vivid memories of interviewed tribespeople, who had regarded the intruders as reincarnated ancestors or ghosts. After making allowance for cultural blindspots on both sides, we cannot come any closer to the emotional reality of America's first encounters than by re-experiencing those of the Papua Highlands.

Understandably, the American encounters that have claimed the most scholarly and public attention during the Quincentenary were those between the Spanish and the natives of the Caribbean. (For lack of evidence and durable effect, we give short shrift to the Norse encounters with the Skraelings in Newfoundland around 1000 A.D.) As Michael Gannon has suggested, some of the most exciting and fruitful scholarship is coming from a union of history and archaeology, often in the same persons.[76] American archaeologists digging in the Caribbean—most of them currently or formerly affiliated with the Florida Museum of Natural History and the University of Florida—are also immersed in the Spanish historical record, printed and manuscript. Their findings substantiate the terrible loss of native life caused by the Spanish incursion; they also establish for the first time a basis for assessing the social meanings of those losses and the changing conditions of Spanish colonial life in the half-century after Columbus's first voyage.

The People Who Discovered Columbus: An Introduction to the Prehistory of the Bahamas by William F. Keegan is a demanding scientific analysis of the geography, ecology, and human lifeways of the twenty-five islands of the Bahama archipelago, where an estimated 80,000 Lucayans lived.[77] Unfortunately, its daunting tables, graphs, and technical terminology will keep it from reaching a large audience. It needs a popularization, because it establishes with unmistakable authority the socio-cultural baseline of Lucayan life that was so thoroughly destroyed within a short generation—so quickly that Columbus was the only

European to record first-hand observations of it. In 1509 King Ferdinand ordered the wholesale deportation of Lucayan slaves to solve Hispaniola's severe shortage of native labor. Amerigo Vespucci forcibly stole 232 natives when he left for Spain in 1500. Between 1502 and 1520, when the Lucayans were finally exterminated, an estimated four hundred caravel loads were needed to remove some 40,000 people from the islands.

Keegan also comes down firmly on San Salvador (Watling's Island) as the site of Columbus's landfall. Unlike that of other debaters, most of whom are sailors and come at the question seaward through Columbus's problematic *diario*, Keegan's conclusion is based on an extensive coastal survey of native archaeological sites in all the Bahamas. This knowledge, combined with a keen geographical and ecological sense of the various candidates, enables him to make more sense of Columbus's observations and directions than do his competitors. By finding Spanish artifacts of the exact types described by Columbus as having been given to the Lucayans, other archaeologists on San Salvador have supported Keegan's view.[78]

More accessible because it relies primarily on written documents is Samuel M. Wilson's brief narrative ethnohistory *Hispaniola: Caribbean Chiefdoms in the Age of Columbus*.[79] Wilson describes how the perhaps one million Taínos of the island were divided into *cacicazgos* or chiefdoms of dozens of villages, ruled by hereditary caciques who directed the manioc-based economy of their people and played a central role in mediating between their subjects' physical and spiritual worlds. When the Spanish invaded, some caciques allied themselves with the newcomers in order to expand or consolidate their bases of power; others saw the handwriting on the wall more clearly and launched armed uprisings against the usurpers. In the end, neither tactic was successful and native culture was obliterated by the combined effects of disease, oppression, and starvation. By 1540 the Taínos were nearly extinct.

For lack of anything sounder, Wilson provisionally accepts R. A. Zambardino's estimate of one million Hispaniolans in 1492, while noting the critiques and cautions of Carl Sauer and David Henige.[80] Only an archaeological survey of native sites in Hispaniola (now Haiti and the Dominican Republic) will endow population estimates, which range from 60,000 to 14.5 million, with credibility. As John Daniels shows, estimates of Indian populations in the Americas have been steadily on the rise, especially (and not coincidentally) since the 1960s and the deadly and unpopular Vietnam War.[81] The escalating "body count" of the war, together with an historiographical shift toward social and quantitative history that focused on the inarticulate victims of the past, fueled the inflation of native losses to implausible heights. It was as though we could not bring ourselves to condemn the moral enormities of the past without an accompaniment of numerical enormities.

The Quincentenary trend toward condemnation of the evils of Columbian, Spanish, European, and Western imperialism, racism, and genocide will do nothing to dampen our moral enthusiasm for huge native numbers. We have yet to outgrow our fondness for the hectoring bishop of Chiapas, Las Casas, and the "Black Legend" of exceptional Spanish cruelty that his writings helped create. But it is time we did so; until we do, we will not be able to get the whole complex story straight or to render fair and impartial judgment upon all of the participants, "winners" as well as "losers," Spaniards as well as Taínos. To do any less is to abnegate our most important duties as historians, amateur or professional.[82]

The lives of ordinary Spanish settlers in the Caribbean are also being reconstructed by historians and archaeologists. The first Spanish settlement was La Navidad on the

northern coast of Haiti, where the *Santa Maria* broke up
on Christmas Eve, 1492. With timbers from the ship, the
Spanish built a fortified enclosure, complete with moat,
palisade, and probably watchtower, in the heart of the
nearest Taíno town. The local cacique, Guacanagarí, not
only helped the sailors salvage their goods but stored the
goods in his own house and then gave the house to them as
the centerpiece of their fort. When Columbus sailed back
to Spain, he left behind thirty-nine men, who were directed to collect gold in the region. But when he returned
the following year, the men had all died, the fort had
burned to the ground, and its supplies were scattered far
and wide.

Since 1983 a University of Florida team under the direction of Kathleen Deagan has been excavating a large
native/Spanish site in northern Haiti called En Bas Saline,
which was located by Dr. William Hodges, a medical missionary and avocational archaeologist. In addition to vast
amounts of native material, excavations to date have un-
covered the burned remains of a substantial wooden and
clay daub structure, eighteen European artifacts dating to
the Columbian era, and, in a well nearby, the teeth of a
European pig and a rat bone. Isotopic analysis of the teeth
concluded that the pig was raised near Seville in Spain.
Both animals probably disembarked while La Navidad was
being unintentionally founded by Columbus.[83]

Less than a mile from En Bas Saline are the ruins of
Puerto Real, a Spanish town occupied from 1503 to 1578
on the edge of cattle country. Four hundred years after the
town's population was relocated to quash its hide smug-
gling with Spain's enemies, University of Florida archaeologists began to dig there, making it the most extensively
excavated site of initial European occupation in the Caribbean. Like La Isabela before it, the town was laid out in a
grid pattern, which Spanish law eventually mandated for

all colonial towns. Surrounding the central plaza were a cathedral, festooned with large limestone gargoyles, and other public buildings, some fortified. Of the fifty-seven masonry structures detected by survey, only the foundations of the cathedral, a cemetery, three domestic buildings, and, downwind from most of the town, a beef-and-hide-processing workshop have been thoroughly exposed and studied.[84]

In this "bovine utopia," beef and pork (from fast-breeding imported pigs) rather than local species were the faunal staples of the colonists' diet, accounting for 95 percent of their fleshy intake.[85] Pond turtles and certain fish were the major dietary adaptations of the Catholic settlers, whose church calendar officially prescribed 165 meatless days. By contrast, the faunal diet of the natives at neighboring En Bas Saline was 68 percent fish and only 20 percent mammal. Fragments of Taíno-style ceramic griddles suggest that early in the town's history native women baked cassava bread made from manioc. Large amounts of crude, unglazed "colono-ware," often made in Hispanic shapes but from local materials and with non-Hispanic decorations, also confirm a major hypothesis about Spanish acculturation in the Americas, namely, that "Spanish domestic adaptive strategy was consistently based on the incorporation of unmodified Indian cultural elements in kitchen activities, probably through Indian mates. This resulted in a genuinely new, multicultural expression that ultimately crystallized as New World criollo culture and stands in sharp contrast to Anglo-American culture."[86] When the native population was exterminated, particularly after the island-wide smallpox epidemic of 1518–19, African slaves replaced Taíno and enslaved Lucayan women in the kitchens, a transition reflected in the colono-wares.

A second, increasingly confirmed, hypothesis about the

"Spanish colonial pattern" is that, while Indian and later African cultural elements were readily incorporated in the socially non-visible infrastructural areas such as diet and food preparation, which were the province of women, visible symbols of social identification such as architecture, tablewares, and personal adornment remained characteristically Spanish because dominated by men. Rectangular Iberian-style buildings (unlike circular Taíno *bohios*), metal lacing tips and buckles for Spanish-style clothing, ornate brass and enamel book clasps, traditional *majolica* vessels with owner's stamps, and delicate glass goblets lend strong support to this useful observation, which had its origins in Deagan's extensive study of St. Augustine.[87]

The Spanish were not the only Europeans to leave their cultural mark on the Caribbean. In *Cannibal Encounters: The Meeting of European and Island Carib Cultures, 1492–1763*, Philip Boucher describes English and French contacts and conflicts with the Caribs of the Lesser Antilles, believed by Columbus and all but the most recent scholarship to be fierce cannibals.[88] Boucher puts the lie to this belief and explains why the Caribs sided with the French in the colonial wars beginning in 1666. Through missionaries and *coureurs des îles*—fishermen, hunters, trappers, and traders—who spoke the Carib language and appreciated Carib war tactics, the French wove a strong web of contact with the natives, which the English could never duplicate. And when English freebooters and vigilantes provoked the Caribs into conflict, the more centralized French colonial administration kept its colonists in line and conflicts to a minimum. The sad irony is that the land hunger of both French and English led to the brutal removal of the Caribs from most of the islands by the eighteenth century, just as European *philosophes* were beginning to romanticize them.

Another important growth industry of the Quincentenary is the study of the Spanish Borderlands, once made famous by Herbert Bolton and his legions of graduate students and now enjoying a renaissance, particularly in the understudied Southeast.[89] What is emerging from the new scholarship is the crucial importance of the sixteenth century in North American history for both colonists and natives. That formative century was filled with Spanish activity—coastal explorations, entradas, mission foundations, failed and enduring colonies, town building, defensive wars with European competitors, and a long series of cultural engagements with native peoples, sometimes as sovereign allies or enemies, more often as tributaries and subjects. In the process, native societies were radically reshaped by warfare, enslavement, resettlement, disease, Christian proselytizing, material novelties, intermarriage, and a host of other acculturative forces. The French and English colonizers who followed later in the century found their tasks lightened or burdened by the conditions—geopolitical, demographic, and emotional—created by previous Spanish-Indian encounters. If the Spanish had magically disappeared from North America in 1599, that legacy alone would make the history of the Borderlands a major key to the history of colonial America.

So much scholarship has been produced since the publication in 1970 of John Francis Bannon's ethnocentric and (for the date) curiously old-fashioned *The Spanish Borderlands Frontier, 1513–1821* that a new synthesis has been needed. David J. Weber has produced a brilliant one in *The Spanish Frontier in North America, 1513–1821,* which makes the Indians as central to the plot as the Spanish.[90] For the eastern Borderlands, Paul E. Hoffman has written a detailed, archivally based synthesis entitled *A New Andalusia and a Way to the Orient: The American Southeast During the Sixteenth Century.* He emphasizes the motivational role of Lucas Vazquez de Ayllon's tale of Chicora, a promised land of abundance and wealth somewhere in the

Southeast, and Giovanni da Verrazzano's tale of an eastern isthmus leading to the Pacific. "All the explorations and the attempts at colonization by the Spanish, French, and English" in the sixteenth century, he argues, "were linked by the belief of their leaders and promoters in these two legends from the 1520s as they had been altered over the decades." Hoffman also explains in often tragic detail "how men's hopes and wishes for North America were contradicted by the difficult reality of the coastal zone of the southeast."[91]

For the general reader, Jerald T. Milanich and Susan Milbrath have edited a sumptuously illustrated set of thirteen essays, *First Encounters: Spanish Explorations in the Caribbean and the United States, 1492–1570,* partly to accompany a traveling exhibition prepared by the Florida Museum of Natural History.[92] Nine essays are devoted to greater La Florida: Hernando de Soto's entrada in 1539–43, the Tristán de Luna expedition of 1559–61, the founding of St. Augustine by Pedro Menéndez in 1565, and the effects of these and other incursions upon the natives. Ten essays were written by historical archaeologists, who not only broaden but often rewrite the histories of encounter from subterranean evidence.

Soto's wandering route through the Southeast is a case in point. In 1939 the U.S. De Soto Expedition Commission, chaired by John R. Swanton, published its final report on the route taken by the Spaniards from Tampa Bay through the southern interior to the Mississippi.[93] Once Swanton's line of march leaves Florida, however, it has been proven to be almost all wrong. The commission lacked three crucial types of evidence which have matured only in the last few decades: historical geography (because the landscape has been substantially altered by human use since the sixteenth century), documentation from other sixteenth-century Spanish expeditions that revisited native towns on Soto's route, and archaeology of native sites just before and after contact.

By combining these sources with contemporary accounts of the expedition and modern topographical maps, Charles Hudson and a number of colleagues have totally reconstructed Soto's route, piece by piece. Hudson and Milanich have collaborated on the readable and ingenious narrative *Hernando De Soto and the Indians of Florida,* and Hudson, Chester B. DePratter, and Marvin T. Smith have summarized their reconstruction of the whole route in *First Encounters.*[94] In addition to giving us historical accuracy, their reconstruction enables us to assess the entrada's full impact on the native Southeast because Soto and his comrades were the first Europeans to encounter the impressive Indian chiefdoms in the interior, and virtually the last to see them at the apex of their development and power. In subsequent decades, the social disorder and depopulation unleashed by imported disease and the military ruthlessness of the entrada sent these hierarchical chiefdoms into decline and eventual collapse.[95]

As an offshoot of his Soto research, Hudson has also written the ethnohistory of *The Juan Pardo Expeditions: Exploration of the Carolinas and Tennessee, 1566–68,* with Hoffman's editions and translations of four known and three new primary documents.[96] These narratives have value as windows on Spanish-Indian relations; they are also important because Pardo visited at least five of the towns visited by Soto. For archaeologists, the documents are useful for the detailed lists of trade goods that the Spaniards gave to the townspeople along their route. These goods help archaeologists date the occupation of native sites in order to measure cultural change accurately.

Two useful collections of scholarly essays by historians and archaeologists also help put the sixteenth century on the historiographical map. *The Forgotten Centuries: Euro-*

peans and Indians in the American South, 1513–1704, edited by Hudson and Carmen McClendon, is the result of an NEH Summer Institute for College Teachers at the University of Georgia in 1989.[97] More ambitious in scope and content are three volumes edited by David Hurst Thomas under the general title *Columbian Consequences.* Volume One is devoted to interdisciplinary perspectives on the Spanish Borderlands West, from Baja California to East Texas. Two Indian scholars discuss the survival strategies employed by their ancestors in coping with the European invaders. In the second volume, forty-five scholars dissect the southeastern Borderlands in three sections: the Soto entrada, the impact of Spanish colonization in the Southeast and the Caribbean, and the Spanish missions of La Florida. Volume Three places the Borderlands in pan-American perspective, assesses recent breakthroughs in the demography of contact, and takes a sobering look at previous Columbian observances. All three volumes bow to the general reader by heading each section with a substantial overview designed to make the succeeding specialized chapters accessible.[98]

Discoveries of new documents and improved translations of known ones are also extending our understanding of the Borderlands. James E. Kelley, Jr., one of the editor-translators of Columbus's *diario,* retranslated Herrera's unique narrative of *Juan Ponce de Leon's Discovery of Florida* to inform Douglas Peck's re-creation of the voyage in June 1990. The new text is augmented by critical essays by David Henige, Oliver Dunn, Donald McGuirk, and Peck himself.[99] The University of Alabama Press will publish new translations of three of the four known accounts of the Soto entrada and a fragment of a fifth recently found in Seville by Eugene Lyons, along with an excellent older translation of the fourth.[100] Finally, Ignacio Avellaneda has patiently assembled and collated the known facts about

257 of the 300-plus survivors of the Soto entrada who sailed to New Spain in 1543. Partly from a new list of 700 volunteers who left Spain with Soto in 1538, Avellaneda concludes that the typical conquistador with Soto was

> a male Spaniard born either in Extremadura or Castilla, 24 years old at the beginning of the expedition, and literate or at least knew how to sign his name. He was most likely a commoner by birth and, in a few cases, an hidalgo. Not being a military leader or an administrator, his chances of survival were reduced to roughly fifty percent. From Florida he went to the port of Pánuco in New Spain, and most likely he arrived in the great city of Tenochtitlan which was subsequently renamed Mexico City. He remained in Mexico or proceeded to Peru, married a daughter of a known conqueror and settled down.[101]

We can expect many more documentary discoveries after 1992 because of two major efforts to collect and make accessible in the United States copies of relevant records in Spanish archives. With multiple sponsors in Spain and the United States, the Institute of Early Contact Period Studies has undertaken a massive job of copying on laser-disk the complete archives of noble Spanish families that had a role in the colonization of the Americas. The first archive copied was that of the counts of Revillagigedo, the family that founded Florida in 1565 and provided the most important viceroys of Mexico. Next in line are the papers of the dukes of Infantado, in which Martín de Navarrete discovered Las Casas's abridged copy of Columbus's *diario* in 1715 and Eugene Lyon more recently found a previously unknown Columbus (Colón) genealogy. To make archival collections such as these more accessible to scholars, the Library of Congress, the American Historical Association, and the NEH sponsored a conference of librarians, archivists, scholarly users, and technical experts to plan a survey of reproduced documents from Spanish and Latin American archives already in the United States libraries. That survey is now under way at the Library of Congress.

The multiplication of texts and documents, official and unofficial, raises a general question about the colonial history of the Americas: whose history is it and how is it to be written? Historians could well profit during the Quincentenary and beyond from the work of literary scholars who study "colonial discourse." The new study of colonial discourse is perhaps only ten or fifteen years old, but its intellectual roots lie in the anticolonial, *négritude* writers of the 1930s and 1940s, and its crystallization in Edward Said's *Orientalism* of 1978.[102] With more recent borrowings from Continental poststructuralism, students of colonial discourse hold that dichotomies between Europe/Third World and Self/Other, as with Civilized/Savage before them, are not ontologically given by nature but historically constituted by the colonizing West. "Minorities" are the creations of power politics; they are cultural, not simply numerical, inferiors. Colonial powers define the world according to their best interests, not lights; their canonical judgments of Literature, Humanity, and Civilization are grounded in dominance, not in superior morality or knowledge. Colonial writing, therefore, is an instrument of the colonizing process, not objective disinterested reportage. In such circumstances, the history of the colonization and conquest of the Americas remains a hegemonic monologue, incomplete, self-serving, and suspect.[103]

To remedy these deficiencies, students of colonial discourse would advise all of us who use colonial texts and documents to make several changes in our assumptions and procedures. First, we should realize that "the native— colonized or indomitable—stands always at the heart of colonial writings, even when not explicitly mentioned," for it was the native's land, life, and labor that were at issue.[104] Second, to rewrite the history of the Americas, "to find the

buried roots of its culture," we must retrace the lost steps,
listen to other voices that could have related the history of
a truly new world, not of the specious discovery of the
invaders' own dreams, desires, and errors. For Hispanic
America particularly, where the conquest was so total and
sudden, we must strive to resurrect the submerged sound
of resistance: "the lying captives, the false guides and informants, the tireless weavers of fables, myths, and lies."[105]

To recapture America's reality, we must therefore conceive of colonial literary culture "not as a series of monuments but as a web of negotiations taking place in a living
society." The notion of canonical "literature" should give
way to that of "discourse," polyvocal and interactive.[106] As
Aimé Cesaire put it, "no race has a monopoly on beauty, on
intelligence, on strength / and there is room for everyone
at the convocation of conquest."[107] We must also pay close
attention to the "locus of enunciation" from which observers—and we ourselves as historians—understand and articulate the colonial situation, for no one born of a particular culture and time has a completely innocent eye.[108] Finally, in opening our ears to the voice of the "other," we
should suspend traditional literary categories and genres
and aesthetic criteria to admit native forms of discourse
that do not necessarily fit Western paradigms.[109] Most natives were speakers, not writers, and oral discourse has
rules and measures different from those of literacy. Several native cultures had sophisticated non-alphabetic writing systems, while others employed simpler pictographs to
the same end. In failing to understand the natives in their
own terms, the colonists simultaneously lost part of their
own identity in "the irreducible challenge of the Other."[110]
After five hundred years, we should not continue to run
the same risk.

No whirlwind tour of Quincentenary scholarship would
be complete without reference to work on the impact of

the Americas upon Europe and the rest of the world—the closing of the Columbian circle. With few exceptions, the best work on the influence of the New World predates the Quincentenary. In 1970 J. H. Elliott published his brilliant Wiles Lectures at Queen's University, Belfast, on the "uncertain impact" of Hispanic America on Europe before 1650. "In material terms," he argued, the Old World "had gained much from America; in spiritual and intellectual terms it had gained less. . . . Europeans had discovered something about the world around them, and a good deal more about themselves. Ironically, the impact of this discovery was blunted by the very extent and completeness of their successes overseas" because they "ministered to the vanity of Europe," which was "unlikely to show itself unduly receptive to new impressions and experiences." Only another, dissident Europe would continue to turn to America as a source of inspiration and hope. "For if America nurtured Europe's ambitions, it also kept its dreams alive."[111]

In 1975, as if to expand Elliott's measured conclusion, Germán Arciniega's panoramic *America in Europe: A History of the New World in Reverse* appeared in Spanish. Translated in 1986 for the English-speaking Quincentenary audience, it makes the unabashed claim that "with America, the modern world begins. Scientific progress begins, philosophy thrives. By means of America, Europe acquires a new dimension and emerges from its shadows."[112] Similarly, in the same year, William Brandon argued that "the New World insidiously engraved upon the Old World—especially via seventeenth- and eighteenth-century France—changes as profound in some respects as those suffered by the New" and that "garbled influences from the New World are in fact ascendant in certain noteworthy areas of social thought in our present world."[113]

The most comprehensive treatment of the question is

still *First Images of America: The Impact of the New World on the Old,* edited by the late Fredi Chiappelli and published in 1976 in two volumes.[114] This work presents fifty-five papers from an important conference at UCLA, covering perceptions, governance of the new lands, international politics, the arts, books, language, geography, movements of people, and science and trade. Its collective contribution will not soon be superseded.

Our understanding of the intellectual consequences of discovery was greatly enhanced by a five-day conference, "America in European Consciousness, 1493–1750," at the John Carter Brown Library in June 1991. Geoffrey Scammell's argument that the "experiences of empire, in which the Americas loomed so large, intensified or exacerbated a number of ominous traits long present in European civilization, most notably absolutism, racism, and intolerance," serves as a useful check on Arciniega's and Brandon's assertions of America's unique force for good in the world. David Cressy also pricks the New World bubble by arguing that "English appreciation of America in the colonial period ranged from ignorance to indifference, from misapprehension to benign (and not so benign) neglect. . . . Generations of colonial development did little to enhance understanding or appreciation of America in the minds of the majority of Englishmen."[115]

That the divination of America's impact on Europe was far from finished became obvious with the publication of the six-volume *European Americana: A Chronological Guide to Works Printed in Europe Relating to the Americas, 1493–1750,* by the JCB.[116] If nothing else, its 32,000 entries will stand as a perpetual challenge to scholars who like their research neat and narrow and their generalizations high and wide. Dennis Channing Landis, editor of the collection, provides an inviting glimpse of it in *The Literature of the Encounter: A Selection of Books from European Ameri-*

cana, the catalogue of an exhibition mounted for the JCB conference in 1991.[117] The printed and pictorial contents of sixty-one titles receive substantial and first-class treatment.

It comes as a pleasant surprise that the quality as well as the quantity of Quincentenary scholarship is very high. With few exceptions, scholars, publishers, and museums have resisted the temptation to capitalize on the bullish Columbian market by producing junk. Colleges and universities have done almost as well. The task now is to ensure that the benefits accrued during the five hundredth anniversary of Columbus's landing continue to pay educational and cultural dividends long after the event. What should we do beyond 1992 to maintain and augment our Quincentenary gains? My survey of the Columbian Encounter field suggests the following prescriptions:

(1) We should focus on Columbus as a man of extraordinary vision, perseverance, skill, and luck, but a man nonetheless—flawed and imperfect like all men. Rather than caricaturing him as an oversized hero or villain, we should see him in full perspective, pre- and post-1492, and measure him only against the men, ideas, and mores of his own time.

(2) We should pay more attention to Europe on the eve of colonization as the locus of experience, goals, and methods for the American incursions.

(3) We should pay much more attention to pre-contact America: its complexity, variety, demography, and deep reservoirs of human experience. We should make greater efforts to hear, not merely listen to, native voices from the past and in the present, not only for Clio's sake but to advance our own necessary and liberating education in "otherness."[118]

(4) In our teaching and study of colonial history, we should rescue the sixteenth century from undeserved ne-

glect. Without it, we have no hope of making sense of its more familiar sequel.[119]

(5) We must learn to do justice to Hispanic America, first, by ridding ourselves of the "Black Legend," and then by pursuing its history beyond the short conquest phase into the less sanguinary settlement period of city-building, imperial bureaucracy, sugar plantations, cattle ranches, and widespread acculturation.[120] We should also do a better job of integrating the Spanish Borderlands with the histories of North America and the United States.

(6) By the same token, we should incorporate the history of the Caribbean, where Europe often fought its inter-colonial wars before landing on North American soil because the sugar islands were so valuable.[121]

(7) We should continue to pay due attention to the role of disease and "biological imperialism" in the conquest and depopulation of the Americas. But we should refine our estimates of mortality to accord with the best available evidence and with common sense.[122]

(8) While well-publicized historical anniversaries invariably provide occasions for them, we should curb the temptation to make premature or, worse, predetermined moral judgments on the past. There will be time enough after we have done our homework thoroughly.[123]

(9) Whenever possible, we should resort to the insights and viewpoints of other disciplines, such as anthropology, archaeology, ethnohistory, cartography, historical geography, and "colonial discourse." Even the historical fiction of Latin American novelists such as Abel Posse, Alejo Carpentier, and Antonio Benítez-Rojo stretches the imaginative limits of our understanding of the Spanish and Indian heritages of that first, vast, "other" America.[124]

(10) On a similar tack, we should employ whenever possible a comparative perspective on the American Encounter—comparing French, Spanish, English, Dutch,

Portuguese, Swedish, and Russian efforts with one another, and American efforts with colonial efforts in other parts of the world—in order to separate the unique from the typical.[125]

(11) Clearly, the well-modulated public and scholarly success of the Quincentenary should inspire us to design future historical anniversaries as opportunities less for celebration than for cerebration. We must also be very careful about who is included in, and who feels excluded from, "We the People." Ethnic, gender, and racial sensitivities are only likely to grow; parity of treatment and attention—and, perhaps as important, the appearance of parity—must be extended to all citizens, past and present. We should start by rethinking our historical vocabulary: *Old* and *New World, discoverer, discovery, Indian, America, American, Latin American,* and the *West,* are factually, morally, or culturally problematic.

(12) Finally, we should all study to become better citizens of the "global village" we now inhabit, the foundations of which Columbus laid in 1492. If we do not learn to protect, respect, and sustain its people and to conserve and renew its resources, it will be much poorer when the Columbian sexcentenary occurs. Perhaps some of the lessons we draw from our study of the first Encounter will prevent such a fate.

Notes

CHAPTER ONE

1. (New York, 1959), 12.
2. Commission on the Humanities, *The Humanities in American Life* (Berkeley and Los Angeles, 1980), 3.
3. Miguel de Cervantes Saavedra, *Don Quixote*, 2 vols. (Everyman ed., London and New York, 1906), 2:22 (pt. 2, ch. 3).
4. Quoted in C. V. Wedgwood, *Truth and Opinion: Historical Essays* (New York, 1960), 62.
5. George Steiner, review of Georges Duby, *William Marshal: The Flower of Chivalry* (New York, 1986), in *The New Yorker*, May 26, 1986, 104.
6. Johann Gustav Droysen, Appendix to *Outline of the Principles of History* (1868), in Fritz Stern, ed., *The Varieties of History* (New York, 1956), 139.
7. Quoted in Robert M. Kingdon, "Garrett Mattingly," *The American Scholar*, 51:3 (Summer 1982), 399.
8. George Macaulay Trevelyan, "The Present Position of History" (1927), in *Clio, A Muse and Other Essays* (London, 1930), 196.
9. John Livingston Lowes, "Teaching and the Spirit of Research," *The American Scholar*, 2:1 (January 1933), 28–38 at 34–35.
10. Henry Glassie, *Passing the Time in Ballymenone: Culture and History of an Ulster Community* (Philadelphia, 1982), 621.
11. Barbara W. Tuchman, "In Search of History" (1963), in *Practicing History: Selected Essays* (New York, 1982), 21.

12. Paul Horgan, "Journey to the Past—and Return: Reflections on the Work of the Historian," *Texas Quarterly*, 13 (Summer 1970), 34–51 at 46.

13. Garrett Mattingly, "A Portrait of Cranmer" (review), *Saturday Review of Literature*, 9:28 (Jan. 28, 1933), 399.

14. Edmund S. Morgan, *The Gentle Puritan: A Life of Ezra Stiles, 1727–1795* (New Haven, 1962), 146, Stiles to Thomas Hutchinson, Nov. 26, 1767.

15. L. P. Hartley, *The Go-Between* (New York, 1954), 3.

16. Marguerite Yourcenar, *Memoirs of Hadrian*, trans. Grace Frick (New York, 1963), 330–31.

17. J. H. Hexter, *The History Primer* (New York, 1971), 80.

18. Horgan, "Journey to the Past," 47.

19. John Updike in George Plimpton, ed., *Writers at Work: The Paris Review Interviews. Fourth Series* (New York, 1976), 432.

20. Hugh Trevor-Roper, "History and Imagination," in Hugh Lloyd-Jones, Valerie Pearl, and Blair Worden, eds., *History & Imagination: Essays in Honour of H. R. Trevor-Roper* (London, 1981), 365.

21. I failed to take note of the source of this quotation when I first saw it and added it to my commonplace book; in any event, it came from a review or article rather than directly from one of Solzhenitsyn's works: *mea culpa*.

22. William Bouwsma, "The Renaissance and the Drama of Western History," *American Historical Review*, 84:1 (Feb. 1979), 14.

23. Bernard Bailyn, *History and the Creative Imagination* (St. Louis: Washington University, [1985]), 10.

24. Perry Miller, *Errand into the Wilderness* (Cambridge, Mass. 1956), vii–ix.

25. Walter J. Ong, "The Writer's Audience Is Always a Fiction," *PMLA: Publications of the Modern Language Association of America*, 90 (1979), 9–22.

26. Louis B. Wright, *The Folger Library: Two Decades of Growth: An Informal Account* (Charlottesville, 1968), 69 (Nov. 8, 1951).

27. Margaret Atwood, *Second Words: Selected Critical Prose* (Boston, 1984), 346.

28. L. B. Namier, "History," in *Avenues of History* (London, 1952), 8.

29. John Updike in *The New Yorker*, Dec. 24, 1984, 57.

30. Philip Larkin, *Required Writing: Miscellaneous Pieces 1955–1982* (New York, 1984), the page eludes me; I caught the quotation from a review, which also failed to provide a reference for the curious.

31. Horgan, "Journey to the Past," 44.
32. Wallace Stegner, ed., *The Letters of Bernard DeVoto* (Garden City, N.Y., 1975), 288.
33. Harold Nicolson, *Diaries and Letters. Volume 3: The Later Years, 1945–1962,* ed. Nigel Nicolson (New York, 1968), 175.
34. Hayden White, "The Historical Text as Literary Artifact," in Robert H. Canary and Henry Kozicki, eds., *The Writing of History: Literary Form and Historical Understanding* (Madison, 1978), 41–62.
35. Stegner, *Letters of DeVoto,* 288.
36. James Axtell, *The European and the Indian: Essays in the Ethnohistory of Colonial North America* (New York, 1981); Axtell, *The Invasion Within: The Contest of Cultures in Colonial North America* (New York, 1985); Axtell, *After Columbus: Essays in the Ethnohistory of Colonial North America* (New York, 1988).
37. Alfred North Whitehead, *The Aims of Education, and Other Essays* (New York, 1949, c. 1929), 23.
38. Quoted in Mark Van Doren, *Nathaniel Hawthorne* (New York, 1949), 267.
39. Carl L. Becker, "The Art of Writing" (1942), in Phil L. Snyder, ed., *Detachment and the Writing of History: Essays and Letters of Carl L. Becker* (Ithaca, N.Y., 1958), 134.
40. J. H. Hexter, *Doing History* (Bloomington, 1971), 45.
41. Quoted in Gay Wilson Allen, ed., *The New Walt Whitman Handbook* (New York, 1986, 1975), 245.
42. Whitehead, *Aims of Education,* 13, 97, 100.
43. Jay Leyda, *The Years and Hours of Emily Dickinson,* 2 vols. (New Haven, 1960), 2:393. Thanks to Richard Sewall and Ralph Franklin for their expert sleuthing.

CHAPTER TWO

1. Philip L. Barbour, ed., *The Jamestown Voyages Under the First Charter, 1606–1609,* Hakluyt Society Publications, 2d ser. 136–37 (Cambridge, 1969), 1:133–34. See James Axtell, "Europeans, Indians, and the Age of Discovery in American History Textbooks," *American Historical Review,* 92:3 (June 1987), 621–32, for more recent treatments; see below Chapter 8.
2. Charles Horton Cooley, *Life and the Student* (New York, 1927), 201–2.

3. Donald M. Frame, ed. and trans., *The Complete Works of Montaigne* (Stanford, 1948), 80, 152; Corinthians I, 14:10–11.

4. Richard Bernheimer, *Wild Men in the Middle Ages: A Study in Art, Sentiment, and Demonology* (Cambridge, Mass., 1952); John Block Friedman, *The Monstrous Races in Medieval Art and Thought* (Cambridge, Mass., 1981); Olive Patricia Dickason, *The Myth of the Savage and the Beginnings of French Colonization in the Americas* (Edmonton, 1984).

5. James Axtell, *The Invasion Within: The Contest of Cultures in Colonial North America* (New York, 1985), ch. 1.

6. David B. Quinn, ed., *New American World: A Documentary History of North America to 1612*, 5 vols. (New York, 1979), 1:428, 2:127; David B. Quinn, *North America from Earliest Discovery to First Settlements: The Norse Voyages to 1612*, New American Nation Series (New York, 1977), 196.

7. Edmund Berkeley and Dorothy Smith Berkeley, eds., *The Reverend John Clayton: A Parson with a Scientific Mind: His Scientific Writings and Other Related Papers* (Charlottesville, 1963), 39; William Strachey, *The Historie of Travell into Virginia Britania (1612)*, ed. Louis B. Wright and Virginia Freund, Hak. Soc. Pubs., 2d ser. 103 (London, 1953), 104–5.

8. Thomas Shepard, *The Clear Sun-shine of the Gospel Breaking Forth upon the Indians in New-England* (London, 1648), in *Collections of the Massachusetts Historical Society*, 3d ser. 4 (1834), 44. See also William S. Simmons, *Spirit of the New England Tribes: Indian History and Folklore, 1620–1984* (Hanover, N.H., 1986), 68.

9. Reuben Gold Thwaites, ed., *The Jesuit Relations and Allied Documents*, 73 vols. (Cleveland, 1896–1901), 5:119–21.

10. Father Chrestien Le Clercq, *New Relation of Gaspesia* [Paris, 1691], ed. and trans. William F. Ganong (Toronto: Champlain Society, 1910), 109.

11. Ella Elizabeth Clark, ed., *Indian Legends of Canada* (Toronto, 1960), 150–51.

12. John Heckewelder, *History, Manners, and Customs of the Indian Nations Who Once Inhabited Pennsylvania and the Neighbouring States* [1818], ed. William G. Reichel (Philadelphia, 1876), 71–75.

13. L. A. Vigneras, ed., *The Journal of Christopher Columbus*, trans. Cecil Jane (New York, 1960), 196; also Oliver Dunn and James E. Kelley, Jr., ed. and trans., *The Diario of Christopher Columbus's First Voyage to America, 1492–1493* (Norman, Okla., 1989), 137, 235.

14. Quinn, *New American World*, 2:41, 46, 47, 51.

15. *Ibid.*, 2:112, 130, 139, 141.
16. David B. Quinn and Alison M. Quinn, eds., *Virginia Voyages from Hakluyt* (London, 1973), 69–73; Louise Phelps Kellogg, ed., *Early Narratives of the Northwest, 1634–1699*, Original Narratives of Early American History [ONEAH] (New York, 1917), 74–75; Ruth Lapham Butler, ed. and trans., *Journal of Paul Du Ru . . . Missionary Priest to Louisiana* (Chicago, 1934), 5–6.
17. Dunn and Kelley, *Columbus's Diario*, 137; Quinn, *New American World*, 2:45.
18. Kellogg, *Early Narratives of the Northwest*, 75, 107, 108, 240, 242.
19. Alexander S. Salley, Jr., ed., *Narratives of Early Carolina, 1650–1708*, ONEAH (New York, 1911), 132; Clarence W. Alvord and Lee Bidgood, eds., *The First Exploration of the Trans-Allegheny Region by the Virginians, 1650–1674* (Cleveland, 1912), 212–13.
20. Dunn and Kelley, *Columbus's Diario*, 267; Quinn, *New American World*, 2:322; H. P. Biggar, ed. and trans., *The Voyages of Jacques Cartier*, Publications of the Public Archives of Canada 11 (Ottawa, 1924), 147, also 172; Kellogg, *Early Narratives of the Northwest*, 85.
21. Quinn, *New American World*, 2:42, 45.
22. Biggar, *Voyages of Cartier*, 56, 62, 162; Quinn, *Virginia Voyages from Hakluyt*, 4; Quinn, *New American World*, 4:235, 236, 240, 242.
23. Salley, *Narratives of Early Carolina*, 91, 117, 132; Richebourg Gaillard McWilliams, ed. and trans., *Fleur de Lys and Calumet: Being the Pénicaut Narrative of French Adventure in Louisiana* (Baton Rouge, 1953), 5; *Iberville's Gulf Journals*, ed. and trans. Richebourg Gaillard McWilliams (University, Ala., 1981), 40, Jay Higginbotham, ed. and trans., *The Journal of Sauvole* (Mobile, 1969), 31; Kellogg, *Early Narratives of the Northwest*, 85, 115.
24. Kellogg, *Early Narratives of the Northwest*, 242.
25. McWilliams, *Fleur de Lys and Calumet*, 5, 24, 57; *Iberville's Gulf Journals*, 46. See also Ian W. Brown, "The Calumet Ceremony in the Southeast and Its Archaeological Manifestations," *American Antiquity*, 54 (1989), 311–31.
26. Kellogg, *Early Narratives of the Northwest*, 85, 129; Butler, *Journal of Du Ru*, 18; Walter James Hoffman, "The Menomini Indians," Bureau of American Ethnology, *14th Annual Report* (Washington, D.C., 1896), pt. 1: 214–16; Quinn, *New American World*, 1:240.

27. Dunn and Kelley, *Columbus's Diario*, 295, 297; Biggar, *Voyages of Cartier*, 164.
28. Biggar, *Voyages of Cartier*, 132–33, 143–44, 188.
29. *Iberville's Gulf Journals*, 86n.141, 112, 113.
30. Buckingham Smith, ed. and trans., *Memoir of D°. d'Escalente Fontaneda Respecting Florida* [c. 1575] (Miami, 1944), 17–19, 24; Quinn, *New American World*, 2:339; James Axtell, "The White Indians of Colonial America," in *The European and the Indian: Essays in the Ethnohistory of Colonial North America* (New York, 1981), ch. 7.
31. Quinn, *New American World*, 2:132.
32. Salley, *Narratives of Early Carolina*, 51, 105.
33. McWilliams, *Fleur de Lys and Calumet*, 24.
34. Quinn, *Virginia Voyages from Hakluyt*, 9–10; Lawrence C. Wroth, *The Voyages of Giovanni da Verrazzano, 1524–1528* (New Haven, 1970), 134, 135; McWilliams, *Fleur de Lys and Calumet*, 4.
35. McWilliams, *Fleur de Lys and Calumet*, 4, 112; Kellogg, *Early Narratives of the Northwest*, 75.
36. Biggar, *Voyages of Cartier*, 165; Quinn, *New American World*, 2:31–32, 38, 40, 47, 130 (Soto).
37. Quinn, *Virginia Voyages from Hakluyt*, 36, 71–72, 73.
38. Vigneras, *Journal of Columbus*, 196; Quinn, *Virginia Voyages from Hakluyt*, 10; Higginbotham, *Journal of Sauvole*, 40–41.
39. Wroth, *Voyages of Verrazzano*, 137.
40. Biggar, *Voyages of Cartier*, 134–35; Kellogg, *Early Narratives of the Northwest*, 46, 50, 73, 75, 77, 243; *Father Louis Hennepin's Description of Louisiana* [Paris, 1683], ed. and trans. Marion E. Cross (Minneapolis, 1938), 98.
41. Quinn, *Virginia Voyages from Hakluyt*, 70.
42. *Hennepin's Description of Louisiana*, 82, 96, 98, 105, 108–9, 130; William Wood, *New England's Prospect* [London, 1634], ed. Alden T. Vaughan (Amherst, Mass., 1977), 96.
43. Vigneras, *Journal of Columbus*, 196; Quinn, *New American World*, 2:331, 482, 4:236, 250; David B. Quinn and Alison M. Quinn, eds., *The English New England Voyages, 1602–1608*, Hak. Soc. Pubs., 2d ser. 161 (London, 1983), 274.
44. James Axtell, *After Columbus: Essays in the Ethnohistory of Colonial North America* (New York, 1988), 270n.22; Dunn and Kelley, *Columbus's Diario*, 67.
45. Dunn and Kelley, *Columbus's Diario*, 93, 117, 227, 251; Vigneras, *Journal of Columbus*, 201; Salley, *Narratives of Early Carolina*, 91.

46. Vigneras, *Journal of Columbus*, 191; Quinn, *New American World*, 2:392–93, 5:438; Biggar, *Voyages of Cartier*, 155; Arthur J. Krim, "Acculturation of the New England Landscape: Native and English Toponomy of Eastern Massachusetts," in Peter Benes, ed., *New England Prospect: Maps, Place Names, and the Historical Landscape*, Annual Proceedings of the Dublin Seminar for New England Folklife (Boston, 1980), 69–88; Quinn, *New American World*, 2:292, 296. See also George R. Stewart, *Names on the Land: A Historical Account of Place-Naming in the United States* (New York, 1945).

47. Dunn and Kelley, *Columbus's Diario*, 63, 79; Vigneras, *Journal of Columbus*, 191.

48. Barbour, *Jamestown Voyages*, 1:88.

49. Biggar, *Voyages of Cartier*, 64–65.

50. Quinn, *New American World*, 2:295, 309, 314, 316, 321.

51. *Ibid.*, 2:291.

52. Quinn, *English New England Voyages*, 154, 272; Quinn, *New American World*, 2:289; *Iberville's Gulf Journals*, 46.

53. Dunn and Kelley, *Columbus's Diario*, 243; Quinn, *English New England Voyages*, 275, also 272, 279, 283–84.

54. Quinn, *New American World*, 3:190, 4:29, 235; Quinn, *English New England Voyages*, 220; McWilliams, *Fleur de Lys and Calumet*, 106–7, 109–10, 115.

55. Wilbur R. Jacobs, *Wilderness Politics and Indian Gifts: The Northern Colonial Frontier, 1748–1763* (Stanford, 1950); Cornelius J. Jaenen. "The Role of Presents in French-Amerindian Trade," in Duncan Cameron, ed., *Explorations in Canadian Economic History: Essays in Honour of Irene M. Spry* (Ottawa, 1985), 231–50.

56. Dunn and Kelley, *Columbus's Diario*, 243; Biggar, *Voyages of Cartier*, 53, 166; Quinn, *New American World*, 2:288.

57. Wroth, *Voyages of Verrazzano*, 138; Quinn, *Virginia Voyages from Hakluyt*, 8; Thomas Hariot, *A briefe and true report of the newfound land of Virginia* (Frankfurt, 1590); original painting in Paul Hulton, ed., *America 1585: The Complete Drawings of John White* (Chapel Hill, 1984), pl. 65.

58. Vigneras, *Journal of Columbus*, 200; Strachey, *Historie of Travell in Virginia*, 71; Albert Cook Myers, ed., *Narratives of Early Pennsylvania, West New Jersey, and Delaware, 1630–1707*, ONEAH (New York, 1912), 230; see also Winthrop D. Jordan, *White Over Black: American Attitudes Toward the Negro, 1550–1812* (Chapel Hill, 1968), 14, 22, 27.

59. Philip L. Barbour, ed., *The Complete Works of Captain John Smith* (*1580–1631*), 3 vols. (Chapel Hill, 1986), 2:115; Quinn, *Virginia Voyages from Hakluyt*, 64. See also David Beers Quinn, *The Elizabethans and the Irish* (Ithaca, N.Y., 1966); Nicholas P. Canny, *The Elizabethan Conquest of Ireland: A Pattern Established, 1565–76* (New York, 1976); James P. Myers, Jr., ed., *Elizabethan Ireland: A Selection of Writings by Elizabethan Writers on Ireland* (Hamden, Conn., 1983).

60. H. C. Porter, *The Inconstant Savage: England and the North American Indian, 1500–1660* (London, 1979); Karen Ordahl Kupperman, *Settling with the Indians: The Meeting of English and Indian Cultures in America, 1580–1640* (Totowa, N.J., 1980); Bernard W. Sheehan, *Savagism and Civility: Indians and Englishmen in Colonial Virginia* (Cambridge, 1980); Dickason, *Myth of the Savage*.

61. Kellogg, *Early Narratives of the Northwest*, 185.

62. Philippe Jacquin, *Les Indiens blancs: Français et Indiens en Amérique du Nord (XVIe–XVIIe siècle)* (Paris, 1987), ch. 3; James M. Crawford, *The Mobilian Trade Language* (Knoxville, Tenn., 1978), 30–32.

63. Quinn, *New American World*, 2:104, 137.

64. Dunn and Kelley, *Columbus's Diario*, 207; Vigneras, *Journal of Columbus*, 196; Biggar, *Voyages of Cartier*, 65–67, 225–27; Quinn, *Virginia Voyages from Hakluyt*, 12, 102; David Beers Quinn, *Set Fair for Roanoke: Voyages and Colonies, 1584–1606* (Chapel Hill, 1985), 232–36.

CHAPTER THREE

1. Charles Horton Cooley, *Life and the Student* (New York, 1927), 201–2.

2. William S. Simmons, *Spirit of the New England Tribes: Indian History and Folklore, 1620–1984* (Hanover, N.H., 1986), 65.

3. John Pickering, ed., "A Dictionary of the Abnaki Language, in North America, by Father Sebastien Rasles," *Memoirs of the American Academy of Arts and Sciences*, n.s. 1 (1833), 539 ("Englishmen," here used in a generic sense for Europeans).

4. William Wood, *New England's Prospect* [1634], ed. Alden T. Vaughan (Amherst, 1977), 95–96; Roger Williams, *A Key into the Language of America* (London, 1643), 59. In 1869 the Micmacs

remembered that the first white men they had seen arrived on a small floating island with tall trees. The next day they awoke to find a number of bears crawling about the tree limbs. Grabbing weapons, they rushed to hunt them, but found men instead (Silas Tertius Rand, *Legends of the Micmacs* [New York, 1894], 225-26).

5. [Edward] *Johnson's Wonder-Working Providence, 1628-1651*, ed. J. Franklin Jameson, ONEAH (New York, 1910), 39-40.

6. *The Complete Works of Captain John Smith (1580-1631)*, ed. Philip L. Barbour, 3 vols. (Chapel Hill, 1986), 1:324, 340, 381.

7. *Ibid.*, 1:381, 402; James W. Bradley, "Native Exchange and European Trade: Cross-Cultural Dynamics in the Sixteenth Century," *Man in the Northeast*, 33 (Spring 1987), 37-38; Samuel Purchas, *Hakluytus Posthumus, or Purchas His Pilgrimes*, 20 vols. (Glasgow, 1906), 13:347.

8. David B. Quinn, ed., *New American World: A Documentary History of North America to 1612*, 5 vols. (New York, 1979), 1:148-51.

9. *Ibid.*, 1:273-79.

10. *Ibid.*, 1:274, 277.

11. *Ibid.*, 1:273, 279.

12. *Ibid.*, 1:149, 151.

13. Lawrence C. Wroth, *The Voyages of Giovanni da Verrazzano, 1524-1528* (New Haven, 1970), 137-39.

14. *Ibid.*, 138.

15. *Ibid.*, 139-40.

16. *Ibid.*, 140-41.

17. *Ibid.* (my emphasis).

18. Quinn, *New American World*, 4:304, 306-8.

19. David Beers Quinn, ed., *The Voyages and Colonising Enterprises of Sir Humphrey Gilbert*, Hakluyt Society Publications, 2d ser. 83-84 (London, 1940), 82:309-10, 464.

20. Bruce J. Bourque and Ruth Holmes Whitehead, "Tarrentines and the Introduction of European Trade Goods in the Gulf of Maine," *Ethnohistory*, 32 (1985), 327-41.

21. David B. Quinn and Alison M. Quinn, eds., *The English New England Voyages, 1602-1608*, Hakluyt Soc. Pubs., 2d ser. 161 (London, 1983), 117-18.

22. *Ibid.*, 125, 127, 131, 134, 154.

23. *Ibid.*, 130, 133-36, 154, 158.

24. *Ibid.*, 221, 222, 227.

25. *Ibid.*, 267-68, 269.

26. *Ibid.*, 270, 272-73, 275.

27. *Ibid.*, 270. See Quinn, *New American World*, 2:349, 4:62.
28. Quinns, *English New England Voyages*, 273; James Axtell, "The Power of Print in the Eastern Woodlands," *William and Mary Quarterly*, 3d ser. 44 (1987), 300–309.
29. Quinns, *English New England Voyages*, 274.
30. *Ibid.*, 277–78 and 278n.2.
31. *Ibid.*, 279–81.
32. *Ibid.*, 282–85, 287–88, 293–95, 303.
33. *Ibid.*, 349–50, 351, 413.
34. *Ibid.*, 344, 438–39, 455–56, 470–76; David D. Smits, "'We Are Not to Grow Wild': Seventeenth-Century New England's Repudiation of Anglo-Indian Intermarriage," *American Indian Culture and Research Journal* 11:4 (1987), 1–31 at 9.
35. Quinns, *English New England Voyages*, 456.
36. *Ibid.*, 409–12.
37. Henry O. Thayer, *The Sagadahoc Colony*, Gorges Society Publications (Portland, Me., 1892), 108–9.
38. *Collections of the Massachusetts Historical Society . . . 1792*, 1 (Boston, 1806), 252. Thanks to Emerson Baker for the last two references.
39. P. -André Sévigny, *Les Abénaquis: Habitat et migrations (17ᵉ et 18ᵉ siècles)*, Cahiers d'histoire des Jésuites 3 (Montreal: Les Éditions Bellarmin, 1976); Kenneth M: Morrison, *The Embattled Northeast: The Elusive Ideal of Alliance in Abenaki-Euramerican Relations* (Berkeley and Los Angeles, 1984); Emerson Woods Baker II, "Trouble to the Eastward: The Failure of Anglo-Indian Relations in Early Maine" (Ph.D. diss., College of William and Mary, Dept. of History, 1986); Harald E. L. Prins, "Turmoil on the Wabanaki Frontier, 1524–1678," in Richard Judd, ed., *The History of Maine* (forthcoming).

CHAPTER FOUR

1. James Axtell, *The Invasion Within: The Contest of Cultures in Colonial North America* (New York, 1985), ch. 7.
2. See above p. 320n.4.
3. Axtell, *The Invasion Within*, 15–19.
4. *Ibid.*, 9–10, 78–79; James Axtell, *After Columbus: Essays in the Ethnohistory of Colonial North America* (New York, 1988), 132–33.
5. Axtell, *After Columbus*, 134–36.

6. See above Chapter 2, pp. 40–52.

7. Axtell, *After Columbus*, 152–56.

8. James Axtell, *American Encounter: The Confluence of Cultures in Colonial North America* (forthcoming), ch. 2, "Babel of Tongues."

9. Axtell, *After Columbus*, 148–52.

10. Neal Salisbury, "Squanto: Last of the Patuxets," in David G. Sweet and Gary B. Nash, eds., *Struggle and Survival in Colonial America* (Berkeley and Los Angeles, 1981), 228–46; David Beers Quinn, *Set Fair for Roanoke: Voyages and Colonies, 1584–1606* (Chapel Hill, 1985), 233–35.

11. H. P. Biggar, ed. and trans., *The Voyages of Jacques Cartier*, Publications of the Public Archives of Canada, No. 11 (Ottawa, 1924), 187.

12. Clifford M. Lewis and Albert J. Loomie, *The Spanish Jesuit Mission in Virginia, 1570–1572* (Chapel Hill, 1953), 15–18, 39–49.

13. Philip L. Barbour, ed., *The Jamestown Voyages Under the First Charter, 1606–1609*, Hakluyt Society Publications, 2d ser. 136–37 (Cambridge, 1969), 133–34 (continuous pagination).

14. Dwight B. Heath, ed., *A Journal of the Pilgrims at Plymouth: Mourt's Relation [1622]* (New York, 1963), 22, 26, 27–29, 35–37, 52; William Bradford, *Of Plymouth Plantation, 1620–1647*, ed. Samuel Eliot Morison (New York, 1952), 65–66, 69–70, 81.

15. James Axtell, *The European and the Indian: Essays in the Ethnohistory of Colonial North America* (New York, 1981), 248–49.

16. *Ibid.*, 249–50.

17. *Ibid.*, ch. 7, "The White Indians of Colonial America"; Daniel K. Richter, "War and Culture: The Iroquois Experience," *William and Mary Quarterly*, 3d ser. 40 (Oct. 1983), 528–59.

18. Judith Reynolds, "Marriages Between the English and the Indians in Seventeenth Century Virginia," Archaeological Society of Virginia, *Quarterly Bulletin*, 17:2 (Dec. 1962), 19–25; James Hugo Johnston, *Race Relations in Virginia and Miscegenation in the South, 1776–1860* (Amherst, Mass., 1970), ch. 11; J. Leitch Wright, *The Only Land They Knew: The Tragic Story of the American Indians in the Old South* (New York, 1981), 234–37; Cornelius J. Jaenen, "Miscegenation in Eighteenth-Century New France" (Paper presented at the Second Laurier Conference on Ethnohistory and Ethnology, London, Ontario, May 12, 1983); Olive Patricia Dickason, "From 'One Nation' in the Northeast to 'New Nation' in the Northwest: A Look at the Emergence of the Métis," *American Indian Culture and Research Journal*, 6:2 (1982),

1–21; Kathleen A. Deagan, *"Mestizaje* in Colonial St. Augustine," *Ethnohistory,* 20 (1973), 55–65.

19. Salisbury, "Squanto," in Sweet and Nash, *Struggle and Survival,* 235–37.

20. David Landy, "Tuscarora Among the Iroquois," in William C. Sturtevant, gen. ed., *Handbook of North American Indians,* Vol. 15: *Northeast,* ed. Bruce G. Trigger (Washington, D.C., 1978), 518–20.

21. James H. Merrell, *The Indians' New World: Catawbas and Their Neighbors from European Contact through the Era of Removal* (Chapel Hill, 1989), ch. 3.

22. Colin G. Calloway, *The Western Abenakis of Vermont, 1600–1800: War, Migration, and the Survival of an Indian People* (Norman, Okla., 1990); Helen C. Rountree, *Pocahontas's People: The Powhatan Indians of Virginia Through Four Centuries* (Norman, Okla., 1990), chs. 4–5.

23. Bruce G. Trigger, *Natives and Newcomers: Canada's 'Heroic Age' Reconsidered* (Kingston and Montreal, 1985), 204, 312, 314, 318.

24. Axtell, *The Invasion Within,* chs. 2–6, 11.

25. Richebourg Gaillard McWilliams, ed. and trans., *Fleur de Lys and Calumet: Being the Pénicaut Narrative of French Adventure in Louisiana* (Baton Rouge, 1953), 98, 102–3, 125–26.

26. *Ibid.,* 129–30, 162, 219–20.

27. Daniel H. Usner, Jr., "The Deerskin Trade in French Louisiana," in Philip P. Boucher, ed., *Proceedings of the Tenth Meeting of the French Colonial Historical Society, April 12–14, 1984* (Lanham, Md., 1985), 75–93; Richard White, *Roots of Dependency: Subsistence, Environment, and Social Change Among the Choctaws, Pawnees, and Navajos* (Lincoln, Neb., 1983), chs. 3–4; Michael James Forêt, "On the Marchlands of Empire: Trade, Diplomacy, and War on the Southeastern Frontier, 1733–63" (Ph.D. diss., College of William and Mary, Dept. of History, 1990), chs. 2, 4–8.

28. Immanuel Wallerstein, *The Modern World-System: Capitalist Agriculture and the Origins of the European World Economy in the Sixteenth Century* (New York, 1974); Eric R. Wolf, *Europe and the People Without History* (Berkeley and Los Angeles, 1982).

29. Shepard Krech III, ed., *Indians, Animals, and the Fur Trade: A Critique of* KEEPERS OF THE GAME (Athens, Ga., 1981).

30. White, *Roots of Dependency,* ch. 3; Anthony F. C. Wallace, *The Death and Rebirth of the Seneca* (New York, 1970), ch. 5; Verner W. Crane, *The Southern Frontier, 1670–1732* (Ann Arbor, 1929);

Forêt, "On the Marchlands of Empire"; Allen W. Trelease, *Indian Affairs in Colonial New York: The Seventeenth Century* (Ithaca, N.Y., 1960), 51–58; Denys Delage, *Le Pays renversé: Amérindiens et européens en Amérique du nord-est, 1600–1664* (Montreal, 1985).

31. Peter A. Thomas, "Cultural Change on the Southern New England Frontier, 1630–1665," in William W. Fitzhugh, ed., *Cultures in Contact: The Impact of European Contacts on Native American Cultural Institutions, A.D. 1000–1800* (Washington, D.C., 1985), 131–57 at 157.

32. Daniel R. Mandell, "Change and Continuity in a Native American Community: 18th Century Stockbridge" (M.A. thesis, U. of Virginia, Dept. of History, May 1982), 42–44.

33. K. G. Davies, ed., *Documents of the American Revolution, 1770–1783 (Colonial Office Series)*, 21 vols. (Shannon and Dublin, 1972–81), 5:113–17.

34. See, for example, *Records of the Town of East-Hampton, Long Island, Suffolk Co., N.Y.*, vol. 1 (Sag Harbor, N.Y., 1887), 3–4, for a deed of sale dated April 29, 1648, in which the local Indians retain the right to "fish in any or all the cricks and ponds, and hunt up and downe in the woods without Molestation, . . . [and] libertie to fish in all convenient places, for Shells to make wampum."

35. Robert S. Grumet, "An Analysis of Upper Delawaran Land Sales in Northern New Jersey, 1630–1758," in *Papers of the Ninth Algonquian Conference*, ed. William Cowan (Ottawa: Carleton U., Dept. of Linguistics, 1978), 25–35.

36. Arthur J. Ray, *Indians in the Fur Trade: Their Role as Trappers, Hunters, and Middlemen in the Lands Southwest of Hudson Bay, 1660–1870* (Toronto, 1974); Davies, *Documents of the American Revolution*, 2:109; W. L. McDowell, ed., *Journals of the Commissioners of the Indian Trade, September 20, 1710–August 29, 1718*, Colonial Records of South Carolina, Series 2 (Columbia, S.C., 1955), 52, 133, 181, 188, 203, 237.

37. *Collections of the Massachusetts Historical Society*, 4th ser. 6 (1863), 228, Roger Williams to John Winthrop, April 16, 1638.

38. William S. Willis, Jr., "Divide and Rule: Red, White, and Black in the Old South," in Charles M. Hudson, ed., *Red, White, and Black: Symposium on Indians in the Old South* (Athens, Ga., 1971), 99–115.

39. Richard R. Johnson, "The Search for a Usable Indian: An Aspect

of the Defense of Colonial New England," *Journal of American History*, 64 (1977), 623–51; I. K. Steele, *Guerillas and Grenadiers: The Struggle for Canada, 1689–1760* (Toronto, 1969); Douglas Edward Leach, *Arms for Empire: A Military History of the British Colonies in North America, 1607–1763* (New York, 1973), index, s. v. "Indians: as allies."

40. Daniel Vickers, "The First Whalemen of Nantucket," *William and Mary Quarterly*, 3d ser. 40 (Oct. 1983), 560–83; T. H. Breen, *Imagining the Past: East Hampton Histories* (Reading, Mass., 1989), 161–89.

41. Axtell, *After Columbus*, 157, 174; Brian L. Evans, "Ginseng: Root of Chinese-Canadian Relations," *Canadian Historical Review*, 66 (1985), 1–26.

42. Edmund B. O'Callaghan and Berthold Fernow, eds., *Documents Relative to the Colonial History of the State of New-York*, 15 vols. (Albany, 1856–87), 2:157; Albert Cook Myers, ed., *Narratives of Early Pennsylvania, West New Jersey, and Delaware, 1630–1707*, Original Narratives of Early American History (New York, 1912), 401.

43. John A. Sainsbury, "Indian Labor in Early Rhode Island," *New England Quarterly*, 48 (1975), 378–93.

44. Theda Perdue, "Cherokee Women: A Study in Changing Gender Roles" (Paper presented at the annual meeting of the American Historical Association, San Francisco, Dec. 29, 1989).

45. Wright, *The Only Land They Knew*, 234–37; Merrell, *Indians' New World*, 3, 30–31, 63–64, 86–87; Philippe Jacquin, *Les Indiens blancs: Français et Indiens en Amérique du Nord (XVIᵉ–XVIIIᵉ siècle)* (Paris, 1987), ch. 7.

46. Pierre Pouchot, *Memoir upon the Late War in North America, Between the French and English, 1755–60*, trans. Franklin B. Hough, 2 vols. (Roxbury, Mass., 1866), 2:237; *Travels of William Bartram*, ed. Mark Van Doren (New York, 1955), 215.

47. David Hurst Thomas, ed., *Columbian Consequences. Volume 2: Archaeological and Historical Perspectives on the Spanish Borderlands East* (Washington, D.C., 1990), chs. 24–35; Axtell, *The Invasion Within*.

48. Axtell, *The Invasion Within*, 69, 191, 193, 194, 212.

49. Many, perhaps most, tribes called themselves something like "the original people" or "real people [men]"; for example, Lenni Lenape (Delaware), Diné (Navajo), Penobscot, Anishanabe (Chippewa). The Seneca word for "Indians" in general (as distin-

guished from white or black people) is *ó-gweh 'o-weh*, real men. Wallace L. Chafe, *Seneca Morphology and Dictionary*, Smithsonian Contributions to Anthropology, 4 (Washington, D.C., 1967), 77.

50. Axtell, *After Columbus*, ch. 3; Axtell, *The Invasion Within*, ch. 11.

51. Axtell, *The Invasion Within*, 283–86.

52. *Ibid.*, ch. 8; Margaret Connell Szasz, *Indian Education in the American Colonies, 1607–1783* (Albuquerque, N.M., 1988).

53. Carolyn Thomas Foreman, *Indians Abroad, 1493–1938* (Norman, Okla., 1943); Richard N. Ellis and Charlie R. Steen, eds., "An Indian Delegation in France, 1725," *Journal of the Illinois State Historical Society*, 67 (Sept. 1974), 385–405.

54. Davies, *Documents of the American Revolution*, 1:40, John Stuart to Governor Lord Botetourt, Jan. 13, 1770.

55. Lt. Lion Gardener in Charles Orr, ed., *History of the Pequot War* (Cleveland, 1897), 142–43.

56. Axtell, *The European and the Indian*, 257–59; Craig MacAndrew and Robert B. Edgerton, *Drunken Comportment: A Social Explanation* (Chicago, 1969); Thomas W. Hill, "Ethnohistory and Alcohol Studies," in Marc Galanter, ed., *Recent Developments in Alcoholism*, 2 (New York, 1984), 313–37.

57. Charles E. Hunter, "The Delaware Nativist Revival of the Mid-Eighteenth Century," *Ethnohistory*, 18:1 (Winter 1971), 39–49; Wallace, *Death and Rebirth of the Seneca*, 114–22.

58. See below Chapter 9. James Axtell, "The Columbian Mosaic in Colonial America," *Humanities* [N.E.H.], 12:5 (Sept./Oct. 1991), 12–18, is a shorter version.

59. Luis Villoro, *Sahagún or the Limits of the Discovery of the Other*, 1992 Lecture Series, Working Papers, No. 2, Dept. of Spanish and Portuguese, U. of Maryland (College Park, 1989), 7, 16.

60. Douglas H. Ubelaker, "North American Indian Population Size, A.D. 1500 to 1985," *American Journal of Physical Anthropology*, 77 (1988), 289–94; Barbara Vobejda, "American Indians' Population Boom," *Washington Post*, Feb. 11, 1991, A1, A4.

CHAPTER FIVE

1. For the British phase of the revolution, see Neil McKendrick, John Brewer, and J. H. Plumb, eds., *The Birth of a Consumer Society: The Commercialization of Eighteenth-Century England* (Bloomington, Ind., 1982); Lorna Weatherill, *Consumer Behav-*

iour and Material Culture in Britain, 1660–1760 (London, 1988); Joan Thirsk, *Economic Policy and Projects: The Development of a Consumer Society in Early Modern England* (Oxford, 1978); Eric Jones, "The Fashion Manipulators: Consumer Tastes and British Industries, 1660–1800," in Louis P. Cain and Paul J. Uselding, eds., *Business Enterprise and Economic Change: Essays in Honor of Harold F. Williamson* (Kent, Ohio, 1973), 198–226; Carole Shammas, *The Pre-industrial Consumer in England and America* (Oxford, 1990).

    On the American side, see Shammas, *ibid.;* T. H. Breen, "An Empire of Goods: The Anglicization of Colonial America, 1690–1776," *Journal of British Studies,* 25 (Oct. 1986), 467–99; Breen, "'Baubles of Britain': The American and Consumer Revolutions of the Eighteenth Century," *Past and Present,* no. 119 (1988), 73–104; Breen, "The Meaning of Things: Interpreting the Consumer Economy in the Eighteenth Century" (William Andrews Clark Memorial Library Lectures: The Birth of Consumer Societies, 1988–89); Gloria L. Main and Jackson T. Main, "Economic Growth and the Standard of Living in Southern New England, 1640–1774," *Journal of Economic History,* 48:1 (March 1988), 27–46; Lois Green Carr and Lorena S. Walsh, "The Standard of Living in the Colonial Chesapeake," *William and Mary Quarterly,* 3d ser. 45:1 (Jan. 1988), 135–59; Carr and Walsh, "Consumer Behavior in the Colonial Chesapeake," in Cary Carson, Ronald Hoffman, and Peter J. Albert, eds., *Of Consuming Interests: The Style of Life in the Eighteenth Century* (Charlottesville, forthcoming 1992); Cary Carson, "The Consumer Revolution in Colonial British America: Why Demand?," *ibid.*

2. William Eddis, *Letters from America,* ed. Aubrey C. Land (Cambridge, Mass., 1969), 51–52.

3. Breen, "'Baubles of Britain'," 88, 90.

4. George T. Hunt, *The Wars of the Iroquois: A Study in Intertribal Trade Relations* (Madison, Wis., 1940), 33; Allen W. Trelease, *Indian Affairs in Colonial New York: The Seventeenth Century* (Ithaca, N.Y., 1960), 43, 131.

5. Marcel Trudel, *Histoire de la Nouvelle-France. II: Le comptoir, 1604–1627* (Montreal, 1966), 207; Bruce G. Trigger, *The Children of Aataentsic: A History of the Huron People to 1660,* 2 vols. (Montreal, 1976), 286, 336–37, 603–5 (continuous pagination); Conrad Heidenreich, *Huronia: A History and Geography of the Huron Indians, 1600–1650* (Toronto, 1971), 280.

6. William Bradford, *Of Plymouth Plantation, 1620–1647*, ed. Samuel Eliot Morison (New York, 1952), 286–89; Ruth A. McIntyre, *Debts Hopeful and Desperate: Financing the Plymouth Colony* (Plymouth, Mass.: Plimoth Plantation, 1963).

7. Verner W. Crane, *The Southern Frontier, 1670–1732* (Ann Arbor, 1956, 1929), 111, 330 (table 4); Joel W. Martin, "The Creek Indian Deerskin Trade, 1670–1805" (manuscript), table 1.

8. Gary C. Goodwin, *Cherokees in Transition: A Study of Changing Culture and Environment Prior to 1775*, U. of Chicago, Dept. of Geography, Research Paper No. 181 (Chicago, 1977), 98.

9. John Hardman, Liverpool merchant, 1749, quoted in E. E. Rich, "The Indian Traders," *The Beaver*, outht 301 (Winter 1970), 5–20 at 18.

10. Joseph and Nesta Ewan, eds., *John Banister and His Natural History of Virginia, 1678–92* (Urbana, Ill., 1970), 42.

11. *The Essayes of Michael Lord of Montaigne*, trans. John Florio, 3 vols., Everyman ed. (London and Toronto, 1910), 1:170 ("Of cannibals").

12. Nicolas Denys, *The Description and Natural History of the Coasts of North America (Acadia)*, ed. and trans. William F. Ganong (Toronto: The Champlain Society, 1908), 441.

13. Reuben Gold Thwaites, ed., *The Jesuit Relations and Allied Documents*, 73 vols. (Cleveland, 1896–1901), 6:297, 299.

14. Roger Williams, *A Key into the Language of America* (London, 1643), 163.

15. *Father Louis Hennepin's Description of Louisiana*, ed. and trans. Marion E. Cross (Minneapolis, 1938), 167.

16. Quoted in Albright G. Zimmerman, "European Trade Relations in the 17th and 18th Centuries," in Herbert C. Kraft, ed., *A Delaware Indian Symposium*, Pennsylvania Historical and Museum Commission, Anthropological Series No. 4 (Harrisburg, 1974), 57–70 at 66.

17. James Phinney Baxter, ed., *Documentary History of the State of Maine. III: The Trelawny Papers* (Portland, Me., 1884), 25–26, 29.

18. Marion Tinling, ed., *The Correspondence of the Three William Byrds of Westover, Virginia, 1684–1776*, Virginia Historical Society Documents 12–13 (Charlottesville, 1977), 29, 30, 57, 60, 64, 66.

19. Thomas Morton, *New English Canaan* (London, 1632), in Peter Force, comp., *Tracts and Other Papers, Relating Principally to the Origin, Settlement, and Progress of the Colonies in North America*, 4 vols. (Washington, D.C., 1836–47), vol. 2, no. 5, p. 40.

20. Governor Johan Rising, June 14, 1655, in Albert Cook Myers, ed., *Narratives of Early Pennsylvania, West New Jersey, and Delaware, 1630–1707*, Original Narratives of Early American History (New York, 1912), 157. See also Toby Morantz, "'So Evil a Practice': A Look at the Debt System in the James Bay Fur Trade," in Rosemary E. Ommer, ed., *Merchant Credit and Labour Strategies in Historical Perspective* (Fredericton, N.B., 1990), 203–22.

21. Robert C. Wheeler *et al.*, eds., *Voices from the Rapids: An Underwater Search for Fur Trade Artifacts, 1960–73*, Minnesota Historical Archaeological Series No. 3 (Minneapolis: Minnesota Historical Society, 1975).

22. James Axtell, *After Columbus: Essays in the Ethnohistory of Colonial North America* (New York, 1988), ch. 9, esp. p. 154.

23. Kenneth E. Kidd, "The Cloth Trade and the Indians of the Northeast during the Seventeenth and Eighteenth Centuries," Royal Ontario Museum, Division of Art and Archaeology, *Annual* (Toronto, 1961), 48–56; Louise Dechêne, *Habitants et marchands de Montréal au XVIIe siècle* (Paris, 1974), 507 (graphique 11); Peter A. Thomas, "Cultural Change on the Southern New England Frontier, 1630–1665," in William W. Fitzhugh, ed., *Cultures in Contact: The Impact of European Contacts on Native American Cultural Institutions, A.D. 1000–1800* (Washington, D.C., 1985), 146; Joel W. Martin, *Sacred Revolt: The Muskogees' Struggle for a New World* (Boston, 1991), 57–58; Dean L. Anderson, "Perishable Trade Goods: Documentary Material Data and Historical Period Indian Research" (paper presented at the annual meeting of the Society for Historical Archaeology, Savannah, Jan. 7–11, 1987).

24. Axtell, *After Columbus*, 135.

25. *Peter Kalm's Travels in North America: The English Version of 1770*, ed. Adolph B. Benson, 2 vols. (New York, 1966), 520 (continuous pagination); William Wood, *New England's Prospect* [London, 1634], ed. Alden T. Vaughan (Amherst, Mass., 1977), 84; Stanley Pargellis, ed., "The Indians in Virginia . . . 1689," *William and Mary Quarterly*, 3d ser. 16 (1959), 230.

26. James Axtell, *The European and the Indian: Essays in the Ethnohistory of Colonial North America* (New York, 1981), 58.

27. Trigger, *Children of Aataentsic*, 358–59; Bruce G. Trigger, *Natives and Newcomers: Canada's "Heroic Age" Reconsidered* (Kingston and Montreal, 1985), 138, 204, 238; Paul A. Robinson, Marc A. Kelley, and Patricia E. Rubertone, "Preliminary Biocultural

Interpretations from a Seventeenth-Century Narragansett Indian Cemetery in Rhode Island," in Fitzhugh, *Cultures in Contact*, 119.

28. Axtell, *After Columbus*, ch. 9.

29. Brian J. Given, "The Iroquois Wars and Native Arms," in Bruce Alden Cox, ed., *Native People, Native Lands: Canadian Indians, Inuit and Métis*, Carleton Library Series No. 142 (Ottawa, 1988), 3–13; Axtell, *The European and the Indian*, 259–63; Thomas Abler, "European Technology and the Art of War in Iroquoia," in Diana Claire Tkaczak and Brian C. Vivian, eds., *Cultures in Conflict: Current Archaeological Perspectives*, Proceedings of the Twentieth Annual Conference of the Archaeological Association of the U. of Calgary (Calgary, 1989), 273–82.

30. James Sullivan *et al.*, eds., *The Papers of Sir William Johnson*, 14 vols. (Albany, N.Y., 1921–62), 12:952 (Johnson to Arthur Lee, March 28, 1772).

31. Cadwallader Colden, *The History of the Five Indian Nations of Canada* (London, 1747), 13–14.

32. Axtell, *The European and the Indian*, 257–59. There are only two sources for the much-cited connection between inebriation and the dream or vision quest, and neither provides direct evidence that the natives themselves took to alcohol as a short cut to visions: Edmund S. Carpenter, "Alcohol in the Iroquois Dream Quest," *American Journal of Psychiatry*, 116:8 (Aug. 1959), 148–51, and André Vachon, "L'eau-de-vie dans la société indienne," *Canadian Historical Association*, *Report* (1960), 23. R. C. Dailey, "The Role of Alcohol Among North American Indian Tribes as Reported in The Jesuit Relations," *Anthropologica*, 10 (1968), 48–50, and Maia Conrad, "From Visions to Violence: Iroquoian Alcohol Use in the Seventeenth Century" (paper presented at the annual meeting of the American Society for Ethnohistory, Chicago, Nov. 5, 1989) are more circumspect about the lack of direct evidence.

33. [François Vachon de] Belmont's History of Brandy," ed. and trans. Joseph P. Donnelly, *Mid-America*, 34 (1952), 60.

34. Kalm, *Travels in North America*, 520–21.

35. Thwaites, *Jesuit Relations*, 44:283.

36. Nicholas Perrot, "Memoir on the Manners, Customs, and Religion of the Savages of North America," in Emma Helen Blair, ed. and trans., *The Indian Tribes of the Upper Mississippi Valley and Region of the Great Lakes*, 2 vols. (Cleveland, 1911), 1:142.

37. [James] *Adair's History of the American Indians* [London, 1775], ed. Samuel Cole Williams (New York, 1966), 245.

38. Ralph Davis, "English Foreign Trade, 1660–1700," *Economic History Review*, 2d ser. 7:2 (Dec. 1954), 150–66.

39. James W. Bradley, *Evolution of the Onondaga Iroquois: Accommodating Change, 1500–1655* (Syracuse, N.Y., 1987), 130; Charles F. Wray, "The Volume of Dutch Trade Goods Received by the Seneca Iroquois, 1600–1687 A.D.," *New Netherland Studies*, Bulletin KNOB, 84:2/3 (June 1985), 100–112.

40. Papers of Eleazar Wheelock, Dartmouth College Library, Hanover, N.H., catalogued in *A Guide to the Microfilm Edition of the Papers of Eleazar Wheelock* (Hanover, N.H.: Dartmouth College Library, 1971), 766554 (Theophilus Chamberlain to Wheelock, Oct. 4, 1766), 768672 (Wheelock to Dartmouth, Dec. 22, 1768). See also *Travels of William Bartram* [Philadelphia, 1791], ed. Mark Van Doren (New York, 1955), 401: "As to the mechanic arts or manufactures, at present [the Indians of the Southeast] have scarcely any thing worth observation, since they are supplied with necessaries, conveniences, and even superfluities by the white traders."

41. William C. Sturtevant, "Two 1761 Wigwams at Niantic, Connecticut," *American Antiquity*, 40:4 (Oct. 1975), 437–44; Kathleen J. Bragdon, "The Material Culture of the Christian Indians of New England, 1650–1775," in Mary C. Beaudry, ed., *Documentary Archaeology and the New World* (Cambridge, 1988), 126–31; Daniel Mandell, "'To Live More Like My Christian English Neighbors': Indian Natick in the Eighteenth Century," *William and Mary Quarterly*, 3d ser. 48 (Oct. 1991), 552–79.

42. Carl Bridenbaugh, ed., *Gentleman's Progress: The Itinerarium of Dr. Alexander Hamilton, 1744* (Chapel Hill, 1948), 98.

43. John A. Sainsbury, "Indian Labor in Early Rhode Island," *New England Quarterly*, 48 (1975), 378–93.

44. Robert Beverley, *The History and Present State of Virginia* [London, 1705], ed. Louis B. Wright (Charlottesville, 1968), 233.

45. Albert Henry Smyth, ed., *The Writings of Benjamin Franklin* (New York, 1907), 10:97; John Phillip Reid, *A Better Kind of Hatchet: Law, Trade, and Diplomacy in the Cherokee Nation During the Early Years of European Contact* (University Park, Pa., 1976), 194–95.

46. Anthony F. C. Wallace, "Revitalization Movements: Some Theoretical Considerations for Their Comparative Study," *American Anthropologist*, 58 (1956), 264–81.

47. Richard L. Haan, "The 'Trade Do's Not Flourish as Formerly': The Ecological Origins of the Yamassee War of 1715," *Ethnohistory*, 28:4 (Fall 1981), 341–58.

48. Howard H. Peckham, *Pontiac and the Indian Uprising* (New York, 1970, 1947); Charles E. Hunter, "The Delaware Nativist Revival of the Mid-Eighteenth Century," *Ethnohistory*, 18:1 (Winter 1971), 39–49; Anthony F. C. Wallace, *The Death and Rebirth of the Seneca* (New York, 1969), 114–22. Gregory Evans Dowd, "The French King Wakes Up in Detroit: 'Pontiac's War' in Rumor and History," *Ethnohistory*, 37:3 (Summer 1990), 254–78 at 259–61, reminds us that Neolin, the major Delaware prophet, made a partial exception for the gift-giving French.

49. Peckham, *Pontiac and the Indian Uprising*, 101–2; Michael McConnell, *A Country Between: The Upper Ohio Valley and Its Peoples, 1724–1774* (Lincoln, Neb., forthcoming).

CHAPTER SIX

1. Alice B. Kehoe, "The Invention of Prehistory," *Current Anthropology*, 32:4 (1991), 467–76.

2. Neal Salisbury, "American Indians and American History," in Calvin Martin, ed., *The American Indian and the Problem of History* (New York, 1987), 46–54; Bruce G. Trigger, "American Archaeology as Native History: A Review Essay," *William and Mary Quarterly*, 3d ser. 40 (July 1983), 413–52.

3. Russell Thornton, *American Indian Holocaust and Survival: A Population History Since 1492* (Norman, Okla., 1987); Ann F. Ramenofsky, *Vectors of Death: The Archaeology of European Contact* (Albuquerque, N.M., 1987); Daniel T. Reff, *Disease, Depopulation, and Culture Change in Northwestern New Spain, 1518–1764* (Salt Lake City, 1991).

4. Jacques Gernet, *China and the Christian Impact: A Conflict of Cultures*, trans. Janet Lloyd (Cambridge, 1985), 1.

5. Louis J. Puhl, ed., *The Spiritual Exercises of St. Ignatius* (Chicago, 1951), 43, 44.

6. Saint Ignatius of Loyola, *The Constitutions of the Society of Jesus*, ed. and trans. George E. Ganss (St. Louis, 1970), 66, 68, 69, 71–72, 92, 238, 262.

7. *Ibid.*, 159, 319.

8. *Ibid.*, 161.

9. James Axtell, *The Invasion Within: The Contest of Cultures in Colonial North America* (New York, 1985), 75–77.

10. Reuben Gold Thwaites, ed., *The Jesuit Relations and Allied Documents*, 73 vols. (Cleveland, 1896–1901), 33:143, 51:265.

11. James Axtell, "A Moral History of Indian-White Relations Revisited," in *After Columbus: Essays in the Ethnohistory of Colonial North America* (New York, 1988), ch. 1.

12. Virgil J. Vogel, *American Indian Medicine* (Norman, Okla., 1970), 267.

13. Axtell, *The Invasion Within*, 17–19, 93, 98–99, 227–30.

14. Thwaites, *Jesuit Relations*, 1:275, 277 (Joseph Jouvency, 1710).

15. *Ibid.*, 6:195.

16. James Axtell, "The Power of Print in the Eastern Woodlands," in *After Columbus*, ch. 6.

17. Axtell, *The Invasion Within*, 93–101.

18. *Ibid.*, 100–104.

19. Loyola, *Constitutions*, 275.

20. P. Richard Metcalf, "Who Should Rule at Home? Native American Politics and Indian-White Relations," *Journal of American History*, 61 (Dec. 1974), 651–65; Robert F. Berkhofer, Jr., "The Political Context of a New Indian History," *Pacific Historical Review*, 40:3 (August 1971), 357–82.

21. Axtell, *The Invasion Within*, 119–24.

22. Reff, *Disease, Depopulation, and Culture Change*, 253–59; Edward H. Spicer, *Cycles of Conquest: The Impact of Spain, Mexico, and the United States on the Indians of the Southwest, 1533–1960* (Tucson, 1962), 291–92, 294–97; Richard Schmutz, "Jesuit Missionary Methods in Northwestern Mexico," *Journal of the West*, 8:1 (1969), 76–89.

23. Reff, *Disease, Depopulation, and Culture Change*, 254–59, 266; Spicer, *Cycles of Conquest*, 291, 294.

24. Reff, *Disease, Depopulation, and Culture Change*, 251, 267–68; Schmutz, "Jesuit Missionary Methods," 81–82.

25. Pierre de Charlevoix, *Journal of a Voyage to North America*, 2 vols. ([Paris, 1744], London, 1761), 1:154; Baron de Lahontan, *New Voyages to North-America*, ed. Reuben Gold Thwaites, 2 vols. ([London, 1703], Chicago, 1903), 1:326.

26. Eleanor Leacock, "Montagnais Women and the Jesuit Program for Colonization," in Mona Etienne and Leacock, eds., *Women and Colonization: Anthropological Perspectives* (New York, 1980), 25–42; Karen Anderson, *Chain Her By One Foot: The Subjugation*

of Women in Seventeenth-Century New France (London and New York, 1991).

27. Axtell, *The Invasion Within*, 56–57, 69; Richard C. Trexler, "From the Mouths of Babes: Christianization by Children in 16th-Century New Spain," in J. Davis, ed., *Religious Organization and Religious Experience*, Association of Social Anthropologists, Monograph 21 (New York, 1982), 115–35; Olive Patricia Dickason, "Campaigns to Capture Young Minds: A Look at Early Attempts in Colonial Mexico and New France to Remold Amerindians," Canadian Historical Association, *Historical Papers 1987* (Hamilton, Ontario), 44–66.

28. Spicer, *Cycles of Conquest*, 291, 324–25, 332; Charles W. Polzer, *Rules and Precepts of the Jesuit Missions of Northwestern New Spain* (Tucson, 1976), 23, 29, 50, 62, 68, 109, 123–24; Axtell, *The Invasion Within*, 125.

29. Axtell, *The Invasion Within*, ch. 11; Axtell, "Were Indian Conversions *Bona Fide?*" in Axtell, *After Columbus*, ch. 7.

CHAPTER SEVEN

1. James Axtell, "A Moral History of Indian-White Relations Revisited," in *After Columbus: Essays in the Ethnohistory of Colonial North America* (New York, 1988), ch. 1.

2. Marion E. Cross, trans., *Father Louis Hennepin's Description of Louisiana*, introd. Grace Lee Nute (Minneapolis, 1938), 159; John Lawson, *A New Voyage to Carolina*, ed. Hugh T. Lefler (Chapel Hill, 1967), 216.

3. Gabriel Sagard, *Histoire du Canada*, 4 vols. (Paris, 1865 [1636]), 2: 379; Reuben Gold Thwaites, ed., *The Jesuit Relations and Allied Documents*, 73 vols. (Cleveland, 1896–1901), 6: 283–85.

4. Henri Joutel, *A Journal of La Salle's Last Voyage*, introd. Darrett B. Rutman (New York, 1962), 133.

5. Charles H. Lincoln, ed., *Narratives of the Indian Wars, 1675–1699*, Original Narratives of Early American History (New York, 1913), 39. See Seymour Feiler, trans. and ed., *Jean-Bernard Bossu's Travels in the Interior of North America, 1751–1762* (Norman, Okla., 1962), 115, for a similar incident.

6. Christopher Levett, "A Voyage into New England," in *Forerunners and Competitors of the Pilgrims and Puritans*, ed. Charles H. Levermore, 2 vols. (Brooklyn, N.Y., 1912), 2: 623–24; William

Wood, *New England's Prospect,* ed. Alden T. Vaughan (Amherst, Mass., 1977), 115–16.

7. David B. Quinn and Alison M. Quinn, eds., *The English New England Voyages, 1602–1608,* Hakluyt Society Publications, 2d ser., 161 (London, 1983), 134; Thwaites, *Jesuit Relations* 44: 279–81; Feiler, *Bossu's Travels,* 154.

8. Richebourg Gaillard McWilliams, ed. and trans., *Fleur de Lys and Calumet: Being the Pénicaut Narrative of French Adventure in Louisiana* (Baton Rouge, 1953), 8.

9. *Ibid.,* 7–8.

10. John Heckewelder, *History, Manners, and Customs of the Indian Nations Who Once Inhabited Pennsylvania and the Neighbouring States,* ed. William C. Reichel (Philadelphia, 1876), 74.

11. Sagard, *Histoire du Canada* 3: 676 (bk. 3, ch. 3).

12. Edward Porter Alexander, ed., *The Journal of John Fontaine: An Irish Huguenot Son in Spain and Virginia, 1710–1719* (Williamsburg, 1972), 99.

13. McWilliams, *Fleur de Lys and Calumet,* 106–10, 113.

14. H. P. Biggar, ed. and trans., *The Voyages of Jacques Cartier,* Publications of the Public Archives of Canada, No. 11 (Ottawa, 1924), 185; Thomas Birch, *The History of the Royal Society of London,* 4 vols. (London, 1756–57), 3: 45 (thanks to Toby Morantz for this reference).

15. Gabriel Sagard, *The Long Journey to the Country of the Hurons,* ed. George M. Wrong, trans. H. H. Langton, Champlain Society Publications, No. 25 (Toronto, 1939), 125–26.

16. Thwaites, *Jesuit Relations* 3: 197, 7: 93; François Du Creux, S.J., *The History of Canada or New France,* ed. James B. Conacher, trans. Percy J. Robinson, Champlain Society Publications, Nos. 30–31 (Toronto, 1951–52), 1: 160.

17. Thwaites, *Jesuit Relations* 44: 297.

18. Quinn and Quinn, *English New England Voyages,* 303. I remain unconvinced by Richard Kania and Carol Clear's sobersided attempt to provide circumstantial "evidence for James Rosier's 1605 claim of Native American butter and cheese production" in a paper entitled "Did the Indians of Maine Domesticate Deer and Caribou?" presented at the 1988 Williamsburg meeting of the American Society for Ethnohistory.

19. Thomas Shepard, "The Clear Sun-shine of the Gospel Breaking Forth upon the Indians of New England," *Collections of the Massachusetts Historical Society,* 3d ser., 4 (1834), 55.

20. William L. Saunders, ed., *The Colonial Records of North Carolina*, vol. 5 (Raleigh, 1887), 142, 143.
21. William K. Boyd, ed., *William Byrd's Histories of the Dividing Line betwixt Virginia and North Carolina* (New York, 1967), 29, 115, 122, 123, 286.
22. Louis-Philippe, *Diary of My Travels in America*, trans. Stephen Becker (New York, 1977), 77, 84–85 (thanks to Theda Perdue for this spirited comeback).
23. L. A. Vigneras, ed., *The Journal of Christopher Columbus*, trans. Cecil Jane (New York, 1960), 143.
24. David B. Quinn, ed., *New American World: A Documentary History of North America to 1612*, 5 vols. (New York, 1979), 2: 125. About the same time, Coronado was also being unseated in Indian country, but only during a horserace with one of his officers. His head injury, however, caused him to withdraw from the Pueblo Southwest (*ibid.*, 1: 398, 417, 420; thanks to William Swagerty for this suggestion).
25. Dwight B. Heath, ed., *A Journal of the Pilgrims at Plymouth: Mourt's Relation* (New York, 1963), 23 (thanks to Kathleen Bragdon for reminding me of this incident).
26. Philip L. Barbour, ed., *The Complete Works of Captain John Smith (1580–1631)*, 3 vols. (Chapel Hill, 1986), 2: 168.
27. *Ibid.*, 2: 182–83.
28. *Ibid.*, 2; 183–84.
29. Colonel [Henry] Norwood, "A Voyage to Virginia," in *Tracts and Other Papers, Relating Principally to the Origins, Settlement, and Progress of the Colonies in North America*, comp. Peter Force, 4 vols. (Washington, D.C., 1836–47), vol. 3, no. 10, p. 44.
30. Lawrence C. Wroth, *The Voyages of Giovanni da Verrazzano, 1524–1528* (New Haven, 1970), 140–41.
31. Barbour, *Complete Works of John Smith*, 2: 150.
32. Richard M. Dorson, "Comic Indian Anecdotes," *Southern Folklore Quarterly* 10 (1946), 123.
33. Joseph François Lafitau, *Customs of the American Indians Compared with the Customs of Primitive Times*, ed. and trans. William N. Fenton and Elizabeth L. Moore, Champlain Society Publications, Nos. 48–49 (Toronto, 1974–77), 1: 234.
34. Milo Milton Quaife, ed., *John Long's Voyages and Travels in the Years, 1768–1788*, Lakeside Classics (Chicago, 1922), 112–13.
35. Pierre de Charlevoix, *Journal of a Voyage to North America*, 2 vols. (London, 1761), 1: 154; Baron de Lahontan, *New Voyages to*

North-America, ed. Reuben Gold Thwaites, 2 vols. (Chicago, 1905), 1: 326; Sagard, *Histoire du Canada* 3: 698 (bk. 3, ch. 4).

36. George Percy, "'A Trewe Relacyon': Virginia from 1609 to 1612," *Tyler's Quarterly Historical and Genealogical Magazine* 3 (1922), 277.

37. Louise Phelps Kellogg, ed., *Early Narratives of the Northwest, 1634–1699*, Original Narratives of Early American History (New York, 1917), 85; Ruth Lapham Butler, ed. and trans., *Journal of Paul Du Ru, Missionary Priest to Louisiana* (Chicago, 1934), 18; Walter James Hoffman, "The Menomini Indians," Bureau of American Ethnology, *Fourteenth Annual Report* (Washington, D.C., 1896), pt. 1: 215.

38. Sagard, *Histoire du Canada* 2: 280 (bk. 2, ch. 25).

CHAPTER EIGHT

1. *American Historical Review*, 92:3 (June 1987), 621–32.

2. *Ibid.*, 93:1 (Feb. 1988), 283–86.

3. Thomas A. Bailey et al., *The American Pageant*, 7th ed. (Lexington, Mass.: D. C. Heath, 1983); Bernard Bailyn, et al., *The Great Republic: A History of the American People*, 3rd ed. (Lexington, Mass.: D.C. Heath, 1985); T. H. Breen et al., *America, Past and Present* (Glenview, Ill.: Scott, Foresman, 1984); Richard H. Current et al., *American History: A Survey*, 6th ed. (New York, Alfred A. Knopf, 1983); John A. Garraty, *The American Nation: A History of the United States*, 5th ed. (New York, Harper & Row, 1983); Rebecca Brooks Gruver, *An American History*, 4th ed. (New York, Alfred A. Knopf, 1985); James A. Henretta et al., *America's History* (Chicago: Dorsey Press, 1987); Winthrop D. Jordan et al., *The United States: Conquering a Continent*, 5th ed. (Englewood Cliffs, N.J.: Prentice-Hall, 1982); Robert Kelley, *The Shaping of the American Past*, 4th ed. (Englewood Cliffs, N.J.: Prentice-Hall, 1986); Edmund S. Morgan et al., *The National Experience: A History of the United States*, 6th ed. (San Diego, Calif.: Harcourt Brace Jovanovich, 1985); Samuel Eliot Morrison et al., *The Growth of the American Republic*, 6th ed. (New York: Oxford University Press, 1969); Gary B. Nash et al., *The American People: Creating a Nation and a Society* (New York: Harper and Row, 1986); Mary Beth Norton et al., *A People and a Nation: A History of the United States* (Boston: Houghton Mifflin, 1986);

Stephan Nissenbaum et al., *The Pursuit of Liberty: A History of the American People* (New York: Alfred A. Knopf, 1984); George Brown Tindall, *America: A Narrative History* (New York: W. W. Norton, 1984); Irwin Unger, *These United States: The Questions of Our Past*, 3d ed. (Englewood Cliffs, N.J.: Prentice-Hall, 1986). For multi-authored texts, I have referred only to the author of the "discovery" chapter(s).

4. Morison, *Growth of the American Republic;* Nissenbaum, *Pursuit of Liberty;* and Tindall, *America: A Narrative History,* feature full-page texts.

5. Bailey, *American Pageant,* 5; Current, *American History: A Survey,* 1; Morison, *Growth of the American Republic,* 9.

6. Breen, *America, Past and Present,* 6: Jordan, *The United States: Conquering a Continent,* 5.

7. William C. Sturtevant, gen. ed., *Handbook of North American Indians,* vol. 15: *Northeast,* Bruce G. Trigger, ed. (Washington, D.C., 1978), 322.

8. See, for example, Henretta, *America's History,* 33; Current, *American History: A Survey,* 18; Gruver, *An American History,* 10; and Nissenbaum, *Pursuit of Liberty,* 27.

9. Bailey, *American Pageant,* 5; Unger, *These United States,* 5; Gruver, *An American History,* 9.

10. Bailyn, *Great Republic,* 28; Current, *American History: A Survey,* 17; Morison, *Growth of the American Republic,* 12; Tindall, *America: A Narrative History,* 10.

11. Henretta, *America's History,* 44; Jordan, *The United States: Conquering a Continent,* 5; Unger, *These United States,* 5.

12. Morgan, *The National Experience,* 12; Garraty, *The American Nation,* 8.

13. Morison, *Growth of the American Republic,* 19.

14. Bailey, *American Pageant,* 2, 9, 42.

15. Bailyn, *Great Republic,* 28.

16. Norton, *A People and a Nation,* 23.

17. Philip L. Barbour, *Pocahontas and Her World* (Boston, 1970), ch. 10.

18. Bailyn, *Great Republic,* 6–14.

19. Current, *American History: A Survey,* 8.

20. Breen, *America, Past and Present,* 16, 18; Current, *American History: A Survey,* 9.

21. *Cambridge History of Latin America, II: Colonial Latin America,* Leslie Bethell, ed. (Cambridge, 1984), 16.

22. Bailyn, *Great Republic*, 12; Gruver, *An American History*, 19; Morison, *Growth of the American Republic*, 22.

23. Unger, *These United States*, 17; Nissenbaum, *Pursuit of Liberty*, 35; Garraty, *The American Nation*, 10; Morgan, *The National Experience*, 13.

24. Morison, *Growth of the American Republic*, 32.

25. Breen, *America, Past and Present*, 19.

26. Unger, *These United States*, 17.

27. Morgan, *The National Experience*, 13.

28. Bailey, *American Pageant*, 42 (picture caption).

29. Current, *American History: A Survey*, 19; Bailey, *American Pageant*, 43.

30. Bailey, *American Pageant*, 43.

31. William Eccles, *The Canadian Frontier, 1534–1760*, rev. ed. (Albuquerque, N.M., 1974); *France in America* (New York, 1972), and others.

32. Bailey, *American Pageant*, 43–47; Breen, *America, Past and Present*, 19; Gruver, *An American History*, 23; Henretta, *America's History*, 36–37; and Morison, *Growth of the American Republic*, 13.

33. Bailey, *American Pageant*, 45.

34. Bailey, *American Pageant*, is the worst offender (43–45, 48, 51), but see Henretta, *America's History*, 19, 32, and Morgan, *The National Experience*, 14 ("roamed"). On the importance of language, see James Axtell, "Forked Tongues: Moral Judgements in Indian History," *Perspectives: AHA Newsletter*, 25 (Feb. 1987): 10, 12–13.

35. Jacques Barzun, "Teaching and Research in History Today," *History Teacher*, 19 (1986): 523.

36. Bailyn, *Great Republic*, 7, 29. The Bailyn text has at least two poorly cropped pictures that run into the binding (19, 67).

37. Nash, *American People*, 5 (baskets), 19 (Tenochtitlán), 21 (Potosí); Norton, *A People and a Nation*, 30 (bowl); Bailey, *American Pageant*, 8 (couple); Henretta, *America's History*, 43 (seal).

38. Norton, *A People and a Nation*, 6; Breen, *America, Past and Present*, 5.

39. Nash, *American People*, 9 (ports), 20 (smallpox); Norton, *A People and a Nation*, 12 (village), 18 (smallpox); Jordan, *The United States: Conquering a Continent*, 7; Bailey, *American Pageant*, 3 (1492); Henretta, *America's History*, 37 (1650); Unger, *These United States*, 7 (spices), 20 (Dürer); Tindall, *America: A Narrative*

History, 31 (Luther); and Breen, *America, Past and Present,* 20 (canoes).

40. Breen, *America, Past and Present,* 7, 10 (disease), 8–9 (acculturation), 25–26 (Ireland); Kelley, *Shaping of the American Past,* 9, 12 (Ireland); Nash, *American People,* 9–11, 63–74 (Africa), 20 (disease); Norton, *A People and a Nation,* 9–13, 47–53 (Africa); Tindall, *America: A Narrative History,* 19–22 (acculturation and disease).

41. Nissenbaum, *Pursuit of Liberty,* 1–15; Morison, *Growth of the American Republic,* 15–22.

42. *The Complete Works of Captain John Smith (1580–1631),* Philip L. Barbour, cd., 3 vols. (Chapel IIill, N.C., 1986), 2: 338.

43. Current, *American History: A Survey,* 15–16.

44. James Axtell, "Colonial America Without the Indians: Counterfactual Reflections," *Journal of American History,* 73 (1987): 981–96.

45. Philip Wayne Powell, *Tree of Hate: Propaganda and Prejudices Affecting United States Relations with the Hispanic World* (New York, 1971), 6.

46. Carl Bridenbaugh, "The Neglected First Half of American History," *AHR,* 53 (1947–48): 506–17; James Axtell, "A North American Perspective for Colonial History," *History Teacher,* 12 (1979): 549–62.

47. Frances FitzGerald, *America Revised: History Schoolbooks in the Twentieth Century* (New York, 1980), 42.

48. David B. Quinn, ed., *New American World: A Documentary History of North America to 1612,* 5 vols. (New York, 1979); John H. Parry and Robert G. Keith, eds., *New Iberian World: A Documentary History of the Discovery and Settlement of Latin America to the Early 17th Century,* 5 vols. (New York, 1984).

CHAPTER NINE

1. John S. Ezell, ed., *The New Democracy in America: Travels of Francisco de Miranda in the United States, 1783–84,* trans. Judson P. Wood (Norman, Okla., 1963), 111.

2. Louis-Philippe, King of France, 1830–1848, *Diary of My Travels in America,* trans. Stephen Becker (New York, 1977), 51.

3. *Moreau de St. Méry's American Journey [1793–1798],* ed. and

trans. Kenneth Roberts and Anna M. Roberts (Garden City, N.Y., 1947), 293, 300.

4. Johann David Schoepf, *Travels in the Confederation* [*1783–84*], trans. Alfred J. Morrison, 2 vols. (Philadelphia, 1911), 2:40, 149.

5. *Moreau de St. Méry's American Journey*, 309.

6. *Luigi Castiglioni's Viaggio: Travels in the United States of America, 1785–87*, ed. and trans. Antonio Pace (Syracuse, N.Y., 1983), 165.

7. *Moreau de St. Méry's American Journey*, 276.

8. *Chateaubriand's Travels in America*, trans. Richard Switzer (Lexington, Ky., 1969), 175.

9. J. P. Brissot de Warville, *New Travels in the United States of America, 1788*, ed. Durand Echeverria, trans. Maria Soceanu Vamos and Durand Echeverria (Cambridge, Mass., 1964), 82n.6.

10. Marquis de Chastellux, *Travels in North America in the Years 1780, 1781 and 1782*, ed. and trans. Howard C. Rice, Jr., 2 vols. (Chapel Hill, 1963), 1:209.

11. *Historical Statistics of the United States: Colonial Times to 1970*, 2 pts. (Bicentennial ed., Washington, D.C., 1975), Series A 1–5, 43–56, 57–72, 91–104, 335–49; Z 20–23.

12. Peter H. Wood, "The Changing Population of the Colonial South: An Overview by Race and Region, 1685–1790," in Wood, Gregory A. Waselkov, and M. Thomas Hatley, eds., *Powhatan's Mantle: Indians in the Colonial Southeast* (Lincoln, Neb., 1989), 38–39.

13. *Historical Statistics of the United States*, Series A 91–104; Z 1–23.

14. Leslie B. Rout, Jr., *The African Experience in Spanish America: 1502 to the Present Day* (Cambridge, 1976), 22.

15. Kirkpatrick Sale, *The Conquest of Paradise: Christopher Columbus and the Columbian Legacy* (New York, 1990).

16. James Axtell, *After Columbus: Essays in the Ethnohistory of Colonial North America* (New York, 1988), ch. 1, "A Moral History of Indian-White Relations Revisited."

17. *Ibid.*, ch. 2, "Forked Tongues: Moral Judgments in Indian History."

18. Nicolás Sanchez-Albornez, "The Population of Colonial Spanish America," in Leslie Bethell, ed., *The Cambridge History of Latin America, Volume II: Colonial Latin America* (Cambridge, 1984), 15–19; Magnus Mörner, "Spanish Migration to the New World Prior to 1800: A Report on the State of Research," in Fredi Chi-

appelli, ed., *First Images of America: The Impact of the New World on the Old*, 2 vols. (Berkeley and Los Angeles, 1976), 2:737–82.

19. R. Cole Harris and John Warkentin, *Canada Before Confederation: A Study in Historical Geography* (New York, 1974), 19–21, 32–37; Jacques Henripin and Yves Péron, "The Demographic Transition of the Province of Quebec," in D. V. Glass and Roger Revelle, eds., *Population and Social Change* (London, 1972), 213, 217, 220; Hubert Charbonneau *et al.*, *Naissance d'une population: Les Français établi au Canada au XVIIe siècle*, Institut National d'Études Démographiques, Travaux et Documents, Cahier no. 118 (Montreal, 1987), 15–16: Mario Boleda, "Trente mille Français à la conquête du Saint-Laurent," *Histoire Social-Social History*, 23 (May 1990),153–77; Leslie Choquette, "Recruitment of French Emigrants to Canada, 1600–1760," in Ida Altman and James Horn, eds., *"To Make America": European Emigration in the Early Modern Period* (Berkeley and Los Angeles, 1991), 131–71.

20. *Historical Statistics of the United States*, Series A 91–104; Z 1–23.

21. R. C. Simmons, *The American Colonies: From Settlement to Independence* (New York, 1976), 174–85; A. Roger Ekirch, *Bound for America: The Transportation of British Convicts to the Colonies, 1718–1775* (Oxford, 1987), 26–27.

22. Jim Potter, "Demographic Development and Family Structure," in Jack P. Greene and J. R. Pole, eds., *Colonial British America: Essays in the New History of the Early Modern Era* (Baltimore, 1984), ch. 5; John J. McCusker and Russell R. Menard, *The Economy of British America, 1607–1789* (Chapel Hill, 1985), ch. 10.

23. Benjamin Franklin, *The Interest of Great Britain Considered . . .* [and] *Observations concerning the Increase of Mankind, Peopling of Countries, &c.* [1751] (London, 1760), 51.

24. Simmons, *The American Colonies*, 174, 179–81; Potter, "Demographic Development," 148–50.

25. Carville V. Earle, "Environment, Disease, and Mortality in Early Virginia," in Thad W. Tate and David L. Ammerman, eds., *The Chesapeake in the Seventeenth Century: Essays on Anglo-American Society* (Chapel Hill, 1979), ch. 3; Simmons, *The American Colonies*, 24, 76; Wood, "The Changing Population of the Colonial South," 38; Helen C. Rountree, *Pocahontas's People: The Powhatan Indians of Virginia Through Four Centuries* (Norman, Okla., 1990), 96, 104.

26. Simmons, *The American Colonies*, 24, 175, 178.

27. *Ibid.*, 124, 176, 178.

28. John White, *The Planters Plea* (London, 1630), quoted in David Cressy, *Coming Over: Migration and Communication between England and New England in the Seventeenth Century* (Cambridge, 1987), 85.

29. James Axtell, *The Invasion Within: The Contest of Cultures in Colonial North America* (New York, 1985).

30. *Historical Statistics of the United States*, Series A 91–104.

31. William D. Phillips, Jr., *Slavery from Roman Times to the Early Transatlantic Trade* (Minneapolis, 1985).

32. Rout, *The African Experience in Spanish America*, 61–66, ch. 3; Frederick P. Bowser, "Africans in Spanish American Colonial Society," in Bethell, *Cambridge History of Latin America*, 2:357–79.

33. Marcel Trudel, *L'Esclavage au Canada français: Histoire et conditions de l'esclavage* (Quebec, 1960), ch. 3; Robin Winks, *The Blacks in Canada: A History* (Montreal and New Haven, 1971), ch. 1; "Slavery in New France, 1628–1760."

34. Daniel H. Usner, Jr., "From African Slavery to American Slavery: The Introduction of Black Laborers to Colonial Louisiana," *Louisiana History*, 20 (Winter 1979), 25–48.

35. Donald R. Wright, *African Americans in the Colonial Era: From African Origins Through the American Revolution* (Arlington Heights, Ill., 1990), ch. 1.

36. *Historical Statistics of the United States*, Series Z 1–23.

37. Simmons, *The American Colonies*, 87, 125, 186; Wright, *African Americans in the Colonial Era*, 17–18, 20.

38. Bernard W. Sheehan, *Seeds of Extinction: Jeffersonian Philanthropy and the American Indian* (Chapel Hill, 1973).

39. Wood, "The Changing Population of the Colonial South, " 38–39.

40. Alfred W. Crosby, "Virgin Soil Epidemics as a Factor in the Aboriginal Depopulation in America," *William and Mary Quarterly*, 3d ser. 33 (April 1976), 289–99; Crosby, "'God . . . Would Destroy Them, and Give Their Country to Another People . . . ,'" *American Heritage*, 29:6 (Oct.–Nov. 1978), 39–42; Sherburne F. Cook, "The Significance of Disease in the Extinction of the New England Indians," *Human Biology*, 45 (1973), 485–508; John Duffy, "Smallpox and the Indians of the American Colonies," *Bulletin of the History of Medicine*, 25 (1951), 324–41; Peter H. Wood, "The Impact of Smallpox on the Native Population of the 18th century South," *New York State Journal of Medicine*, 87 (Jan. 1987), 30–36; Russell Thornton, *American Indian Holocaust and*

Survival: A Population History since 1492 (Norman, Okla., 1987), ch. 4.

41. Thomas Morton, *New English Canaan* (London, 1632), in Peter Force, comp., *Tracts and Other Papers Relating Principally to the Origin, Settlement, and Progress of the Colonies in North America . . . ,* 4 vols. (Washington, D.C., 1836–47), vol. 2, no. 5, pp. 18–19.

42. Alexander S. Salley, Jr., ed., *Narratives of Early Carolina, 1650–1708,* Original Narratives of Early American History (New York, 1911), 284–85.

43. Quoted in Duffy, "Smallpox and the Indians," 332.

44. [James] *Adair's History of the American Indians* [London, 1775], ed. Samuel Cole Williams (New York, 1966), 244–45.

45. Sherburne F. Cook, "Interracial Warfare and Population Decline Among the New England Indians," *Ethnohistory,* 20:1 (Winter 1973), 1–24.

46. Almon Wheeler Lauber, *Indian Slavery in Colonial Times Within the Present Limits of the United States,* Columbia University Studies in History, Economics, and Public Law, vol. 54, no. 3 (New York, 1913); William Robert Snell, "Indian Slavery in Colonial South Carolina, 1671–1795" (Ph.D. diss., U. of Alabama, 1972); Robert P. Wiegers, "A Proposal for Indian Slave Trading in the Mississippi Valley and Its Impact on the Osage," *Plains Anthropologist,* 33 (May 1988), 187–202.

47. Paul Chrisler Phillips, *The Fur Trade,* 2 vols. (Norman, Okla., 1961); above, Chapter 5.

48. William Hand Browne et al., eds., *Archives of Maryland,* 72 vols. to date (Baltimore, 1883–), 2:14–15 (Proceedings and Acts of the General Assembly, April 12, 1666).

CHAPTER TEN

1. Alfred W. Crosby, "Reassessing 1492," *American Quarterly,* 41 (1989), 661–69 at 665–66; J. H. Parry, *The Discovery of the Sea* (Berkeley and Los Angeles, 1981), xi, xiv.

2. Lewis Hanke, *The Spanish Struggle for Justice in the Conquest of America* (Washington, D.C., 1949; Boston, 1965); Hanke, "A Modest Proposal for a Moratorium on Grand Generalizations: Some Thoughts on the Black Legend," *Hispanic American Historical Review* [*HAHR*], 51 (1971), 112–27; Charles Gibson, "Reconquista and Conquista," in Raquel Chang-Rodríguez and Donald

A. Yates, eds., *Homage to Irving A. Leonard: Essays on Hispanic Art, History and Literature* (East Lansing: Latin American Studies Center, Michigan State University, 1977), 19–28; Gibson, "Conquest and So-Called Conquest in Spain and Spanish America," *Terrae Incognitae*, 12 (1980), 1–19.

3. Bartolomé de Las Casas, *History of the Indies*, ed. and trans. Andrée Collard (New York, 1971), 183–86.

4. *Motolinia's History of the Indians of New Spain*, ed. and trans. Francis Borgia Steck (Washington, D.C., 1951), 87–94.

5. Alonso de Zorita, *Life and Labor in Ancient Mexico: The Brief and Summary Relation of the Lords of New Spain*, ed. and trans. Benjamin Keen (New Brunswick, N.J., 1963), 202–18. See also Ralph H. Vigil, *Alonso de Zorita: Royal Judge and Christian Humanist, 1512–1585* (Norman, Okla., 1987).

6. Charles Gibson, ed., *The Spanish Tradition in America* (New York, 1968), 106. On the "Black Legend" of Spanish cruelty and the uses to which it was put by Spain's European enemies, see Charles Gibson, ed., *The Black Legend: Anti-Spanish Attitudes in the Old World and the New* (New York, 1971); Philip Wayne Powell, *Tree of Hate: Propaganda and Prejudice Affecting United States Relations with the Hispanic World* (New York, 1971); William S. Maltby, *The Black Legend in England: The Development of Anti-Spanish Sentiment, 1558–1660* (Durham, N.C., 1971); Benjamin Keen, "The Black Legend Revisited: Assumptions and Realities," *HAHR*, 49 (1969), 703–19; Keen, "The White Legend Revisited: A Reply to Professor Hanke's 'Modest Proposal,'" *HAHR*, 51 (1971), 336–55; John Paddock, "The War of the Myths—Spanish and English Treatment of the Native Americans," *América Indígena*, 18 (1958), 281–92.

7. Miguel Leon-Portilla, ed., *The Broken Spears: The Aztec Account of the Conquest of Mexico* (Boston, 1962), 51.

8. [Arthur C.] *Parker on the Iroquois*, ed. William N. Fenton (Syracuse, N.Y., 1968), 17–18.

9. Wendy Rose, "For Some, It's a Time of Mourning," *The New World* [Smithsonian Institution], 1 (Spring 1990), 4.

10. *The Web* [Newsletter of the American Indian Program, Cornell University], April 1990, [5], [7].

11. "First Nations to Mark Discovery of America," [Toronto] *Globe and Mail*, January 10, 1989.

12. *The Boston Magazine*, May 1784, 281–85, reprinted in Gerald A. Danzer, "Has the Discovery of America Been Useful or Hurtful

to Mankind? Yesterday's Questions and Today's Students," *The History Teacher*, 7 (1974), 192–206 at 203.

13. Paul E. Lovejoy, "The Impact of the Atlantic Slave Trade on Africa: A Review of the Literature," *Journal of African History*, 30 (1989), 365–94 at 368.

14. Francis D. Adams and Barry Sanders, eds., *Three Black Writers in Eighteenth Century England* (Belmont, Calif., 1971), 81, 86.

15. Henry Kamen, "The Mediterranean and the Expulsion of Spanish Jews in 1492," *Past and Present*, no. 119 (May 1988), 30–55.

16. J. H. Elliott, *Imperial Spain, 1469–1716* (London, 1963), 98; *Quincentennial of the Discovery of America: Encounter of Two Worlds* [Organization of American States newsletter], 17 (Oct. 1989), 3. Toledan chauvinism notwithstanding, the "School of Translators" was not a building or even a congress of experts but an uncoordinated, peninsula-wide effort of Jewish scholars to translate Arabic works into Castilian and later Latin. In fact, most Jewish scholarship was original rather than in translations and was especially important in science and mathematics. Norman Roth, "Jewish Collaborators in Alfonso's Scientific Work," in Robert I. Burns, ed., *Emperor of Culture: Alfonso X the Learned of Castile and His Thirteenth-Century Renaissance* (Philadelphia, 1990), 59–71, 223–24n.1 (thanks to William D. Phillips, Jr. for this reference).

17. "Spain Honoring Jews 500 Years After Expulsion," *New York Times*, International section, June 3, 1990, 5.

18. William H. McNeill, "How Columbus Remade the World," *Humanities* [National Endowment for the Humanities], 6:6 (Dec. 1985), 3–7 at 4.

19. William Cronon, *Changes in the Land: Indians, Colonists, and the Ecology of New England* (New York, 1983), 161–62.

20. Alfred W. Crosby, *The Columbian Voyages, the Columbian Exchange, and Their Historians*, Essays on Global and Comparative History (Washington, D.C.: American Historical Association, 1987), 24–25; Crosby, *The Columbian Exchange: Biological and Cultural Consequences of 1492* (Westport, Conn., 1972). See also Crosby, *Ecological Imperialism: The Biological Expansion of Europe, 900–1900* (Cambridge, Eng., 1986) and "Reassessing 1492," *American Quarterly*, 41 (1989), 661–69.

21. *What's to Celebrate?* (Newsletter of the Columbus in Context Clearinghouse), 1:1 (Fall 1989), [1]–[2] (thanks to Jesse Lemisch for a copy).

22. Gibson, "Conquest and So-Called Conquest," *Terrae Incognitae*, 12 (1980), 1–19 at 2.

23. Mario Gongora, *Studies in the Colonial History of Spanish America*, trans. Richard Southern (Cambridge, Eng., 1975), ch. 1, esp. 6–8; James Lockhart, *The Men of Cajamarca: A Social and Biographical Study of the First Conquerors of Peru* (Austin, 1972), ch. 2 and p. 62. See also Ignacio Avellaneda, *Los Sobrevivientes de la Florida: The Survivors of the De Soto Expedition*, ed. Bruce S. Chappell, Research Publications of the P. K. Yonge Library of Florida History No. 2, University of Florida Libraries (Gainesville, 1990), 67–74, for a similar profile.

24. Margaret Atwood, *Second Words: Selected Critical Prose* (Boston, 1984), 397.

25. Luis Villoro, *Sahagún or the Limits of the Discovery of the Other*, 1992 Lecture Series, Working Papers No. 2, Dept. of Spanish and Portuguese, University of Maryland (College Park, 1989); Tzvetan Todorov, *The Conquest of America: The Question of the Other*, trans. Richard Howard (New York, 1984).

26. James Axtell, "Forked Tongues: Moral Judgments in Indian History," *After Columbus: Essays in the Ethnohistory of Colonial North America* (New York, 1988), 34–44 at 35.

27. Frank Chalk and Kurt Jonassohn, "The History and Sociology of Genocidal Killings," in Israel W. Cherny, ed., *Genocide: A Critical Bibliographical Review* (New York, 1988), 40; Chalk and Jonassohn, *The History and Sociology of Genocide: Analyses and Case Studies* (New Haven, 1990), 23.

28. Francis Jennings, *The Invasion of America: Indians, Colonialism, and the Cant of Conquest* (Chapel Hill, 1975), ch. 13; Steven T. Katz, "The Pequot War Reconsidered," *New England Quarterly*, 64:2 (June 1991), 206–24; Andrew C. Albrecht, "Indian-French Relations at Natchez," *American Anthropologist*, n.s. 48:3 (July–Sept. 1946), 321–54; Patricia D. Woods, "The French and the Natchez Indians in Louisiana: 1700–1731," *Louisiana History*, 19 (1978), 413–35; Joseph L. Peyser, "The Fate of the Fox Survivors: A Dark Chapter in the History of the French in the Upper Country, 1726–1737," *Wisconsin Magazine of History*, 73:2 (Winter 1989–90), 83–110.

29. General Philip H. Sheridan at Fort Cobb, Indian Territory, Jan. 1869: John Bartlett, *Familiar Quotations* (Boston, 1955), 653b.

30. Edmund Burke quoted in Lord Acton, *Essays on Freedom and Power*, ed. Gertrude Himmelfarb (New York, 1955), 52.

31. Bernard Knollenberg, "General Amherst and Germ Warfare," *Mississippi Valley Historical Review,* 41 (1954–55), 489–94, 762–63; P. M. Ashburn, *The Ranks of Death: A Medical History of the Conquest of America,* ed. Frank D. Ashburn (New York, 1947); Crosby, *The Columbian Exchange,* ch. 2; William H. McNeill, *Plagues and Peoples* (Garden City, N.Y., 1976), ch. 5; Henry F. Dobyns, *Native American Historical Demography,* Newberry Library Center for the History of the American Indian Bibliographical Series (Bloomington, Ind., 1976); Dobyns, *Their Number Become Thinned: Native American Population Dynamics in Eastern North America* (Knoxville, Tenn., 1983); Russell Thornton, *American Indian Holocaust and Survival: A Population History since 1492* (Norman, Okla., 1987).

32. Lord Bolingbroke, *Letters on the Study and Use of History* (new ed., London, 1779), 14 (letter 2).

33. Gordon Wright, "History as a Moral Science," *American Historical Review,* 81 (1976), 9.

34. Adrian Oldfield, "Moral Judgments in History," *History and Theory,* 20 (1981), 260–77 at 271.

35. James Axtell, "A Moral History of Indian-White Relations Revisited," *After Columbus,* ch. 1, esp. 19–25.

CHAPTER ELEVEN

1. Jesse Lemisch, "Bicentennial Schlock," *New Republic,* Nov. 6, 1976, 21–23.

2. Diane Ravitch and Chester E. Finn, Jr., *What Do Our 17-Year-Olds Know? A Report of the First National Assessment of History and Literature* (New York, 1987), 75, 99; *A Survey of College Seniors: Knowledge of History and Literature,* conducted for the National Endowment for the Humanities (Princeton, N.J.: The Gallup Organization, 1989).

3. Kenneth J. Cooper, "Test Suggests Students Lack Grasp of Civics," *Washington Post,* April 3, 1990, A5; Ravitch and Finn, *What Do Our 17-Year-Olds Know?,* 265.

4. Carla Rahn Phillips and William D. Phillips, "The Textbook Columbus: Examining the Myth," *Humanities* [National Endowment for the Humanities], 12:5 (Sept.–Oct. 1991), 27–30.

5. Foster Provost, *Columbus: An Annotated Guide to the Scholarship on His Life and Writings, 1750–1988* (Detroit: Omnigraphics, 1991).

6. (Detroit: Omnigraphics, 1991).

7. Silvio A. Bedini, ed., *The Christopher Columbus Encyclopedia*, 2 vols. (New York: Simon and Schuster, 1991).

8. *Raccolta di documenti e studi pubblicati dalla R. Commissione colombiana pel quarto centenario della scoperta dell'America*, 3 vols. in 4 (Rome, 1892–96); only 560 copies were published.

9. Comitato Nazionale per le Celebrazioni del V. Centenario della Scoperta dell'America, *Nuova Raccolta Colombiana*, 27 vols. (Rome, 1988–   ).

10. 3rd rev. ed. (Madrid, 1986).

11. *The Diario of Christopher Columbus's First Voyage to America, 1492–1493* (Norman: University of Oklahoma Press, 1989). On the superiority of this edition and the value of its concordance, see David Henige, "Edited . . . and not Precipitated: Three Recent Editions of Columbus's *diario*," *Terrae Incognitae*, 22 (1990), 93–104. See also Henige, *In Search of Columbus: The Sources of the First Voyage* (Tucson: University of Arizona Press, 1991) on the limitations of the *diario* in general.

12. Juan Gil, ed. and trans., *El libro de Marco Polo: ejemplar anotado por Cristóbal Colón y que se conserva en la biblioteca capitular y colombina de Sevilla* (Madrid, 1986).

13. Delno C. West and August Kling, ed. and trans., *The Libro de las profecías of Christopher Columbus* (Gainesville: University Presses of Florida, 1991), 2, 5, 87. See also Pauline Moffitt Watts, "Prophecy and Discovery: On the Spiritual Origins of Christopher Columbus's 'Enterprise of the Indies,'" *American Historical Review*, 90 (1985), 73–102, and "Columbus's Crusade," *Humanities* [NEH], 6:6 (Dec. 1985), 15–17.

14. Eugene Lyon, "15th-Century Manuscript Yields First Look at Niña," *National Geographic*, 170:5 (Nov. 1986), 600–605; Lyon, "Niña, Ship of Discovery," in Jerald T. Milanich and Susan Milbrath, eds., *First Encounters: Spanish Explorations in the Caribbean and the United States, 1492–1570* (Gainesville: University of Florida Press, 1989), ch. 4.

15. James Parrent et al., "Zeroing In on the *Capitana* and the *Santiago*," *Archaeology*, 44:1 (Jan.-Feb. 1991), 53–54.

16. Donald H. Keith and Toni L. Carroll, "The Hunt for the *Gallega*," *ibid.*, 55–59. See also Roger C. Smith, "Ships of Exploration," *ibid.*, 48–52, for other 16th-century shipwrecks recently studied.

17. See Provost, *Columbus: Annotated Guide*, items 286, 602, 604. As early as 1942, Emiliano Jos suggested syphilis as the cause of

Pinzón's death. Jeffrey Burton Russell provides a longer and more entertaining footnote in *Inventing the Flat Earth: Columbus and Modern Historians* (New York: Praeger, 1991), which shows how the "flat earth" myth was concocted in the 19th century by Washington Irving and a French *érudit*.

18. Kathleen Deagan, "The Archaeology of the Spanish Contact Period in the Caribbean," *Journal of World Prehistory*, 2:2 (1988), 206–8; Deagan, "La Isabela, Foothold in the New World," *National Geographic*, 181:1 (Jan. 1992), 40–53; John Noble Wilford, "Dominican Bluff Yields Columbus's First Colony," *New York Times*, Nov. 27, 1990, C1, C6; José Maria Cruxent, "The Origin of La Isabela: First Spanish Colony in the New World," in David Hurst Thomas, ed., *Columbian Consequences. Vol. 2: Archaeological and Historical Perspectives on the Spanish Borderlands East* (Washington, D.C.: Smithsonian Institution Press, 1990), 251–59.

19. *Admiral of the Ocean Sea: A Life of Christopher Columbus*, 1-vol. ed. and 2-vol. ed. (Boston, 1942); Morison, *Christopher Columbus, Mariner* (Boston, 1955). Both titles are still in print.

20. *Christopher Columbus: The Grand Design* (London: Orbis, 1985), originally published in Italian in 1974; *The Voyages of Columbus: The Great Discovery*, trans. Marc A. Beckwith and Luciano F. Farina, 2 vols. (Novara: Instituto Geografico de Agostini, 1991), based on the 2nd Italian edition of 1990; *Columbus: The Great Adventure*, trans. Farina and Beckwith (New York: Orion Books, 1991), published in Italian in 1989.

21. (New York: Alfred A. Knopf, 1990). For critical reviews see William H. McNeill in the *New York Times Book Review*, Oct. 7, 1990, 28; Edwards Park in the *Washington Post Book World*, Oct. 7, 1990, 5; and *The Economist*, Jan. 5, 1991, 69.

22. (New York: Alfred A. Knopf, 1991).

23. (Oxford, 1991), viii, x.

24. *Imagining the New World: Columbian Iconography*, eds. Irma B. Jaffe, Gianni Eugenio Viola, and Franca Rovigatti (Rome and New York: Instituto della Enciclopedia Italiana Treccani, 1991).

25. Carla Hill, "Christopher Columbus—the Lawsuit," *Washington Post*, Nov. 27, 1990, C1, C5; Alan Riding, "6 Ships, 2 Queens, Many Headaches," *New York Times*, March 15, 1992, H17, H20–21.

26. (New York: William Morrow, 1991). John Dyson and Peter Christopher's *Columbus: For Gold, God, and Glory* (New York: Simon & Schuster, 1991) is a colorful but inferior lookalike.

27. See, for example, the differing views of the contributors to *Columbus and His World: Proceedings of the First San Salvador Conference, Oct. 30–Nov. 3, 1986,* ed. Donald T. Gerace (Ft. Lauderdale: College Center of the Finger Lakes, Bahamian Field Station, 1987).

28. Taviani, *Columbus: The Grand Design.*

29. Stuart B. Schwartz, *The Iberian Mediterranean and Atlantic Traditions in the Formation of Columbus as a Colonizer* (Minneapolis: Associates of the James Ford Bell Library, 1986), 19.

30. Carla Rahn Phillips and William D. Phillips, Jr., *The Worlds of Christopher Columbus* (New York: Cambridge University Press, 1992). See also J. R. S. Phillips, *The Medieval Expansion of Europe* (Oxford: Oxford University Press, 1988).

31. Franco Cardini, *Europe 1492: Portrait of a Continent Five Hundred Years Ago* (New York: Facts on File, 1989). The subheadings of Sale's chapter on Europe are "Violence," "Disease," and "Famine"; its epigraph is "The End of the World Is Near" (Sale, *The Conquest of Paradise,* ch. 2). Several essays in *The Spanish World,* ed. J. H. Elliott (New York: Harry N. Abrams, 1991), and many of its 320 illustrations, paint a fairer portrait of Columbus's adopted country.

32. Jay A. Levenson, ed., *Circa 1492: Art in the Age of Exploration* (New Haven: Yale University Press, 1991). The Library of Congress also mounted an exhibition "Old World/New World: The Worlds of Columbus."

33. On the question of Columbus's alleged Jewish background, see Provost, *Columbus: Annotated Guide,* 167–70. A traveling exhibition "Golden Threads: A Tapestry of Sephardic Experience" opened at the Smithsonian's S. Dillon Ripley Center in the spring of 1992. The University of Michigan devoted the whole year of 1992 to lectures, symposia, and concerts on "Jews and the Encounter with the New World, 1492–1992."

34. Philip P. Argenti, *The Occupation of Chios by the Genoese . . . (1346–1566),* 3 vols. (Cambridge: Cambridge University Press, 1958). See also Taviani, *Columbus: The Grand Design,* ch. 8.

35. John Vogt, *Portuguese Rule on the Gold Coast, 1469–1682* (Athens: University of Georgia Press, 1979). See also Taviani, *Columbus: The Grand Design,* ch. 22.

36. David B. Quinn, "Columbus and the North: England, Iceland, and Ireland," *William and Mary Quarterly,* 3d ser. 49 (April 1992), 278–97. See also Taviani, *Columbus: The Grand Design,* ch. 15.

37. Alfred W. Crosby, *Ecological Imperialism: The Biological Expansion of Europe, 900–1900* (Cambridge: Cambridge University Press, 1986), 80. The last Guanche died in the late 17th century.

38. Felipe Fernández-Armesto, *Before Columbus: Exploration and Colonization from the Mediterranean to the Atlantic, 1229–1492* (Philadelphia: University of Pennsylvania Press, 1987), 213; Fernández-Armesto, *The Canary Islands After the Conquest: The Making of a Colonial Society in the Early Sixteenth Century* (Oxford: Oxford University Press, 1982); John Mercer, *The Canary Islanders: Their Prehistory, Conquest, and Survival* (London: Rex Collings, 1980); Antonio Tejera Gaspar and Eduardo Aznar Vallejo, "Lessons from the Canaries. The First Contact Between Europeans and Canarians: ca. 1312–1477," paper read at conference "Rethinking the Encounter: New Perspectives on Conquest and Colonization, 1450–1550," U. of Florida, April 17–20, 1988; Aznar Vallejo, "Contacts in the Conquest of the Canary Islands," paper read at conference "Implicit Ethnographies: Encounters between Europeans and Other Peoples in the Wake of Columbus," U. of Minnesota, Oct. 4, 1990; John Kicza, "Patterns in Early Spanish Overseas Expansion," *William and Mary Quarterly*, 3d ser. 49 (April 1992), 229–53. For Columbus's experiences in the Canaries, see Taviani, *Columbus: The Grand Design*, 376–77.

39. Raymond D. Fogelson, "The Red Man in the White City," in David Hurst Thomas, ed., *Columbian Consequences. Vol. 3: The Spanish Borderlands in Pan-American Perspective* (Washington, D.C.: Smithsonian Institution Press, 1991), ch. 4; Ricardo Gonzalez Leandri, "Crónica de un desencuentro," *92 America* (Revista del Quinto Centenario), no. 6 (Oct.–Dec. 1990), 85–88; *Report of the United States Commission to the Columbian Historical Exposition at Madrid, 1892–93* (Washington, D.C., 1895).

40. "500 Years: Preliminary Results of a Quincentenary Survey," *Northeast Indian Quarterly*, 7:3 (Fall 1990), 21–22.

41. George P. Horse Capture, "An American Indian Perspective," in Herman J. Viola and Carolyn Margolis, eds., *Seeds of Change: A Quincentennial Commemoration* (Washington, D.C.: Smithsonian Institution Press, 1991), 186–207; *Northeast Indian Quarterly*, 7:3 (Fall 1990).

42. *Northeast Indian Quarterly*, 4:4–5:1 (Winter 1987–Spring 1988); 6:1–2 (Spring/Summer 1989).

43. Robert F. Berkhofer, Jr., "Native Americans and United States History," in William H. Cartwright and Richard L. Watson, Jr.,

eds., *The Reinterpretation of American History and Culture* (Washington, D.C., 1973), 37–52.

44. (New York: Crown, 1988, 1991).

45. (New York: Facts on File, 1986).

46. (Washington, D.C.: Smithsonian Books, 1986).

47. (New York: Alfred A. Knopf, 1991). The Newberry Library also sponsored an exhibition, lecture series, and teachers' workshops in conjunction with the publication of the book.

48. (New York: Facts on File, 1990).

49. (London and New York: Thames and Hudson, 1991).

50. "Museums and Politics: *The Spirit Sings* and the Lubicon Boycott," *Muse* (Autumn 1988), 12–16.

51. (Toronto: McClelland and Stewart for the Glenbow Museum, 1987), 7.

52. (Washington, D.C.: Smithsonian Institution Press, 1988).

53. (New York: Cambridge University Press, forthcoming). The Meso-American volume is being edited by R. E. W. Adams and Murdo J. MacLeod; Frank Salomon and Stuart B. Schwartz are supervising the South American volume.

54. For virtually an alternative history of North America, see Peter Nabokov, ed., *Native American Testimony: A Chronicle of Indian-White Relations from Prophecy to the Present, 1492–1992* (New York: Viking, 1991), a rich and freshly illustrated anthology.

55. Herman J. Viola and Carolyn Margolis, eds., *Seeds of Change: A Quincentennial Commemoration* (Washington, D.C.: Smithsonian Institution Press, 1991).

56. (Forthcoming).

57. For other Quincentenary projects in Indian history supported by the NEH, see Malcolm Richardson, "1992 Opportunities for Indian History," *History News*, 45:3 (May/June 1990), 10–11.

58. (Edmonton: University of Alberta Press, 1989); (New York: Oxford University Press, 1990), 325. See also Patricia Seed, "Taking Possession and Reading Texts: Establishing the Authority of Overseas Empire," *William and Mary Quaterly*, 3d ser. 49 (April 1992), 185-209.

59. J. B. Harley, *Maps and the Columbian Encounter* (Milwaukee: Golda Meir Library, University of Wisconsin, 1990), xii, 56; Harley, "Deconstructing the Map," *Cartographica*, 26:2 (Summer 1989), 1–20.

60. The catalogue of the same title was published in Portland by the Maine Humanities Council in 1988.

61. (Chicago: Rand McNally, 1991).
62. (Lincoln: University of Nebraska Press, forthcoming).
63. (Chicago: University of Chicago Press, 1991), ix, 14, 25.
64. Bruce Trigger has published his thought-provoking paper from the Florida conference, "Early Native North American Responses to European Contact: Romantic versus Rationalistic Interpretations," *Journal of American History,* 77:4 (March 1991), 1195–1215.
65. Gary H. Gossen and J. Jorge Klor de Alva, eds. (Albany, N.Y. and Austin: Institute of Mesoamerican Studies and University of Texas Press, 1992).
66. (Washington, D.C.: Smithsonian Institution Press, 1991).
67. An exception to the rule is the National Museum of American History's April 1989 symposium "After Columbus: Encounters in North America," whose papers were, however useful, apparently too eclectic to publish.
68. (Washington, D.C.: Smithsonian Institution Press, 1992).
69. Barbara Sweetland Smith and Redmond J. Barnett, eds. (Tacoma: Washington State Historical Society, 1990), 9. A more sumptuous but less historical catalogue, *Soft Gold: The Fur Trade & Cultural Exchange on the Northwest Coast of America* by Thomas Vaughan and Bill Holm (Portland: Oregon Historical Society, 1982, 1990), accompanied a joint Oregon Historical Society-Peabody Museum, Harvard, exhibition in 1982 and was revised in 1990 to contribute to the Quincentenary.
70. (New York: W. H. Freeman, 1984).
71. Trans. Richie Robertson (Stanford: Stanford University Press, 1989).
72. (Washington, D.C.: Smithsonian Institution Press, 1985).
73. Essays on the Columbian Encounter (Washington, D.C.: American Historical Association, 1991); see above Chapter 2. See also my *After Columbus: Essays in the Ethnohistory of Colonial North America* (New York: Oxford University Press, 1988), chs. 8–9.
74. Trigger, "Early Native North American Responses to European Contact," *Journal of American History,* 77:4 (March 1991), 1195, 1197, 1210 (my emphasis).
75. (New York: Viking Penguin, 1987). Edward L. Schieffelin and Robert Crittenden's *Like People You See in a Dream: First Contact in Six Papuan Societies* (Stanford: Stanford University Press, 1991) is a similar reconstruction of a 1935 expedition's first encounter.

76. Michael Gannon, "The New Alliance of History and Archaeology in the Eastern Spanish Borderlands," *William and Mary Quarterly*, 3d ser. 49 (April 1992), 321–34.

77. (Gainesville: University Presses of Florida, 1992). Equally technical is Irving Rouse's brief *The Tainos: Rise and Decline of the People Who Greeted Columbus* (New Haven: Yale University Press, 1992). Keegan has also edited *Hispanic/Native American Interactions in the Caribbean: A Sourcebook* (New York: Garland, 1992), part of a 27-volume set of article ⸳reprints, The Spanish Borderlands Sourcebooks, ed. David Hurst Thomas.

78. Charles A. Hoffman, "Archaeological Investigations at the Long Bay Site, San Salvador, Bahamas," in *Columbus and His World*, ed. Gerace, 237–45; Robert Brill, "Laboratory Studies of Some European artifacts Excavated on San Salvador Island," *ibid.*, 247–92 (with illustrations).

79. (Tuscaloosa: University of Alabama Press, 1990).

80. David Henige, "On the Contact Population of Hispaniola: History as Higher Mathematics," *Hispanic American Historical Review*, 58 (1978), 217–37; R. A. Zambardino, "Critique" of Henige, *ibid.*, 700–708; Henige, "Reply" to Zambardino, *ibid.*, 709–12; Carl O. Sauer, *The Early Spanish Main* (Berkeley: University of California Press, 1966), 198–204.

81. John D. Daniels, "The Indian Population of North America in 1492," *William and Mary Quarterly*, 3d ser. 49 (April 1992), 298–320.

82. See above Chapter 10.

83. Kathleen A. Deagan, "The Search for La Navidad, Columbus's 1492 Settlement," in Milanich and Milbrath, eds., *First Encounters*, ch. 3; Deagan, "Initial Encounters: Arawak Responses to European Contact at the En Bas Saline Site, Haiti," in *Columbus and His World*, ed. Gerace, 341–59.

84. Deagan, "The Archaeology of the Spanish Contact Period in the Caribbean," *Journal of World Prehistory*, 2:2 (1988), 211–16; Charles Ewen, "The Rise and Fall of Puerto Real," in Thomas, ed., *Columbian Consequences*, 2:261–68; Ewen and Maurice A. Williams, "Puerto Real: Archaeology of an Early Spanish Town," in Milanich and Milbrath, eds., *First Encounters*, 66–76; Deagan, ed., *Puerto Real: The Archaeology of a Sixteenth-Century Spanish Town in Hispaniola* (Washington, D.C.: Smithsonian Institution Press, 1992).

85. Charles R. Ewen, *From Spaniard to Creole: The Archaeology of Cul-*

tural Formation at Puerto Real, Haiti (Tuscaloosa: University of Alabama Press, 1991), 4.

86. Deagan, "Accommodation and Resistance: The Process and Impact of Spanish Colonization in the Southeast," in Thomas, ed., *Columbian Consequences*, 2:309.

87. Ewen, *From Spaniard to Creole*, 46, 73, 79, 82–83; Deagan, *Spanish St. Augustine: The Archaeology of a Colonial Creole Community* (New York: Academic Press, 1983). See also Deagan, *Artifacts of the Spanish Colonies of Florida and the Caribbean, 1500–1800. Vol. 1: Ceramics, Glassware, and Beads* (Washington, D.C.: Smithsonian Institution Press, 1987).

88. (Baltimore. The Johns Hopkins University Press, 1992?)

89. David J. Weber, *Myth and the History of the Hispanic Southwest* (Albuquerque: University of New Mexico Press, 1988), chs. 3–4.

90. (New Haven: Yale University Press, 1992).

91. (Baton Rouge: Louisiana State University Press, 1990), x, xi.

92. (Gainesville: University of Florida Press, 1989).

93. John R. Swanton, *Final Report of the United States De Soto Expedition Commission* (Washington, D.C., 1939) (76th Cong., 1st sess. House Doc. 71). In 1985 the Smithsonian Institution Press issued a reprint with an update of Soto studies by Jeffrey Brain.

94. (Gainesville: University Presses of Florida, forthcoming); "Hernando de Soto's Expedition through the Southern United States," in Milanich and Milbrath, eds., *First Encounters*, ch. 6; see also chs. 7, 8, and 10 for related aspects of the entrada, such as the damage inflicted by Spanish swords and the diagnostic value of the trade goods left along the route.

95. Marvin T. Smith, *Archaeology of Aboriginal Culture Change in the Interior Southeast: Depopulation During the Early Historic Period* (Gainesville: University Presses of Florida, 1987); Robert L. Blakely, ed., *The King Site: Continuity and Contact in Sixteenth-Century Georgia* (Athens: University of Georgia Press, 1988).

96. (Washington, D.C.: Smithsonian Institution Press, 1990).

97. (Athens: University of Georgia Press, 1992).

98. David Hurst Thomas, ed., *Columbian Consequences. Vol. 1: Archaeological and Historical Perspectives on the Spanish Borderlands West* (Washington, D.C.: Smithsonian Institution Press, 1989); *Columbian Consequences. Vol. 2* (Washington, D.C., 1990); *Columbian Consequences. Vol. 3* (Washington, D.C., 1991). Thomas has also published museum reports on and a popular summary of his own discovery and excavation of the Spanish mission of Santa

Catalina de Guale on St. Catherines Island off the Georgia coast. The summary and a film produced by the Georgia Endowment for the Humanities are both entitled *St. Catherines: An Island in Time* (Atlanta, 1988).

99. *Juan Ponce de Leon's Discovery of Florida: Herrera's Narrative Revisited* (forthcoming).

100. Lawrence A. Clayton and Vernon J. Knight, eds., *The De Soto Chronicles: The Expedition of Hernando de Soto to the United States, 1539–1543,* 2 vols. (Tuscaloosa: University of Alabama Press, forthcoming).

101. *Los Sobrevivientes de la Florida: The Survivors of the De Soto Expedition,* ed. Bruce S. Chappell, Research Publications of the P. K. Yonge Library of Florida History No. 2 (Gainesville: University of Florida Libraries, 1990).

102. Edward Said, *Orientalism* (New York: Pantheon, 1978); Peter Hulme, "Subversive Archipelagos: Colonial Discourse and the Break-up of Continental Theory," *Dispositio,* 14:36–38 (1989), 1–23.

103. *Ibid.;* Edward Said, "Representing the Colonized: Anthropology's Interlocutors," *Critical Inquiry,* 15 (1989), 205–25; Benita Parry, "Problems in Current Theories of Colonial Discourse," *Oxford Literary Review,* 9 (1987), 27–58; Beatriz Pastor, "Silence and Writing: The History of the Conquest," in René Jara and Nicholas Spadaccini, eds., *1492–1992: Re/Discovering Colonial Writing, Hispanic Issues,* 4 (1989), 121–63; Abdul JanMohamed and David Lloyd, "Introduction: Toward a Theory of Minority Discourse," *Cultural Critique,* 6 (Spring 1987), 5–12.

104. Rolena Adorno, "New Perspectives in Colonial Spanish American Literary Studies," *Journal of the Southwest,* 32:2 (Summer 1990), 173–91 at 181. See also Patricia Seed, "Colonial and Postcolonial Discourse," *Latin American Research Review,* 26:3 (1991), 181–200.

105. Pastor, "Silence and Writing," *Hispanic Issues,* 4 (1989), 147, 153.

106. Adorno, "New Perspectives," *Journal of the Southwest,* 32 (1990), 173.

107. Aimé Cesaire, *The Collected Poetry,* trans. Clayton Eshleman and Annette Smith (Berkeley and Los Angeles: University of California Press, 1983), 77.

108. Walter D. Mignolo, "Afterword," *Colonial Discourse,* ed. Adorno and Mignolo, *Dispositio,* 14:36–38 (1989), 335; Said, "Representing the Colonized," *Critical Inquiry,* 15 (1989), 211–14.

109. Adorno, "New Perspectives," *Journal of the Southwest*, 32 (1990), 184; Peter Hulme, *Colonial Encounters: Europe and the Native Caribbean, 1492–1797* (London: Methuen, 1986), xiii, 9–10. The practice of the students of colonial discourse is even more impressive than their preaching. On their recovery of native voices, see, for example, Adorno, *Guaman Poma: Writing and Resistance in Colonial Peru* (Austin: University of Texas Press, 1986); Adorno, ed., *From Oral to Written Expression: Native Andean Chronicles of the Early Colonial Period*, Foreign and Comparative Studies/Latin American Series No. 4, Maxwell School of Citizenship and Public Affairs, Syracuse University (Syracuse, N.Y., 1982); Frank Salomon and George L. Urioste, *The Huarochiri Manuscript: A Testament of Ancient and Colonial Andean Religion* (Austin: University of Texas Press, 1991); Bruce Mannheim, *The Language of the Inka Since the European Invasion* (Austin: University of Texas Press, 1991).

110. Pastor, "Silence and Writing," *Hispanic Issues*, 4 (1989), 153.

111. J. H. Elliott, *The Old World and the New, 1492–1650* (Cambridge: Cambridge University Press, 1970), 103–4.

112. Trans. Gabriela Arciniegas and R. Victoria Arana (San Diego: Harcourt Brace Jovanovich, 1986), 2.

113. *New Worlds for Old: Reports from the New World and Their Effect on the Development of Social Thought in Europe, 1500–1800* (Athens: Ohio University Press, 1986), ix, 3–4.

114. (Berkeley and Los Angeles: University of California Press, 1976).

115. G. V. Scammell, "The Other Side of the Coin: The Discovery of the Americas and the Spread of Intolerance, Absolutism, and Racism in Early Modern Europe"; David Cressy, "The Limits of English Enthusiasm for America."

116. (New York and New Canaan, Conn.: Readex Books, 1980–92).

117. (Providence, R.I.: John Carter Brown Library, 1991).

118. Tzvetan Todorov, *The Conquest of America: The Question of the Other*, trans. Richard Howard (New York: Harper and Row, 1984); Luis Villoro, *Sahagún or the Limits of the Discovery of the Other*, 1992 Lecture Series, Working Papers No. 2, Dept. of Spanish and Portuguese, University of Maryland (College Park, 1989).

119. Joseph Judge, "Exploring Our Forgotten Century," *National Geographic*, 173:3 (March 1988), 330–63; James Axtell, review of David B. Quinn, *New American World*, in *William and Mary Quarterly*, 3d ser. 37 (July 1980), 497–99.

120. James Axtell, "Europeans, Indians, and the Age of Discovery in

American History Textbooks," *American Historical Review*, 92:3 (June 1987), 625–26, 630; see above Chapter 8, pp. 204–6, 212.

121. Jack P. Greene, "Society and Economy in the British Caribbean During the Seventeenth and Eighteenth Centuries," *American Historical Review*, 79 (Dec. 1974), 1499–1517; John J. McCusker and Russell R. Menard, *The Economy of British America, 1607–1789* (Chapel Hill: University of North Carolina Press, 1985), ch. 7.

122. Alfred W. Crosby, Jr., *The Columbian Exchange: Biological and Cultural Consequences of 1492* (Westport, Conn.: Greenwood Press, 1972); Crosby, *Ecological Imperialism*, ch. 9; Henry F. Dobyns, *Their Number Become Thinned: Native American Population Dynamics in Eastern North America* (Knoxville: University of Tennessee Press, 1983); Russell Thornton, *American Indian Holocaust and Survival: A Population History Since 1492* (Norman: University of Oklahoma Press, 1987); Ann F. Ramenofsky, *Vectors of Death: The Archaeology of European Contact* (Albuquerque: University of New Mexico Press, 1987); Daniel T. Reff, *Disease, Depopulation, and Culture Change in Northwestern New Spain, 1518–1764* (Salt Lake City: University of Utah Press, 1991); Douglas H. Ubelaker and John W. Verano, eds., *Disease and Demography in the Americas: Changing Patterns Before and After 1492* (Washington, D.C.: Smithsonian Institution Press, forthcoming).

123. See above Chapter 10.

124. Posse, *The Dogs of Paradise,* trans. Margaret Sayers Peden (New York: Atheneum, 1989); Carpentier, *The Harp and the Shadow,* trans. Thomas Christensen and Carol C. Christensen (San Francisco: Mercury House, 1990); Benítez-Rojo, *Sea of Lentils,* trans. James Maraniss (Amherst: University of Massachusetts Press, 1990). Spain on the eve of America's discovery is vividly evoked by Homero Aridjis in *1492: The Life and Times of Juan Cabezón of Castile,* trans. Betty Ferber (New York: Summit Books, 1991).

125. One of the most sumptuous publications to emerge from the Quincentenary is *Portugal-Brazil: The Age of Atlantic Discoveries,* designed by Franco Maria Ricci (New York: The Brazilian Cultural Foundation, 1990). It catalogues a major exhibition at the New York Public Library in the summer of 1990, adding several essays by scholars such as Wilcomb Washburn and Francis M. Rogers.

Index

Abenaki Indians, 65, 90, 92–96, 108, 131, 183
Abstinence, Catholic days of, 191–92, 303
Acculturation: European, 312–13; Indian, 146–47, 149, 163–64, 250, 336n.40; Spanish, 303–4
Adair, James, 237–38
Adoption, Indian, of Europeans, 50, 102
Africa: explored by Portuguese, 31; Gold Coast, 279; Indian corn in, 210; slave trade, 252–53
Africans, compared with Indians, 68. *See also* Marriage, Indian-African; Slaves, African.
Alcohol, 35, 36, 38, 65, 91, 100, 170, Indian women sell, 115; Indian uses, 142–43; in Iroquois tradition, 250; and vision quest, 335n.32
Alexander VI, pope, 99, 206, 245
Allen, John, 291
Allouez, Claude, S.J., 41, 47
America: Europeans claim, 60, 62–63; Europeans compare to known world, 59; renamed, 59–60, 61
American Council of Learned Societies, 4
Americas: books on, 313–14; impact upon Europe, 311–13
Amooret, 93
Anderson, Robin, 298

Andrews, Charles McLean, 14
Animals, overhunted, 111, 147, 150, 239
Anniversaries, historical, 242–43, 266, 268, 283–84, 315, 316
Anthropologists, use of imagination, 12
Apalachee Indians, 109
Aqua vitae. See Alcohol.
Arciniega, Germán, 312
Argenti, Philip, 281
Aridjis, Homero, 364n.124
Armies, of conquest. *See Entradas.*
Armor: European, 93, 192; Indian, 141, 142
"Artificial wants," 128, 132, 150
Assembly of First Nations, 251
Association, the, 128, 150
Atwood, Margaret, 16, 259
Audience, the historian's, 15
Audiencia, in New Spain, 248, 283
Avellaneda, Ignacio, 308–9
Axes. *See* Trade goods, tools.
Axtell, James, 297
Ayllón, Lucas Vazquez de, 305
Aztec Indians, 245–46, 249

Bailey, Thomas, 208
Bailyn, Bernard, 14, 203–4, 204–5
Baldness, 53
"Bambaras" (Senegalese slaves), 233
Bancroft, George, 17

Bannon, John Francis, S.J., 305
"Barbarians," 30
Barlowe, Arthur, 44, 52, 54, 68, 71–72
Barreiro, José, 285
Barzun, Jacques, 209. 211
Bashabes, 93, 94
Basque: pidgins, 87; ships, 87
"Baubles of Britain," 128, 151
Bayogoula Indians, 40, 49, 51, 65
Beards, 34, 36, 101
Beaver, as theological fish, 191–92
Becker, Carl, 20–21
Bedini, Silvio, 271
Belching. See Breaking wind.
Belknap, Jeremy, 251
Bellenger, Étienne, 86
Benitez-Rojo, Antonio, 315
Benson, Elizabeth, 286
Beverley, Robert, 150
Bible, 31
Bienville, Jean Baptiste LeMoyne de, 49
Biloxi Indians, 52–53, 178–79
Bitterli, Urs, 296
"Black Legend," 204, 205, 212, 215, 262, 301, 315
Blankets, dreams of, 190
Bolingbroke, Henry St. John, 1st viscount, 264
Bolton, Herbert Eugene, 305
Books, impress Indians, 56, 159–60
Boston, Mass., 228
Boucher, Philip, 304
Bourque, Bruce, 86
Bouwsma, William, 13–14
Bradford, William, 186–87
Brandon, William, 312
Breaking wind, 175–76
Bressani, Francesco, S.J., 141
Brissot de Warville, Jacques Pierre, 221
Burials, Spanish colonial, 275
Burke, Edmund, 262
Byrd, William, II, 133, 183–84

Cabeza de Vaca, Alvar Núñez, 38–39, 41, 43–44, 53–54
Calumet, 46, 47, 48, 51, 102, 192
Canada, "a few acres of snow," 226

Canary Islands, 59, 279, 282–83
Cannibals, 245, 304
Cardini, Franco, 280
Cards, playing, 57, 250
Carey (Irish interpreter), 185
Carib Indians, 304
Caribbean. See West Indies.
Carpentier, Alejo, 315
Cartier, Jacques, 42, 43, 53, 66–67, 181; crowned, 48–49; erects cross, 62; fires cannon, 55; kidnaps Indians, 71–72, 103; names St. Lawrence River, 59; in textbooks, 206
Cartography. See Maps.
Casqui, 50, 54
Castiglioni, Luigi, 220
Catawba Indians, 107, 183, 221
Cattle, 119–20, 164; in Indian fields, 239–40; Spanish, 302, 303
Census, U.S. Federal (1790), 222
Cervantes Saavedra, Miguel de, 6
Cesaire, Aimé, 311
Champlain, Samuel de, 207–8
Change: directed, 163; in history, 157; in Indian culture, 154, 163–68
Charleston, S.C., 131
Chastellux, François-Jean de Beauvoir, marquis de, 221
Chateaubriand, François-René de, 221
Chequamegon, 41
Cherokee Indians, 42, 112, 119, 131; mortality, 235, 237; sexual behavior, 185
Chesapeake Indians, 29, 35, 104
Chiappelli, Fredi, 313
Chicaça, 186
Chickasaw Indians, 235
Chicora, 305–6
Chinese explorers, vii
Chios, 59, 279, 281
Chitimacha Indians, 109
Choctaw Indians, 235
Christianity: book religion, 160; explanatory power, 168; as social catalyst, 155
"Civility," 116
Cloth. See Trade goods, cloth.
Coe, Michael, 286
Colapissa Indians, 181

Colden, Cadwallader, 142
"Colonial discourse," 310–11
"Colono-ware," Spanish, 303
Colors, Indian preferences, 138
Columbian Encounter, 269; aptness
of name, 289; archaeology of, 274–
76, 299–304, 306–8; between
farmers, 236; biological, 254–55;
comparisons, 296–99, 315–16; conferences, 292–93; counterfactual,
99; mixed results, viii; moral judgments upon, ix, 244, 284; in museums, 293–96; mutuality of, 26–
27, 98
"Columbian exchange," 255
Columbian Quadricentenary, 27, 283
Columbian Quincentenary, 126, 268–
69; agenda, viii–ix; Indian views,
249–51, 284–85; Jewish views, 254;
newsletters, 269–70; radical views,
256
Columbus, Christopher (Cristoforo
Colombo), 57, 58, 65, 98, 120, 314;
accelerates Indian change, 154;
American palacio, 275–76; anti-
hero, 271; biographies, 276–77,
279–80; chamberpot, 276; claims
America, 60; crowned, 48; genealogy, 309; gifts to Indians, 66;
humor, 185–86; and Indian slavery, 223; in Iroquois tradition, 250;
kidnaps Taínos, 38, 71; lack of Jewish background, 281; lands on Guanahaní, 26, 59, 60, 300; media
views of, 278–79; pre-American experience, 279–83; portraits, 277–
78; providentialist, 272–73; ships,
273–75; in textbooks, 199, 211
Columbus Caravel Archaeological
Project, 274
"Columbus in Context Clearinghouse," 256, 257
Columbus Quincentenary Committee
(American Historical Association),
x, 26, 199
Columns, stone, French, 62, 63
Comet (1618), 81
Connolly, Bob, 298
Constitution, U.S., 222

Consumer revolution: British, 126–
28; Indian, 129
Conversion, Indian, 245–46; benefits,
168–69; cultural changes required
by, 163; methods, 159–61; reasons
for, 117–18
Conversos, Spanish-Jewish, 253, 281
Cornell University American Indian
Program, 251
Coronado, Francisco Vázquez de, 34,
341n.24
Corte-Real, Gaspar, 82–83, 135, 139
Cortés, Hernán, 258
Coureurs de bois, 208
Coweta Indians, 178
Credit. See Fur trade, credit.
Cree Indians, 181–82; Lubicon Lake,
287
Creek (Muskogee) Indians, 112, 119,
131, 150
Cressy, David, 313
Cronon, William, 255
Crosby, Alfred, 255
Crosses, to claim America, 60–61, 92
Crowell, Aron, 287
Crusades, Christian, 31
Cuguano, Ottobah, 252–53
Culture, encoded, 16
Current, Richard, 212

Dale, Sir Thomas, 204
Dancing: French, 181; Indian, 92,
181
Danforth, Susan, 291
Daniels, John, 301
Dartmouth, William Legge, 2nd earl
of, 146
Davis, John, 44, 48, 65–66
De Bry, Theodor, 62, 68, 69, 205,
210
DePratter, Chester B., 307
De Smet, Pierre Jean, S.J., 294–95
De Soto. See Soto.
DeVoto, Bernard, 18, 19
Deagan, Kathleen, 302, 304
Deer snare, 186
Delaware Indians, 37–38, 112–13,
150, 179
Denevan, William, 289
Depardieu, Gerard, 278

Dickason, Olive P., 290
Dickens, Charles, 172
Dickinson, Emily, 22
Diseases: divine providence, 237;
    European, 39, 49, 53, 54, 59, 105,
    118, 131, 154–55, 168, 210, 230,
    236–38, 239, 255, 262, 307, 315;
    Indian, 93, 99, 210, 275; Indian
    responses to, 106–7, 238; plague,
    35, 79, 81, 107, 155, 237; shock
    troops of invasion, 72, 155; small-
    pox, 105, 145, 155, 237–38, 262–
    63, 303
Disinterestedness, historical, 224, 244
Dissertations, doctoral, 16
Dogs, 89–90, 92
Domagaya, 72, 103
Donkeys, 180
Donnacona, 49, 55, 72, 86, 103
Dor-Ner, Zvi, 278
Droysen, Johann Gustav, 7
Du Ru, Paul, 48, 192
Duffels. See Trade goods, cloth.
Dunn, Oliver, 272, 308
Dürer, Albrecht, 210

Eccles, William J., xvi, 208
Eliot, John, 146
Elizabeth I, queen of England, 60
Elliott, John H., 312
Emigration, to Americas: economic,
    231; English, 227; French, 226–27;
    German, 227; reasons for, 229–31;
    religious, 229–30; Scotch-Irish,
    227; Sephardic Jews, 227; Spanish,
    206, 226
Empathy, historical, 11
Emplotment, narrative, 19
En Bas Saline, 302, 303
Encomienda, in New Spain, 206, 246,
    248, 283
Engagés. See Indentured servants.
English colonists: emigrate to Amer-
    ica, 227; fecund, 228; marry young,
    227–28
Entradas, Spanish, 34, 39, 186, 258–
    59, 306–7, 308–9
Epidemics. See Diseases.
Eskimos (Inuit), 44, 48, 65–66
Estevánico, 38

Etchemin Indians, 86–87
Ethnohistory, bifocal, x
Europeans: "civilized," 27; dominate
    Indians, 72–73; "gods," 33–34, 37,
    38, 39–40, 53, 55, 56, 101; hairi-
    ness, 36, 101; hospitable, 64–67;
    skin color, 36, 52–53, 101; steal
    from Indians, 88, 89, 104

Facts, historical, 7–8, 10; limita-
    tions, 9
Fagan, Brian, 286–87, 296
Farting. See Breaking wind.
Fasting. See Abstinence.
Ferdinand, king of Aragon, 300
Ferdinand and Isabella, 60, 99, 253,
    273, 281
Fernández-Armesto, Felipe, 277
Filles du roi. See "King's girls."
First encounters, 297–98; Europeans
    assimilated, 45–52, 101–2; Euro-
    peans carried, 42–43, 176; Euro-
    peans crowned, 48; Europeans
    married, 50–52; Europeans wel-
    comed, 40–45, 101–2; Indians en-
    tertained, 65–66; languages
    learned, 70–72; in Mass., 79–82;
    oral traditions of, 35–38, 79–81,
    324n.4; peaceful, 58, 100–101; in
    textbooks, 29
Fishing: European, 87; with frying
    pans, 186
Fitzhugh, William, 287, 296–97
"Flat earth," myth of, 355n.17
Flathead Indians, 144, 295
Food: European, 65, 84, 139; In-
    dian, 45, 92, 110. See also Ship's
    biscuits.
Forts: Biloxi, 47, 55; Christanna, 180;
    Orange, 130; St. George, 95, 96;
    Toulouse, 178
Fox Indians, 47, 261
Francis I, king of France, 60
Franklin, Benjamin, 150, 227
Free will, 13
French colonists: in Canada, 206–8;
    in Caribbean, 304; emigrate to
    Americas, 226–27; in Florida, 63,
    207; in Louisiana, 40, 209
Frye, Northrop, 19

Fur trade, 129–34; credit, 111–12, 133–34, 147, 150, 190, 239; depletion of game, 111, 147, 150, 239; Dutch, 130–31; French, 108, 130–31; haggling, 92; Indian income, 130–31; Indians as consumers, 132–33; Louisiana, 110; maritime, 81–82, 87; records, 134–35; Russian, 294; South Carolina, 131

Furs and skins: beaver, 129, 130–31, 132; deer, 110, 130, 131, 150; moose, 86; otter, 130–31, 294; "small furs," 129

Gannon, Michael, 299
Gastaldi, Giacomo, 43
Genocide, 224, 250, 256, 261–63, 284, 288; defined, 261
Gibbon, Edward, 15, 17
Gift-giving, 64, 66–67, 88, 102, 179, 188
Gil, Juan, 273
Gilbert, Sir Humphrey, 65
Ginseng, 114
Glassie, Henry, 8–9
"Global village," the world as, viii, 223, 266, 316
Gold, Spanish love of, 249, 275
Goldman, James, 281
Gomes, Estevão, 82–83
Gorges, Sir Ferdinando, 94
Gosnold, Capt. Bartholomew, 65, 87–88, 178
Granganimeo, 44
"Great Migration," to New England, 229
Green, L. C., 290
Greenblatt, Stephen, 291
Griffin, Owen, 91–92
Guacanagarí, 48, 302
Guanahaní, 26, 59, 60
Guanches, 279, 282–83
Gunpowder, 96, 189–90, 192
Guns, 108, 141, 178–79; arquebuses (matchlocks), 55, 95, 192; cannon, 55, 80, 96; Indian views of, 36, 55–56, 84; and Indian warfare, 142; Indians fall flat at report, 91; superiority to bow and arrow, 56, 140, 142

Hamilton, Dr. Alexander, 147
Handkerchiefs, 182–83
Handsome Lake, 120, 249
Harley, J. Brian, 290–91
Harriot, Thomas, 54, 56, 68
Hartley, L. P., 10
Hats, beaver, 129, 131
Hawthorne, Nathaniel, 20
Heckewelder, John, 179
Henige, David, 301, 308
Hennepin, Louis, 56
Henretta, James, 200
Herodotus, 31
Hexter, Jack H., 12, 21
Hilton, William, 51
Hispaniola, 300–301
History: books, 5; ecological, 254–55; as "exact imagining," 7; facts as, 7–8; Indian, 154; as interpretation, 19; national uses, 243; not the past, 8–9; "objective," 5; one of the humanities, 4, 6; poetry of, 7; popular, 17; social, 126; as social science, 5; students' ignorance of, 268
Hochelaga, 48, 53
Hodges, Dr. William, 302
Hoes, 135, 136
Hoffman, Paul E., 305–6, 307
Horgan, Paul, 10, 12, 18
Horse Capture, George P., 285
Horses, 42, 180, 186, 341n.24; of conquest, 258
Hostages, 51, 92; Indian students as, 116, 167
Houma Indians, 109
Hudson, Charles, 307, 308
Hudson's Bay Company, employees, 181–82
Huguenots, French, 63, 207
Humor, in history: Indian sense of, 181–83; sexual, 184–85, 187; uses, 172–74
Hunt, Thomas, 104
Huron Indians, 57, 131, 141, 261; and silver spoon, 193

Iberville, Pierre LeMoyne d', 44, 47, 51–52, 65, 179
"Ideal reader," the historian's, 16
Illinois Indians, 45

Imagination: in history, 6, 10, 12, 13, 14, 16; key to moral understanding, 259; as social fact, 30, 77

Imperialism, European, 289–90; cartography of, 290–91

Indentured servants, 219, 220, 226

Indian corn, in Africa, 210

Indian economy, 108; dependence on Europeans, 150; diet, 303; division of labor, 114, 236; farming, 210, 236, 288–89; wealth, 129

Indian government, 202–3; chiefs, 48, 300; factions, 100, 118, 161; goals, 100

Indian housing, 35, 148–49, 304

Indian medicine, adopted by colonists, 158

Indian reactions to Europeans: armed resistance, 119, 151; convert to Christianity, 115–18; drinking, 120; incorporation, 101–2; play off European rivals, 110–11, 118, 132; relocation, 107–10; revitalization, 120, 150–51; sell land, 111–13; work in colonial economy, 113

Indian religion: afterlife, 165; dances, 92; deities (gods), 33, 93; dreams, 190–91, 335; European misconceptions, 203; guardian spirits, 142; offerings, 47, 55–56, 192–93; shamans, 34, 37, 38, 53, 91, 158, 160, 164; spirits (souls, *manitous*), 33–34, 54, 117, 158, 161, 203; syncretism, 117–18; vision quests, 335n.32

Indian warfare: alliances, 119; effect of guns, 142; intertribal, 131; "mourning wars," 106

Indian women, 84, 87, 102, 106, 303–4; in colonial economy, 114–15; Christian role models for, 166; enslaved, 83; European sexual partners, 94, 184; farmers, 236

Indians: Anglo-American view of, 262; cannibals, 245, 304; in colonial literature, 310; color, 52; compared with Africans, 68; compared with Irish, 68; contributions to American culture, 285; ethnocentric, 33; in Europe, 83; European views of,

67–68, 85–86; hair, 53, 184; hospitable, 40–45; in media, 288; in museums, 287–88, 288–89, 293–96; "Parched Corn," 107; in Quadricentenary, 283–84; in Quincentenary, 284, 308; resist Europeans, 86, 90, 119; "savages," 27, 68, 73, 74, 101, 209; sexually free, 166; share, 65, 91, 129; vain, 143–45

Industrial Revolution, 127–28

Infantado, dukes of, 309

Inquisition, Spanish, 226, 253

Institute of Early Contact Period Studies, 309

Interpreters: European, 51, 70–71, 185; Indian, 38, 49, 70, 71–72, 92, 93, 103, 113

Irish, "Wild," compared with Indians, 68

Irony, 19, 173, 266

Iroquois Indians, 106, 190, 202, 221, 249, 261; and Founding Fathers, 285. *See also* Mohawk Indians; Seneca Indians.

Irving, Washington, 355n.17

Jacobs, Wilbur, 197

Jameson, J. Franklin, 18, 82

Jamestown Settlement, 295–96

Jesuits, 294–95; agents of social change, 163–68, 169–70; cultural relativism, 157; dress, 162; education, 156–57; educators, 166–67, 169; geographers, 169, 294; goals, 156; healers, 160; historians, 169; learn Indian languages, 182; methods, 159–61; military organization, 156; missions, 163, 164, 166, 295; nurture neophytes, 161; origins, 155; political leaders, 164; supplant shamans, 158, 160; use of technology, 160–61

Jews: and Columbian Encounter, 356n.33; emigrate to Americas, 227, 253; expelled from Spain, 212, 226, 253–54, 281; and Holocaust, 261; views on Quincentenary, 254

Johnson, Edward, 80

Johnson, Dr. Samuel, 6, 7

Johnson, Sir William, 142, 190–91

Jones, Howard Mumford, 4
Jos, Emiliano, 355n.17
Josephy, Alvin, 286
Joutel, Henri, 176–77

Keith, Robert, 215
Kelley, James E., Jr., 272, 308
Kelley, Robert, 197–98
Kickotank Indians, 188
Kidnapping: of Europeans, 183; of
    Indians, 38, 71–72, 82–83, 86, 92,
    93, 103, 183, 204, 291, 300, 303
King Hagler (Catawba chief), 183
King Hendrick (Theyanoquin), 137,
    190–91
King Philip (Metacomet), 177, 238
"King's girls" (filles du roi), 227
Kissing, 181
Kling, August, 273
Kopper, Philip, 286

La Isabela, 302
La Navidad, 48, 301–2
La Salle, René-Robert Cavelier, sieur
    de, 176
Labadists, 113
Lahontan, Louis-Armand de Lom
    D'Arce, baron de, 191
Land, Indian, 202, 204; lost to Euro-
    peans, 110–13, 120, 191, 235, 239–
    40, 304; use of former, 329n.34
Landis, Dennis Channing, 313–14
Language, morally loaded, 260
Languages: classical, 118; differences
    between, 30; French, 181; Indian,
    83, 182, pidgin, 80, 87, 95, 102,
    177–78; sign, 70, 102, 188
Larkin, Philip, 17
Las Casas, Bartolomé de, 205, 248–
    49, 301; editor of Columbus's di-
    ario, 272, 309
Laws, Spanish, to protect Indians,
    246, 248
Le Jeune, Paul, S.J., 176, 182
Le Moyne de Morgues, Jacques, 62
Le Page du Pratz, Antoine Simon, 47
Lead seals, for cloth, 138
Levett, Christopher, 177
Library of Congress, 310
Long, John, 190

Louis XIV, king of France, 203
Louis-Philippe, king of France, 184–
    85, 219
Louisiana, Indian relocations, 108–9
Lowes, John Livingston, 7
Loyola, Ignatius, S.J., 155
Lucayans. See Taínos.
Luis, Don (Indian), 103–4
Luna y Arellano, Tristán de, 306
Luther, Martin, 210
Lyons, Eugene, 273, 308, 309

Macanoche, 51
McClendon, Carmen, 308
McGuirk, Donald, 308
McNeill, William, 254–55
Madariaga, Salvador de, 212
Madeira Island, 282
Manatees, as "sirens," 186
Manioc, 303
Manitous. See Indian religion, spirits.
Manteo, 72, 103
Maps: Indian, 87, 291; instruments of
    imperialism, 290–91
Marquette, Jacques, S.J., 41, 45
Marriage: age of first, 228; English
    colonial, 227–28; Indian-African,
    106, 114; Indian-European, 50–52,
    102, 106, 114, 182, 226
Mascouten Indians, 43
Matchcoat, 138
Mathes, Michael, 278
Mattagund, 239–40
Mattingly, Garrett, 7, 10
Maw, Robin, 288
Mawooshen, 94
Menominee Indians, 48, 53, 193
Menéndez de Avilés, Pedro, 306
Mercury, 275
Mestizos, 50, 226. See also Métis.
Metacomet. See King Philip.
Métis, 294. See also Mestizos.
Micmac Indians, 35–36, 44, 62, 87,
    324n.4
"Middle Passage," on slave voyages,
    234
Milanich, Jerald T., 306, 307
Milbrath, Susan, 306
Miller, Perry, 14, 15
Miranda, Francisco de, 219

Mirrors, trade, 39, 85, 91, 143–45; lead to suicide, 238
Missionaries, 72, 116, 182, 230; Dominican, 246–47, 248; Franciscan, 247. *See also* Jesuits.
Missions: benefits, 168; discipline, 168; Jesuit, 163, 164, 166, 295; Spanish, 308
Mobile, 109, 131
Mobilian Indians, 47
Mochila, 51
Mohawk, John, 285
Mohawk (Iroquois) Indians, 57
Moheege, Elizabeth and Phebe, 146, 149
Monsters, medieval, 31, 32
Montagnais Indians, 35, 131, 182
Montaigne, Michel de, 30, 32, 291–92
Montauk Indians, 119
Montesinos, Antonio de, 246–47
Montezuma, 248, 249
"Moon over Monhegan," 86, 189
Moors, expelled from Spain, vii, 212, 226
Moral judgments: of Columbian Encounter, 224–25, 231–32; and guilt, 263; in history, 257–58, 260; of Jesuits, 157; language, 260; reasons for, 264–65; standards, 265–66
Moreau de St.-Méry, Médéric-Louis-Elie, 219, 220, 221
Morgan, Edmund S., 207
Morison, Samuel Eliot, 4, 201, 206, 208, 211, 276
Mortality: alcohol-related, 142–43; colonial, 219, 228; "gate," 227; Indian, 105, 155, 235, 236, 247, 249, 255; Jewish, 262; war-related, 239
Morton, Thomas, 133
Motolinía, Toribio de, 247
Mouth (Jew's) harps, 140
Music: European, 65–66; Indian, 66
Mustard, 65, 88, 178

Nahaneda, 92, 93, 94, 95
Names: descriptive, for European colonists, 225; Europeans change American, 59–60; Indian, for Europeans, 57, 80, 102; Indian, for tribes, 33, 330n.49; of Indian groups, 202
Namier, Lewis, 14, 17
Nansemond Indians, 192
Narragansett Indians, 57, 84–85, 119, 133
Narváez, Pánfilo de, 38
Nash, Gary B., 200
Nassitoche Indians, 181
Natchez Indians, 46, 47, 235, 261
National Endowment for the Humanities, 269
Nauset Indians, 29, 35
Navarrete, Martin de, 309
Nazis, 258, 262
Nebenzahl, Kenneth, 291
Neolin, 120, 337n.48
Newport, Capt. Christopher, 187
Nicolson, Harold, 18
Ninigret, "King George," 147
Nissenbaum, Stephen, 211
Norridgewalk Indians. *See* Abenaki Indians.
Norse (Vikings), vii, 299
North America, 16th-century, 305
Norton, Mary Beth, 200
Norumbega, 78
Norwood, Col. Henry, 188
Novelists, 18; Latin American, 315; use of imagination, 12

Ojibwa Indians, 36–37
Ong, Walter, S.J., 15
Oral traditions, Indian, 34–38, 76, 79, 95–96, 154, 324n.4
Ortiz, Juan, 71
"Others," x, 311, 314; European ideas of, 30–32, 73, 259; Indian ideas of, 32–34, 73
Ottawa Indians, 119
Ovando, Nicolás de, 223

Pacaha, 50
Panama, conquerors of, 258
Papua, New Guinea, 298–99
Pardo, Juan, 307
Parkman, Francis, 17, 208, 215
Parry, John H., 215
Pascagoula Indians, 44–45

Past, the: as a foreign country, 10, 16; not history, 8–9
Patuxet Indians, 107
Paul, apostle, 30
Pease Y, Franklin, 293
Peck, Douglas, 308
Pénicaut, André, 52–53, 109, 178
Pensacola, 108, 109
Pequot Indians, 119, 238, 261
Perrot, Nicolas, 39–40, 41, 42–43, 47–48, 55–56, 192
Philadelphia, Pa., 229
Phillips, Carla Rahn and William D., 280
Picard (French violinist), 66, 181
Picts, 68, 69
Pilgrims, Plymouth, 29, 35, 104, 186
Pinzón, Martin Alonso, 275
Pizarro, Francisco, 258–59
Plow, English, 56–57
Plymouth Colony, 131. See also Pilgrims.
Pocahontas, 187, 204
Pocumtuck Indians, 57
Poets, contrasted with historians, 6
Point, Nicolas, S.J., 294
Polo, Marco, 31, 273
Polygamy, Indian, 163
Ponce de León, Juan, 308
Pontiac (Ottawa chief), 151, 238
Population: black, 222, 232, 233–34; colonial Southeast, 222; English mainland colonies, 227; Hispaniola, 301; Indian, 121, 203–4, 221, 235; Mass., 222–23, 228; New France, 208, 226–27; New Spain, 226; Pa., 219, 228–29; U.S., 222, 223; Va., 228
Port Royal Indians, 51
Porter, John, 218
Portuguese exploration, 364n.125
Posse, Abel, 315
Potawatomi Indians, 39, 41, 53
Potosí, 210
Powhatan (chief), 34–35, 60, 187–88, 204
Powhatan Indians, 108, 119, 189, 228, 295; uprising of 1622, 228, 238
"Praying Indians," 117

"Praying towns," 146, 230
"Prehistory," 153–54
Prescott, William Hickling, 17, 215
Pring, Capt. Martin, 66, 88–90
Printing. See Books.
Property, Indian concepts of, 202
Prophecies, Indian, Europeans in, 34–37
Provost, Foster, 269, 271
Ptolemy, Claudius, 31
Puccoon, 184
Puerto Real, 302–3
Puzo, Mario, 278
Pynchon, John, 111

Quakers (Society of Friends), 113
Quinn, David B., xvi, 215, 282

Radisson, Pierre, 55
Ralegh, Sir Walter, 54, 203
Ranke, Leopold von, 6, 7
Reconquista, of Spain, 211, 245, 280, 282, 283
Records: archaeological, 79, 134, 145, 274–76, 299–304, 306–8; historical, 9, 77; limitations of, 12–13, 30, 77
Reisch, Gregor, 32
Repartimiento, 283
Requerimiento, 246, 247, 283
Research, seductive, 9
Reserves (Catholic Indian), 108, 165
Residencia, 283
Revillagigedo, counts of, 309
Ribault, Jean, 63, 64, 65, 66
Roanoke colonists, 29, 39
Roanoke Indians, 54, 68, 72
Rockefeller Foundation, 4–5
Rogers, Francis M., 364n.125
Rolfe, John, 204
Roman Catholic Church, patriarchal, 165–66
Rose, Wendy, 250–51
Rosier, James, 91, 340n.18
Russell, Jeffrey Burton, 355n.17
Russian-American Company, 294
Russian colonists, and Indians, 294

Sabbath, Christian, 92
Sabenoa, 95
Sagadahoc colony, 90, 94–96

Sagamité, 45
Sagard, Gabriel, 176, 182, 191–92; on
  silver spoon, 193
Said, Edward, 310
St. Augustine, Fl., 304, 306
Sale, Kirkpatrick, 276–77, 280
Salkind, Alexander and Ilya, 278
Salmoral, Manuel Lucena, 286
San Salvador (Watling's Island), 300.
  See also Guanahaní.
Saõ Jorge da Mina, 279, 282
Saponi Indians, 180
Sassafras, 88, 89, 114
Sauer, Carl, 254, 301
Sauvole, Antoine de, 44–45, 55
"Savages," Indians as, 27, 68, 73, 74,
  101, 209
Savannah, Ga., 131
Scalps, 37
Scammell, Geoffrey, 313
Schoepf, Johann David, 220
Scholarship, foibles of, 174–75
"School of Translators," Toledo, 253,
  351n.16
Schools: corporal punishment, 167;
  curriculum, 118, 167; Indian, 116,
  118, 166–67; Jesuit, 166–67
Schwartz, Stuart, 279
Scott, Ridley, 278
"Second contacts," between Indians
  and Europeans, 104
"Second record," the historian's, 12
Seneca (Iroquois) Indians, 56, 143
Ships, 212; *Archangel*, 91; as calumet,
  47; *Capitana*, 274; *Dauphine*, 84;
  Gallega, 274; Indian use of, 87; In-
  dian views of, 36, 37, 54–55, 80;
  Nīna (*Santa Clara*), 270, 273, 275;
  Nonsuch, 182; *Pinta*, 270, 275;
  Santa Maria, 270, 274, 302;
  Santiago, 274; *Susan Constant*,
  295–96
Ship's biscuits, 35, 65, 92, 139
Shipwrecks, 50, 57, 188
Silver spoon, Huron theft of, 193
Sin, Catholic sense of, 166
Sioux Indians, 56
Skidwarres, 93, 95
Skraelings, 299
Slave trade, African, 252–53

Slaves, African, 113, 220, 223,
  239; in English colonies, 233–34;
  protest slave trade, 252–53; spread
  disease, 237–38; replace Indians,
  247, 303; "seasoned," 233; in Virginia, 295
Slaves, Indian, 83, 104, 113, 223, 239,
  247; *panis*, in French colonies, 232–
  33; in Spanish colonies, 248, 303
Smallpox. *See* Diseases, smallpox.
Smith, Capt. John, 68, 81–82, 104;
  captured, 189; fishing with frying
  pans, 187; on geography, 212
Smith, Marvin T., 307
Snow, Dean, 286
Solzhenitsyn, Alexander, 13
Sorbonne, 191
Soto, Hernando de, 34, 39, 50–51,
  54, 71; route of, 306–7, 309; un-
  horsed, 186
Space, Catholic sense of, 165
Spanish Borderlands, 304–9, 315
Spanish colonists, 204–6; archaeologi-
  cal evidence of, 301–4; *conquis-
  tadores*, 258–59; criticisms of, 246–
  49; diet, 303; emigrate to Americas,
  206, 226; goals, 245–46; *See also*
  "Black Legend."
Spanish Empire, 246
Spicebox, 210
Squanto, 103
Stadacona Indians, 44, 181
Stamp Act, 128
Steiner, George, 6–7
Stiles, Ezra, 10, 149
Stockbridge, Mass., 111–12
Style, literary, 20–21
Suicide, Indian, 145
Swagerty, Jacqueline Peterson, 294
Swanton, John R., 306
Swearing, Indian, 177–78
Sweatlodges, Indian, 105, 182, 237
Syme, Ronald, 14

Taignoagny, 72, 103
Taínos, 58, 274, 285, 299–301; kid-
  napped, 38, 300, 303; trade with
  Spanish, 57
Taviani, Paolo Emilio, 276
Tawasa Indians, 109

Taylor, William B., 293
Technology, European, 35, 90–91, 101; superiority of, 54–57, 132
Tenochtitlán, 210, 247, 249
Textbooks, American history, 29, 250; anachronistic, 200, 214; chronological divisions, 214; deficiencies, 198; factual errors, 201–10; illustrations, 209–11, 216; omissions, 211–13; prose, 211, 213; reviews, 198, 216; shortchange colonial period, 201; team-written, 199, 214–15; views of Indians, 209
Theyanoquin. See King Hendrick.
Thomas, David Hurst, 308
Thomas, Peter, 111
Three Rivers Reserve, Ohio, 288
Time, Catholic sense of, 165
Timucua Indians, 62
Tobacco, 181, 192–93. See also Indian religion, offerings.
Towns, Spanish, grid plan, 302–3
Trade goods, 110, 132; cloth, 36–37, 57, 82, 112, 130, 136–39, 146, 179, 188; decorative, 48, 82, 85, 90, 139–40; exported from England, 145; food, 139; Indian adaptations, 139–40; Indian preferences, 133, 138; on Indian sites, 145–46, 307; Italian, 82, 135; kettles, 81, 136; novelties, 140; relative values, 132; Spanish, 307; tools, 36, 48, 82, 103, 135, 189; weapons, 36, 57, 58, 88, 140
"Trading girls," 114–15
Travelers, in America, 219–22; limitations, 221–22
Treaties: Alcáçoyas, 282; Tordesillas, 245
Trevelyan, George Macaulay, 7
Trevor-Roper, Hugh, 13
Trigger, Bruce G., 297–98
Tuchman, Barbara, 9
Tunica Indians, 109
Tuscarora Indians, 107, 119, 238

Universities, purpose of, 21
Updike, John, 13, 17
Urination, Indian, 138
U.S. Pharmacopaeia, 158

Vacuum domicilium, 204, 290
Varela, Consuelo, 271, 273
Verdigris, 139
Vermilion, 139
Verrazzano, Giovanni da, 52, 55, 306; in New England, 68, 84–86, 189; in textbooks, 206
Vespucci, Amerigo, 300
Vikings. See Norse.
Violins, 66, 181, 250
"Virgin" land, 203
"Virgin soil" populations, 154, 237
Vogt, John, 282
Voltaire, François Marie Arouet de, 226

Walker, John, 86
Wampanoag Indians, 119
Wampum, 102, 329n.34
Wanchese, 72
Wars: Anglo-Indian, 238–39; intercolonial ("French and Indian"), 238; King Philip's, 177, 238–39; Pequot, 119, 238; Pontiac's Rebellion, 151, 238; Powhatan uprising (1622), 228, 238; Tuscarora, 107, 119, 238; Yamasee, 119, 150, 238
Washburn, Wilcomb, 364n.125
Washington, George, 184–85
Watts, Pauline Moffitt, 278
Waymouth, Capt. George, 57, 65, 90–91, 183
Weatherford, Jack, 286
Weber, David J., 305
Werowocomoco, 187
West, Delno, 273
West Indies, 212–13, 315
Westo Indians, 41–42
Whaling, Indians in, 114, 115
Wheelock, Eleazar, 146
White, Hayden, 19
White, John (of Roanoke), 68, 210
White, John (of Mass.), 229
Whitehead, Alfred North, 20, 21
Whitehead, Ruth, 86
Whitman, Walt, 21
Wig, 177
Wilde, Oscar, 21
Wilford, John Noble, 277
Williams, Robert A., Jr., 290

Williams, Roger, 132
Wilson, Samuel M., 300–301
Windmill, 56
Wingina, 54
Winthrop, John, 203–4
Wonder, discourse of, 291
Wood, Peter, 222
Wood, William, 79–80
Woodward, Henry, 42, 51
Wright, Gordon, 265
Wright, Louis B., 15
Writing, historical, 9–10, 16; akin to

fiction, 18; emplotted, 19; qualities, 21; style, 20–21
Writing, impresses Indians, 56, 91
Writing, Indian, 311
Wrong, George M., 208

Yamasee Indians, 119, 150, 238
Yourcenar, Marguerite, 11

Zambardino, R. A., 301
Zeitgeists, 11
Zorita, Alonso de, 248